Real Estate Appraisal

REAL ESTATE APPRAISAL
REVIEW AND OUTLOOK

Paul F. Wendt

University of Georgia Press

Library of Congress Catalog Card Number: 72–97939
International Standard Book Number: 0–8203–0317–8

The University of Georgia Press, Athens 30602

Printed in the United States of America

CONTENTS

PREFACE

Every real estate decision involves an appraisal. These range in difficulty and sophistication from the informal house-inspection tour, the "windshield" appraisal for loan purposes, or the multiple-listing "caravan" house tour, to the most detailed appraisal team analyses of economic background, market sales, income, expense, and cost data for large and complex investment properties. The quality of the final appraisal result does not depend upon the hours spent on the job, nor on the cost, bulk, and appearance of the final report.

The valuation of real estate is an art involving the exercise of judgment and, in many cases, long-term forecasting. The appraiser must know his product — property — which implies that he must be able to identify the legal rights of ownership and the public restrictions on those rights, as well as the physical characteristics of the myriad property types that are the subjects of his appraisals. He must be able to sense the "pulse" of the real estate market and to understand the complex motivations of buyers and sellers under a wide range of competitive pricing conditions. He must also understand the relationships between financing terms and property valuation, and the close linkages between property values and the general economy. In other words, the appraiser must be an economist.

The jingle "the worth of a thing is what it will bring" is deceptively simple, for there is no cookbook approach to the art of real estate appraising. The appraiser, like the scientist, does not lack specialized tools and techniques. His problem, like theirs, is to know how and when to use the multitude of techniques, methods, and data available to him. The capacity to formulate valuation judgments is the product of accumulated wisdom, and the appraiser, like the investment analyst, builds upon the foundation of previous knowledge and experience in the field.

This book has a dual objective — first, to provide a review of the development of appraisal theory and practice and, second, to evaluate the present state of the appraisal art and to project its future.

The first three chapters draw heavily on the author's previous writings. A review of recent developments in appraisal practice, with emphasis on new techniques and approaches, dominates the balance of the book. Reflecting their contemporary and future importance, the computer and cash-flow analysis stalk through the newer parts of this work, furnishing a much-needed link between real estate investment counseling and appraisal.

The book is directed toward the professional appraiser and the college-level student of real estate appraisal. The author's indebtedness to others is acknowledged in many portions of this work. Many of the classics in the real estate appraisal field are now out of print, and the author, therefore, has quoted extensively from the pioneering work of Hurd, Dorau, Babcock, Bonbright, Ratcliff, Hoyt, and others. It is only through an understanding of the background of appraisal theory and practice that we can assess the present state of knowledge in the field.

The American Institute of Real Estate Appraisers, through its official textbook and the *Appraisal Journal*, provides a continuous developmental strand of appraisal theory and practice in the United States. This important source of documentation has aided the author in his attempt to evaluate critically the present state and the future outlook of the appraisal art.

Special acknowledgment is made to my colleagues, Dr. Wallace F. Smith of the University of California and Dr. William Shenkel of the University of Georgia, and to the many professional appraisers who have aided and encouraged the author at various stages of this work.

Richard Mallory, Peter Tsong, and David Walters assisted in preparing computer program descriptions and output. Special thanks are due to Colonel Ernest W. Smith, Assistant Director, Division of Research, College of Business Administration, University of Georgia for editorial and other assistance in an earlier draft. Mrs. Rosemary Klei assisted in typing the manuscript.

CHAPTER 1

WHAT IS VALUE?

The naive reader may come to the study of valuation with the belief that the word *value* has some specific and restricted meaning. Very soon, however, he will accept the dictum of Justice Brandeis that "value is a word of many meanings."[1]

A brief excursion into the literature on the theory of value will convince the reader that the economic conception of value is partial and narrow in its scope compared with the ancient classification of values by the philosophers as "the True, the Beautiful, and the Good."[2] In discussing the various specialized uses of the term *value*, one philosopher emphasizes the breadth of meaning of the term and takes particular issue with the narrowness of the economic concept of value.

> The principal objection to the term "value" arises from its use in economics. In that science it has long been used in a narrow sense to distinguish commodities commanding a price from "free goods" possessing utility. In other words, value in the economic sense is a species of value in the general sense, and we must take pains not to confuse the two. . . . On the whole, then, value appears to be the most colorless word that can be borrowed from common speech, and the word that lends itself most readily to new technical use.[3]

It is important to review some of the literature on the meaning and concepts of value as a prelude to an examination of appraisal theory and techniques. As will be seen in the chapters that follow, the precise meaning attached to the term *value* is the most important single influence affecting both the method of valuation to be employed and the final valuation estimate.

Economists

Economists have not been unaware of the confusing word meanings associated with the term *value*. It has been stated that "the scientific development of economic theory began with the attempt to solve the value problem."[4]

The writings of Edwin R. A. Seligman reveal the acceptance in economic writings of the universality of the value concept: "Since value implies capacity to satisfy wants, there are as many kinds of value as there are classes of wants. Things have a scientific value, an aesthetic value, a religious value, a philosophic value, a political value, and so on. The value with which economics has to deal is economic value, a small subdivision of the whole."[5]

Let it not be thought, however, that economic value itself is a word with any single and unchanging connotation. The history of economic thought contains a long record of controversy over "real" or "natural" versus "exchange" value, and "objective" versus "subjective" value. These conflicts were more or less resolved by the neoclassical economists who held that so-called subjective value, relative marginal utility, or relative subjective worth was incapable of measurement and that "market" value is the "objective resultant or equilibrium point of all the different subjective values implicated in the market."[6]

Medici, head of the Department of Appraisal at the University of Naples, quotes Pareto as saying: "I deliver the whole of my course on political economy without using the term value."[7] According to Medici, Pareto sought only to investigate the phenomenon of price.

Generally speaking, modern economists have abandoned arguments concerning the meaning of the term *value* and considered the word to be synonymous with the term *market price* for purposes of economic investigation. This point of view was adopted in one of the early books in the field of urban land economics. In the chapter on urban land valuation Dorau and Hinman stated that "value is the market price of land. It is exactly what the land will bring through free sale in an open market."[8] The degree to which so-called value theory in economics has given way to price theory is evident from the observation that a paper read at the 1953 annual meeting of the American Economic Association entitled "The Value of Value Theory" was presented in a session on "Industrial Pricing" and dealt exclusively with an evaluation of price theory.[9]

Appraisers

Before the depression of the 1930s appraisers generally adhered closely to market prices as the central measure of real estate values. As appraisers gradually assumed a professional identity apart from those engaged solely in real estate brokerage and as the occasions for valuing real estate multiplied, appraisers began to recognize many different concepts of value for varying purposes. The collapse of the real estate market during the depression of the 1930s and the broadened influence of the government in the establishment of appraisal values for purposes of real estate mortgage loan insurance and guaranty aided in the tendency to reject market price as the central concept of value. The development of a body of literature in the appraisal and valuation field by lawyers, engineers, and accountants furthered the gradual acceptance of multiple value concepts.

The strong reliance upon market price as the prime measure of real estate value is illustrated in some of the early appraisal literature in the United States. In his book *Principles of City Land Values*, published in 1903, Hurd stated that "as ordinarily expressed, 'value' means exchange value, average sales being considered the best test of value."[10] Following much the same view, Zangerle, writing in the early 1920s, identified the "real value of real estate" as "the money price which it will sell for in the open market in the particular locality." Zangerle also identified the "economic" or "intrinsic" value as resulting from the capitalization of net income from the property and "exchange value" as a price agreed upon between a willing buyer and a willing seller.[11]

A similar reliance upon market price is evidenced in the *Standards of Appraisal Practice*, edited by the National Association of Real Estate Boards in 1929: "The market value of a property at a designated date is that competitively established price which represents the present worth at that date of all the rights to future benefits arising from ownership."

Frederick M. Babcock in his *Valuation of Real Estate*, published in 1932, attempted to develop a unified body of appraisal theory around a concept of "warranted" or "justified" market value, which was similar to the concept of "exchange value" employed by Zangerle. Babcock's efforts to develop a unified body of theory were handicapped by two factors: (1) his basic distrust and consequent rejection of market prices as reliable indicators of real estate values; (2) the acceptance of multiple value concepts by courts of law and by valuation experts.

Babcock attempted to resolve the first difficulty by drawing a distinction between market price and market value. The latter concept implies the existence of the willing buyer and willing seller, while the former refers to actual transaction prices in the real estate market.

The second problem proved a major obstacle in the development of a unified body of appraisal theory. Because of the many value concepts in common use, Babcock was forced to conclude that the method of valuation would vary with the purpose of the appraisal. He made a strong plea for emphasis upon a concept of warranted market value and deplored the variety of meanings attached to the word *value*:

> Value may be defined as the ratio in which goods exchange. In common usage the word "value" is used to denote other concepts, and as a result considerable difficulty and ambiguity frequently arise in discussions of value problems because different individuals are prone to attach different meaning to the word. It is not to be supposed that the different concepts for which we use the word "value" are without significance. But it is regrettable that the concept of value in exchange has not been provided with a distinctive word to prevent confusion. . . . Prices are, then, values expressed in terms of a common medium of exchange, such as dollars.
>
> From time to time court decisions, statutes, and constitutions have attempted to define value for taxation and other purposes. In connection with real estate, the legal definitions of value have usually been built upon the exchange or market concept of value.

3

At best, market value is a term difficult to apply in practical cases. . . .

For the purpose of developing a practical theory of real estate valuation, a distinction will be made in this book between value and market price. Value will be used to designate the concept in which the thoroughly informed buyer is present and market price will be used to designate the prices which properties actually do bring in the real estate market.

. . . the purposes of valuation can very well require one estimate of value for one purpose and another for some other purpose. . . . Of course it may be stressed that the real value of a property is represented solely by the value estimate which represents the price which the typical buyer is warranted in paying and that values to specific owners for specific purposes do not come within the scope of the definition of value. It may also be urged that the recognition of the possibility that a single property may have a variety of values is dangerous and confusing in many practical situations.[12]

Since the publication of Babcock's book, the view has persisted in appraisal literature that market value and market price are different. There has also been increasing acceptance of the idea that there are as many value concepts as there are purposes and occasions for establishing values.

McMichael cites some fifty of the commoner types of value which have become accepted and warns that in some cases several kinds of value must be considered to obtain the answer sought in a given appraisal problem. These terms range the alphabet from "attached business value" to "warranted value." McMichael cautions the appraiser in these words: "Value of real estate is so varied and at times so intangible in character that the appraiser must keep in mind specific definitions of the kind of value he is asked, or decides, to establish."[13]

Similarly, Arthur May in his book *The Valuation of Residential Real Estate* emphasizes the importance of defining the value concept to be employed in an appraisal. It is quite obvious, however, that May deplored this heterogeneity of value concepts and subscribed to Babcock's view that a willing buyer–willing seller kind of market value should be the central value concept in appraisal theory.

The appraisal of real estate is a problem. The value estimate is its solution. There can be no logical solution unless the problem has been defined. . . . Thus the principal asks the appraiser to make an appraisal of property to find: (1) market value, (2) sales price, (3) purchase price, (4) fair rental value, (5) fair trading value, (6) insurance coverage, and (7) fair compensation for damages suffered.

In each of these instances a different result may be obtained (not, by the way, a different "value"). And in each of these instances a different appraisal pattern will evolve.[14]

There are many definitions [of value]: one text lists thirty-eight. "Fair," "present," "insurable," "economic," "sound," "assessed," "taxable," and a host of other kinds of "value" have all been defined, discussed and are alleged to have their specific application to the problem and the field of usage in which their proponents are engaged.

We shall not pause to debate the logic of such practice, although a sizable volume might be written around the thesis that real estate has, or has not, more than one "value." The bull's eye of our target is "market value," and we must have specific and clear-cut delineation of the target, or we shall be wide of the mark. To aim at a variety of "market values" is to get nowhere in our discussion that follows.[15]

The particular market value concept which May supports is similar to that proposed by Babcock and recommended by the American Institute of Real Estate Appraisers. The latter definition, quoted below, also bears close relation to the definition adopted for use by the Federal Housing Administration in its loan insurance program.

> Market Value: (1) As defined by the courts, the highest price estimated in terms of money which a property will bring if exposed for sale in the open market allowing a reasonable time to find a purchaser who buys with knowledge of all the uses to which it is adapted and for which it is capable of being used. (2) Frequently, it is referred to as the price at which a willing-seller would sell and a willing-buyer would buy, neither being under abnormal pressure. (3) It is the price expectation if a reasonable time is allowed to find a purchaser and if both seller and prospective buyer are fully informed.[16]

George Schmutz joined the ranks of those appraisal writers who hold that justified or warranted market value is the central value concept. He maintained that "market value is market price provided: (a) A reasonable time is allowed to find a purchaser; and (b) He buys with knowledge of the uses and purposes to which the property is adaptable and for which it is capable of being used."[17]

It is interesting to observe that valuation theory in England has not been so concerned with the distinction between market value and market price. According to the authors of a British work on valuation the "market value or market price of a particular property may therefore be defined as that amount of money which at any given time can be obtained for the property from persons able and willing to purchase it."[18]

Typical of European valuation theories was that of Medici which distinguished between price as a historic occurrence — an accomplished fact — and estimated value as a judgment. Market price, according to this author, is synonymous with market value. Medici held that a property may have diverse values for different purposes and distinguished the following: "(1) The most probable market value (which he held to be not distinguishable from the most probable capitalization value); (2) the most probable cost of reproduction; (3) the most probable price (value) of transformation (i.e., the expense in-

5

volved in converting property into another form); (4) the most probable price (value) of substitution (i.e., the price paid to purchase a substitute); or (5) the most probable complementary price (value) (i.e., price of a portion of the whole)." According to Medici any appraisal judgment presupposes a knowledge of prices and of the market.[19]

Not all appraisers in the United States have unanimously accepted the view that market price should be rejected in favor of warranted or justified market value. Percival V. Bowen criticized the view that appraisers should exercise their judgment in adjusting market prices to some "warranted" or "justified" level during the depression years: "The time may come when we can scientifically appraise what the market value should be. Until the time comes, I believe that we should limit ourselves in the public service to appraising of what the market value really is."[20]

He took pains to point out that market prices were the indicators of this value. A very similar view was expressed by the managing editor of the leading professional journal in the appraisal field in 1950. Robert H. Armstrong called attention to the dividing influence of such value abstractions as "normal," "stabilized," "mortgage loan," and other similar value concepts and recommended a return to the basic concept of market value.[21] An editorial in the *Appraisal Journal* for January 1946 closed with these words: "Why not let market value mean what the words obviously connote – the price obtainable in the market under outlined circumstances. Better still, why not speak of the market price obtainable under such circumstances instead of the market value – and use value only in conjunction with descriptive words that express the underlying assumptions made by the speaker."[22]

Post–World War II appraisal literature has increasingly emphasized market value as the central appraisal concept. In an earlier work the author recommended that market value should provide the central concept about which appraisal theory should be developed and that the market-comparison technique, based upon market selling prices, was the most logical and simple technique for establishing the values of real property.[23] Writing a decade later, Ratcliff argued that "almost every variety of problem faced by real estate investors and requiring an investment decision calls for an estimate of the Most Probable Selling Price of the property." Ratcliff takes pains to distinguish between this concept, which he refers to as V_p, and the conventional definition of "fair market value" cited in the text of the American Institute of Real Estate Appraisers, which he identifies as V_c. He says: "The price which actually clears the market may have little relationship to what a sophisticated buyer might have been willing to pay if it had been necessary, or a sophisticated seller might have been willing to take for his property if no better offer had come along. . . . It follows this line of reasoning that V_p and V_c could be the same but that it is very unlikely."[24] Ratcliff's criticism of the concepts of fair and warranted value embraced in the AIREA is closely similar to those expressed by Bonbright as early as 1937 and the author's views in the 1956 edition of *Real Estate Appraisal*.

The fair market value concept is highly subjective in nature and often results in estimates of hypothetical values as distinct from actual prices in the market place. However Ratcliff's notion that market value or the "Most Probable Selling Price" represents the only significant value concept appears to disregard the idea that the same property may have a higher value to one investor than to another, which is the foundation of Bonbright's concept of "value to the owner." The market at any time presents a range of differing values for different investors for the same property. The values reflecting the different tax positions and preferences of investors can be termed *investment values*, since they are used primarily to guide investment decisions. The most probable selling price represents the classical meeting place of marginal buyers and sellers in the market, but this may differ from other investment values as calculated by individual investors.

Ratcliff's concept of the most probable selling price introduces the important element of probability, referred to above in Medici's *Principles of Appraisal*, but not reflected in conventional concepts of market value. The distinguishing feature of real estate is that individual properties are distinctive and that sales of the identical property under appraisal are seldom available. This underscores the fact that an appraisal is an *estimate* of probable value, regardless of the method employed. It is not a fact to be found, as many have believed in the past. Herein lies a strong justification for the language adopted by Ratcliff. We do not know what values are, but we must estimate them, and the precise nature of one estimate we may make is that it is the most probable selling price under the conditions prevailing in the market at that time.

Henry A. Babcock, brother of Frederick Babcock, identifies three primary kinds of value in his 1968 textbook:[25]

	Value Characteristics	Kinds of Value
1. Investment value	Utility, marketability, self-liquidity	Owner value Market value Investment value
2. Market value	Utility, marketability	Owner value Market value
3. Owner value	Utility	Owner value

He characterizes service properties as those lacking marketability and what he terms self-liquidity, and argues that properties producing only nonpecuniary satisfactions have neither an investment value nor a market value. Babcock says, "In a normal market, investment value and market value are one and the same thing. In an abnormal market, market value may be above or below investment value, but such differences are transitory and are the result of speculative activity."[26] Babcock fails to recognize that properties may have different values for different investors, although he comes close to this recognition in saying that "different prospective purchasers may bid the same price but base it on different earning expectancies and different yield rates; mathematically, there are an infinite number of combinations of earning expectancies and yield rates which result in the same initial investment value." He never explains how or why these differing earning expectancies and yield rates result in the same estimate of investment value.

This author accepts the notion that certain classes of property, such as churches, school buildings, and other special purpose properties, do not have a market value and on this basis can agree with Babcock's delineation of the major concepts of value, investment value, market value, and owner value. Babcock's analysis of the three primary kinds of value boils down to the conclusion that marketable investment properties have an investment value and marketable noninvestment properties have a market value and that these normally bear a close relation in the market. This classification of course is preparatory to presentation of his two major methods of valuation – the "investment analysis method," which he applies to determine investment value, and the "sales analysis," or comparable sales method to determine market value.[27]

Ratcliff's concept of the most probable selling price overcomes many of the shortcomings of the vague and qualified fair market value. His rejection of investment value as a separate concept appears unjustified in the light of the special circumstances surrounding its determination by a rapidly expanding body of differing investor types. Further, since the principal significance of the classification of value concepts lies in the selection of methods of valuation, there is added reason for identifying investment value as a concept distinct from market value.

Proponents of the view that market price should be recognized as a central value concept have met with only grudging acceptance however. This has in part been the result of the very substantial influence which government agencies have exerted in the valuation field. Growing recognition of multiple value concepts in engineering and legal valuation has constituted an additional deterrent to the efforts of those seeking to rally forces about market prices as the central value concept.

Government Agencies

The Federal Housing Administration, through its mortgage-insuring operations, has had an important influence upon the use of value concepts in the residential field. The National Housing Act of 1934, enacted to improve housing standards and to create a sound mortgage market, had as an additional objective "the universal application of a uniform system of appraisal of properties and analysis of the risk involved in individual mortgage transactions."[28] The *Underwriting Manual*, which has guided the appraisal policies of the Federal Housing Administration, was prepared under the supervision of Frederick M. Babcock, who was named chief underwriter of the agency.[29] Echoing his views the *Underwriting Manual* distinguishes between market prices and market value and uses "long-term warranted value" as a central concept: "The word *value*, as used by the Federal Housing Administration, refers to a price which a purchaser is warranted in paying for a property rather than a price for which a property may be sold, and is defined as: The price which typical buyers would be warranted in paying for the property for long-term use or investment, if they were well informed, acted intelligently, voluntarily, and without necessity."[30]

This definition distinguishes between market value and market price. It adds the assumption of purchase for long-term use to the earlier assumption of equal knowledge and absence or duress which were included in the American Institute of Real Estate Appraisers' definition quoted above. In a series of illustrative summaries the *Underwriting Manual* draws attention to the effect upon market prices of different buyers' and sellers' reactions, assuming hypothetical motivations and knowledge on the part of each. No change was made in this section of the *Underwriting Manual* in a revision of part 4, section 13 in 1966.

The concept of "reasonable" value/ which was written into the Servicemen's Readjustment Act of 1944 and which created the system of Veterans Administration guaranteed home loans was originally interpreted to have a meaning similar to FHA's "long-term warranted value." The concept of reasonable value was redefined by the Veterans Administration in 1948, however, as

> that figure which represents the amount a designated appraiser, unaffected by personal interest or prejudice, would recommend as a proper price or cost to a prospective purchaser, whom the appraiser represents in a relationship of trust, as being a fair price or cost in the light of prevailing conditions.
> . . . It is in effect not a determination of value for long-term use or investment but a finding of that amount which is reasonable for the veteran to pay in the light of conditions prevailing locally.[31]

This definition relieved the appraiser of the obligation to consider the long-term future in establishing the "reasonable" value of property for veterans' purchase.

Following the passage of the Housing Act of 1954, which provided for public acquisition of land in urban renewal areas for sale to private investors, two new value concepts were added to the lexicon of land value concepts: acquisition cost and reuse value. These concepts have been defined in instructional pamphlets published by the Urban Renewal Administration and have been accompanied by instructions as to the methods to be employed by appraisers in fixing such values. In this sense they have joined a host of specialized concepts of value with special legal definition prescribed by law or administrative manual.

The Public Land Law Review Commission was established by an act of 19 September 1964 (and amended by an act of 18 December 1967) to study the existing statutes and regulations governing the retention, management, and disposition of the public lands and to review the policies and practices of federal agencies charged with administrative supervision over such lands, insofar as such policies and practices relate to the retention, management, and disposition of those lands. The commission invited proposals in 1969 for a comprehensive study of appraisal practices and procedures of the major federal agencies in connection with their acquisition and disposal of the public lands. This study promises to be the most comprehensive review of appraisal practices in government ever undertaken, although the omission of the Federal Housing Administration and the Veterans Administration is notable. The study is almost certain to reveal a wide disparity in appraisal concepts and methods used in different government agencies. Although some of the differences undoubtedly result from specific legislative intent and language, a considerable portion of the disparity can be attributed to the basic subjectivity in adherence to the concept of fair market value and to the flexibility inherent in the use of the traditional three approaches to valuation.

Engineering and Legal Valuation

The authors of a leading text in engineering valuation accept the view that *value* is a word of many meanings and that the occasion for establishing values will determine the precise nature of the value concept to be used. Somewhat noncommittally, they advise the reader:

> The word value in itself is difficult of precise definition and usage. Value is a relative term by which the desirability of ownership of the property in question is stated in terms of other property or money. The conditions under which the value is arrived at and the conditions under which the value is applicable must be understood, if the expressed value is to have a real significance. The time, place, purpose and parties thereto all affect the measure of the value of the property. . . .
>
> Throughout this book the value of property will be used in the concept of the desirability of ownership or value to the owner. . . . Market price, cost of replacing the service rendered by the property, and present value of the future returns from the property are usually relatively good measures of the value of the property to the owner.[32]

The reluctance of the authors to single out any one concept of value as central to valuation theory can probably be attributed to the fact that such a determination would automatically commit the authors to singling out a particular method of valuation. In the comments quoted above the writers carefully note that all three of the conventional measures or methods of valuation should be employed. If particular emphasis were accorded the market-price concept of value, market price would automatically be raised to a position of preeminence as a *method* of establishing values.

Writers in the field of legal valuation have had an important influence upon valuation theory and have been particularly influential in establishing the view that *value* is a word of many meanings.

Bonbright, in his two-volume work *The Valuation of Property*, held that the first and most important problem in any appraisal was to secure a definition of value acceptable for the purpose of the investigation. According to his analysis there are two basic concepts of value: (1) market value and (2) value to the owner. Of these two major concepts Bonbright seems to lean in favor of value to the owner as the central and more universal concept: "One cannot properly speak of the value of property *in general*; instead, one must speak of its value to some specific person or group of persons. Strictly construed, therefore, property value should mean invariably value to some particular owner."[33] In his subsequent examination Bonbright finds that both of these basic concepts are employed in valuation processes, frequently without setting forth the definitive concept employed and thus resulting in considerable ambiguity.

Bonbright said relatively little about the difficulties of estimating value to the owner. He took strong issue, however, with the identification of value with market price, principally on the grounds of its indeterminate nature.

> The identification of value with market price, for which the classical economists are perhaps primarily responsible, does such violence to the spirit of the word that its abandonment might well be urged, were it not too late to hope for success in this direction.
> . . . "market value," or "exchange value," is a multi-significant phrase, requiring much closer definition than it has generally received in order to constitute even a tolerable standard of legal appraisal. Even the economists have not agreed upon its meaning, while to the courts it has been taken to mean, on occasion, almost anything that the unadorned word "value" might mean.[34]

According to Bonbright the indeterminate nature of the term *market value* is primarily owing to the following terms and conditions of the market being seldom if ever specified: (1) time for negotiation of the sale, (2) time for delivery and payment, (3) degree of coercion by buyers and sellers, (4) type of ownership, and (5) gross or net sales price. He identified the following different concepts of market value which have been recognized by the courts:

11

First Sense: Price Which the Property Would Actually Bring if Presently Offered for Sale, with Reasonable Time for Negotiation.

Second Sense: Valuation Based on Current Market Prices of Substantially Similar Commodities.

Third Sense: Hypothetical Sale Price as Between a Willing Buyer and Willing Seller.

Fourth Sense: Cost of Replacement through Purchase on the Market Place.

Fifth Sense: "Justified Selling Price" or "Normal Selling Price."[35]

Bonbright concluded:

> Our own preference, at least in the field of appraisal, is for the previous definition of market value, under which a valuation of property means merely an attempt to estimate the price for which the property could be sold by some stipulated seller to anyone else the conditions of the assumed sale being left for selection by reference to the purpose for which the valuation is being made. So defined, market value will not qualify as a basis of legal appraisal save in a rather limited number of cases. But no alternative definition of value will serve as a jack-of-all-trades. The use of "market value" as the verbal basis for settling all varieties of legal disputes represents a uniformity of mere words rather than one of principle. The multiformity of value standards is only concealed, not avoided, by the accepted legal definition of market value as the price at which the property would be exchanged between a "willing buyer" and a "willing seller."[36]

According to Bonbright's analysis there is no central concept of value. The occasion for valuation will dictate whether the concept in the particular case is related to market value or to value to the owner. There are an infinite number of variations for each of these two alternative basic concepts. He dismissed the concept of the willing buyer and the willing seller, which furnished the basis for Babcock's work and for much of the federal government appraisal policy, as an obstacle to clear thinking in the appraisal field and maintained that the theory is based upon artificial, hypothetical, and indefinite assumptions.

Another specialist in real property and valuation law, Herman D. Jerrett, expressed similar criticism of the concept of market value.[37] According to Jerrett something he terms *real* value is the primary or basic value that governs all other kinds of value. Following the classical economists he maintains that the basis for real value lies in utility. He holds that market value is merely a very imperfect rule of thumb for determining actual or real values:

> There is no such thing as market value, the word market, as we learned, not being a term of fixed legal significance.
> . . . what is the exchange value of a commodity? The answer is, what it will bring in the open market. What is the best evidence of its exchange value? The answer must be, for what it actually sells.

. . . But, when we attempt to apply these terms to the buying and selling of the natural agents of production, especially the land, it is something entirely different, for we are attempting the ascertainment of market price and exchange value in cases where there is no open market recording numerous transactions of barter and sale and responding automatically to the relative quantities of supply and demand. . . .

. . . market price and exchange value are applicable only to articles for which there are numerous willing buyers and sellers (such as are found in the market places where we have competition in its true form) of things movable, consumable and of use where everyday wants demand.[38]

Both Jerrett and Bonbright are critical of the willing buyer–willing seller concept of value. Different assumptions implied in the valuation process, according to these authors, can lead to an infinite number of conclusions as to value. To this author, these criticisms seem fully justified. If an appraiser looks forward to a decline in values, he may in a given instance reach a decision that the warranted market value is substantially below the present market price. By the same token, if he views the future differently, he might be willing to accept current market prices as indicative of values.

Similar objections can be raised concerning the assumptions implied in the FHA concept of value that buyers and sellers are both willing and equally well informed and purchase for long-term use or enjoyment. The establishment of these conditions automatically introduces wide latitude in the processes of estimation. Just how wide this latitude can be has been graphically illustrated in the FHA scandals of the last two decades.

In an interesting recent editorial comment in "The Legal Angle" in the October 1970 *Appraisal Journal* a well-known attorney supports the view that the measure of value used in condemnation cases is not "the actual market — its cash value on a day certain, but rather the theoretical market value." He says, "This latter value could be considered analogous to the value an investment advisor attributes to a common stock, which might be substantially higher or lower than its daily quoted stock exchange value." This emphasizes anew the flexibility in the concept of warranted value and the continuing debate over the meaning of market value.

Market prices in many real estate markets are a better and more consistent measure of market values than many of the hypothetical market value concepts adopted by appraisers and government agencies. Further, market price represents a value concept with a specific meaning as distinguished from the uncertainty of the concept of value to the owner and the imaginary nature of the willing buyer–willing seller concept. There appear to be good arguments for the use of the market-price concept in the more highly developed real estate markets and the reservation of the willing buyer–willing seller concept for classes of property with poorly organized markets. The concept of value to the owner, for which Bonbright expresses such a strong preference, appears to have primary applicability in the field of condemnation law. Even here, however, its indeterminate nature forces reliance upon either cost or market values.

Critics of the market price concept contend that the varied terms and conditions surrounding market sales render sales data virtually useless. Admitting the difficulties it could be countered that the terms and conditions of real estate sales tend to be similar for similar types of properties at any given time. This is particularly true for residential properties as a result of government mortgage insurance terms. For such classes of property, market price data generally tend to reflect roughly similar terms. To the further objection that individual market sales prices reflect different degrees of knowledge and willingness on the part of buyers and sellers, it might be argued that such is generally true throughout all markets. Further, for many classes of property market information is widely circulated and an assumption of equal knowledge might be fairly assumed. In summary market price, with all its shortcomings, appears to represent the most acceptable general value concept and the most reliable evidence of value.

Summary

The apparent simplicity of the task of defining the concept of value is misleading. The word *value* may be used to mean any monetary statement about property. It has been observed that the word *value* has many different connotations in different fields of study and that part of the confusion with respect to its meaning is due to the common usage of the term.

Economists have long debated the meaning of and basis for value. It was observed that the two main value concepts in economics are distinguished as "subjective" or "use" value and "objective" or "market" value. Economists in recent years have placed chief reliance upon market prices as indicators of values, owing to the difficulties of measuring subjective value.

Relying upon economic theory, appraisers generally accepted market price as a central value concept before 1930. Since the writings of Babcock and Bonbright during the 1930s however, appraisers have become increasingly reluctant to accept market prices as the appropriate measure of market value. Babcock sought a stable measure of value during the depression period of widely fluctuating prices, while Bonbright and other legal writers were concerned with a precise concept to be used in court cases in valuation. Babcock emphasized the distinction between market value and market price and advocated the use of a justified or warranted market value concept. The resulting confusion in appraisal theory has been supplemented by the development of a large number of specialized value concepts for use in particular types of valuation problems. Bonbright's work drew attention to the lack of precision in most commonly used value concepts and to the resulting confusion and ambiguity in legal decisions on value. Appraisers have endeavored to absorb specialized legal and other value concepts into a general appraisal theory. Many value concepts, however, imply narrow and specialized procedures and types of valuation evidence.

Nurtured by the Federal Housing Administration, appraisers have gradually come to accept Babcock's "long-term warranted" market value as a central concept. It was concluded that the criticisms of Bonbright and others that such a concept is hypothetical and elusive are well founded. The author expressed the view that market prices should be accepted as representative of market values. In defense of this viewpoint it was contended that the terms and conditions of the various segments of the market are generally similar and that the market, even without perfect knowledge, furnishes a headstone superior to any hypothetical value concept.

It must be concluded that the word *value* is indeed a word of many meanings. One of these meanings, market value, should be based upon the data of the market place and should provide the central concept about which appraisal theory should be developed. The remainder of the multitude of meanings can be accommodated as special cases requiring special procedures and types of evidence.

The author has argued that market value, more specifically described as the most probable selling price, and investment value represent the two major concepts of value with which the appraiser must be concerned.[39] Beyond these, of course, there are innumerable specialized concepts specified in the law or in administrative practice, in many cases supplemented by instructions as to the methods to be employed in reaching a valuation estimate. The significance of the author's recommendation that the most probable selling price and investment value constitute the fundamental appraisal objectives is that these objectives, so stated, lead logically to a delineation of the methods appropriate to the estimation of the value for the purposes outlined. It is not without good reason that one of the cardinal principles of appraisal theory is that any estimate of value must first be predicated upon a statement of purpose.

The acceptance of these recommendations will have considerable influence upon the structure of appraisal theory, but conclusions as to its probable effects must await an examination of the structure and logic of that theory.

THE DEVELOPMENT OF APPRAISAL THEORY

A theory is an explanation of the principles of an art or science. Modern appraisal theory is eclectic in the sense that it has been built upon the basis of theories of value and valuation developed by economists, supplemented by depreciation and annuity theories contributed by accountants and writers in the fields of corporation finance and investments.

In some sense it seems fair to state that appraisal theory has lost touch with valuation theory in economics since the work of Irving Fisher shortly after the turn of the century. Full recognition has been given in economic writings to the difference between a theory of valuation and the practice of establishing values. Economists' rejection of costs as evidence of value and their recognition of the difficulties of applying the capitalization-of-income method have caused them to rely upon the market as the source of valuation data.

Beginning with the significant work of Babcock, appraisal theorists have attempted to develop an appraisal system based upon the economic theory that the present value of a durable good is equal to the discounted value of its future returns. The preoccupation of many appraisal theorists with the extremely difficult problems of technique in the capitalization-of-income method has resulted in a multiplication of techniques and some confusion with respect to their proper use.

Paralleling their concern with capitalization of income theories, appraisers have actually established values for residential properties since the Great Depression based upon replacement costs. This trend has been influenced in important degree by the entrance of the federal government into the mortgage loan field on a large scale.

It is the purpose of this chapter to trace the contribution of economists and others to valuation theory and to demonstrate the indebtedness of appraisers to work carried on earlier in the fields of economic theory, accounting, corporation finance, investments, and engineering. An attempt will be made to establish that there has been inadequate recognition in appraisal literature of the distinction noted by economists between value and valuation theory and that this has resulted in inordinate attention by appraisal theorists to the development of income-capitalization techniques. Recent developments in appraisal theory will be reviewed and critically evaluated, and important differences between appraisal theory and current practice will be noted.

Contribution of Economists

Arthur M. Weimer, in a review of the history of value theory for the appraiser, concludes, "Fortunately or unfortunately, however, a study of the history of value theories is not likely to supply very much that can be taken over in its entirety and applied to current valuation problems."[1]

The author takes issue with this view. The appraiser inherited from the economists a body of value theory developed over several centuries.[2] Economists, to be sure, were primarily concerned with the sources and bases of value, that is, with value theory, rather than with the methods of estimating value, distinguished as valuation theory. Although value theory was primarily concerned with the sources and bases for value, it furnished the basis for many of the concepts and methods which have been applied in valuation theory. An example of this is found in the doctrine of *justum pretium* (just price) which was developed during the Middle Ages, when prices charged for goods were subject to strong central control. The just price was determined by authorities, based upon the theory that value should equal labor cost. Freely determined market values were considered immoral and required regulation. The roots of two modern approaches to the estimation of value — cost of reproduction and market comparison — are found in this early period, since the just price was the cost of reproduction as distinguished from the exchange value or market price.

Classical Economists   Although the notion of government-regulated prices was gradually supplanted by greater reliance upon the free competitive market following the seventeenth century, the cost-of-production theory of value remained dominant until the middle of the nineteenth century. The cost-of-production theory of value received new support during the eighteenth and nineteenth centuries from such economists as Smith, Mill, Ricardo, and Marx.[3] Although these writers recognized the influence of utility and demand upon exchange values, they looked to cost of production or sacrifice as the basis of value.

Bastiat and other French economists, writing early in the nineteenth century, recognized the importance of the market and emphasized exchange value. The roots of their theories were found in the writings of the Physiocrats, whose economic thinking dominated the previous century and who had recommended reliance upon market or exchange values as a substitute for government-determined just prices.

Austrian School   A further swing away from the cost-of-production theory of value was led by the Austrian school of economists (Menger, Wieser, Böhm-Bawerk), supported by W. S. Jevons in England. Giving primary attention to utility as the basis for value, this group pointed out that market values generally fluctuate either above or below cost, and that the value of many products bears little relationship to the labor cost in producing them. In writing on interest Böhm-Bawerk pointed out that men tend to value present goods more highly than future goods. Thus he furnished an early basis for the principle of discounting future returns to obtain the value of the property.[4]

Neoclassical Economists   Alfred Marshall, writing at the turn of the twentieth century, recognized the relationship between the cost-of-production theories of value employed by the classical economists and the so-called subjective or marginal-utility theories of the Austrian school. He synthesized these two apparently opposing theories into our modern concept of market value as influenced on the demand side by utility and on the supply side by cost of production. Marshall extended his theory of value to explain the distribution of economic wealth, and in that process echoed the classical concepts of normal value and the relationship of this natural price to long-term cost of production. Although he was not directly concerned with developing a theory of valuation, Marshall's writings illustrated the three basic methods of estimating value in use today: replacement cost, market comparison, and capitalization of income.[5]

According to Marshall, "The aggregate 'site value' of any piece of building land is that which it would have if cleared of buildings and sold in a free market. The 'annual site value' — to use a convenient, though not strictly correct form of speaking — is the income which that price would yield at the current rate of interest."[6] Later in the same chapter he states, "The capitalized value of any plot of land is the actuarial 'discounted' value of all the net incomes which it is likely to afford." Marshall describes the competition of various uses for land and in his discussion of the "margin of building" illustrates the process through which the highest and best use of sites is determined.[7] Marshall outlined the "summation" approach to estimating the value of sites developed with new buildings. This value, according to his *Principles* would equal the discounted value of estimated net incomes of the "site value" as it would be sold in a free market, plus the cost of the improvements, which could be equal to both the market price and the discounted future returns from the improvements.[8] This relationship between cost, market price, and cost of production no longer exists, according to Marshall, when the machine (or house) is old. Its value then is simply the discounted value of the future returns which it is expected to earn. Although he did not employ modern terminology, Marshall recognized over- and underimprovement of land and the difficulty of segregating joint returns to land and buildings by the residual process.[9]

It can be seen that Marshall was the first economist to give attention to the techniques of establishing values. Marshall's concern with these techniques was only incidental to his exposition of the central position of the pricing process in the functioning of the economic system. Irving Fisher, writing shortly after the turn of the century, expanded the view advanced by Marshall and others that the value of durable goods is represented by the present worth of future returns. Fisher emphasized the distinction between cost and value, and in his discussion of risk, capitalization rates, and the discounting process he presented in fully developed form the income theory of value which has been the basis for the work of Babcock and much of modern appraisal literature.[10]

Gustav Cassel, a Swedish economist writing shortly before World War I, developed further the Marshallian principle of the tendency for long-run cost, market price, and capitalized income to be equal under conditions of equilibrium. Cassel held that a special theory of value was unnecessary in economic science and should be replaced by a theory of prices. Discussing what he called the principle of cost, Cassel stated that "the principle (of cost) represents, in a measure, a normal condition about which actual pricing oscillates. Any material deviation from the principle of cost provokes, as a rule, counteracting forces."[11] Cassel agrees with the principle set forth by Marshall and Fisher that the value of durable goods equals the discounted value of the future returns, although a critic has held that he introduced a fundamental error in deducting depreciation from income before capitalization.[12]

Urban Land Economics, by Dorau and Hinman, represents the work of a group of economists led by the late Prof. Richard T. Ely, who headed the Institute for Research in Land Economics and Public Utilities at Northwestern University.[13] The authors outline two methods of appraising property: (1) income analysis and (2) comparison. The description of the income method is limited to a description of the land-residual technique. In describing the method of determining net income for capitalization, the authors insist that annual deductions should be made for depreciation and obsolescence. It is interesting that the concept of cost is not mentioned in connection with the determination of value by appraisal. This probably reflects the important influence of Fisher's writings emphasizing income as the basis for estimating values and marks a departure from the emphasis of Marshall and Cassel on long-term costs. Although their presentation of valuation methods was inaccurate and incomplete in some respects, the authors did provide a clear exposition of the competition of uses for land and of the principle of "highest and best use."[14]

Henry George Controversy Economists, from the time of Ricardo to the present, have given considerable attention to the question of whether income from land is "earned" or "unearned." The argument has revolved around the consideration that land is nonreproducible and has no cost of production.

The returns from land, therefore, are monopoly returns, according to one group of economists (the land reformers) and are attributable to population growth and other social and political factors.[15] The views of this group, who held that land value must be considered a distinctly separate theory, have been widely refuted by a long line of economists, including John Bates Clark, Richard T. Ely, Franklin A. Fetter, Edwin R. A. Seligman, and others.[16] Although this controversy has not been fruitful for appraisal theory, it drew attention to the problem of the separation of land and building returns and accounts in some measure for the neglect of replacement cost as a measure of value by economists.

Modern Economic Theory of Value In a modern exposition of the theory of value as developed by Marshall, Cassel, and others Bye summarized the relationship between cost of production, normal value, and market value as follows:

> The theory of value represents only what the equilibrium of demand and supply would be under ideal conditions. It represents what may be called the *normal value*, which may be defined as the value which purely competitive forces, if unimpeded, would bring about. The price which actually prevails at a given time may be called the market value, and will deviate somewhat from the normal value, fluctuating now above, now below it, according to conditions. Corresponding to normal value is normal price, and to market value is market price. Market value is determined in a general way by the equilibrium between marginal demand price and costs of production, and always tends to approach the normal value. . . . a perfect equilibrium value or normal price does not exist in the economic world. . . .
>
> It is the representative costs over a long period — such as those incurred on an average by an ordinarily well managed enterprise — toward which values in the long run tend; but at any particular time, the contributions of high cost producers being necessary to the supply, the value tends temporarily to equal the marginal costs of production.[17]

As will be noted in more detail in chapter 9, this theory has had a profound influence upon appraisal practice, which has emphasized replacement costs.

Economists, meanwhile, convinced of the illusory character of long-term equilibrium, have more and more stressed market price as the sole measure of value. Beginning with the work of Edward Chamberlin and Joan Robinson in 1933, the theory of value in economics has gradually evolved into the examination of price behavior and policy under a variety of conditions affecting demand and supply.[18] This development has brought about a shift in emphasis away from discussions of the basis for value and of normal value under equilibrium conditions, toward empirical study of the behavior of costs and prices for different classes of goods under varying competitive conditions. Present-day economists accept the hypothesis that valuation is price determination. The emphasis, however, has been upon price determination of new production of homogeneous units. Such analysis is difficult to apply to single, differentiated, used, durable assets. The application of modern price theory to real estate valuation is therefore virtually limited to the pricing of newly constructed properties.

Contributions from Investments, Finance, and Accounting

Investments　Although recent economic theorists have been more concerned with price determination than with valuation theory, writers in the fields of investments, corporation finance, and accounting have given considerable attention to valuation methods. Chamberlain's textbook on bond investment, originally published in 1911, sets forth in some detail the technique for obtaining the present value of a bond by the process of income capitalization and discount.[19] Williams emphasized the difference between market price of securities and their investment value in a theoretical work published in 1938. Following Fisher, he points out that investment value depends upon the present worth of future returns and discusses at some length the determination of investment risk and capitalization rates.[20]

Corporation Finance　Dewing addressed himself to problems of valuation in connection with the determination of "going concern value" of corporations. Writing at a time when there was a great deal of controversy over the proper methods of evaluating public utility and other corporation properties for purposes of taxation, rate fixing, and reorganization, Dewing commented:

> Consequently, when attempts are made to set up legal postulates to control economic value — such postulates as original cost of reproduction — nothing but uncertainty and contradiction results. In the end the test of value is pragmatic — where does the judgment of most men meet? It is the composite of many judgments, not the reaching for an illusory fixed and unvarying basis of value on which the judgment of all people should agree. . . .
> The stern, inflexible, and perhaps unpleasant fact is that ultimately rea'
> estate, whether land or structures, like all income producing property, has a value determined by the capitalization of the net income obtainable from it, and not by its original cost, or by the current cost of reproducing it.[21]

The earlier work of Dewing has been followed by more recent extension of valuation theory and practice in the capital budgeting field. An extensive literature has developed in present value theory as applied to corporate investment decisions.

Although somewhat more sophisticated the essential framework of this theory, including cash-flow analysis, closely resembles the capitalization-of-income approach and techniques used in rate of return analysis.[22]

21

Security Valuation   The theory and practice of valuation of corporate assets and corporate securities have close parallels with real estate appraisal. Indeed, it can be argued that the only differences in valuation procedures between the two classes of assets arise from the peculiar physical and legal characteristics of real property. Both real estate and securities are capital assets, deriving their value from some future stream of benefits. In the case of a bond the future benefits are represented by coupon or interest payments, plus a capital or principal amount due at some future date. Thus, a bond is identical with a mortgage and closely similar to a leased fee interest in real estate, with a predetermined residual value at the termination of the lease. Likewise, stocks are closely similar to equity interests in real estate, where the returns are uncertain in amount and duration.

In view of these close similarities it is somewhat surprising to observe that the theory and methods of security evaluation have developed quite independently of those in real estate appraisal. The volume and sophistication of the professional literature in the field of security evaluation has expanded rapidly over the past decade, while the chartered financial analyst has become the recognized professional expert in this field. There are reasons to believe that the professional gap between security evaluation and real estate appraisal may be substantially reduced in the near future. First, many investment firms are broadening their investment research activities to include real estate and real estate securities. Second, many investors who previously confined investments to securities or to real estate are developing combined portfolios.

Investment literature generally has retained this distinction in concepts between market value, as reflected by market prices, and investment values, based upon the use of multipliers or capitalization-of-income methods. Graham, Dodd, and Cottle use the term *intrinsic value*, while others use variations of the expression "long-term investment value." In a recent review of the valuation methods employed by security analysts, the author concluded that most techniques were based upon some modification of an earnings or dividend multiplier or capitalization rate, usually adjusted for anticipated growth in dividends or earnings.[23]

A price-earnings ratio for a stock is essentially the same concept as the price-net income multiple for real estate or its reciprocal, a percentage figure which is usually termed *broker's yield*. Estimated future earnings per share are often used in security analysis, instead of current or past earnings, to represent a price-future earnings ratio. This concept is identical with the use of stabilized future income from real estate expressed as a percentage of market or offering price, or in a reciprocal relationship as a multiplier.

The influence of depreciation policies and taxes upon net income has focused increasing attention on after-tax cash flow in security analysis and in real estate valuation. Cash flow per share is generally reported in corporate financial reports, and security values are often represented as multiples of cash flow per share. Cash flow is generally regarded as the prime measure of the productivity of a real estate investment, and the discounted cash-flow method is widely employed in establishing real estate investment values.

The notion that common stock returns should be treated as a perpetuity, while real estate returns are usually limited to the physical life of improvements, is gradually disappearing, as financial analysts become increasingly reluctant to forecast beyond the foreseeable future. Hence, stock earnings or dividends are customarily discounted over some limited period and a terminal value assumed at the end of that time. This, of course, is identical with the capitalization approach for real estate, where some residual land value is hypothesized at the end of the life of the improvements.

It is significant that some elements that have loomed as important in appraisal theory are almost totally disregarded in security evaluation. The concept of fair market value has only a specialized legal connotation in security valuation. Market values are reflected in the marketplace and there is seldom any debate whether market prices of listed issues are fair or reflect complete knowledge on the part of buyers and sellers. This distinction is not unexpected, of course, since shares of stock of the same company are identical, unlike different real estate parcels, and they enjoy a more active and perfect market generally.

The concept of replacement cost as evidence of the value of securities is given little recognition. Book values, except in special cases of corporations holding primarily liquid assets, are accorded little attention today in estimating the values of securities. Indeed the whole notion of equivalence among the cost, market, and income approaches is completely ignored in security analysis. Recently, however, some authors supporting the random-walk theory of stock market price behavior have argued that the increasing availability of investment information tends to cause market prices to adjust rapidly to inherent investment values, bringing these two concepts closer together.[24] As knowledge about the prospects of corporate earnings improves and becomes more widely disseminated, market prices will conform more closely with investment values, according to these writers. Following similar reasoning it might be contended that as market knowledge concerning real estate income prospects improves, the disparity between market values and investment values will narrow.

Probably the value concepts, theory, and methods of valuation employed in real estate appraisal will gradually conform more generally to those in the field of security valuation, as the basic similarity in the valuation process becomes more apparent. The rationale for the present structure of appraisal theory should thus be examined in the light of its relationship with valuation theory in the field of investment finance. As the close relationship between security and real estate valuation becomes more generally perceived, it is likely that the language and vocabulary used in the two fields will also become more similar. The concept of the rate of return on investment in securities or in real estate will mean the same thing, for instance, as will the terms *cash flow*, *depreciation*, *leverage*, and *net income*.

The psychic equivalence of the three approaches, as well as the outmoded straight capitalization, split rates, and many of the nuances of depreciation calculation and the residual approaches, will easily be recognized by security analysts as irrelevant.

Accountants on Valuation The distinction between conceptual theories of value and the practical problems of valuation is set forth in clear outline in the writings of Canning.[25] He pointed out that theories of value are conceptual but that theories of valuation are statistical, involving measurement. Acknowledging the conceptual validity of Fisher's income theory of value, he stressed the difficulty of estimating future returns from capital goods and rationalized the use of market prices as "working valuations."[26] Another writer on accounting theory expressed a similar view: "The real value of any asset at any given time . . . may be said to be the present (discounted) value of its future services. . . . the values of tangible fixed assets are not usually established by computing the present value of their future services; for the difficulty of imputing values (of services) to specific assets often makes this method very impracticable."[27]

Any discussion of the contribution of accountants to appraisal theory would not be complete without mention of writings on the theory and measurement of depreciation, a key factor in both the replacement-cost and capitalization-of-income methods of valuation. In a review of the accounting theory of depreciation Dewing points out that depreciation charges have been recognized by accounting historians as early as the sixteenth century, and he cites much of the voluminous literature on depreciation theory which has developed in the past two decades.[28]

It has long been recognized that in theory the problem of estimating depreciation is synonymous with the problem of estimating value, and that the accounting theory of depreciation as amortized cost is a necessary compromise because of the difficulties of estimating values. Appraisal theory has adapted much from accounting theory of depreciation. The familiar present-day classification in appraisal theory of physical, functional, and economic depreciation can be recognized in accounting writings as early as 1913.[29] Further such variations in methods of calculating depreciation as the straight-line, sinking-fund, and other annuity methods were first developed in accounting literature.

Modern accounting theory has increasingly emphasized market price as the central criterion of value. Sterling, in a recent work, says:

> The problematic situation that the trader and other interested receivers find themselves in is one of valuation. . . .

THE DEVELOPMENT OF APPRAISAL THEORY

One bit of information is relevant to all these decisions: the present price.[30]

A Statement of Basic Accounting Theory, published by the American Accounting Association in 1966, specifically recommends the use of market price indexes in the estimation of real estate values.[31]

As emphasis on historical and reproduction cost as a measure of value is reduced, it can be expected that much of the language of appraisal theory which was originally adopted from the field of accounting will disappear from general usage in real estate appraisal, including the familiar classification in appraisal theory of physical, functional, and economic depreciation and the use of age-life tables.

Although this review has been brief, it indicates clearly that the contribution to appraisal theory by writers in applied fields of economics has been extensive. In addition to the work of economists a substantial volume of literature has been developed on engineering valuation. Although writers in the engineering field have relied heavily upon the work of economists and accountants for their theory of value, they have made contributions to the mathematics of income capitalization and depreciation which are widely employed in appraisal theory.[32]

Contributions of Appraisers

Lawyers, accountants, engineers, government officials, bankers, and others had developed specialized concepts of value and techniques for establishing values long before appraisers became a recognized professional group.[33] It is important to recognize that appraisal theory inherited a body of concepts and techniques which had been established in practice and accepted by the courts. Writers in the appraisal field have attempted to integrate economic theories of value and valuation with these established valuation principles and practices.

Early Emphasis on Market Sales   One of the early textbooks on valuation procedures in England illustrated the manifold purposes for which valuation was required in that country and emphasized the influence of legal and administrative regulations upon the fixing of an estimate of value.[34] The authors established as a general rule that the capital value of real property shall be estimated by capitalization of net income and presented basic formulas for the construction of capitalization tables, similar to those which had been in use for some time in calculating bond yields and values. Discussing the separate valuation of land and buildings, the authors state that comparable sales will provide an indication of the values obtaining in particular localities. Their discussion of the replacement-cost method is limited to a description of the square-foot and cubic-foot techniques. It is notable that

25

there is no reference in the book to the Marshallian doctrine of the equivalence of normal cost, capitalized income, and market value.

A pioneer book in the valuation field in the United States, written by Richard M. Hurd, has been referred to in chapter 1.[35] Holding that economic rent is the basis of value, Hurd set forth the procedure accepted today for calculating the residual return to land and capitalizing these returns to obtain land value. He pointed out that capitalization rates tend to vary for different classes of property. Hurd thus describes the relationship between market value and capitalized income value: "While intrinsic value is correctly derived by capitalizing ground rent, exchange value may differ widely from it. As ordinarily expressed, 'Value' means exchange value, average sales being considered the best test of value, and since all ownership lies subsequent to the date of purchase, the estimated future prospects form the mastering factor of all exchange values."[36]

Hurd wrote from a wealth of practical experience in the real estate business, and his comments upon the influence of utilities and transportation upon urban values and his presentation of the operating ratios for various classes of buildings and their effect upon values established a standard of enlightened inquiry which has seldom been equaled in this field since he wrote. One of his most important contributions to appraisal theory was his translation of the economic principle of proportionality to investment in real estate.

Contrasted with the sophistication of Hurd's writing, McMichael and Bingham's widely read book, published in 1923, seems to mark a regression in appraisal theory.[37] The authors state that four cardinal factors determine value in land: (1) location, (2) utility, (3) shape and topography, and (4) size. This classification demonstrates their failure to recognize the dependence of utility upon the other factors mentioned. Valuing land, according to McMichael and Bingham, cannot be classed as an exact science, but buildings may be accurately valued. The authors recommend analysis of comparable sales as the proper appraisal procedure. The only mention of the capitalization-of-income method is contained in a statement that "a careful appraiser will consider the income from an improved property."[38] This work illustrates the general reliance of predepression theory upon the market-comparison method.

Attempts to Develop Scientific Assessment Values   The work of Pollock and Scholz portrays the dissatisfaction of the engineer-appraiser plagued by the practical difficulties of establishing scientifically accurate valuations.[39] Their work, like that of Zangerle which is discussed below, grew out of property-assessment procedures developed between 1910 and 1920 by W. A. Somers and others. The authors, pointing out the difficulties of applying the capitalization process and the imperfections of the real estate market, concluded that "neither actual selling price, long-term leases, capitalized rentals, nor so-called 'market values' of land can serve as accurate bases or indices to be used as evidence for purposes of land valuation."[40]

Following this conclusion they outline a complicated procedure for conducting a public opinion survey to ascertain the value of the 100 percent location in a community and, based upon that value, to factor out the values for the 90 percent, 80 percent, and other locations. This technique, which included the preparation of depth- and corner-influence tables, has been referred to as the "Somers System of Land Valuation." Variations of this plan were used as the basis for municipal assessments in New York, Cleveland, Chicago, Philadelphia, and other cities, beginning in 1910.

John A. Zangerle, assessor for the city of Cleveland, developed further the theory of standardized real estate values for assessment purposes in his book published in 1924.[41] Zangerle held that "market value" was the central concept of concern to the appraiser and that "these fifty-seven varieties of appraisal, to suit the purchaser, are not calculated to elevate the profession."[42]

It is interesting to observe that the use of the electronic computer in calculating the values of urban real estate by multiple regression techniques was first proposed for use in tax assessment work by Raoul Freeman in 1959.[43] This represents one of the most advanced and fruitful avenues for improving the reliability of the market-comparison approach to establishing real estate values and is being employed in a number of cities and counties for establishing assessment values. It would appear that the assessors, who have traditionally been the innovators in the processing of mass data for determining assessed values, will once again be in the forefront of change and application of the new computer technology to real estate market data. A detailed review of recent application of multiple-regression analysis in real estate appraisal is included in chapter 5.

Influence of Economists   The influence of economists upon appraisal theory is most clearly evident in the writings of Arthur J. Mertzke, Horace F. Clark, and Frederick M. Babcock.[44] Mertzke employed the Marshallian concept of normal value as the foundation for his appraisal writings. Kingsbury quotes from the mimeographed work:

> It is obvious that all who have long-time interests in property, like owners and lending institutions, are interested primarily in normal value. . . . Buyers, sellers and brokers on the other hand are interested not only in the long-time trend but also in the temporary market fluctuations . . . after the normal value has been computed on the cost basis this must be corrected in the light of market conditions for any given date, in order to show the current market value of the property. . . .
> We may conclude then by saying that the value of a house and lot will be equal to the cost of the lot plus the cost (or cost of replacement) of the house

(subject to qualifications discussed earlier — suitability of site, typicality of construction features for the community, and allowance for depreciation and obsolescence), corrected by a reasonable addition or deduction as indicated by prevailing market conditions.

In the long run . . . it is possible to show that rentals and property values are governed very largely by costs, because the supply of rental properties in the long run tends to adjust itself to a level that will yield a fair return on the cost of the property. When rents are high, the supply of building is increased until rentals fall to the fair return level, and when rents are too low, building tends to ease until the demand has again had time to grow sufficiently to bring rents up to the point where they again represent a fair return on the investment.[45]

Although Mertzke appears to have recognized the controlling importance of market values, his emphasis upon normal cost and the equivalence of the three approaches to value has had a profound influence upon appraisal theory.

Frederick M. Babcock, following the value theory of Marshall and Fisher, developed further the thesis that value represents the present worth of future returns from property. He illustrated this theory by the use of highly developed techniques for capitalizing estimated returns in a series of case problems. Babcock drew heavily from the pioneer work of Grimes and Craigue in the evolution of his income premises and in his derivation of present-value-annuity formulas.[46] The most notable feature of Babcock's work was his rejection of cost as evidence of value and his emphasis upon the capitalization-of-income method. Babcock, rejecting the view held by most economists at that time, emphasized the distinction between value and price, thus furthering the development of an extensive dichotomy over the meaning of value in appraisal literature. Babcock also rejected the view that replacement cost, market value, and capitalized-income value would be equal for other than new buildings and established criteria for the selection of the appropriate method of valuation to be used in specific cases. His exposition of the land and the building residual methods and of methods of estimating capitalization rates and depreciation provided the basic structure upon which most modern appraisal theory rests.

Recent Developments in Appraisal Theory

Until recent years, academicians accepted the body of appraisal theory that had been developed largely by practicing appraisers. This was due, in large measure, to the dominance of professional appraisers and their organizations in the education of appraisers and to the neglect of the field in academic curricula. The status of appraisal teaching in universities can be likened to the situation which prevailed in the accounting field before the 1930s when most university teaching of accounting was carried on by professional accountants on a part-time basis. The fields of real estate appraisal and urban land economics generally still occupy a marginal position in the curricula of most leading universities, although the number of full-time professors teaching these subjects has increased substantially over the past decade.

The publication of *Real Estate Appraisal — A Critical Analysis of Theory and Practice* in 1956 represented one of the early strong dissents by an academician with the body of appraisal theory developed by Schmutz, May, and others that had become institutionalized in the textbooks of the American Institute of Real Estate Appraisers. Since that time several university scholars have given expression to their rejection of many of the doctrines of traditional appraisal theory, including the correlation of the three approaches; straight capitalization; split rates; the residual approaches; the segregation of physical, functional, and economic depreciation; and the use of replacement cost as a measure of value.

E. Holland Johnson, writing in the *Encyclopedia of Real Estate* in 1959, stated, "The Cost Approach is usually a secondary approach to value for cost does not entirely reflect market conditions."[47] Kahn, Case, and Schimmel stated in 1963 that "the insistence among some appraisal theorists that the majority of appraisals require the use of the three approaches and that the three will produce approximately the same estimates has produced some amazingly complex and unrealistic appraisal estimates."[48] And elsewhere Sanders A. Kahn has argued that "the real error of the cost approach is in not seeing clearly that a property established as a going concern is more than merely a pile of arranged materials on a parcel of land; it is also a complex of established economic relationships ready to provide a flow of income out of the relationships of revenue, expense and capital employed."[49] Prof. Wallace F. Smith in his study of *The Low-Rise Speculative Apartment* came to a similar conclusion in reporting that the finished apartment building was in almost all cases worth more than the sum of the prices paid for the parts.[50] In a broad attack on established appraisal doctrine Prof. Richard U. Ratcliff stated in 1965 that "the Cost and Income approaches, as they are conventionally presented, prove to be mainly irrelevant."[51]

Elsewhere in a recent article Ratcliff asserted that the conventional "capitalization formulas do not even closely replicate or simulate the real world system by which market price of income property is established" and hence he argues that "it follows that the conventional residual capitalization formulas are unlikely to produce a value figure which is market value."[52] Having dismissed the cost and income approaches as irrelevant, Ratcliff concluded, based upon a study of a large sample of income property appraisals, that real estate brokers, mortgage lenders, and many appraisers place primary reliance upon the direct conversion ratio (gross income or net income multipliers) in establishing values. He reported that in 77 percent of the appraisals he studied appraisers had placed primary reliance upon the direct conversion ratio and that in the "correlation" step they had adjusted the other approaches so as to produce value figures of respectable consistency.[53]

An interesting insight into the attitude of the courts with respect to the three approaches is found in a recent decision of the California District Court of Appeals which held that the three methods are usually combined. The court quoted from page 66 of *The Appraisal of Real Estate*, published by the American Institute of Real Estate Appraisers.[54]

A "thorough-going, sweeping review of appraisal theory" was called for by Dr. William N. Kinnard in a paper entitled "New Thinking in Appraisal Theory," presented at the Southwest Conference of the Society of Real Estate Appraisers at Dallas, Texas, on 28 April 1966. More recently he has called attention to "The Approaching Crisis in Appraisal Education," in the April 1968 *Appraisal Journal* where he characterized most appraisal courses available as "a repetition of relatively inflexible ideas, techniques and standards which have not kept pace with the development of modern, advanced techniques of investment and market analysis." In an earlier work the author concluded that there had been no major contributions to appraisal theory since the writings of Babcock in 1932 and Bonbright in 1937.[55] The rigid, taxonomic structure of post–World War II appraisal theory is under attack from many sides today and appears to be ripe for a fresh restatement integrating the most recent work in economics, statistics, and computer technology with changes in real estate market structure and information sources.

Mortgage Lenders   Mortgage lenders have made major contributions to appraisal theory in recent years by steps taken to improve market data as well as by sponsoring innovations in capitalization of income techniques. Under the financial sponsorship of mortgage lenders, market price series and current cost data for single- and multiple-family residences were developed in several metropolitan areas beginning soon after World War II.[56] Members of the Society of Residential Appraisers and of the American Institute of Real Estate Appraisers and leading mortgage lending institutions cooperated in the assembly of these market data on sales prices and building costs.

Improved market sales data for many classes of property, including apartment buildings, shopping centers, and office buildings, provided a more reliable statistical foundation for the use of gross income multipliers. The use of gross income multipliers was encouraged by the fact that investors and lenders realized increasingly that net income figures were seldom calculated or reported on a consistent basis and hence could not be relied upon in comparing different properties. This forced mortgage lenders and others to turn to the two figures which were usually both comparable and possible to confirm – gross income and market sales prices. Reported cost figures, which had been relied on to a large extent in FHA and VA lending policies, fell into disfavor when it was realized that costs varied widely among individual builders, were seldom reported correctly, and could be easily overstated in order to qualify for a higher loan.

Leon W. Ellwood, chief appraiser for the New York Life Insurance Company, took issue with many of the widely accepted capitalization-of-income techniques as early as 1956.[57] Ellwood pointed out that real estate could rise or fall in value over time and that the change in market value was the significant measure of depreciation to the investor. *Ellwood Tables for Real Estate Appraising and Financing*, published originally by the author in 1959, set forth a mathematical procedure for deriving overall capitalization rates, given selected mortgage terms, and assumed equity rates and depreciation or appreciation. Ellwood's work spelled the death knell to many established appraisal concepts and techniques such as straight-line depreciation, straight capitalization, declining annuities, split rates, and much of the dichotomy of physical, functional, and economic depreciation which had been under attack from academic circles. This significant break with tradition, designed as a mortgage lender's manual, measured depreciation in market terms rather than by age-life or other techniques and provided an improved method of developing a band-of-investment overall capitalization rate. Ellwood treats depreciation or appreciation as an addition or subtraction of a percentage figure from his overall weighted band-of-investment capitalization rate. Ellwood's technique makes more explicit, even though it does not eliminate, the problem of subjective determination of capitalization rates, which is the source of much of the flexibility in the capitalization-of-income method.[58]

An important shortcoming of Ellwood's technique is that it is designed for use in valuation cases with assumed level incomes over time. Although the concept of a stabilized gross income can be defended, cash flow to the investor, the critical element in his valuation decision, is seldom or never a level amount because of the prevailing use of accelerated depreciation methods and changing income tax liabilities over time. Increasing recognition of the critical importance of after-tax cash flow to the investor and the growing adaptation of the computer to the rapid determination of rates of return and valuation under varying income, depreciation, and tax assumptions have limited the extensive application of Ellwood's techniques in practical investment decisions. A modification of Ellwood's formulation is presented in chapter 6 which overcomes this shortcoming in the Ellwood tables.

The growing participation of life insurance companies and other institutions in equity participation and investment in real estate promises further innovations in valuation techniques. Computer programs are presently available which can compute and print out after-tax cash flows, rates of return, and valuations based upon varied assumptions with respect to the depreciation methods used, mortgage terms, and income tax rates – all within seconds. These techniques will undoubtedly lead to greatly improved market data and sophistication in the application of valuation techniques by real estate brokers and investors.

31

Real Estate Brokers   The real estate broker has never given more than lip service to appraisal theory and to the nuances of differentiating between market price and market value. In company with the mortgage lender his interest centers upon market price, and the most realistic test of the value of any specific property for him is found in the comparable sales of similar properties. Several developments during the past decade have served to improve the flow of reliable market data among real estate brokers. First, the development of multiple listing services in virtually every urban community has provided a means of rapid communication of listing and sales price data that have been widely used by brokers in estimating the value of residential properties. Second, market price indexes for different classes of residences, including multiples, have been initiated over the past decade in a number of metropolitan areas. These price indexes have provided a continuous flow of information to mortgage lenders and brokers on average price trends in the various communities. The third and most recent development has been the initiation of computerized retrieval systems that make it possible for brokers and lenders to have almost instantaneous access to the latest listing and sales information for various types of properties in any specific location.[59] It has been predicted that within the next decade most real estate marketing will be done by computer and that regional real estate markets will soon be linked to form a national real estate exchange.

The American Institute of Real Estate Appraisers was established in 1932 as an affiliate of the National Association of Real Estate Boards. However, the subsequent organization of the Institute of Property Management, the Commerical and Investment Division of the National Institute of Real Estate Brokers, and the Society of Real Estate Counselors — all affiliates of NAREB — reflects the breadth of interest in various aspects of real estate valuation and, to some degree, the brokers' dissatisfaction with the conventional appraisal methodology sponsored by the American Institute of Real Estate Appraisers. The real estate broker, manager, and counselor, in close contact with investors and the market place, have a keen awareness of the importance of depreciation accounting, financing terms, and federal income tax shelter. They have supplanted the traditional appraisers' and brokers' concept of net income before taxes and financing charges with the concept of cash flow to the equity holder after federal and state income taxes and express this for the investor before and after so-called equity buildup (that is, amounts paid off on principal of the mortgage over a period of time). The concept of after-tax income became of increasing importance to investors following the enactment of the Revenue Act of 1954 with its optional depreciation scheduling and has become the critical factor influencing individual and institutional real estate investment decisions since that time.[60] Newly developed computer techniques for calculating rates of return and investment values based upon projected cash flows have brought the real estate broker into the mainstream of new developments in appraisal theory.

Influence of Government Agencies   The influence of government agencies upon appraisal theory and practice has been growing rapidly since World War II. In addition to staff appraisers with the Federal Housing Administration and the Veterans Administration, the appraisal function is carried on in the Departments of the Interior, Agriculture, Defense, Transportation, Justice, and Commerce, as well as the Atomic Energy Commission, General Services Administration, Public Health Service, Federal Communications Commission, and Tennessee Valley Authority. The American Right of Way Association was organized to carry on education programs for those engaged in acquisition of rights of way for public bodies. Urban redevelopment agencies have staff appraisers engaged in property acquisition for urban redevelopment and renewal. Chapters of an organization known as the Society of Government Appraisers have been started in many sections of the country.

The Society of Real Estate Appraisers, formerly known as the Society of Residential Appraisers, has taken the leadership in the training of appraisers for the savings and loan industry, supplementing special courses offered by the American Institute of Real Estate Appraisers, the Mortgage Bankers Association, the American Bankers Association, and other organizations. The very magnitude of the task of training large numbers of appraisers has tended to dampen innovation and freeze the body of theory and knowledge included in course offerings by these groups. The doctrine of the three approaches and their correlation has become institutionalized in publications and courses sponsored by the American Institute of Real Estate Appraisers and in examinations for membership in this and other professional organizations. There has been a natural fear that the process of advancing candidates to membership might be confused by criticism of existing theory, and the tendency to freeze the content of course offerings was encouraged by the use of part-time, professional appraisers as instructors. Textbooks used in institute courses are subject to committee review that tends to reduce the speed and frequency with which new ideas and concepts are widely disseminated. Further, the threat implicit in the existence of so-called appraisal review committees tends to encourage conformity in appraisal practice. However desirable this may seem to a professional organization in improving its image, it most assuredly dampens innovation and criticism of existing theory and practice.

The Federal Housing Administration has been in the forefront of developments in appraisal theory since the contributions of Frederick M. Babcock, Ernest Fisher, and others to early editions of the *Underwriting Manual*. Recent revisions of the valuation section of the *Manual* represent a refreshing statement of the principles and methods of valuation of residential property, free of much of the mumbo-jumbo found in the professional literature.[61]

Courts of law and public agencies reinforce the lag between appraisal practice and theory since professional practitioners are influential upon policies and court decisions. The traditional lag in recognition by the courts of law of changes in valuation theory will most certainly continue in evidence, and it can be expected that existing and widely accepted tenets of appraisal theory and practice will change only slowly in the years immediately ahead, owing in large measure to the institutional drags.

Summary

This brief review has emphasized the eclecticism in the development of appraisal theory. Although economists before the turn of this century were primarily concerned with explaining the nature and causes of value, the three commonly used approaches to the estimation of value were well established in the writings of the neoclassical economists by 1910. Fisher had developed the complete theoretical exposition of the capitalization-of-income method by 1906. Although the theoretical validity of the capitalization-of-income method has had general acceptance, writers in the fields of corporation finance, investments, and accounting have long recognized the difficulties in the establishment of values by that method and its reliance upon market values and, as a result, have turned to costs or to the market as the prime source of value information.

The doctrine of the three approaches to value had its roots in the theoretical relationship between costs, market values, and capitalized income under conditions of stable equilibrium developed by Marshall and his followers. There has been a growing recognition by economists of the important departures from these relationships under dynamic conditions, with the result that the theory has been considered to have limited applicability in practical valuation problems.

The writings of Hurd, Mertzke, and Babcock stand out as milestones in the development of present-day appraisal theory. Hurd concentrated his attention upon market sales as the central concept and prime evidence of value. He accepted the theoretical validity of the capitalization-of-income method, but recognized the practical difficulties in establishing values by use of that method. Mertzke, some twenty-five years later, was influential in introducing the economic ideas of normal value and the equivalence of the three approaches into appraisal theory. Relying heavily upon Fisher's theories and mathematical techniques, Frederick Babcock developed the synthesis which is the basis for modern appraisal theory. He rejected market prices as evidence of value. As a consequence his concept of long-term warranted value has been the central value concept influencing residential appraisals for the past two decades. His emphasis upon the capitalization-of-income method has been gradually rejected in appraisal practice, although it is honored in theory. The extent to which modern appraisal theory differs with Babcock on the question of selection of method will be taken up in more detail in chapter 9.

Members of the American Institute of Real Estate Appraisers have led in the development of appraisal theory since the establishment of the institute in the 1930s. The rejection of Babcock's views on the capitalization-of-income method caused a return to the principle of the three approaches to value which had been advocated by Mertzke in the 1920s. Paralleling this, an added emphasis upon the doctrine of correlation has developed. The origins and evolution of this doctrine will be more thoroughly discussed in chapter 9.

Most modern appraisal writers have refused to accept the conclusion of economists that market value and market price are synonymous. This has brought about further multiplication-of-value concepts and has impeded the development of a unified appraisal theory. Babcock's attempt to develop the concept of long-term warranted value was influential in its effect upon government appraisal practices, but it has served to widen the gap between so-called market values and observed market prices in the marketplace. As a result of Babcock's heritage, the modern appraiser must "dance to many tunes." The three value approaches of neoclassical economics provide a convenient framework with which appraisers are able to choose concepts, and hence values, to suit the purpose at hand. The significance of this built-in flexibility in appraisal theory will be examined in greater detail in the subsequent chapters.

Appraisal theory appears to be on the threshold of a major reorientation and integration with general valuation theory. The major point of this movement, deriving largely from brokers and investors, is to emphasize market price as the primary evidence of value and after-tax cash flow as the investor's primary objective. In the following chapters the author presents a theoretical framework designed to reflect the renewed emphasis upon market prices and their relationship to the concept of investment value.

Cash-flow analysis, with earliest applications in the fields of capital budgeting and investments, has come upon real estate appraisal with a rush and promises to supplant more naive applications of the capitalization approach in the determination of investment value.

Meanwhile, the demand for more accurate valuations for assessment and mortgage loan purposes has given impetus to the improvement of market value estimation by use of multiple regression analysis and computer retrieval of market sales information. Appraisal theory and practice are undergoing rapid innovation and change in the early 1970s.

ECONOMIC BASE ANALYSIS IN APPRAISAL THEORY

The returns from real estate are dependent upon the highly complex interaction of economic forces on the international, national, regional, and local levels. Economic base or background analysis, as it is alternately referred to, is the process of determining the probable impact of these collective forces upon a local area. The broad relationships between economic events and real estate values are recognized in appraisal writings. However, there are substantial differences in the importance attributed to the analysis of the economic base and little attention has been devoted to techniques for analysis. It is the purpose of this chapter to establish more clearly the meaning and significance of economic base analysis in appraisal theory and to review and evaluate the various analytical techniques which have been developed in allied fields.

Meaning of the Term *Economic Base*

Andrews, in a series of articles on the urban economic base, defined the term *economic base* as "the export activities of a community that bring in its *net* earnings and enable it to continue as an independent economic entity."[1] This conception of the economic base had its roots in the writings of F. L. Nussbaum, Homer Hoyt, and others who visualized a city as an economic unit dealing with the outside world. According to this analysis the flow of purchasing power to a city and its volume of employment will depend upon its capacity to produce goods and services demanded by the outside area. Those activities which bring income to a city from outside areas are variously referred to as "urban-growth," "primary," "basic," "export," or "town-builder" activities, as contrasted with "secondary," "service," "residentiary," or "town-filler" activities.

Weimer and Hoyt hold that the growth of an urban economy will depend upon the rate of expansion in its functions and suggest a functional classification:

1. Industrial cities, including those involved chiefly in the manufacturing and processing of commodities.
2. Cities devoted principally to commerce, which includes seaports, lake ports, river cities, and railroad terminals and junctions.
3. Political cities, including all those for which the activities of a state government or the Federal government provide the basic income source.
4. Recreational and health resorts, as well as cities in which retired people reside.

5. Educational, research, and cultural centers.[2]

The above classification is but one of many similar attempts to group cities by types of major activity. Although a few cities may be identified as having a single predominant economic function or activity, most large cities can be recognized as multifunctional.

Andrews drew attention to the fact that the term *economic base* is defined more broadly in other sources.[3] Differences in definition of the term result in part from the fact that the economic base of cities and regions is the subject of study by many groups with varying objectives. Business cycle theorists, marketing specialists, city planners, real estate market analysts, and appraisers are all vitally concerned with analysis of the economic base of urban areas. In each of these fields economic data pertaining to a given locality are studied with somewhat different objectives. The business cycle theorist is primarily interested in the relationship between the movements in national economic series and the movements of these series for individual regions. Marketing specialists, on the other hand, are chiefly concerned with the sales potentialities for various classes of goods in specific areas and with interregional trade. City planners study the economic base in order to forecast future population and to translate it into estimates of future land use requirements. The center of interest in the study of the economic base by the housing market analyst is in the estimation of the future demand for housing.

Weaknesses in the technique of estimating future employment by use of a simple basic-nonbasic ratio were highlighted in the writings of Blumenfield, Pfouts, Curtis, and others in the mid-1950s.[4] It became evident in these writings that the "naive" economic base models, which relied solely upon the extrapolation of future employment by applying a single basic-nonbasic ratio to estimated employment in export industries, rested upon inadequate theoretical foundations.

Charles M. Tiebout, writing in the February 1956 issue of *Land Economics*, concluded that the economic base concept was useful as a framework for analysis of aggregate urban activity, but that it was a serious mistake to emphasize export activities as the only force influencing aggregate urban incomes. He said:

> In summation, the base is simply a modified form of an old economic concept, the multiplier. Its usefulness is derived from the logic of the assumptions made concerning the behavior of the dependent and independent activities. These are yet to be tested fully by empirical research.
>   . . . The definition of basic activities as the exports of goods, services and capital beyond the boundaries of the region can be misleading. If the object of a base study is to show the forces determining the level of income, this concept is too limited in its coverage. This follows from the fact that as the boundaries of a region are expanded, exports become less and less.[5]

The theory of the economic base was so strongly entrenched in appraisal theory that Tiebout's warning that the "base concept cannot explain everything" appears to have gone unheeded. Andrews rationalized the emphasis upon manufacturing as an important part of the economic base of community in 1962.[6]

More recently, Homer Hoyt, one of the early proponents of the use of economic base analysis in forecasting future population trends, has reexamined employment and population growth in fifty-seven metropolitan areas from 1960 to 1968 and concluded that "there is a marked correlation between the increase in factory jobs and population growth."[7] The data which Hoyt cites to support the above conclusions are summarized in tables 3–1 and 3–2.

A least-squares analysis of the data for the fifty-seven metropolitan areas cited by Hoyt for which data were available fails to reveal marked correlation between the increase in factory jobs and population growth. Rather, it appears that the rate of population growth from 1960 to 1967 was negatively

Table 3-1. Percentage of Increase in Manufacturing, Nonagricultural employment except Manufacturing, 1960-1967; Increase in Population, 1960-1968, in Leading U.S. Metropolitan Areas with Population One Million or Over (January 1968)

| | | Percentage of Increase | | |
| | | 1960–1967 | | |
Standard Metropolitan Area	Mfg. Emp. of Total Emp.	Nonagricultural except Mfg.	Manufacturing Employment	1960–1968 Population
New York–N.E. New Jersey	27.71%	16.35%	0.06%	10.30%
Los Angeles–Orange County	32.30	46.71	25.20	29.90
Chicago	33.56	20.05	13.07	16.28
Philadelphia	33.87	19.29	- 0.31	11.56
Detroit	40.90	22.00	11.87	13.17
San Francisco–Oakland	17.25	26.78	2.34	22.12
Seattle–Everett–Tacoma	29.90	36.53	38.30	23.81
Atlanta	22.04	46.05	38.31	39.40
St. Louis	33.50	22.94	11.63	12.86
Washington, D.C.	4.10	43.67	31.63[a]	42.30
Dallas	26.40	. . .	55.00	25.63
Houston	20.34	. . .	26.35	35.72
Kansas City	30.00	24.90	23.98	20.54
Boston	24.93	18.99	0.26	7.03
Baltimore	27.51	27.91	5.43	14.36
Minneapolis–St. Paul	28.19	26.46	35.28	24.56
Denver	18.00	26.49	15.78	30.24
Cleveland	37.93	21.39	9.51	11.88
Cincinnati	35.00	22.72	7.84	11.01
Buffalo	36.79	15.46	0.96	7.81
Pittsburgh	34.79	2.69	- 0.31	4.52
San Diego	19.00	29.00	-11.93	27.10
New Orleans	15.82	26.38	29.30	28.80

[a]Federal government employment.

Source: Homer Hoyt, "Importance of Manufacturing in Basic Employment," *Land Economics* 45 (August 1969): 346.

correlated with the percentage of manufacturing employment to total employment and that growth in nonmanufacturing employment was more closely associated with population growth than was growth in manufacturing employment. The standard errors are small and the t statistic measures indicate that the results have a high statistical reliability.[8] Higher correlation and R^2 coefficients for "nonagricultural employment except manufacturing" indicate that nonmanufacturing employment growth would have been a better predictive variable for estimating population during this period of growth than percentage changes in manufacturing employment. The regression of population change on percentage change in manufacturing employment alone reveals a low coefficient (0.36) and the R^2 measure (0.38) and high standard error indicate that percentage changes in manufacturing employment alone were of little or no value as predictors of population change in the metropolitan areas cited by Hoyt.

Analysis of the stepwise coefficients of multiple determination (R^2) confirms the observation that percentage changes in nonmanufacturing employment account for the largest percentage of the explained variation (48 percent) in population, while the introduction of the variables "percentage employed in manufacturing" and "percentage changes in manufacturing employment" each add only about 10 percent to the explained variation. Separate analysis of the thirty-one metropolitan areas with population under one million leads to the hypothesis that population growth is less responsive to percentage changes in manufacturing employment in large metropolitan areas than in smaller metropolitan areas and vice versa. Conversely, although percentage changes in nonmanufacturing employment in smaller metropolitan areas still appear to have a larger influence upon population growth than do percentage changes in manufacturing, the margin of difference is not as great as compared with the metropolitan areas with population over one million. Further, the percentage of the change in population explained by all three independent variables, as measured by the R^2 coefficient, is markedly lower for the thirty-one smaller metropolitan areas. Apparently other variables had a substantial influence upon population growth for the small metropolitan areas during the period examined.

The observed differences in regression measures for the twenty-one large and thirty-one small metropolitan areas suggest the hypothesis that population growth in the early stages of city growth may have a closer dependency upon changes in manufacturing employment, although the relationship between nonmanufacturing employment growth and population still appears closer. The association between nonmanufacturing employment and population growth appears greatly magnified as metropolitan areas reach the later stages of growth. This conclusion seems quite logical since the larger the metropolitan area, the less it relies upon export income, which is usually associated with manufacturing.[9] It must also be recognized that employment

CHAPTER 3

Table 3-2. Increase in Population Compared with Increase in Manufacturing Employment in Selected Metropolitan Areas with Less than One Million Population, 1960–1968

| Standard Metropolitan Area | Percentage of Increase | | | |
| | 1960–1967 | | | |
	Mfg. Emp. of Total Emp.	Nonagricultural except Mfg.	Manufacturing Employment	1960–1968 Population
Akron	42.0%	26.3%	12.6%	15.6%
Albuquerque	8.4	23.0	7.9	29.7
Allentown	50.0	20.3	7.4	11.3
Ann Arbor	28.9	35.7	24.0	27.6
Birmingham, Ala.	28.8	23.1	18.6	7.9
Charleston, S.C.	28.5	67.5	40.2	28.5
Charlotte, N.C.	25.6	42.2	45.9	25.6
Columbus, Ohio	25.1	30.6	19.1	23.7
Dayton	41.2	25.0	23.0	14.4
Flint	53.4	28.0	10.4	11.9
Fort Worth	...	...	53.1	25.0
Grand Rapids	43.0	22.5	18.1	22.5
Hartford, Conn.	37.7	28.4	30.7	14.7
Jacksonville	13.5	27.4	12.9	12.1
Lexington, Ky.	22.9	24.7	75.3	39.5
Louisville	36.0	21.3	26.5	14.5
Madison, Wis.	14.7	48.2	21.2	27.0
Memphis	22.8	30.8	26.2	22.3
Mobile	21.3	...	14.8	7.4
Newport News	30.0	40.6	28.1	33.6
Norfolk-Portsmouth	10.5	23.6	16.3	26.1
Oklahoma City	13.4	29.9	50.7	26.6
Omaha	20.0	19.4	0.5	15.8
Rochester, N.Y.	44.8	27.1	24.4	16.7
Sacramento	11.2	26.6	-13.5	22.3
Salt Lake City	16.4	22.6	11.4	12.9
San Antonio	12.1	...	20.7	13.1
San Bernardino	18.1	36.9	35.3	34.5
San Jose	35.8	72.0	71.3	55.0
Syracuse	31.0	30.0	- 0.5	5.7
Toledo	35.5	44.6	30.1	9.5
Tucson	10.2	50.6	3.6	33.3
Tulsa	24.4	23.2	40.8	19.3
Youngstown	47.2	11.6	8.9	12.0

Standard Metropolitan Area	Govt. to Total Emp., 1967	Increase Govt. Emp., 1960–1967
Columbus, Ohio	21.2%	46.1%
Madison, Wis.	36.9	61.7
Oklahoma City	29.1	40.2
Sacramento	39.9	46.9
Tucson	28.2	62.4
Salt Lake City	19.2	50.5
Norfolk-Portsmouth	32.3	25.8
Mobile	19.5	-25.8
Washington, D.C.[a]	38.6	32.9

[a]The only metropolitan area in this group in the one million and over population size.

Source: Homer Hoyt, "Importance of Manufacturing in Basic Employment," *Land Economics* 45 (August 1969): 348.

of a service nature has expanded very rapidly over the past decade in most large, growing metropolitan areas.

The traditional theory that manufacturing employment is necessarily linked with export activities needs much closer examination. Growth of employment in research and development, finance, real estate, and government has probably contributed more to the expansion of incomes in California than has manufacturing during the past decade. Prof. Ray Northam asks, "Why does change in the economic base result in decline of urban Center B, while Centers A and C continue to grow even if slowly?"[10] Hoyt's attempt to substantiate traditional economic base theory by reference to recent employment and population trends is unconvincing. The theory of the economic base appears ripe for reexamination. It is to be hoped that the sharpened tools of computer-assisted multiple regression analysis can contribute to this effort.

The above review of population and employment growth in the fifty-two metropolitan areas for which Hoyt provided data suggests that the relationships between employment and population growth will vary with the employment structure of the area, its size, and stage of growth, as well as with external and internal demand forces and its social and political organization. Future relationships between employment and population growth for any metropolitan area may differ substantially from those observed for other areas and from those observed in the past. Basic trends in the national economy support this view. Figure 3–1 shows that trade, finance and service, and government employment have increased more rapidly over the past two decades than has employment in manufacturing and mining. The total number of employees on payrolls of nonagricultural establishments rose from 54,347,000 (monthly average) in 1960 to 71,517,000 in November 1971. During this same period the number of employees on manufacturing payrolls rose from 16,762,000 to 18,685,000. An increase of approximately 31 percent in total nonagricultural employees on payrolls was matched by an increase of only 11.4 percent in employees of manufacturing establishments. (It is important to recognize that national manufacturing employment estimates include office employees of manufacturing concerns and thus tend to overstate the number of production workers.) We are entering a period in which nonmanufacturing employment is expected to increase even more rapidly as compared with employment in manufacturing industries. Two reasons account for this. First, the demand for services tends to increase rapidly as incomes rise in an affluent society. Second, the continued rise in manufacturing productivity will continue to exceed increases in productivity in the government and service sectors.

As the importance of nonmanufacturing employment increases and as metropolitan areas expand, it will be increasingly difficult to classify industries in the traditional basic-nonbasic or export and service categories that have been used in the past. The assignment of proportions of employment

41

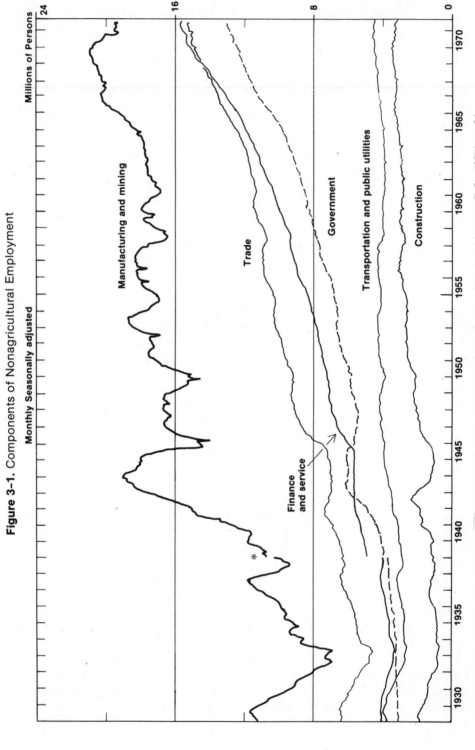

Figure 3–1. Components of Nonagricultural Employment

Monthly Seasonally adjusted

Millions of Persons

Manufacturing and mining

Trade

Finance and service

Government

Transportation and public utilities

Construction

Source: Board of Governors of the Federal Reserve System, *Historical Chart Book, 1971* (Washington, D.C., 1971), p. 81.

in such fields as financial services, trade, and communications to basic and nonbasic categories will become even more difficult as transportation and communication between metropolitan areas is improved. For these and other reasons, land-use simulation models have been designed to forecast population growth and urban development and will be described in chapter 4.

Economic Base Analysis and the Appraiser

The real estate appraiser has need for all of the approaches to the study of the economic base. His forecasts of incomes and market prices of real estate require knowledge of the cyclical sensitivity of local area incomes to economic disturbance. Estimation of the future incomes which may accrue to industrial and commercial property requires a knowledge of market areas and growth trends for industrial products. In the appraisal of these classes of property the appraiser must also be familiar with the locational factors affecting various classes of industrial and commercial enterprises. The estimates of population growth and land use requirements developed by the city planner furnish key data for the appraiser in judging the rates of growth for various districts and their effects upon urban land values. With reference to residential property the concern of the real estate appraiser is practically identical with that of the housing market analyst since they are both interested in forecasting the future demand for and supply of residential space. The all-embracing concern of the real estate appraiser with the analysis of the economic base can be summarized in the observation that since he finds it necessary to forecast future incomes for industrial, commercial, and residential property in a given locality, he must understand the structure of that economy and the probable impact of international, national, and regional economic developments upon it. An important factor which is frequently overlooked, however, is that the appraiser must also assess the influence of supply factors as they will influence future incomes, occupancy ratios, and prices.

It is apparent from the foregoing discussion that economic base analysis is of primary significance to the appraiser in the capitalization-of-income method, since this method requires the long-term forecasting of property incomes. In contrast the market-comparison and replacement-cost methods require limited economic base analysis. It can be assumed that buyers and sellers in the market will give consideration to the economic base in establishing prices. The appraiser, therefore, is not constrained to analyze the national, regional, and local economic outlook in employing this method. Similarly, replacement costs represent market observations, and deductions for depreciation are based upon market observation at the time of the appraisal, rather than upon any forecast of future development. It could be maintained, however, that the appraiser using either the market-comparison or the replacement-cost method might analyze the economic base in order to test, so to speak, the validity of the assumptions concerning the future which appear to be accepted and discounted in the market.

Although there is wide recognition in appraisal literature of the importance of the economic base as an influence upon property values, few writers have recognized the more or less limited applicability of economic base analysis in the appraisal process and its counterpart in the analysis of supply influences. Although economic base analysis is used over the entire range of appraisal problems and methods, it appears to be true that the analysis is of major significance only in the capitalization-of-income method. Estimates of prices of future market sales involve forecasts and hence would require economic base analysis.

Techniques of Analysis

Babcock on Analytical Technique   Limited attention is given to the techniques for analysis of the economic base in appraisal literature. Babcock pointed up the importance of population estimation in appraising property but held that the functions of the appraiser did not necessarily include the prediction of population changes.[11] In his discussion of the various methods for predicting future population of a city, he declared:

> One method makes the prediction of future population proportional to the expected growth of some industry which dominates the city. Thus in Grand Rapids, Michigan, a prediction would be made by projecting the historical growth of the furniture industry into the future and making the estimates of future population proportional to the projected curve. This method is probably tolerably accurate for short predictions but is not generally applicable to cities having a wide diversification of industry.
> Another method which is used assumes that the city increases in population by an absolute number of people each year. . . .
> Another method assumes population to grow geometrically. . . .[12]

Babcock used the classification developed by Hurd in 1903 which grouped cities as commercial, industrial, or farming centers; political capitals; or educational or resort cities. Although Babcock indicated the importance of estimating city growth in appraising property, he paid little heed to the technique for such estimation and appeared satisfied with the advice that "if there are not demonstrable reasons why past forces will not continue to operate, they may be assumed to operate inevitably."[13] Many more sophisticated techniques have been developed for the projection of local population estimates.

May on Analytical Technique   In his textbook *Valuation of Residential Real Estate*, Arthur A. May emphasized the importance of national, regional, and local economic factors in appraisal work, but he provided little or no explanation of the techniques for analysis of the economic factors. In the chapter on "National and Regional Influences on Value" he said:

> The national economy has intimate relation to the value of real property. . . .
>
> The region that surrounds the city – the hinterland – presents a field of study requiring exploration in the data program. Its *population growth* and trend must be subjected to the same type of inquiring analysis as that of the nation and the city.
>
> The *economic background* must be accorded intelligent study as to its effect on the ebb and flow of the prosperity of the city within the region. In the case of the commercial or trading center, the scope of the regional trading area and its ability to continue the production of those commodities that sustain the central city bear investigation. In the case of manufacturing cities, the accessibility of raw materials used in the manufacturing process is important in that it indicates the economic stability of the principal city within the region.[14]

Economic Base Analysis in Recent Appraisal Literature Few, if any, contributions have been made in recent years to the theory of the economic base in appraisal literature. Kahn, Case, and Schimmel, for example, offered the appraiser little practical guidance in their 1963 text: "There is no simple, consistently effective and accurate method of analyzing the economic base of a community. Rather, the appraiser must evaluate several factors and, in the light of his business experience and judgment, decide what impact they will have on property values."[15]

Analysis of the economic base is accorded only brief mention in Alfred Ring's *Valuation of Real Estate*, published in 1970, and is discussed only cursorily in the 1967 edition of *The Appraisal of Real Estate*, published by the American Institute of Real Estate Appraisers. The appraiser must be satisfied with a statement found in the latter work that "the appraiser must keep well informed of economic trends. He must keep in close touch with price levels, purchasing power, population trends, building cycles, government regulations, construction costs and interest rates."[16] Henry Babcock's recent book *Appraisal Principles and Procedures* makes no mention of economic base analysis.[17]

Dasso, writing in the July 1969 *Appraisal Journal*, illustrates the technique for forecasting population growth for the Portland, Oregon, metropolitan area by extrapolating employment trends for the period 1960 to 1967 and estimating an employed participation rate of 45 percent in 1975.[18] His analysis considers trends in total employment and represents a markedly superior technique to traditional economic base analysis which relied upon a forecast of basic employment growth only and the estimation of total employment by

Table 3-3. Employment Projections to 1975 by Major Industry Group for Portland Metropolitan Area

Major Industry Group	1967 Employment Number	Percentage of Change in Employment		Employment in 1975	
		1960–1967 Actual	1967–1975 Estimated	Number	Percentage of Distribution
Agriculture	12,900	-24.12%	- 27.6%	9,300	1.79%
Contract construction	15,600	5.41	33.3 a	20,800	4.00
Manufacturing	81,600	26.71	40.3	114,500	22.00
Durable goods manufacturing	51,700	46.05	61.1	83,300	16.00
Lumber, wood products	9,400	9.30	- 4.3 a	9,000	1.73
Furniture, fixtures	2,400	26.32	30.0	3,100	0.60
Primary metals	6,600	26.92	30.8	8,600	1.65
Fabricated Metals	6,500	44.44	50.8	9,800	1.88
Nonelectrical machinery	6,200	44.19	50.5	9,300	1.79
Electrical machinery	8,400	95.35	109.0	17,600	3.38
Transportation Equipment	7,200	140.00	160.0	18,700	3.60
Other durables	5,000	38.89	44.4	7,200	1.38
Nondurable goods manufacturing	29,900	3.10	4.4	31,200	6.00
Food, kindred products	9,700	- 3.96	- 4.5	9,300	1.79
Textile mill products	2,300	- 11.54	- 13.2	2,000	0.38
Apparel, other textiles	3,300	6.45	7.4	3,500	0.67
Paper, allied products	7,900	6.76	7.7	8,500	1.63
Printing, publishing	3,600	5.83	6.7	3,800	0.73
Other nondurables	3,100	29.17	33.3	4,100	0.79
Transportation, communications, utilities	29,500	7.27	8.3	31,900	6.13
Wholesale trade	29,100	26.52	30.3	37,900	7.29
Retail trade	56,200	28.31	32.4	74,400	14.31
Finance, insurance, realty	21,300	42.95	49.1	31,800	6.12
Services & miscellaneous	53,900	42.59	48.7	80,100	15.40
Government	54,800	37.34	42.7	78,200	15.04
Self-employed, unpaid family, domestics	45,700	3.39	- 10.0	41,100	7.90
Totals	400,600	18.30	28.76	520,000	100.00

[a] Judgment used in projecting rate of change.

Source: Jerome Dasso, "Economic Base Analysis for the Appraiser," *Appraisal Journal* 37 (July 1969): 382.

extrapolating a basic-to-service employment ratio. Dasso's employment projections for the Portland metropolitan area to 1975 are shown in table 3–3.

Urban Land Economics

Ratcliff on Analytical Technique   Urban land economists have developed techniques for analyzing the economic background of cities. These techniques are based upon the conception of "export" or "primary" industries as the key determinants of local economic conditions. Ratcliff asserts:

> A clear understanding of the economic base of a particular city is requisite to an understanding of the demand for land located in it. No prediction of the factors that influence the demand for the services of urban land can be made without forecasting the future trends in the basic economic activities of the area. City planning, planning to meet the housing needs of the community, forecasting population trends, foretelling the real estate market, appraising land values, predicting tax revenues – all these and many other prognostications call for an analysis of the economic base of the area as a first step.[19]

Ratcliff then outlines a procedure for appraising the economic base of a community which includes the following steps: "(1) prepare inventory of local economic resources, (2) identify 'primary' or 'city building' activities, and (3) analyze the characteristics and outlook for 'primary' industries." He points out that the relations between local industries and national economic conditions must be carefully studied. Citing the advantages of a diversified economic base, he concludes that the nature of a city's industries is more important than the degree of diversification.

Weimer and Hoyt on Analytical Techniques   Weimer and Hoyt outlined essentially the same procedure for analyzing the economic base of a city, emphasizing the importance of "urban growth" sources of employment. They recommend the following steps: "(1) determining the relative importance of major present and potential income sources; (2) analyzing each of the basic sources of income – manufacturing, trade, extractive industry, other types; and (3) studying modifying influences – the size of the local market, quality of community facilities and service, governmental factors, and the general 'climate' for local economic activities."[20] This technique has been applied by Homer Hoyt in the economic analysis of the New York metropolitan region; Chicago; Baltimore; Washington, D.C.; Raleigh, North Carolina; Orlando, Florida; Brockton, Massachusetts; and many other cities.

There are important theoretical and practical shortcomings in the application of this technique. First, the authors fail to point out that the geographical area chosen for analysis will alter the classification of different employments as "basic" or "urban service." For example, the services of a large hospital catering to a metropolitan area or of a wholesale auto supply firm may be urban growth employment if the city is viewed as extending only to its corporate limits, but it would be considered as urban service employments if the city is viewed more broadly as encompassing the entire metropolitan area. The identification of basic employments is further complicated by the fact that many concerns "whose production is intended predominantly for the local market" may produce goods which are an integral part of products which are exported from the area. For example, a local firm may manufacture adhesives which are sold entirely in the local market yet are destined for use in products exported from the area.

Finally, this technique and variations of it have essential defects in that they overlook the important differences which exist between the economies of cities and of the nation as a whole. Contrary to some assumptions the proportion of population engaged in trade and service activities is not uniform among cities. The expenditures of the population of New York for amusements or of Los Angeles for automobiles, for example, would most certainly be higher than the national average, and hence employment in these fields would be grossly underestimated by using the technique recommended above.

It should be emphasized that the difficulties referred to thus far involve the relatively simple problem of describing the present structure of employment in an area. The forecasting of future employment in the various urban growth employments presents far greater difficulties. Weimer and Hoyt appear to recognize the nature of these problems in the third recommendation cited above. The obstacles in the preparation of such an exhaustive study of the economic outlook for a city are immeasurable. First, the separate analysis of the economic outlook for each individual firm is virtually impossible in any large city because of the numbers of firms involved. Second, not only are the data lacking for such analysis, but the influences of many of the factors recommended for consideration are indeterminate. Third, almost any conclusions reached could be substantially altered by slightly modified hypotheses regarding the national and regional outlook. It should also be observed that a forecast of changes in the supply factors affecting the particular segment of the real estate market under appraisal are lacking in this analytical framework.

Artle, in a review of various approaches to the analysis of metropolitan economies, drew attention to the fact that the economic base theory improperly assumes one-way relationships; a change in the basic industries is assumed to cause a change in the non-basic industries.[21] He also draws attention to a more fundamental shortcoming in economic base theory, that the "multiplier" or basic-nonbasic ratio, remains constant. Artle points out that changes in household consumption and government expenditures provide capital investment, and other components of income and expenditure act to change the multiplier. In his words, "it would be hard to find any change in technical or organizational know-how which would not imply a change in the base-theory multiplier."[22] The author concludes that the input-output model brings out the interdependence among all the different industries and offers much greater potential development than the economic base model.[23]

Federal Housing Administration Technique   The Federal Housing Administration adopted a technique for analyzing the economic background of cities in connection with its mortgage insurance program. This technique, which was evolved under the guidance of Ernest M. Fisher and Homer Hoyt during the 1930s, was based upon the analysis of the employment trend and cyclical fluctuations in a city's primary or urban growth activities. The first step in the FHA technique was the identification of the basic or primary sources of employment in the locality. The volume of employment in these categories is multiplied by two to give effect to the contribution of basic employment to the support of service activities. The percentage of those engaged in trade was calculated as a residual after deducting the percentage engaged in industry and specialty occupations. The sum of the weighted ratings for each category of employment was finally adjusted for what is referred to as the *scope of the market* in the last step illustrated in the *Underwriting Manual*. According to the description in the latter publication, this term referred to "the degree of marketability or residential properties at current value levels in the economic background area."

According to a recent report, the economic base theory of analysis is no longer applied directly in FHA housing market studies. The report characterizes the economic base theory of urban analysis as "simple enough as a working plan, but it is quite difficult to implement."[24] Because of the problems of basic activity classification and data assembly, the FHA has adopted the concept of total employment as the basis for analysis and projection. Hence, the segmentation of basic and nonbasic employment is eliminated.

The FHA has placed increasing emphasis upon local housing market analysis, encompassing reviews of vacancies and unsold inventories and analysis of new construction, migration, and family formation. Local housing market analyses are published for major metropolitan areas and provide an important source of market data for the appraiser. The general outline of these reports includes reference to the economy of the area, demographic factors, housing market factors, demand for housing, and area summaries, which summarize the demand and supply factors operative in the sales and rental markets in specific subareas. Although these analyses are designed primarily to guide mortgage lenders and the FHA in forecasting short-run market trends, they furnish a highly useful substitute for the traditional economic background analytical technique of the FHA.[25]

Recent Developments in National and Regional Economic Analysis

The complexity of the task of forecasting urban economic growth can be illustrated by figure 3–2, which shows the manner in which physical and human resources are combined through new investment to result in an expanding urban structure. The appraiser seeking to forecast future incomes accruing to real property in any region or metropolitan area must rely upon both national and regional forecasting. As noted above, the traditional approaches to economic forecasting in appraisal theory have relied upon subjective forecasts or naive trend projection techniques.

Several new and improved techniques have been developed recently which are of significance to the appraiser in attempting to forecast the economic growth of the nation or of the region. Among the more important of these are the following: (1) econometric models of the national economy, (2) current national and regional economic projections prepared by governmental and other bodies, (3) refinements in regional income analysis and projections by the U.S. Department of Commerce, (4) regional economic studies published by Federal Reserve banks for individual districts, (5) input-output studies for specific regions, (6) long-range projections for specific regions and metropolitan areas.

Having in mind that economic base analysis has significance primarily in the capitalization-of-income approach and that the appraiser will essentially be a user of the results of projections such as those above, it will suffice to explain the general methods of estimation employed in these various approaches and evaluate their general usefulness in real estate appraisal.

A national econometric model is a mathematical representation of the interrelationships between the various sectors of the national economy. During the late 1950s there was a growing professional interest and sophistication in the construction, interpretation, and use of large-scale macroeconomic models.[26] The Brookings-SSRC econometric model of the United States, developed under a grant from the National Science Foundation during 1961 to 1963, is the most elaborate economic model with a short-run stabilization focus in the United States.[27] This model, which is based on quarterly data, includes more than one hundred fifty equations developed by a team of economists to represent the interrelationships between the purchasing decisions of consumers, the investment decisions of producers and home builders, and government fiscal and monetary policies. The Brookings Institution, which assumed responsibility in 1963 for testing and improving the model, is pursuing studies of the impact of various governmental policy actions and other variables upon personal consumption and business expenditures and upon the national income. Subsequent simulation studies involving the use of this and other econometric models have emphasized the importance of the magnitudes of the exogenously determined variables required for the models' use. In other words, to employ such models for long- or medium-

Figure 3-2. Urban Growth Processes

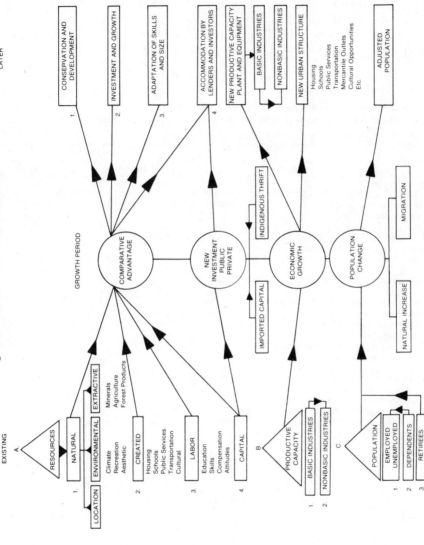

Source: U.S., Department of Housing and Urban Development, Urban Renewal Service, Technical Guide, no. 20, *Economic Factors in Urban Planning Studies* (Washington, D.C.: Government Printing Office, 1966), pp. 18-19.

term forecasts, the user must make explicit assumptions concerning a number of policy and other exogenous variables.

For this reason, most appraisers will choose to rely upon specific forecasts of long-term national or regional economic development under varying assumptions. The Council of Economic Advisers, in its annual economic report to the president of the United States, makes projections of short-term national economic growth in various sectors of the economy.[28]

Table 3-4. Summary of NPA Projections, 1967–1980
(All expenditure figures in billions of 1967 dollars unless otherwise noted)

		Projected		
	Actual	Judgment		Target
Item and Unit	1967	1973	1980	1980
Population (millions)	199.1	213.7	235.2	235.2
Labor force (millions)	80.8	89.3	100.3	100.6
Employment (millions)	77.8	86.0	96.7	97.7
Average weekly hours (hours)	38.34	37.26	36.82	36.79
Unemployment rate (percent)	3.8	3.8	3.7	3.0
Consumption (billion dollars)	492.2	631.6	868.4	924.5
Investment	114.3	158.1	223.0	249.4
Of which: residential construction	24.6	42.0	56.7	65.6
Net experts	4.8	9.5	15.5	16.1
Government purchases of goods and services	178.4	212.1	277.4	300.4
Federal purchases of goods and services	90.6	95.9	113.7	112.6
State-local government purchases of goods and services	87.8	116.2	163.7	187.8
GNP	789.7	1,011.3	1,384.3	1,490.4
In current prices	789.7	1,195.6	1,920.1	1,933.3
GNP deflator (1967 = 100)	100.0	118.3	138.7	129.7
Total government expenditures (billion current dollars)	241.2	359.2	587.2	613.0
FRB index of industrial production (1957–1959 = 100)	158.1	201.6	273.7	. . .
Private residential housing starts (millions)	1.29	1.89	2.42	2.80

Average Annual Growth Rates			
		1967–1980	
	1948–1967	Judgment	Target
GNP[a]	3.9%	4.4%	5.0%
Labor force	1.3	1.7	1.7
Employment	1.4	1.7	1.8
Average weekly hours	-0.4	-0.3	-0.3
Manhours	0.9	1.4	1.5
GNP per manhour	2.9	3.0	3.5

[a]Based on constant dollars.

Source: National Planning Association, Center for Economic Projections, *National Economic Projection Series,* "Report 68-N-1: National Economic Projections to 1978/79" (Washington, D.C., January 1969), p. 16.

The National Planning Association, a nonprofit organization, also makes long-term projections of growth in the national and regional economies of the United States, based upon various assumptions concerning basic population growth, international developments, and other exogenous variables.[29] A summary of their national forecasts to 1980 is shown in table 3–4. The NPA also published *Economic and Demographic Projections for States and Metropolitan Areas* in 1968 and 1969.

Shift-Share Technique The United States Department of Commerce has continued its publication of "Income Payments to Individuals, by Regions," in the *Survey of Current Business*, which reflects the long-run trends in regional economic growth in the nation. Table 3–5 shows the relatively rapid growth in recent years in income payments to individuals in the South and in the West and the relatively slower rates of growth in the Rocky Mountains, New England, Plains, Midwest, and Mideast regions. The Department of Commerce also publishes analyses which show the relative rates of growth of employment by specific category for each region, state, and county, in comparison with the nation as a whole.[30] Table 3–6 illustrates the growth in employment from 1948 to 1969 by decades and by regions. The same reference includes breakdowns of employment changes by counties and by industry.

The shift and share method of analyzing regional growth, originally developed by Edgar S. Dunn, Jr., and Lowell D. Ashby, provides a highly useful technique for explaining differential rates of economic growth among regions.[31]

The heading in table 3–6 entitled "National Growth" represents the theoretical growth which might have occurred in each region if total personal incomes had increased there at the same rate as for the nation as a whole. Thus, since total incomes in the nation as a whole increased by approximately $139.6 billion in the decade from 1948 to 1957, the number for each region in the column under "National Growth" represents that region's share of estimated national personal income change. Similarly, the numbers for 1959 to 1969 represent the share of each region in national personal income change from 1959 to 1969.

The columns in table 3–6 headed "Income Component Mix" represent the change in regional personal incomes which would have occurred if incomes for each component of total employment had increased in the region for the relevant period at the same rate as did each industry's incomes in the nation as a whole. The estimate for "Net Relative Change" is calculated by multiplying 1948 employment in each of 32 SIC employment categories by the percentage increase in national employment in each category for the period, less the national all-industry growth rate. The "Income Growth Factors" are calculated for the periods from 1948 to 1957 and 1959 to 1969.

Table 3–5. State and Regional Change in Total Personal Income

	Percentage of Change		Relative Difference between State (Regional) and National Growth Rates[a]	
	1948–1957	1959–1969	1948-1957	1959–1969[b]
United States	66.8%	34.5%	0 %	0 %
Fast-growing states[c]	79.3	108.8	18.7	15.1
Nevada	137.8	163.9	106.3	73.4
Florida	154.0	140.6	130.5	48.9
Hawaii	. . .	132.7	. . .	40.4
Arizona	130.7	132.4	95.7	40.1
Georgia	75.4	129.1	12.9	36.6
South Carolina	58.0	124.1	- 13.2	31.3
Alaska	. . .	123.8	. . .	31.0
North Carolina	60.2	123.3	- 9.9	30.5
Virginia	75.2	120.8	12.6	27.8
Maryland	89.6	120.4	34.1	27.4
Vermont	52.1	111.9	- 22.0	18.4
Tennessee	60.4	107.4	9.6	13.7
Arkansas	30.9	105.3	- 53.7	11.4
South Dakota	16.6	103.6	- 75.1	9.6
Mississippi	32.5	103.5	- 51.3	9.5
California	101.3	103.4	51.6	9.4
Connecticut	85.4	102.7	27.8	8.7
Texas	80.9	102.6	21.1	8.6
Colorado	84.9	101.6	28.6	7.5
New Hampshire	65.0	100.4	- 2.7	6.2
Michigan	74.1	100.3	10.9	6.1
Washington	63.9	100.2	- 4.3	6.0
Minnesota	49.4	97.8	- 26.0	3.5
Kentucky	53.9	97.7	- 19.3	3.4
North Dakota	11.3	94.9	- 83.1	0.4
Louisiana	87.7	94.9	31.3	0.4
Slow-growing states[c]	58.5	83.1	- 12.4	- 12.1
Alabama	65.7	94.2	- 1.6	- 0.3
Indiana	63.4	93.0	- 5.1	- 1.6
New Jersey	80.5	91.3	20.5	- 3.4
Rhode Island	44.8	90.4	- 32.9	- 4.3
Oregon	50.0	89.8	- 25.1	- 5.0
Nebraska	37.0	89.5	- 44.6	- 5.3
Oklahoma	56.7	89.4	- 15.1	5.4
Massachusetts	57.9	87.2	- 13.3	- 7.7
Utah	83.0	86.9	24.3	- 8.0
Iowa	25.6	85.6	- 61.7	- 9.4
Delaware	109.5	85.5	63.9	- 9.5
Illinois	55.0	83.7	- 17.7	- 11.4
Wisconsin	60.5	83.6	- 9.4	- 11.5
New York	56.7	83.3	- 15.1	- 11.9
Ohio	79.8	82.4	6.0	- 12.8
Kansas	58.5	80.6	- 12.0	- 14.7
Missouri	50.9	79.8	- 23.8	- 15.6
Maine	46.0	75.4	- 31.1	- 20.2
Pennsylvania	59.1	75.0	- 11.5	- 20.6
Idaho	52.3	72.4	- 21.7	- 23.4
District of Columbia	25.4	69.1	- 62.0	- 26.9
New Mexico	120.2	63.4	79.9	- 32.9

Table 3–5—*Continued*

	Percentage of Change		Relative Difference between State (Regional) and National Growth Rates [a]	
	1948–1957	1959–1969	1948–1959	1959–1969[b]
Montana	48.1	61.5	- 28.0	- 34.9
West Virginia	39.6	61.2	- 40.7	- 35.2
Wyoming	50.3	50.1	- 24.7	- 47.0
Coefficient of variation	0.45	0.22	. . .	. . .
	Regions			
Fast-growing regions[c]	79.7	107.1	19.3	13.3
Southeast	70.2	113.6	5.1	20.2
Far West	91.2	102.9	36.5	8.9
Southwest	81.8	100.7	22.5	6.6
Slow-growing regions[c]	60.5	86.9	- 9.4	- 8.0
New England	62.9	92.3	- 5.8	- 2.3
Great Lakes	64.5	87.9	- 3.4	- 7.0
Plains	41.8	87.1	- 37.4	- 7.8
Mideast	62.5	84.9	- 6.4	- 10.2
Rocky Mountain	69.7	84.2	4.3	- 10.9
Coefficient of variation	0.20	0.10	. . .	. . .

[a] [(State or regional growth rate divided by national growth rate) less 1.00] 100.

[b] Regional rates in this column are based on change over the entire period.

[c] Order of states and regions based on 1959–1969 rate of growth.

Source: *Survey of Current Business*, August 1970, p. 17.

The third and final component of the shift and share method of analysis gives effect to the fact that the regional growth rate in specific industry groups may be greater or less than the national growth rate for those industries. The estimates for "Regional Share" are calculated as the difference between the actual increase in regional personal incomes over the relative period and the algebraic sum of the estimated "National Growth" and "Income Component Mix" elements. It might be described as the portion of regional growth in personal incomes not "explained" by national growth trends or by the employment structure per se in a particular region. It represents a residual of all the other manifold influences affecting employment trends in a region.

It will be noted that the components of regional income change may be positive or negative. A negative "Income Component Mix" for a given region indicates that the region had a concentration of employment in industries with incomes growing at rates below the all-industry national level. A negative "Regional Share" component provides an indication that the personal

Table 3-6. Regional Growth Effects

	1948-1957					1959-1969				
	Total Personal Income Change	National Growth	Income Growth Factors		Net Relative Change[a]	Total Personal Income Change	National Growth	Income Growth Factors		Net Relative Change[a]
			Income Component Mix	Regional Share				Income Component Mix	Regional Share	
	(billions of dollars)					(billions of dollars)				
United States	139.6	139.6	0	0	0	361.6	361.6	0	0	0
Fast-growing regions	54.7	45.8	- 2.7	11.5	8.9	148.7	131.3	- 2.4	19.9	17.5
Southeast	22.3	21.2	- 3.1	4.2	1.1	68.6	57.1	- 1.6	13.1	11.5
Far West	21.7	15.9	1.2	4.6	5.8	53.6	49.3	0.3	4.1	4.4
Southwest	10.7	8.7	- 0.8	2.7	2.0	26.5	24.9	- 1.1	2.7	1.0
Slow-growing regions	85.0	93.6	2.5	-11.5	- 8.8	210.3	228.7	2.4	-20.6	-18.2
New England	8.7	9.2	1.2	- 1.8	- 0.5	22.5	23.1	0.8	- 1.3	- 0.5
Great Lakes	30.8	31.9	1.4	- 2.5	- 1.1	73.3	78.8	0.8	- 6.3	- 5.5
Plains	8.3	12.1	- 4.2	- 0.8	- 4.9	26.3	28.6	- 1.0	- 1.2	- 2.3
Mideast	34.0	36.3	4.8	- 7.2	- 2.4	80.9	90.0	2.1	-11.2	- 9.0
Rocky Mountain	3.2	3.1	- 0.7	0.8	0.1	7.3	8.2	- 0.3	- 0.6	- 0.9

Table 3-6—Continued

	Total Personal Income Change	1948-1957 National Growth	Income Growth Factors Income Component Mix	Regional Share	Net Relative Change[a]	Total Personal Income Change	1959-1969 National Growth	Income Growth Factors Income Component Mix	Regional Share	Net Relative Change[a]
		(distribution of dollar change)					(distribution of dollar change)			
United States	100.0%	100.0%	0 %	0 %	0 %	100.0%	100.0%	0 %	0 %	0 %
Fast-growing regions	100.0	83.7	- 4.9	21.0	16.3	100.0	88.3	- 1.6	13.4	11.8
Southeast	100.0	95.1	-13.9	18.8	4.9	100.0	83.2	- 2.3	19.1	16.8
Far West	100.0	73.3	5.5	21.2	26.7	100.0	92.0	0.6	7.6	8.2
Southwest	100.0	81.3	- 7.5	25.2	18.7	100.0	94.0	- 4.2	10.2	6.0
Slow-growing regions	100.0	110.1	2.9	-13.5	-10.4	100.0	108.7	1.1	- 9.8	- 8.7
New England	100.0	105.7	13.8	-20.7	- 5.7	100.0	102.7	3.6	- 5.8	- 2.2
Great Lakes	100.0	103.6	4.5	- 8.1	- 3.6	100.0	107.5	1.1	- 8.6	- 7.5
Plains	100.0	157.8	-50.6	- 9.6	-50.0	100.0	108.7	- 3.8	- 4.6	- 8.4
Mideast	100.0	106.8	14.1	-21.2	- 7.1	100.0	111.2	2.6	-13.8	-11.2
Rocky Mountain	100.0	96.9	-21.9	25.0	3.1	100.0	112.3	- 4.1	- 8.2	-12.3

[a]The sum of "income component mix" and "regional share."

Note: Details may not add to totals because of rounding.

Source: Survey of Current Business, August 1970, p. 20.

incomes in the region's industries grew less rapidly (or declined more rapidly) in the region than in the nation as a whole.[32]

The column headed "Net Relative Change" in table 3–6 measures the difference between the total change in the region for the relevant period and the theoretical "National Growth" shown for the region in the relevant period. A negative figure in this column indicates that the total employment growth in the region has been relatively less than the growth in the nation.

This analytical scheme provides the appraiser with a convenient framework for interpreting the significance of national and regional personal income trends. The shift and share method of analysis has been recently employed in forecasting employment and income trends in the Coastal Plains development region, the Wisconsin Upper Great Lakes region and in the Northeast Georgia region, under the auspices of the Economic Development Administration, U.S. Department of Commerce.[33] The author projects an average annual rate of growth in employment in the Wisconsin Upper Great Lakes region from 1967 to 1980 of 0.9 percent, slightly above the region's 1959 to 1967 growth rate, but lower than the 1.5 percent rate estimated for the remainder of the state and the 1.6 percent growth rate estimated for the nation as a whole to 1980. Using essentially the same techniques, the author projected an employment increase in the Northeast Georgia Region at an annual rate of 2.0 to 2.2 percent for the same period.[34] The estimated rates of employment change by industry were computed from national projections made by the U.S. Bureau of Labor Statistics. The BLS estimated rates of employment change were applied to estimated 1967 employment by industry groups to arrive at national projections of employment by industry as of 1980. These national projections were used to compute "National Growth" and "Industrial Mix" components of regional employment growth to 1980, as shown in table 3–7.

Two alternative methods were employed to estimate the all-important "Regional Share" of employment growth to 1980 for the Northeast Georgia region. The first assumption, which resulted in "A" Projection of a 2.2 percent average annual growth in employment, hypothesized that the "Regional Share" component during the period from 1967 to 1980 would be the same as for the 1959 to 1967 period, after adjustment for a different national employment base and a longer time period. The "B" Projection was based on the assumption that the "Regional Share" component of growth from 1967 to 1980 would decline to 75 percent of the 1959 to 1967 level after adjustment. (See table 3–5 for "A" and "B" Projections.) It is important to observe that the "Regional Share" component is a residual in historical analysis of employment or income trends, but that it represents a subjectively determined but key element in any regional forecast.

The shift and share method of analysis provides the appraiser with a greatly improved tool for analyzing and interpreting historical trends in regional employment and incomes. It is also a useful supplementary technique

Table 3-7. Employment Projections Based upon Application of Shift-Share Analysis—Northeast Georgia, 1967-1980

		Projection 1967 to 1980									
		"A" Projection						"B" Projection			
	Emp. in 1967	Natl. Growth	Ind. Mix.	Reg. Share[a]	Total Change	1980	Annual Change	Reg. Share[a]	Total Change	1980	Annual Change
Agriculture	6,041	1,462	-2,959	-2,668	-4,165	1,876	-8.7%	-2,001	-3,498	2,543	-6.5%
Mining	550	133	- 191	381	323	873	3.6	286	228	778	2.7
Con. cons.	4,044	979	454	2,611	4,044	8,088	5.4	1,958	3,391	7,435	4.7
Food prod.	3,204	775	- 888	1,074	961	4,165	2.0	805	692	3,896	1.5
Textiles	6,433	1,557	-2,122	-1,304	-1,869	4,564	-2.7	- 978	-1,543	4,890	-2.1
Apparel	8,891	2,151	- 515	2,285	3,921	12,812	2.8	1,714	3,350	12,241	2.4
Lumb. & wood	970	235	252	- 284	- 301	669	-2.9	- 213	- 230	740	-2.1
Furniture	150	36	13	- 199	- 150	0	0	- 199	- 150	0	0
Paper	191	46	- 15	53	84	275	2.8	40	71	262	2.4
Print., pub.	452	109	34	253	328	780	4.2	190	265	717	3.6
Chemicals	123	30	8	- 42	- 20	103	-1.4	31	9	114	-0.6
Pet. refin.	0	0	0	0	0	0	0	0	-	0	0
Rub., plas.	237	57	51	451	559	796	9.7	338	446	683	8.4
Leather	0	0	0	0	0	0	0	0	0	0	0
Stone, clay	1,402	339	2	461	798	2,200	3.5	346	683	2,085	3.0
Prim. met.	178	43	43	326	326	504	8.3	244	244	422	6.8
Fab. met.	437	106	61	531	576	-1,013	6.6	398	443	880	5.5
Machinery	480	116	7	310	419	899	4.9	233	342	822	4.2
Elec. mach.	725	175	44	72	203	928	1.9	54	185	910	1.7
Trans. equip.	309	75	68	482	489	798	7.5	361	368	677	6.2
Instr., misc.	1,565	379	115	1,464	1,728	3,293	5.8	1,098	1,362	2,927	4.9
Trans. serv.	947	229	- 301	- 282	- 354	593	-3.6	- 211	- 283	664	-2.7
Comm., p.u.	1,420	344	- 165	- 794	973	2,393	4.0	596	775	2,195	3.4
Trade	9,968	2,412	127	1,750	4,289	14,257	2.7	1,312	3,851	13,851	2.5
Fin., ins., R.E.	1,534	371	66	783	1,220	2,754	4.6	587	1,024	2,558	4.0
Services	9,961	2,410	2,366	-2,433	2,343	12,304	1.6	1,825	2,951	12,912	2.0
Fed., civ., & mil.	2,043	494	- 207	168	455	2,498	1.5	126	413	2,456	1.4
State & local	9,429	2,282	2,768	1,883	6,993	16,362	4.3	1,412	6,462	15,891	4.0
Total	71,684	17,345	-2,152	7,332	24,113	95,797	2.2	6,641	21,833	93,517	2.0
				Relative change = 6,702					Relative change = 4,489		

[a] "B" Projection assumes a decline in regional share to 75 percent of the 1959-1967 level after adjustment.

Source: Charles F. Floyd, *Employment and Income: Its Structure and Change in Northeast Georgia*, prepared for Northeast Georgia Area Planning and Development Commission, Athens, Ga., August 1970, table A-18. Northeast Georgia includes the eleven counties of Clarke, Jackson, Barrow, Walton, Newton, Morgan, Oconee, Greene, Oglethorpe, Elbert, and Madison.

in estimating basic employment in the conventional economic base multiplier analysis.

These government studies have resulted in a technique of regional economic analysis termed the *shift technique* which is based on projection of the regional differences in rates of economic growth in various categories. This technique, as will be illustrated in chapter 4, is widely used in regional and metropolitan economic studies.

Other Forecasting Studies　The Federal Reserve banks also carry on studies of trends in economic activity in their several districts. While these studies often focus upon the influence of monetary influences, they are directed to the analysis of changes in production and employment relative to national trends. Special studies of the economies of major metropolitan areas within the districts have been published by the Federal Reserve banks of Minneapolis, St. Louis, Chicago, and Philadelphia. These studies provide the appraiser with a valuable source of information concerning economic trends in regional and metropolitan areas.

Growing recognition of the significant differences in regional economic growth trends has given rise to a number of major regional economic studies in recent years. These studies, which have been described elsewhere in detail, generally rely upon one or two analytical approaches, or upon a combination of these with traditional trend-projection methods.[35]

A recent study of metropolitan income in Detroit for the period from 1950 to 1969 represents a significant extension of traditional economic base analytical techniques.[36] The author estimates what he refers to as "total effect multipliers" for the area's principal basic employment sectors, identified as (1) motor vehicles and equipment, (2) machinery (including electrical), (3) fabricated metal products, and (4) primary metal products. The economic base model employed by the author assumes that the level of activity in the export industries of Detroit is determined largely by national demand factors. Local service sector activity is expressed as a function of the aggregate level of export activity. As would be expected, the author found that metropolitan employment in Detroit is highly sensitive to changes in national demand for motor vehicles.

Based upon analysis of data from 1950 to 1969, the author reports total effect multipliers of 1.913 for the local machinery industry and 1.482 for the motor vehicle and equipment industry.[37] The higher multiplier for the local machinery industry is attributed to the fact that this industry relies more heavily on local sources of inputs and hence has greater secondary and tertiary effects on total employment.

However, the author finds that the estimated "exogenous variable impact multipliers," which measure the impact of a given change in national demand on the total income of the Detroit economy, are in striking contrast to the apparent ranking of the total effect multipliers. As a result of the much larger absolute size of the local motor vehicle industry in Detroit relative to the machinery industry, he reports that each additional dollar of national demand for automobiles will add approximately thirty-six cents to Detroit's total income, while a dollar of change in the national demand for durable goods will add only seven cents.[38]

Economic base studies of this general type, which have been undertaken in California, Massachusetts, Ohio, and in other areas, illustrate the wealth of economic research which contributes to the appraiser's understanding of the relationships between the local, regional, and national economies.

A recent study by Victor Zarnowitz concludes that the national business forecasting record of business, economic, and government forecasters was extremely poor during the decade from 1952 to 1963.[39] He concluded that "(1) the average error in forecasting the annual average change in the GNP from 1953 to 1963 was approximately 40 percent; (2) there is no evidence that the forecasters' performance improved steadily over the period 1953 to 1963; (3) most forecasts underestimate the future growth of GNP; (4) forecasts for greater than one year ahead are not superior to simple extrapolations of the recent trend; and (5) forecasts of GNP are typically much better than those of its components."

The dismal record of national economic forecasting over the past decade has caused many practicing appraisers to lose faith in many of the more sophisticated techniques for both national and regional forecasting. If, as appears to be true, trends in national growth are the most important factor influencing regional growth, how can we hope to forecast the latter effectively if we cannot forecast the GNP with any accuracy?

The appraiser appears to be left with three alternatives: (1) rely upon the traditional approach of extrapolating past growth trends for the national and regional economies; (2) adopt a consensus of national and regional economic forecasts; and (3) employ a modified economic base approach that seeks to identify linkages among the local, regional, and national economies, with explicit assumptions regarding national and regional growth hypothesized. In the author's opinion, the last of these alternatives, which integrates national and regional economic analysis with urban growth and neighborhood analysis, holds great promise for use in real estate appraisal. Its principal value lies in the fact that the national and regional growth assumptions are made explicit in the urban growth forecast, and that, through the use of computer simulation models, they can be varied with ease to provide a range of estimates subject to probability analysis. This alternative will be described in detail in the following chapter.

Difficulties in preparing meaningful analyses of the economic base and forecasts of national and regional economic growth heighten the difficulties in the use of the capitalization-of-income method, where such forecasts are of important consequence.

CHAPTER 3

Summary and Conclusions

It has been seen that the interrelationships between international, national, regional, and local economies are extremely complex. Although our knowledge of these relationships has increased substantially in recent decades, neither the quality or quantity of data available nor the degree of refinement of techniques permit more than highly generalized descriptions.

The volume of basic or primary employment in a city is considered so significant in economic base analysis that some authors refer to such employment as constituting *the* economic base of a community. Both the long-term growth of a community and its responsiveness to national and regional economic influences appear to be conditioned in major part by the character and volume of its basic employment. The analysis of the economic base in early appraisal theory was confined to the projection of past population growth by simple techniques. Modern techniques for forecasting population integrate economic forecasting with the analysis of age distribution, birth, and mortality data.

The broad similarity between national, regional, and local trends in business activity appears to have been confirmed by a number of different economic studies and to provide an appropriate starting place for the analysis of a local economic base. Although none would maintain that growth trends and cyclical responses do not vary widely among different urban economies, the studies examined point to national economic conditions as the number one factor influencing local employment and income trends. It was recommended that predictions of changes in national income provide the most convenient framework for viewing the probable effects of national business conditions upon a local economy. Unfortunately, the record of national and regional economic forecasting is unimpressive. The appraiser, in using such forecasts, must recognize their limitations and give particular attention to the sensitivity of local economic activity to changes in the national economy.

Several techniques were examined for determining the historical relationships between national, regional, and local business conditions. Particular attention was drawn to the findings by the Department of Commerce that the economic differences among regions are becoming relatively less pronounced. The comparison of local estimates of effective buying power and national income in the manner outlined by Rapkin, Winnick, and Blank recommends itself as an interesting technique, particularly since Department of Commerce income and employment data are available for most regions. Continuing studies of business trends in the individual Federal Reserve districts and economic subregions of the United States furnish a historical basis for future estimation of regional economic conditions. The current volume of empirical research on regional economic structures and trends holds additional promise for future economic analysis of the region.

The highly detailed procedure for analyzing the economic base of a local area recommended and employed by Weimer and Hoyt appears adaptable only to a large-scale investigation of the economic base of a community. Even under these circumstances, the practicality and usefulness of employing the detailed forecasting procedures which they recommend appear highly questionable, considering the nature of the assumptions required and the large *probable statistical* errors. Both this technique and the earlier one employed by the FHA furnish inadequate linkage between national and regional economic analysis and the analysis of the local economic base. Notably lacking in any of the techniques explored was the consideration of future changes in supply factors influencing real estate.

Recent studies have sought to integrate national, regional, and local economic forecasting. Although time has not demonstrated their effectiveness, logic suggests that the appraiser endeavor to ride on the shoulders of the regional economist.

The relationship between the economic base and real estate values is clearly recognized in most appraisal literature, and the appraiser is concerned with a multitude of approaches to the analysis of the local economic base. However, the prediction of local economic trends and the assessing of their influence upon incomes and property values is an extremely difficult problem of economic analysis. It is to be carefully noted that the application of all the analytical techniques examined requires the exercise of skillful judgment. Many appraisal reports employ the simple device of assuming that past trends will be continued in the future and assume, on that basis, constant rates of urban growth or decline. In the absence of evidence to the contrary or substantially better methods, this may be a logical decision. It should be recognized, however, that any forward estimate of property incomes or values can be no better than the economic forecast upon which it is based. The improvement in techniques for analysis of the economic base represents an important key to the improvement of appraisal practice in the use of the capitalization-of-income method.

Fortunately for the appraiser, the extensive need for employment and population projections for economic and physical planning purposes will undoubtedly result in continuous and increasingly sophisticated population projections for most metropolitan areas. It will be necessary, however, for appraisers to develop sufficient familiarity with the techniques and pitfalls of employment and population forecasting to evaluate the alternative projections made by others and judgmatically select those which appear to him to be the most defensible.

The conclusions may be reached from this review that economic conditions in a local area and its surrounding region will depend largely upon national economic developments. The sheer numbers of organizations carrying on the work of national business forecasting and the great variety in specific techniques employed recommend that the student of the economic base of a specific area rely upon the national economic forecasts of others, tempered with his own judgment, rather than engage in the details of applying various forecasting techniques.

That he will rely upon national economic forecasts of others in no way diminishes the importance of the integration of the study of national economic background with that of the regional and local area. It might even be said that any attempt to predict future economic developments in a local area will be of little or no value without taking into consideration probable national developments.

Traditionally, the appraisal process proceeds from the consideration of national and regional influences to the separate analysis of city and neighborhood growth. In the following chapter, the present status of urban growth theory is reviewed and an integrated approach to forecasting economic base, population, and land use development is recommended.

ANALYZING THE INTERNAL STRUCTURE OF CITIES

The appraisal process involves the successive consideration by the appraiser of regional, city, and neighborhood influences upon the value of a subject property. The effects of national and regional economic trends and of the expansion in basic employment upon urban growth have been noted in chapter 3. The manner in which urban growth will proceed and influence the individual districts of a community will depend upon the physical characteristics of the area, historical trends, types of economic functions undergoing expansion, character of population growth, the nature of technological advances in the area, local governmental policies, and many other factors. These factors will determine the aggregative effect of urban growth upon total property values in a city and the selective effect of this growth upon values in the different urban districts, sections, or neighborhoods. The specific objectives of this chapter will be (1) to evaluate present theories of urban growth and structure as an aid to the appraiser and (2) to describe and critically evaluate techniques for analysis of the internal structure of cities.

Present Theories of Urban Growth and Structure

Urban land economists, sociologists, geographers, appraisers, and city planners have made contributions to the extensive literature on urban growth and structure. The participation of so many groups in the investigation of urban structure is itself evidence that cultural factors, geography, economic motivation, and political decisions all have important influences upon the internal structure and property values in a city. It is difficult for the appraiser to gain insight into the contributions of these various disciplines, however, because of the barriers of terminology peculiar to each field. The sociologists refer to the dynamics of the spatial distribution of persons and institutions in the city as *human ecology* and speak of the theory of urban growth as *typological analysis*.[1] Geographers distinguish between *external morphology* as the study of the physical and functional relationships between the city and outside areas and *internal morphology* as the study of the relationships between the component parts of the city itself.[2] Urban land economists use a more simplified terminology in referring to the field of inquiry as the *theory of urban growth and structure*. However, economic writings in the field are replete with such terms as *competition of uses*, *succession of uses*, *highest and best use*, and others confusing to the lay reader.

The most fruitful attack upon the theory of urban growth and structure had its origins in the trail-blazing work of Richard M. Hurd, a mortgage banker who assembled a large volume of empirical data on the growth of over fifty American cities in 1903. Hurd explained the growth process of cities in these words:

> Cities originate at their most convenient point of contact with the outer world and grow in the lines of least resistance or greatest attraction, or their resultants. The point of contact differs according to the methods of transportation, whether by water, by turnpike or by railroad. . . . The influence of topography, all-powerful when cities start, is constantly modified. . . . The most direct results of topography come from its control of transportation. . . .
>
> Growth in cities consists of movement away from the point of origin in all directions, except as topographically hindered, this movement being due both to aggregation at the edges and pressure from the centre. Central growth takes place both from the heart of the city and from each subcentre of attraction, and axial growth pushes into the outlying territory by means of railroads, turnpikes and street railroads. All cities are built up from these two influences, which vary in quantity, intensity and quality, and resulting districts overlapping, interpenetrating, neutralizing and harmonizing as the pressure of the city's growth bring them in contact with each other. . . . Residences are early driven to the circumference, while business remains at the centre, and as residences divide into various social grades, retail shops of corresponding grades follow them, and wholesale shops in turn follow the retailers, while institutions and various mixed utilities irregularly fill in the intermediate zone, and the banking office section remains at the main business centre. Complicating this broad outward movement of zones, axes of traffic project shops through residence areas, create business subcentres, where they intersect, and change circular cities into star-shaped cities. Central growth, due to proximity, and axial growth, due to accessibility, are summed up in the static power of established sections and the dynamic power of their chief lines of intercommunication.[3]

Extensive research and writing in the field have been carried on during the seventy years since Hurd wrote. However, no more comprehensive analysis of the dynamics of city growth has appeared since his work.

Concentric Circle Theory Prof. E. W. Burgess led a group of sociologists in what they termed "ecological" studies early in the 1920s and advanced the theory that cities tend to expand in concentric circles from their point of origin.[4] Professor Burgess offered a recent defense for his theory as an idealized construction, claiming that it described tendencies which might prevail in the absence of topographical, climatic, institutional, and other influences. Commenting upon the present state of the theory of urban structure, he said, "Today, after almost thirty years of use, criticism and research, there is still need for a comprehensive typological analysis of the growth of the city. This research must answer two basic questions: To what extent is urban growth radial (i.e., outward from the center), and to what extent is it agglomerative (from the outside in) or peripheral (at the rim, at the expense of the center)?"[5]

Sector Theory of Growth   The so-called sector theory of city growth was advanced by Homer Hoyt, based upon the empirical analysis of rental data for over sixty-four cities by the Federal Housing Administration.[6] Not only did the results of this study, published in 1939, confirm Hurd's earlier work, but, in addition, many of the principles of city growth which Hoyt developed from the study bear close resemblance to Hurd's earlier conclusions. From the trends observed in the FHA study and in studies of other cities, Hoyt developed the following fundamental hypotheses, which he expanded into a set of principles of urban growth:

1. The various groups in the social order tend to be segregated into rather definite areas according to their incomes and social positions. . . .

2. The highest income groups live in the houses which command highest prices and rents, while the lower-income groups live in houses which are offered for the lower prices and rents. Generally the low-rent areas are located first near the business and industrial center of the city and then tend to expand outward on one side or sector of the city occupying the land which is not preempted by higher-rent residential areas or by business and industrial districts.

3. The principal growth of American cities has taken place by new building at the periphery rather than by the rebuilding of older areas.[7]

In a 1966 study Hoyt found "pronounced sectors of high income concentration" in many leading cities.[8] It is significant that Weimer and Hoyt carefully qualify their theory as a "statement of general tendency varying with the unique characteristics of individual cities."

Critics of Hoyt's hypotheses have pointed out that his generalizations express only past tendencies and do not provide a sufficiently precise framework of theory to guide the analysis of urban growth trends.[9] Firey claimed that Hoyt's theory could be only partially confirmed in the growth of the city of Boston and held that the role of social and cultural institutions is not accorded adequate recognition in Hoyt's principles of growth. Rodwin contended that (1) Hoyt fails to define sectors with sufficient clarity to permit their ready identification in the growth patterns of cities, (2) Hoyt's arbitrary division of income classes into high, low and intermediate fails to recognize the intricate ethnic, religious, and nationality groups occupying residential areas, and (3) Hoyt fails to recognize the important influence of public intervention upon urban structure. In spite of these criticisms, Rodwin concluded that "an adequate substitute for Hoyt's basic generalizations on residential location has not been formulated. Firey's studies only graze Hoyt's empirical conclusions; and though Firey's emphasis on social and cultural systems is more complex and sophisticated than Hoyt's simple explanation, there is no necessary inconsistency between the two."[10]

Contribution of Economists   Economists view competition as the guiding force influencing urban land use and structure. Dorau and Hinman, writing in the 1920s, characterized the competition of uses as the process through which the highest and best use of land was to be achieved in these words:

> Urban land is put to many different uses and often it is apparently optional which use shall be chosen. A business site might be used for a department store or an office building; a residential site for a single-family dwelling or an apartment house, and so on. Yet, after the site is committed to one use or the other, it may be found to have been a mistake. With several optional uses for a site, only the most careful analysis will reveal which is the best. The situation is made still more difficult by the fact that urban land uses are constantly changing. Cities grow and districts shift. What may be a good retail store section today may be a wholesale section five years from now; a high-class residential section may become a low-class residential section or a retail store section, and so on.[11]

In a study of the changing patterns of business location in New York City, Haig summarized the influence of economic motivation on urban structure as follows: "An economic activity seeking a location finds that, as it approaches the center, site rents increase and transportation costs decline. As it retreats from the center, site rents decline and transportation costs increase. The sum of the two items, the costs of friction, is not constant, however. On the contrary, it varies with the site. The theoretically perfect site for the activity is that which involves the lowest costs of friction."[12]

Haig's analysis, which followed closely von Thunen's theories of agricultural location, had wide acceptance in the literature of economics and planning until recent years. This author took issue with Haig's emphasis upon transportation costs as the sole determinant of location, land values and rents, in 1957 and 1958.[13] More recently Alonso concluded that

> the minimum aggregate costs of friction hypothesis is not valid when it is interpreted strictly in economic terms, . . . There is, moreover, fundamental objection to its use as a guide for urban planning. The logic that would have the minimizing of the costs of friction be a planning objective is faulty in the same way that Haig's view of the location of the urban firm is faulty. The minimizing of a certain type of costs would be a valid approach only if all other costs and revenues (economic and psychological) remain constant.[14]

Recently, Goldberg has shown that since the price elasticity of demand for land is high the total revenues to land and aggregate land values can be expected to increase with transportation improvements. He cites several recent empirical studies to defend his conclusion. One such study states "that a transportation improvement will have the effect of bringing large supplies of cheap, raw land on the market. This in turn will lead to cheaper houses. People will buy more land than previously, thus increasing their aggregate expenditure on land and raising the aggregate value of such land in the urban area."[15]

Ratcliff emphasized the operation of the principle of competition of uses in stating that the physical form and ecology of the city are the products of the forces of demand and supply operating within the framework of the real estate market and conditioned by economic, social, and legal institutions.[16] According to his analysis, the market price of urban land reflects economic decisions with respect to its future productivity as measured by its net income for various uses. Ratcliff points out that many uses of land are noncompetitive, since level land is best adapted to industrial sites or to low-cost residential housing, while hillside land is most desirable for higher-priced, single-family use.

Continuing his analysis of the competition of uses for urban land, Ratcliff points out that the demand for retail space in a city depends upon the number of potential customers and upon their buying habits. Influenced by transportation and population factors and the location and relative importance of central shopping districts, string-street commercial developments and outlying nucleations will change over time. Following Haig, he explains the location of wholesale districts convenient to transportation facilities and accessible to the central retail district.[17] Ratcliff calls attention to the decline in the proportion of the urban area devoted to the wholesaling function as a result of changes in the methods of distribution.

Urban land economists explain the shifts in urban districts in terms of changing locational demands for different land uses. The relative importance of the distance traveled by customers and employees and the necessity for interbusiness communication influence the changing demands for office space. According to this analysis, large-scale manufacturing is no longer considered a typical central city use since the incentives of lower taxation, larger space, lesser congestion, accessibility to labor supply, and improved transportation have caused a major shift in this type of activity to outlying areas. There is a wide variation, however, in the degree to which these factors attract industries to the outlying districts of cities.

Route of Wedge Theory The process of change in urban land uses, according to economic theory, is carried on through the principle of succession of uses. Babcock superimposed a "radial" or "axis of transportation" theory upon a modified concentric circle theory (allowing for constant traveling times to the downtown district) and held that this described "the grand pattern upon which cities are built." He termed this the *route and wedge* *structure*. Ratcliff pointed out that a new use will succeed "when the return on the site after the removal of the original structure and its replacement for the new use is greater than the return on the entire property, land and building, under the original use."[18]

Babcock aptly described this process:

> As cities grow, the uses to which individual sites are put change, usually in the direction of more intensive uses. What the successive uses will be depends upon the operations of the competititon of uses.
>
> In the growth of a city we find that the original districts tend to disappear gradually and to be replaced by other districts. In some cases, the districts expand and encroach upon others, driving them to new locations. . . .
>
> The shift and flux and change in the details of this city pattern are not utterly haphazard. The several types of districts seem to follow very definite life cycles in which, for given kinds of districts, the principal differences are found in the rate at which the cycles advance.
>
> The net result of this process is, from the valuator's point of view, that individual parcels of land go through a succession of different uses.[19]

Babcock categorized the various ways in which urban districts move as *sliding*, *bursting*, and *jumping*. As he described the process, districts usually expand by gradually encroaching upon neighboring districts in a sliding manner. At other times an expanding district will find it necessary to overcome a barrier by jumping a well-established district or some other restriction hindering its expansion. By the term *bursting*, Babcock referred to the scattering of district additions to several locations. He cited the decentralization of shopping facilities on the peripheries of cities as an example of bursting and also identified this as the typical manner of growth for small towns.

The movements of districts are accelerated by the inexorable factors of old age and depreciation. Advancing age of commercial, industrial, and residential structures results in physical depreciaiton and, even more important, functional obsolescence, and these developments encourage the selection of new locations for modern structures. Changing technologies and social and living habits add further impetus to the processes of urban change. Examples of such influences are found in the rise of automobile transportation and the individually owned home, the extension of public utility and educational facilities to new areas, and the concomitant decentralization of suburban housing and shopping centers.

Urban locational theory is handicapped by the lack of well-organized data portraying long-term changes in land use and by the complicated nature of the decision-making process in the selection of urban locations. As a result, economists have not as yet translated the relatively bare principles of competition of uses, succession of uses, and reducing the costs of friction into a unified theory which can be used as a guide to the determination of future changes in the internal structure of the city.

Lowdon Wingo, in his 1961 book, attempted to construct a model of the interaction of housing demand, travel behavior and residential land-supply factors. Commenting upon the use of his model to predict the future of cities, Wingo said, "To get an answer that is even mildly satisfying, we find that we have to feed it a lot of guesses about the parameters."[20] Later, he made an interesting forecast of future urban structure: "The unfolding picture, then, is one of low density urban sprawl reaching out along the radial freeways far into the hinterland and nucleated by commercial and industrial development at the interchange points. At the center, densities will tend to decline — radically in the more obsolescent areas — with declining densities go declining land values. At the very center a more highly specialized central business district appears likely, vigorous and healthy as a whole, but less dominant in the Gestalt of the urban region."[21]

William Alonso, in his recent work, provides a reformulation of urban land market theory in essentially Marshallian terms, applying a static model to the city of the classical "featureless plain" with no zoning and with a single center.[22] In evaluating the success of an empirical test of his theory, in which some of the restrictive assumptions are relaxed, Alonso says, "Confirmation of the validity of our theory must await more ambitious empirical studies."[23]

Other studies by Herbert and Stevens, Muth, Kain, and others have focused on the residential location decision, portraying the consumer trade-off between distance from the center of cities and the amount and type of space demanded.[24] Mohring and Horwitz, in their succinct review of the relationships between residential land values and highway improvements, concluded, "Before much faith can be placed on empirically derived rent gradients as highway planning tools, models will have to be developed that take into account the facts that real world communities typically have more than one center of economic activity, that the demands for both land and transportation are not totally inelastic and that differences in tastes do exist."[25]

Urban geographers have led in the synthesis of what they term *central-place theory* since World War II. Berry provides a useful summary of the important contributions of two German scholars, geographer Walter Christaller and economist August Losch, and discusses the relationship of these contributions to modern economic location theory.[26] Citing the contrasts in retail distribution between unplanned developments of the predepression period and planned shopping centers, discount stores, and planned ribbons constructed since the end of World War II, he speculates that we may be witnessing the emergence of new metropolitan forms accompanied by more extreme types of specialization.[27] Supporters of this point of view argue that the country is gradually becoming a set of metropolitan regions with a population of three hundred thousand or larger located within two hours' commuting time of a core area on modern expressway systems.

The dynamics of functional and physical change in urban and metropolitan areas and the increasing complexity and individuality of the site-selection process force the appraiser to rely upon the historical methods of analysis carried on by Hurd and Hoyt and continued by city planners and urban geographers. Careful current observation, supplemented by time-map analytical techniques, can provide the appraiser with operationally useful insights into the overall growth of the community and the shifts of its major districts.

The ability to anticipate public policy decisions has become of increasing importance in appraisal work as the scope and influence of these decisions has widened. The long-range master plan is now a requisite for obtaining federal financing assistance in most large urban communities, and in many cases the law requires that these plans be consistent with metropolitan or state master plans. To the extent that these foretell and dictate zoning, urban renewal and public building, and street and highway construction, they provide highly useful guidelines to the future development of an urban area.

Recent Analysis of Metropolitan Growth   Empirical study of the process of urban growth and the analysis of these data by sociologists, economists, and others provide a reasonably good explanation of the factors of change in the internal structure of cities and the way in which they have operated in the past. However, the theories and hypotheses which have been developed must be subject to close scrutiny by the appraiser who seeks to employ them as a basis for predicting future incomes and values for urban real estate.

First of all, the fundamental structure of the large American urban community is undergoing rapid change as the metropolitan area replaces the municipality as the unit of analysis. This expansion in geographical area, brought about by the revolution in transportation, has been accompanied by growth and change in the basic economic functions of large metropolitan centers. As a result of these factors, the geographical areas within which the principles of competition of uses or segregation of social groups come into play have been greatly expanded. The core of a metropolitan area may carry on functions for urban and rural areas a hundred or more miles away, while large urban communities may develop serving exclusive functions as industrial or "bedroom" areas. Bogue provided insight into the nature of the new metropolis-centered interurban community in his 1950 study: "When the metropolis centered activities of wholesale trade and manufacturing do 'go to the hinterland,' they tend to cling to their metropolitan moorings and choose a location which will permit them ready access to the metropolis. . . . It can only be surmised that wholesale trade and manufacturing in the hinterland are highly integrated with an extensive system, the center of which is located in the central city."[28] This conception of the modern urban community makes the analysis of intraurban structure more difficult. The conception of a downtown district of an urban community from which expansion will take place outward must give way to a new conception of multiple nuclei with a high degree of specialization and subspecialization and with growth and district changes initiated both locally in the individual nuclei and more broadly from the metropolitan center.

This change in the extent of the urban area subject to analysis must be considered in combination with the revolution in transportation currently being witnessed in American cities, since much of our present theory of city growth rests upon the importance of transportation facilities and the related topographical features of cities. There is no question that the growth of American cities during the past fifty years has been greatly influenced by the existence of mass transportation routes leading from the center of the city to outlying open country. It is also logical to judge (following Hurd, McMichael and Bingham, Babcock, Hoyt, and others) that these axes have provided the routes for gradual extension of the newer residential areas of cities and that businesses catering to these groups have been attracted in the same direction. Because of their historical influence, it should be noted that transportation routes and methods are undergoing substantial alteration in almost every city of the United States, as systems of express highways supplant former rapid transit routes as major transportation arteries. Mitchell and Rapkin conclude that the analysis of past traffic movements does not provide a guide to probable future developments.[29] New routes are encouraging new types of suburban residential, commercial, and industrial development. Commercial enterprises, not content with inching their way outward from the central city along former rapid transit routes, frequently jump large areas devoted to mixed residential and industrial uses to locate in the center of new, large, residential nucleations. The scope of land development operations has become so large that entire communities of high-, intermediate-, or low-priced dwellings are being created with little or no regard for past directions of growth for each class of home. Industrial firms have abandoned many older central locations in favor of more expansive areas outside of town on the dual assumption that workers prefer to use automobiles to come to work and that residential builders will locate homes for workers in proximity to new plant locations.

Such developments place a severe strain upon the analyst seeking to interpret urban growth in terms of existing theories. The attempt to identify the high-, intermediate-, or low-rent sectors of New York, Chicago, San Francisco, or Los Angeles finds the cartographer lost in Westchester County, Lake County, San Mateo County, or in the San Fernando Valley. The general tendency for urban districts to slide, which was typical of city development for the past half century, seems to have given way to a dominant tendency for them to jump or burst.

The important assumption in existing theories of urban growth that all cities will continue to grow from within may also be challenged. According to the theory of Hurd, Babcock, Hoyt, and others, the growth of the central commercial district inevitably alters land uses on the borders of such districts and gradually forces out so-called lower uses. In turn the invasion of single-family residential areas by apartment or commercial structures alters the characteristics of such districts and forces residential growth outward. Thus, the expansion from within furnishes the motivating force behind the movements of districts and growth on the periphery. Many large cities have already faced the fact that their central business districts have stopped their lateral expansion. Factors in this trend include competition from new outlying commercial districts, the decline in demand for industrial space in central districts, the decline in the importance of the wholesaling function, tendencies toward vertical rather than lateral expansion, and more restrictive commercial zoning. To the extent that these tendencies become general, the entire process of urban expansion, succession of uses, invasion by commercial enterprises of residential districts, and gradual outward extension of urban areas is likely to be fundamentally altered in the years ahead.

One of the most significant changes affecting urban growth has been the tremendous growth of light industry which depends on trucks rather than on ships and rails. Since most small cities are close to at least one major superhighway, this change has made smaller cities more attractive to industry. Even more important, the physical and social problems of the larger cities have made most large cities unattractive as places to live and work, with the result that employers often find it difficult to attract employees to such an environment.

The full significance of this trend is not yet completely apparent, but it appears likely that future urban growth will be attracted to smaller cities and that, given the proper financial and institutional investment climate, new communities will spring up in response to the need for an improved urban environment.

David L. Birch, in a provocative paper prepared for the Committee for Economic Development, sheds interesting light on the changing functions and structure of American cities.[30] The burden of his analysis, which will undoubtedly be confirmed in greater detail by the results of the census of 1970, is that large American cities are becoming more specialized. He points out that although there have been recent absolute declines in retail trade employment and relatively slow growth in wholesaling and manufacturing in most central cities, the growth in service employment has offset these trends.[31] More importantly, he draws attention to the fact that white-collar jobs in service categories are expected to provide a large share of future employment growth in the nation and will undergird certain of the older and larger central cities as elite service centers. Based upon analysis of data from the U.S. census, Birch develops the thesis that the changes in central city employment will vary according to the size and age of metropolitan areas, with the young SMSA's continuing to expand rapidly in most categories of employment and shifting to more specialized functions as they go through the life cycle of growth and eventual decline.[32]

He speculates that increasingly the poor and the blacks will move to the suburbs following job opportunities and that the inner suburbs may face the same social and fiscal problems experienced by the central cities during the first half of this century. As this movement occurs, the author expects that there may be increasing incentives for wealthier families to reclaim larger sections of the central cities for their own use, close to the centers of high income service employment.[33] The implications of this type of analysis are of course of utmost importance for the appraiser, who in many respects is an urban land-market forecaster.

Appraisal Techniques and District Analysis

Few modern appraisal texts integrate the analysis of the economic base and urban growth of a city with the analysis of the districts within a city. The books by Hurd and by McMichael and Bingham pointed out the important effects of changes in urban structure upon city land value.[34] Although most of the factors influencing the directions of growth of a city and changes in its districts were recognized by Hurd and the other authors cited, no attention was given to the techniques by which this process of movement could be analyzed. Babcock pointed out even more clearly the significance of district analysis in the appraisal process in his chapter on "City Growth and Development":

> The real estate appraiser is interested in districts because districts undergo changes which result in value changes. The creation and continued existence of movement of city districts are not independent or even fundamental in city growth. District development is secondary to the route and wedge structure already discussed above.
>
> The approximate locations of the borders (of districts) are important to appraisers because district growth takes place at the boundaries, usually, however, only on one side of a district.[35]

Rating of Residential Areas Because of the complexity of forces affecting other types of districts and the consequent difficulties in presenting analytical techniques, Babcock confined his recommendations to techniques for the analysis of residential neighborhoods. These techniques were most fully developed in the procedure adopted by the Federal Housing Administration for rating of residential location. In an article describing this procedure, Babcock commented:

> Neighborhoods experience a change in quality directly related to the changing types of persons coming successively into occupancy. . . . Every

change of occupancy in a neighborhood tends to increase, stabilize, or de-crease the desirability of the area. The cumulative effect is reflected in the actions of the market and influences the growth pattern of a city.

Neighborhoods tend to decline in investment quality. The exception to this observation is partially developed new neighborhoods. If such areas are well planned, favorably situated, adequately protected, and properly priced, they often improve for a period.

City growth is directional. The directions which it takes arise from favora-ble market attitudes toward selected areas. New residential districts are the product of city expansion, and, if they enjoy a favorable position in relation to the general direction of city growth, they will possess a higher degree of appeal to the market. If they do not enjoy this favorable geographic position, they are apt to remain sparsely developed or experience sporadic development over a long period before becoming substantially built-up. The latter condi-tions tend to accelerate adverse influences which produce neighborhood insta-bility.

As the degree of appeal for owner occupancy declines, some districts become rental areas. Others experience a gradual transition to higher uses. When transition to the higher use begins, only a few of the sites change in use, while the remainder become much less attractive for the formerly established residential purposes. This effect of the competition of uses tends to hasten the decline of the neighborhood. . . .

The economic forces which affect the values of residential properties are significant factors in residential location rating. These factors affect the broad metropolitan area of the entire community and its total population. Resi-dential neighborhoods within such an area will reflect the general income and employment advantages in varying degrees. Even against the most stable economic background, there are some neighborhoods which derive little bene-fit from their location in such areas.[36]

The rating technique which Babcock developed from these hypotheses is designed to give consideration to the economic stability of the residents and to particular locational attributes of each neighborhood. The factors entering into the rating of a given neighborhood under this technique are summarized: (1) relative economic stability (stability of family incomes, sufficiency of family incomes, social characteristics of neighborhood occupants, stage and trend of neighborhood development, and probability of forced sales and foreclosures); (2) protection from adverse influences (zoning, restrictive cove-nants, natural physical protection, surrounding homogeneous neighborhood, quality of neighboring development, ribbon developments, and nuisances); (3) freedom from special hazards (topography, subsidence, earthquake, torna-do, or hurricane hazard, flood hazard, traffic hazard, fire and explosion hazard, and hazards to health); (4) adequacy of civic, social and commercial centers (quality and accessibility of schools, quality and accessibility of shop-ping centers and amusements, quality and accessibility of churches, clubs and recreation centers); (5) adequacy of transportation (diversity of available services, quality and frequency of services, cost of service, distance from location to service, time required to destinations, and condition of streets and roads); (6) sufficiency of utilities and conveniences (presence of required utilities, quality of utilities, and cost of services); (7) level of taxes and special assessments (relationship of tax burden with competitive locations and nature, cost, and duration of special assessments); and (8) appeal (natural physical charm and beauty of location, geographical position of location, layout and plan of neighborhood, architectural attractiveness of buildings, social attractiveness, and nuisances).[37]

The Federal Housing Administration recommended a grid technique for the rating of location, based in large measure upon the factors listed above, until the *Underwriting Manual*'s sections on location analysis were revised, effective December 1968. The effect of the change and of the elimination of the grid-rating procedure, which had provided for outright rejection of certain locations, was to broaden the classes of locations eligible for FHA mortgage insurance and to eliminate any implication in the former rating procedure that properties in inner city or low-income neighborhoods were not eligible for FHA insurance.[38] The revised framework for analysis of location, however, still follows closely the outline proposed by Babcock and incorporated in the earlier editions of the *Underwriting Manual*. The abandonment of the grid technique appears to be a belated recognition of the basically subjective assignment of weights to the various site-desirability features identified.

Neighborhood Homogeneity Arthur May suggested a long list of factors for consideration in analyzing the residential neighborhood, many of which are included in the above list of location factors used in the FHA rating procedure. He follows Babcock in offering the major premise that "the general trend of residential districts is always down," attributing this tendency, in part, to the outward movement of population from the center of cities.[39] May gives primary attention to homogeneity as the basic criterion in neighborhood analysis, concluding somewhat remarkably: "This supports the sociological truth that contentment of living is present in greater abundance in that circumstance where the inhabitants of a particular district have the same level of income, social attributes, ethnics, culture, and education."[40] The doctrine of homogeneity and its corollary that the infiltration of nonhomogeneous racial or ethnic groups into neighborhoods destroys values have been under attack from many quarters.[41] The arguments on both sides of the latter question have been thus far inconclusive, with the weight of general opinion on the side of May's position, but with recent evidence that the doctrine of homogeneity is not universal and that social attitudes may be changing. At the least, recent studies have shown that property values have not declined in the degree commonly supposed in areas where racial infiltration has been studied. One factor adding to the difficulty of appraising the significance of recent statistical comparisons of selling prices before and after racial infiltration is that terms of sale have been observed to change radically with changes in race of purchasers. According to recent interviews with lenders, sales prices have been rising rapidly in many areas experiencing Negro infiltration. This reflects the growing affluence of some blacks and pressure which will continue upon areas from which blacks have been excluded.

The *Wall Street Journal* of 11 January 1972 reported upon a study of the feasibility of federal government efforts to house subsidized inner-city families in suburban neighborhoods. According to this report, a panel of experts appointed by the National Research Council and led by Dr. Amos Hawley reported to the Department of Housing and Urban Development that "little is known about whether people of different economic levels, regardless of race, can live together harmoniously." The panel concluded, according to this press report, that federal housing desegregation policies should be directed primarily toward "matching" socioeconomic levels.

The appraiser must be guided by the market and not by his personal social philosophies in appraising the effects of neighborhood influences upon values. The author hypothesizes that the influence of race on property values will differ among cities and neighborhoods and may be expected to vary over time. If the forecasts of Birch and others are realized, we may expect accelerated movements of blacks to the suburbs in the next decade. It is to be hoped that improved market data and analytical techniques may provide the appraisers with the much needed knowledge of the complex neighborhood influences affecting market prices.

Useful Guides to Analysis of Cities   It is no criticism of present theories of urban growth to point out that any set of hypotheses based upon the growth tendencies of American cities during the first half of this century will almost inevitably prove inadequate for explaining future growth. At the same time, many of the principles of urban growth which have been formulated by empirical observation of past tendencies will continue to serve as guides in the analysis of urban structure. Among those which the author considers the most useful are the following: (1) the rate of expansion of economic functions in the core of large urban areas has declined substantially and the growth of such areas will proceed slowly, if at all; (2) the physical topography of an urban area will continue as a major determinant of urban structure, influencing land utilization directly and through its related effect upon transportation routes. Advancing technology and public investment will modify the future importance of topography; (3) major transportation routes will continue to have a dominant influence upon the directions of urban growth; (4) the revolution in transportation has changed the geographical unit for analysis of urban structure from the corporate municipality to the metropolitan district. New transportation developments may alter historical growth trends; (5) public controls will play an increasingly important part in determining the urban structure of the future; (6) the principle of residential segregation of ethnic and income groups will continue to have an important influence upon the characteristics of individual districts; and (7) the combined influence of these factors may alter substantially the historical processes of extension, growth, and decay which have been characteristic of urban growth during the past half-century.

These principles offer a tenuous base for the analysis of the internal structure of cities by appraisers. Fundamentally, the discussion thus far has emphasized that the appraiser must link the internal analysis of the districts of a city with his assumptions regarding the economic base outlook for that city. Following in the footsteps of Hurd and Hoyt, he must carry on an empirical analysis of past trends, looking for evidence of historical similarity with trends in other cities. In his analysis he should give prime consideration to study of the topographical and other physical characteristics of the area as they affect locational policies and future transportation developments. Major consideration should be given to planning, zoning, public acquisition of land, and other public controls as they will affect the growth and development of the community under analysis. Finally, recognizing the key importance of the principle of competition of uses, he must integrate the conclusions drawn from the above with a detailed knowledge of locational trends and factors affecting the decisions of builders, investors, and developers. Starting at this level of analysis of urban structure, the appraiser is prepared to review critically urban growth forecasts.

The need for improved, long-range urban and metropolitan growth forecasts has resulted in an increase in both the number and sophistication of metropolitan planning studies in recent years. This improvement reflects a growing recognition by the planning profession of the need to integrate economic analysis with the traditional emphasis upon design and public investment aspects of planning. The very existence of master plans, which have often been adopted as policy goals by legislative bodies, makes them to a degree self-justifying, since public and private investment decisions are often guided by the plans. The appraiser, however, must be able to evaluate the realism of the economic growth assumptions hypothesized and the political uncertainties which underlie such plans. He must also be able to comprehend the interaction of changes in important elements of a master plan upon the future land use patterns which will emerge. A recent analysis of projections for the Atlanta metropolitan area illustrates the sophistication and detail of such plans as well as the problems of interpretation.[42]

The commission's employment projections for the Atlanta metropolitan area, summarized in table 4–1, reflect a forecast of continued absolute growth in the central Atlanta area of Fulton County but more rapid rates of growth in the outlying counties. These trends toward metropolitan decentralization, as observed earlier, are characteristic of most large metropolitan areas of the United States.

Table 4-1. Atlanta Metropolitan Area Planning Projections, 1961–1983; Employment by Counties

Counties	1961	Percent	1983	Percent
Clayton	13,767	3	41,183	5
Cobb	35,577	8	90,512	10
DeKalb	57,037	14	158,939	18
Fulton	306,523	73	576,847	65
Gwinnett	6,396	2	22,919	2
Total region	419,300	100	894,400	100

Source: Atlanta Region Metropolitan Planning Commission, *Population and Employment* (Atlanta, 1969), table 6, p. 25.

The most significant observations of concern to the appraiser in referring to the 1969 Atlanta Region Metropolitan Planning Commission report are that (1) in 1969 the commission abandoned its earlier objectives of a "contained growth–Satellite City" concept; (2) new objectives for 1988 regional directions of growth were adopted, based upon an extension of historical growth trends; and (3) the commission explicitly cautioned users of the plan that planned freeway and airport expansion developments in the Atlanta region were not incorporated in its master plan and that these could have a major impact on future development and population distribution in the region. These observations underline the problems faced by the appraiser in evaluating so-called official master plans. He must not only be able to evaluate the realism of the basic economic growth assumptions used in the plan, but he must as well be able to measure the political uncertainties underlying key forecasts.

Fortunately, the market comparison approach does not require that the appraiser forecast future development and land uses. It can be assumed that market sales prices implicitly reflect the views of buyers and sellers about the future. However, the determination of investment value by the capitalization of income method explicitly requires forecasts of rental income in the future and these in turn must rest upon forecasts of growth and development and neighborhood characteristics in the future. It is clearly not sufficient for the appraiser to quote at length from local or regional planning reports without a critical analysis of the underlying economic assumptions and of the political uncertainties involved. Unfortunately, the growing sophistication of planning studies does not lessen the need for this type of critical analysis by the appraiser, although it makes his task more difficult.

Land-Use Simulation Models

Land-use simulation models are designed to project future patterns of land development by assigning urban activities to subareas of a region. The development of these models requires the integration of a wide range of disciplines and techniques for forecasting regional population, employment, incomes, industry structure, and housing demand. Assumptions must be made concerning consumer travel and shopping behavior; residential, industrial, and commercial locational decisions; and government housing, investment, transportation, and land-use policies.

The pioneering work of the Pittsburgh Regional Plan Association in developing a prototype land-use assignment model provided the basis for the construction and implementation of a considerably more sophisticated model for the San Francisco Bay area, which has proven operationally useful.[43] The BASS model, as it is called, integrates national and regional economic forecasts of employment and population with a land-use assignment model to provide estimates of land use for six categories of residental use, as well as for manufacturing and wholesaling, agricultural, commercial, and public use for two areas, one composed of nine counties and the other of thirteen, surrounding the San Francisco Bay.[44] The BASS model is a set of integrated submodels made up of an employment and population submodel, shown in figure 4-1, and employment location and residential location submodels, shown in figure 4-2. The model makes predictions of future land use by five- and ten-year periods to the year 2020 for 617 tracts in nine counties and for 777 tracts in thirteen counties in the San Francisco Bay area. The authors of the report emphasize that the forecasts of land absorption for different classes of industrial, residential, and commercial usage by tracts are subject to wide margins of error because of the quality of the data inputs and should be regarded as indicated probabilities rather than exact predictions. It might be asked: How then can an appraiser make use of such approximations? The answer lies in the inherent flexibility with which such models can be used, since the assumptions underlying any set of forecasts can be altered with considerable ease to produce alternative forecasts. Employing the techniques of probability analysis, the appraiser can adopt some forecast as the most probable in his judgment. It can be seen that the land-use simulation model does not eliminate the appraiser's judgment but rather provides an independent check upon other forecasts and upon his own subjective analysis and a framework within which the assumptions underlying any estimate are made explicit.

Data from the BASS report *Jobs, People and Land* can be used to illustrate the use of the output of land-use simulation models in appraisal analysis. Table 4-2 shows a comparison of the population and employment forecasts of the BASS model with those in the *Preliminary Regional Plan* for the nine-county San Francisco Bay area, which were based upon trend projections. Although the estimates of total population and employment for the entire nine-county area are closely similar, notable differences can be observed in the forecasts of growth of individual counties and employment groups. The BASS model forecasts somewhat lower growth for Contra Costa, San Mateo, Marin, and Sonoma counties and higher rates of growth for Solano and Alameda counties. The principal significance to the appraiser of these differences is found in the resulting forecasts in the BASS report that the volume of

Figure 4–1. Bay Area Simulation Model (BASS): Employment and Population Submodels

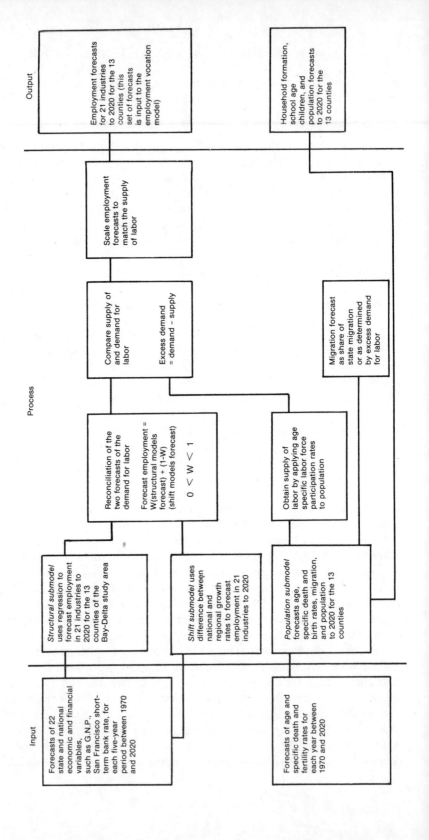

Figure 4–2. Bay Area Simulation Model (BASS): Employment and Residential Location Submodels

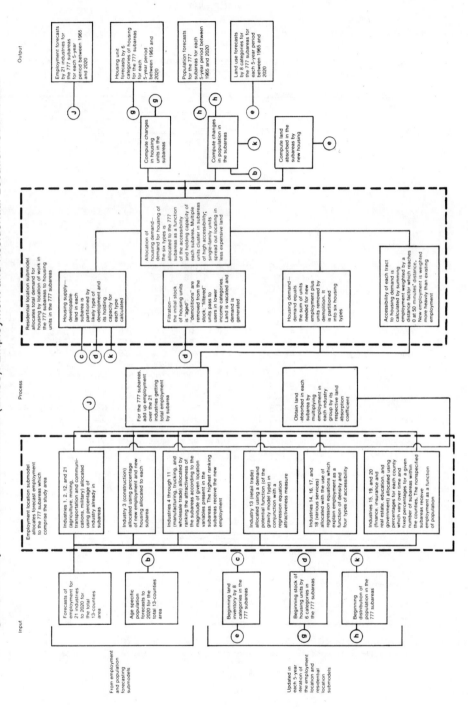

Table 4-2. Comparison of Population and Employment Forecasts, 1960–1990; BASS Medium Forecast and ABAG *Preliminary Regional Plan* (in thousands)

		Actual 1960	Forecast 1970	Forecast 1980	Forecast 1990	1960 to 1970	1970 to 1980	1980 to 1990
Population								
Total nine-county Bay area								
ABAG		3,639	4,869	6,071	7,207	33.8%	24.7%	18.7%
BASS		...	4,819	5,907	6,952	24.5	22.6	17.0
By counties								
Alameda	ABAG	908	1,150	1,350	1,505	26.6	17.4	11.5
	BASS		1,115	1,357	1,583	22.8	21.7	16.0
Contra Costa	ABAG	409	605	860	1,138	47.9	42.1	32.3
	BASS		588	736	885	43.8	25.2	20.2
Marin	ABAG	147	232	330	450	57.8	42.2	36.4
	BASS		238	321	388	61.9	34.9	20.9
Napa	ABAG	66	87	117	150	31.8	34.5	28.2
	BASS		85	103	113	28.8	21.2	9.7
San Francisco	ABAG	740	760	815	850	2.7	7.2	4.3
	BASS		765	802	856	3.4	4.8	6.7
San Mateo	ABAG	444	600	745	860	35.1	24.2	15.4
	BASS		577	668	730	30.0	15.8	9.3
Santa Clara	ABAG	642	1,033	1,290	1,500	60.9	24.9	16.3
	BASS		1,042	1,314	1,523	62.3	26.1	15.9
Solano	ABAG	135	180	220	254	33.3	22.2	15.4
	BASS		190	295	436	40.7	55.3	47.8
Sonoma	ABAG	147	222	344	500	51.0	54.9	45.3
	BASS		220	312	427	49.0	42.5	36.9
Employment								
Total nine-county Bay area								
ABAG		1,427	1,924	2,455	2,926	34.8	27.6	19.2
BASS			1,940	2,422	2,940	36.0	24.9	21.4
Manufacturing—BASS groups 4–10								
Total nine-county Bay area								
ABAG		284	368	489	591	29.6	32.9	20.9
BASS			358	441	528	26.1	23.2	19.7

Source: *Jobs, People and Land,* Bay Area Simulation Study (BASS), Special Report no. 6 (Berkeley: University of California, Center for Real Estate and Urban Economics, 1968), p. 297.

single-family housing in Solano County would approximately double between 1965 and 1990, while over one hundred thousand units would be added in Alameda County. Contra Costa County was estimated to add less than eighty thousand single-family units and San Mateo County to add approximately forty-three thousand units.

The BASS model also forecasts the volume of multi-family housing to be added during the period by county, city, and census (BASS) tracts and the total amount of land to be absorbed for each class of housing: for commercial, manufacturing, and wholesale use; for public and recreational purposes; and for agricultural, mining, and construction uses. Such estimates can be particularly useful in evaluating the feasibility and effect of large-scale industrial, commercial, or residential developments since they provide rough estimates of the total absorption of land for these purposes by areas over several decades.

Flexibility and sensitivity in the use of land-use simulation models as a basis for forecasting is illustrated by comparison of the estimated increments in housing development under two population assumptions – the medium forecast and the so-called low-pop forecast (low population). This comparison provides the appraiser with some insight into the effect of a change in the basic assumptions regarding population growth in the area upon the forecasts of housing requirements by area. The appraiser who has access to such a range of estimates can exercise his own judgment as to the acceptability of either the medium- or low-population projections, or he may use some estimates of the subjective probabilities of one or the other. If, for example, he thinks there is a fifty-fifty chance of either the medium- or low-population projections, he may average these and adjust his estimates of housing requirements accordingly. Of course, if his resources permitted, it would be possible to run the simulation model for any specific population and employment projection and use the output estimates.

The appraiser can also make use of land-use simulation models to assess the influence of major changes in public policy upon land prices and future development. Illustration of this is found in a recent application of the BASS model to test the impact of a major proposal for reserving land for open-space usage in the San Francisco Bay area.[45]

Land-use simulation models also greatly facilitate urban growth and neighborhood analysis by the appraiser. Table 4–3 compares the forecasts of growth in Alameda County by planning areas from 1970 to 1985. Such estimates permit the appraiser to construct time maps projecting present population for major planning areas into the future. The output of the land-use simulation model provides information for these same areas for single-family and multi-family housing for high-, middle-, and low-income groups. The model also permits the estimation of employment and land use for residential, commercial, manufacturing and wholesale, agricultural, and pub-

Table 4-3. Comparison of BASS Medium Forecast and Alameda County General Plan Estimates of Population and Employment, 1970–1990; Alameda County and County Planning Units (in thousands)

County planning units	1970 General Plan 1966 Est.	1970 General Plan 1967 Est.[a]	1970 BASS Medium Forecast	1980 General Plan 1966 Est.	1980 General Plan 1967 Est.[a]	1980 BASS Medium Forecast	1990 General Plan 1966 Est.	1990 General Plan 1967 Est.[a]	1990 BASS Medium Forecast
Alameda County									
Total population	1,168	1,143	1,115	1,477	1,350	1,357	1,770	1,550	1,583
Civilian employment	433	443	424	549	552	518	658	639	621
Manufacturing empl.	95	89	86	118	105	95	142	121	107
Central metropolitan									
Total population	617	605	602	661	635	598	713	665	593
Civilian employment	240	234	296	256	273	352	273	290	410
Manufacturing empl.	43	40	51	43	36	55	45	36	60
Eden									
Total population	318	295	293	379	339	358	425	370	410
Civilian employment	116	123	80	145	140	99	159	156	121
Manufacturing empl.	31	27	22	36	29	24	38	32	26
Washington									
Total population	167	155	152	270	225	253	348	280	341
Civilian employment	55	56	29	94	100	40	127	122	53
Manufacturing empl.	17	18	12	27	29	14	33	33	16
Livermore-Amador									
Total population	92	88	67	192	151	149	310	235	240
Civilian employment	30	30	19	63	54	27	108	87	38
Manufacturing empl.	17	4	1	27	19	3	33	21	5

[a]Revised population estimates for Alameda County Planning areas were released in December 1967 by the Alameda County Planning Department, "Population and Housing: 10." (Mimeographed). The revised figures as of 1 July 1967 were Alameda County, 1,074,000; Central metropolitan, 597,500; Eden, 283,000; Washington, 129,000; Livermore-Amador Valley, 64,700.

Source: *Jobs, People and Land,* Bay Area Simulation Study (BASS), Special Report no. 6 (Berkeley, Center for Real Estate and Urban Economics, University of California, 1968), p. 308.

lic and recreational use for these or other small areas simply by grouping of BASS tract output.

Their greatest value to the appraiser lies in the flexibility of computerized land-use simulation models. They should be regarded and used as sophisticated analytical devices rather than as precise forecasting tools. Used in this manner, they provide an invaluable aid to the appraiser's knowledge and judgment.

Up to the present, these models have been designed to forecast future development and land use. Conceptually, however, it would be feasible to extrapolate future values from the density forecasts. This would add substantially to the adaptability of land-use simulation models in appraising.

Summary and Conclusions

Urban growth and intraurban structural shifts have important influences upon real estate values. Although the growth of a city will usually result in an overall increase in property values, changes in values are usually unevenly distributed over the entire city and over time. Values in newer districts may rise precipitously, while properties in older districts suffer a decline. The encroachment of a new use in an old district may result in an upward adjustment in values of properties on the edge of the district encroached upon, while values in the remainder of the district may decline. It is important, therefore, for the appraiser to understand the dynamics of urban growth and to develop techniques for predicting future growth trends and shifts in urban districts.

Present theories of urban growth are based upon the analysis of past historical trends. The theories that have been developed emphasize the pressure caused by the expansion of central city functions and the key influence of topography and transportation routes in determining the directions of outward growth. Although the principles of city growth which have evolved provide a workable explanation of historical growth in American cities, they are less satisfactory as a framework for predicting the growth patterns of the future, owing to the revolution in interurban transportation and its effects upon urban functions and structure. For these reasons, the conclusion was reached that the appraiser must study past historical trends in analyzing future development, but he cannot assume that they will provide an infallible guide to the future. He can assume, however, that urban growth will depend upon the expansion of the economic base and that transportation and topography will continue to be dominant factors influencing urban structure. The major factors of change which he must consider are transportation developments and the influence of public policy upon urban structure.

Generally, appraisal literature fails to integrate analysis of the economic base and overall growth of the city with analysis of its internal structure. Hurd and Babcock recognized the importance of these interrelationships but gave only limited attention to the development of techniques of analysis in early writings. Babcock developed the technique for rating of residential location used by the Federal Housing Administration. This has served as a pattern for most appraisal literature on the analysis of residential neighborhoods. Prime attention in this technique is accorded to the internal factors within a neighborhood which will tend to maintain stability and values, rather than to the dynamics of urban growth and district shifts. Lacking a better standard, appraisers have generally emphasized the importance of economic, cultural, and ethnic homogeneity. This general principle has been under sharp attack by empirical researchers in recent years.

Weimer and Hoyt suggest that the analysis of any residential, commercial, and industrial district should proceed from certain basic hypotheses as to the rate and direction of growth of the various districts of a city. Although they do not present a comprehensive theory of urban location, their recommended technique furnishes a framework with which the appraiser may proceed to consider special locational factors for various land uses in a city.

Although it can be argued that urban growth theory has not changed significantly in the past decade, the quality of data has been greatly improved and new techniques of analysis employing the computer have provided the appraiser with challenging and powerful tools. Land-use simulation models, the outcome of transportation and planning studies in selected metropolitan areas, represent a significant and rich potential contribution to the appraisal process. Most importantly, these models provide an analytical framework which integrates national, regional, and local economic background analysis with traditional neighborhood analysis. As the quality of data inputs to these models improves, their usefulness in appraisal work will be greatly enhanced and a major shortcoming of appraisal theory and practice may be overcome.

Economic background, city, and neighborhood analysis provide valuable insights into past and future growth trends affecting property values. The final test of the validity of any forecast is in the market place. The following three chapters review in some detail the rationalization and techniques underlying the use of the market comparison, income, and cost approaches to value.

THE MARKET-COMPARISON METHOD

The market-comparison, comparable-sales, or market-data method, as it is variously called, permits the establishment of values of real estate by reference to actual sales of a subject property or of a comparable property. It will be recalled from earlier chapters that market price gradually lost its central position in appraisal theory. This development resulted from a gradual decline in emphasis, rather than from a formal or outright rejection of the market-comparison method. It was accompanied by greater reliance upon and refinements in the capitalization-of-income and the replacement-cost methods. The decline in the importance of the market-comparison method can be attributed, in large measure, to the rapid gyrations in market prices of real estate during the depression and World War II years. These wide price movements occurred at a time when there was a growing need for stability in real estate value measurement. The development of specialized value concepts, the continuing lack of organized real estate price series, and the increasing recognition of the many factors influencing the real estate market structure have been contributing factors.

The market-comparison method has experienced a marked resurgence since World War II. Increasing emphasis on market prices in appraisal theory and extensive augmentation in the quantity and quality of real estate market data have combined to reestablish the market-comparison method as the central valuation technique.

It is the purpose of this chapter to reexamine the position of the market-comparison method in appraisal theory. In that connection, underlying theoretical problems involved in the use of the method will be considered. Market data and techniques of valuation will be described and evaluated, and conclusions will be drawn as to the applicability of the market method to appraisal problems today.

Problems in Using the Market-Comparison Method

It has been maintained that "the market has not now, nor has it ever had, a monopoly of pecuniary valuation."[1] This statement focuses attention upon the lack of acceptance of market valuations for many purposes. The accountant may be interested in original cost; the tax assessor or fire insurance adjuster in replacement cost; and the long-term investor or mortgage lender may be primarily interested in some concept such as "normal" or "intrinsic" value. The conclusion follows that any concept or method of valuation must be significant for the purpose at hand. The acceptance of market sales as evidence of value is dependent in the first analysis, therefore, on the purpose of the valuation estimate.

The economic law of substitution would lead us to believe that in competitive markets equal market prices would be established for real estate as well as for other commodities which furnish equivalent amenities or prospects for income. As a result of the working of this principle, the market-comparison method is by all odds the most widely used method in establishing values in the economy as a whole. The myriad prices paid for food, gasoline, clothing, automobiles, and practically every commonly purchased commodity are established by comparing the prices in the market for the same or substitute articles. Upon reflection, one will observe that the market-comparison method has far greater applicability in the pricing of standardized, new commodities that are bought and sold continuously on a large scale. To illustrate, the method is much better adapted to the determination of the value of Number 2 cash red wheat, prime steers, or Idaho potatoes than it is to the valuation of a used guitar, a six-ounce fly rod, or the Empire State Building. The former group of commodities are considered to be new and uniform in grade and characteristics. They are dealt in continuously by large numbers of highly informed individuals. By contrast, the latter group of commodities are highly individualized, have suffered varying degrees of depreciation, and enjoy limited markets.

The efficiency with which the real estate markets, in fact, establish similar values for properties with the same amenities, risks, and prospective incomes is dependent upon the class of real estate under consideration, its market structure, and the efficiency of the means of market communication. The basic nonhomogeneity of real estate and the wide variations in the degree of real estate market organization underlie many of the problems in the application of the comparable sales or market-comparison method. Three types of problems that have their roots in the characteristics of real estate and its markets are discussed below under the following headings: (1) defining market value, (2) establishing terms and conditions of comparable sales, and (3) determining comparability.

Defining Market Value   It has already been observed that the market-comparison method is adaptable only when the value sought is market value. The jingle "the worth of a thing is the price it will bring" is misleading in its apparent simplicity. Real estate, because of its bulk, high unit value, and individuality, is not bought and sold like other commodities. Ordinarily, it requires considerable time to effect a real estate transaction, and it cannot be assumed that the market knowledge of buyers and sellers is complete or equal. As a result of the imperfections in the various markets for real estate, wide variations are observed in the market prices of identical properties over short periods, and more extreme differences are noted in the market prices of seemingly close substitutes. Because of these variations, it becomes necessary to establish some criteria for determining when a market sale will be acceptable evidence of market value. Such criteria have been set forth in some detail by courts of law, mortgage lenders, tax officials, and government mortgage-insuring agencies. It would seem to go without saying that these attempts to define the meaning of the term *market value* are not mutually consistent. Clear illustration of these difficulties is found in the definitions of the term by the New York and Pennsylvania courts, quoted by Alfred D. Jahr:

> But what is the meaning of this "fair market value"? The definitions vary between fact and fancy. Generally speaking, when the courts refer to market value in eminent domain they mean the value of the property which it would bring in the market between a willing buyer and a willing seller under ordinary circumstances. The definition itself raises more questions than it answers.
>
> Let us now examine some of these definitions of market value. One of the New York Courts defines market value of real property as "the amount which one desiring but not compelled to purchase would pay under ordinary conditions to a seller who desires but is not compelled to sell." The same court further stated: "Fair market value means neither panic value, auction value, speculative value, nor a value fixed by depressed or inflated prices. A fair market value is not established by sales where prices offered are so small that only sellers forced to sell will accept them. The mere absence of competitive buyers does not establish lack of a real market. But a market in fact may be established only where there are willing buyers and sellers in substantial number." The Court went on to say: "Fair market value of property actually taken as of the date of appropriation resides in an estimate and a determination of what is the fair, economic, just and equitable value under normal conditions. . . . All elements of value that inhere in the property should be considered."
>
> In Pennsylvania the Supreme Court defines market value as follows: "It is nothing more or less than what the subject would sell for in the open market, exposed to all bidders in the regular course of trade and competition which ordinarily obtain with respect to that particular class of subject. Nothing short of an actual sale of a tract of land in the open market can fix definitely and certainly its market value. Until so sold, what it will bring in a fair and open market, is mere matter of opinion, and while divergence of view is in most cases to be expected, rarely, however, so marked as in the present case [*sic*]. Nevertheless, it is from these opinions, based on the general selling price of land, however divergent, that the laws seek to arrive at an estimate that will serve the ends of practical justice.[2]

These definitions illustrate the difficulties which arise when it is assumed that going market prices represent unsuitable measures of value, for obviously the appraiser under these circumstances must resort to hypothetical market prices. To an increasing extent, both in the law and in appraisal practice generally, the concept of comparable sales value has come to mean a "justified" or "normal" sales price. Bonbright has said that the fair market value so established by the courts "is likely to be not quite 'fair' on the one hand, and not quite 'market' on the other hand, but something in between the two."[3]

The broad influence of this tendency to reject going market sales prices as evidence of value is found in appraisal literature of the depression years. A. J. Mertzke, writing in 1933, distinguished three general market conditions in real estate: (1) the normal or usual market when the market is firm and dependable, (2) the period of speculative boom and activity, and (3) the period of deflation and depression. It is only under the first condition that selling prices approximate true values, in his opinion. Commenting on the values then current in the market, he stated:

> In a period of depression the true appraiser has the more pleasant task of seeing beyond the illusions of the moment that blind the multitude and pointing out the vital elements in real estate values which emerge unharmed from every period of depression. . . .
> Following the psychology of the crowd, many appraisers' valuations are as unstable as chips riding the waves, instead of holding to a steady course in stormy as well as placid waters.[4]

One might question Mertzke's idealized "three general market conditions." Most real estate market analysts are in agreement that we do not have a single unified real estate market but rather a large number of more or less closely related markets. Fisher and Fisher point out that the real estate market is composed of many submarkets which may be distinguished by classification as to use, tenure, location, and physical characteristics.[5] Thus, markets for office space, housing, and industrial and commercial sites have distinguishing characteristics. Within these submarkets different markets can be distinguished for rental as compared with fee ownership.

The geographical boundaries of real estate markets also vary for each type of use, with close price relationships observable for particular use types within the boundaries of a given geographical area. Finally, real estate markets can be broken down by the physical characteristics and price classes of property involved. Large office buildings, loft buildings, and combination office-store buildings are examples of the submarkets by type of structure within a single broad use classification.

It is quite apparent that divergent price trends may prevail from time to time in many of these submarkets since each is influenced by special demand and supply conditions. It would be difficult indeed to identify any period within the past two decades of the housing market as a "normal or usual market when the market is firm and dependable," to use Mertzke's words. Early postwar market weakness in some sections of the country contrasted with rapidly rising prices in other regions. At certain times, older homes appear to reflect market weakness, while the market for new homes is firm.

Casual observation belies any such simple classification of market conditions as that proposed by Mertzke. Further, his proposition that market prices represent true values *only* when the market is firm and dependable appears to be little more than a naive rationalization for his rejection of depression market prices. Peter Hanson, in an article written at about the same time, objected to the philosophy of market values and "chips on the waves," as expressed by Mertzke, in these words: "We are not appraising market value — we are appraising what market value ought to be."[6]

The more or less general view that market value in the comparable-sales method represents the price which a property would sell for under some idealized market conditions rather than the price it actually sells for has required that appraisers study the terms and conditions of comparable sales in some detail before accepting such sales as evidence of value. Such a detailed examination must proceed from a clear conception of the market-value concept suited to the appraisal problem at hand, be it *normal, long-term, actual, fair cash,* or *fair* market value. Unfortunately for the appraiser, these terms mean different things to different people.

Establishing Terms and Conditions of Comparable Sales The selling price of a parcel of real estate will almost certainly vary with the period of time allowed for consummating the sale, with the relative knowledge of buyers and sellers in the market, and with the terms of financing specified in the sale. The FHA *Underwriting Manual* describes the variations to be expected in selling prices of residential real estate with different degrees of knowledge and conditions of duress affecting buyers and sellers. It is because of these influences, specified in figure 5–1, that the Federal Housing Administration has fashioned a definition of *value* which prescribes fairly precise conditions of knowledge and duress on the part of buyers and sellers: "The word Value (excluding closing costs) used by the Federal Housing Administration refers to a Price which a purchaser is warranted in paying for a property rather than a price for which a property may be sold, and is defined as: The price which typical buyers would be warranted in paying for the property for long-term use or investment, if they were well informed, acted intelligently, voluntarily and without necessity."[7]

The need for applying criteria of knowledge and duress to market sales varies with the characteristics of the market. The price of Number 2 cash red wheat in Chicago is usually accepted as evidence of its value without considering whether buyers and sellers are acting with or without equal knowledge or duress. This is true for many types of goods enjoying mass markets. Individual real estate markets, however, differ substantially. For example, the conditions of knowledge are generally more uniform in the markets for commercial and industrial property than for residential real estate since these markets are characterized by a much higher degree of professional participation. Sectors of the real estate market in which properties are dealt in actively

Figure 5-1. Market Effects of Buyers' Reactions

Buyers who are well informed and act intelligently and without necessity.	Buyers who act without necessity but are not well informed or act unintelligently.	Buyers who are motivated by necessity or who act to secure special benefits which will accrue to them as specific users.
Buyers will pay current market prices if they are not more than the present worth of future long-term benefits that will accrue to typical users.	Buyers will pay current market prices even though they may exceed present worth of future long-term benefits that will accrue to typical users.	Buyers will, or must, pay current or higher than the current market prices, even though they exceed the present worth of future long-term benefits that will accrue to typical users.
Prices paid are influenced by an adequate understanding of existing and prospective market conditions.	Prices paid are influenced by an inadequate knowledge of existing and prospective market conditions.	Prices paid are influenced by existing market conditions, by degree of necessity, and by available alternatives.
The buyers' actions tend to hold market prices at levels not in excess of the present worth of future long-term benefits that will accrue to typical users.	The buyers' actions tend to cause market price levels to rise above the present worth of future long-term benefits that will accrue to typical users.	The buyers' actions tend to create and support a market at inflated price levels.

Market Effects of Sellers' Reactions

Sellers who are well informed and act intelligently and without necessity.	Sellers who act without necessity but are not well informed or act unintelligently.	Sellers who are motivated by necessity or who act to secure special benefits which will accrue to them specifically.
Sellers will sell for available market prices if they are not less than the present worth of future long-term benefits that will accrue to typical users.	Sellers will sell for available market prices even though they may be less than the present worth of future long-term benefits which will accrue to typical users.	Sellers will, or must, sell for any available price, even if less than present worth of future long-term benefits that will accrue to typical users.
Prices received are influenced by an adequate understanding of existing and prospective market conditions.	Prices received are influenced by an inadequate knowledge of existing and prospective market conditions.	Prices received are influenced by existing market conditions, by degree of necessity, and by lack of alternatives.
The sellers' actions tend to hold market prices at levels not less than the present worth of future long-term benefits that will accrue to typical users.	The sellers' actions tend to cause market price levels to decline below the present worth of future long-term benefits that will accrue to typical users.	The sellers' actions tend to depress and retard upward movements of market price levels.

Source: Federal Housing Administration, *Underwriting Manual*, loose-leaf rev. ed. (Washington, D.C., February 1966). pt. 4, sec. 13, 71306.6.

approximate ideal markets. At the other extreme are sectors of the real estate market in which property changes hands infrequently and in which buyers and sellers have very imperfect knowledge.

If the appraiser is able to establish the criteria of knowledge and duress to be used in analyzing comparable sales of real estate, he is then confronted with the more difficult task of adjusting sales which fail to meet the desired qualifications. What adjustment should the appraiser make in a sale of industrial land by a business concern that needs working capital? What dollar allowance should be made for lack of knowledge on the part of a buyer of subdivision property? These adjustments can be determined with some ease if sales data on similar property under conditions close to the ideal are available. However, in the absence of such sales information, the appraiser must make some judgmental percentage allowance.

Since the war, the application of the market-comparison method has been complicated by the varying financing terms under which residential property has been sold. Two factors that have been notable influences are (1) the existence of favorable mortgage loan terms on specific properties and (2) the acceptance by sellers of second mortgages in partial payment for homes sold. The first factor has been a particularly noticeable influence upon market sales prices during periods of mortgage-money stringency.

Tables 5–1 and 5–2 show that FHA-insured and VA-guaranteed loans have been a gradually decreasing proportion of total mortgage debt outstanding and loans made on nonfarm, one- to four-family properties since the early 1960s. The total dollar volume of new FHA-insured and VA-guaranteed loans made on both new and existing homes has not exceeded $13 billion in any year since 1964. The volume represented a small proportion of total new loans made nationally, although it rose in 1970 and early 1971.

Appraisers have found it necessary to distinguish carefully between the VA (otherwise known as the GI) market and the market for homes without VA home loans and to make adjustments in sales prices to allow for the buyer's preferences for homes with the more liberal financing terms. Although the appraiser has been able to recognize this phenomenon in the market without too great difficulty, the determination of the exact dollar adjustment allowance has proved substantially more difficult.

The making of appropriate adjustments for the existence of VA loans on residences was complicated by a parallel tendency for sellers to accept second or purchase-money mortgages as a portion of selling price. Generally speaking, sellers would expect to receive a higher price for a home if they were required to accept second-mortgage paper in lieu of cash. Although some evidence of the amount of discount can be obtained by reference to market sales of second mortgages, wide variations will be found to exist, as can be expected, in the quality and value of such mortgages. The appraiser is also required, therefore, to exercise his judgment in making adjustments in market sales prices to allow for variations in financing terms.

Table 5-1. Mortgage Debt Outstanding on Nonfarm, One- to Four-Family Properties (billions of dollars)

| End of Period | Total | Government-Underwritten | | | Conventional |
		Total	FHA	VA	
1954	18.6	4.3	4.1	0.2	14.3
1963	182.2	65.9	35.0	30.9	116.3
1964	197.6	69.2	38.3	30.9	128.3
1965	212.9	73.1	42.0	31.1	139.8
1966	223.6	76.1	44.8	31.3	147.6
1967	236.1	79.9	47.4	32.5	156.1
1968	251.2	83.8	50.6	33.2	167.4
1969	266.8	90.1	54.5	35.6	176.9
1970 (2d qtr.)	271.7	92.1	56.1	36.0	179.9

Table 5-2. Government-Underwritten Residential Loans Made (millions of dollars)

| Period | Total | FHA-insured | | | | Total | VA-guaranteed | |
| | | Mortgages | | Projects | Property Improve-ments | | Mortgages | |
		New Homes	Existing Homes				New Homes	Existing Homes
1945	665	257	217	20	171	192		
1964	8,130	1,608	4,965	895	663	2,846	1,023	1,821
1965	8,689	1,705	5,760	591	634	2,652	876	1,774
1966	7,320	1,729	4,366	583	641	2,600	980	1,618
1967	7,150	1,369	4,516	642	623	3,405	1,143	2,259
1968	8,275	1,572	4,924	1,123	656	3,774	1,430	2,343
1969	9,129	1,551	5,570	1,316	693	4,072	1,493	2,579
1970 Jan.-June	5,133	1,065	2,414	1,365	289	1,536	654	882

Source: *Federal Reserve Bulletin*, December 1970, p. A 52.

The mortgage credit crunch of 1969–1970 stimulated renewed interest among appraisers in the influence of differing financing terms upon market values. J. L. Doherty reported in the July 1970 *Appraisal Journal* that a 1 percent difference in interest rate accounted for differences of 7 to 10 percent in the probable sales prices of single family homes with loans of twenty thousand dollars in Richmond, Virginia.[8]

Although the interest rate alone is not an acceptable criterion of financing terms from the viewpoint of the potential buyer of residential properties, other conditions of comparability and credit availability being the same, a property with the lowest interest rate should command the highest price. The problem is that these are usually not the market circumstances. Properties bearing low interest rate loans usually were financed at an earlier date and hence the loans are partially amortized. This means that the down payment required will usually be higher for properties with low interest rate loans. The addition of a second mortgage loan may result in higher total monthly payments than would be required under a single new first mortgage made at higher interest rates for a higher percentage of market sales price. The entire loan package must be considered in judging the influence of financing terms on market sales prices. The principal criterion in judging loan terms should be the amount of the monthly loan payments per thousand dollars of loan. The most attractive loan terms are not necessarily consistent with the lowest interest rate. Estimates such as those obtained in the survey by Doherty should be used with great caution since they are based upon a questionnaire survey with a low response rate and the questions posed relatively unrealistic conditions of financing availability.

Two solutions are offered to the appraiser seeking to determine current market value and faced with varying terms of sale in the market: (1) having fixed upon the terms of sale considered typical in the market and suited to the value concept sought, choose *only* comparables which satisfy these terms, and (2) adjust all comparable sales to a cash equivalent basis. The choice between these alternatives will depend upon the purpose and value definition. If the most probable selling price is the appraiser's objective, the gross sales prices of properties with generally similar financing terms may be employed. However, increasing diversity in financing terms might justify adopting a definition of the most probable selling price adjusted to a cash-equivalent basis, under some circumstances. Garcia, writing in the January 1972 *Appraisal Journal,* makes a strong case for the use of "cash equivalent."[9]

Timing of Comparable Sales   The appraiser using the market-comparison method must also reach a decision as to the relative significance of recent sales as compared with sales more distant in time and as to the means of making adjustments in sales for differences in the timing of transactions. Various sectors of the real estate market differ in the relative frequency with which sales occur. Large office buildings sell very infrequently, while single-family tract homes and smaller income properties may have a relatively rapid turnover. Further, the amount and quality of market data concerning the various sectors of the real estate market vary considerably. As will be pointed out below, computer analysis of multiple-listing data has made it possible to adjust market sales prices for differences in the time of sale with considerably greater reliability than heretofore.

Determining Comparability   The determination of the comparability of individual sales gives rise to the most general and difficult problems in the application of the market-comparison method. Each parcel of real estate is not only distinctive as to the land on which it is situated but also varies in type of structure and neighborhood influence. Land may vary in its locational features, topography, or soil conditions, while structures differ in age, condition, or type. Consequently, the appraiser employing the market-comparison method must take all of these factors into consideration in using market sales of differing parcels to measure the value of a subject property.

97

Elaborate techniques have been devised for determining comparability of residential real estate. Many of these are adaptations of the so-called grid technique, wherein different attributes of the land and buildings are given percentage ratings in comparison with the subject property. The prime difficulty, of course, is in assigning dollar importance to the differences observed. Is a property with a beautiful view worth 110 percent of one lacking such a view, or 150 percent? Can the relative value of a sloping lot be measured by the increased costs of building, or must other factors be taken into consideration? The problem of adjusting for differences in condition of buildings recalls the difficulties noted in the measurement of depreciation in the cost approach. Differences in the value of neighborhood amenities are the subject of wide dispute. Some appraisers consider proximity to schools and shopping facilities a desirable feature; others do not. The whole question of value adjustments for nonhomogeneity of types of structures, income, family, and racial status is likewise unresolved.

The institute text illustrates a rating grid for adjusting comparable sales for differences in time of sale, location and neighborhood, and physical characteristics, but this long-used technique provides little basis for determining the all-important dollar adjustments to be made in each case.[10] Multiple-regression techniques provide the most acceptable statistical basis for determining the dollar value adjustments to be made in comparable sales.

The question of the geographical boundaries of real estate markets is usually raised in the consideration of comparability. Should sales of homes in Westchester County, New York, be compared with home sales in Brooklyn for purposes of establishing value? This and a host of similar questions can be answered only by comparing price performance over time by geographical areas. Here, again, rigorous statistical analysis of new sources of sales data provides the only basis for reliable answers.

The foregoing review of some of the basic problems involved in the use of the market-comparison method emphasizes anew the various points in the appraisal process at which the factor of judgment must be applied. Although sales in the real estate market recommend themselves as prime evidence of values, the nonhomogeneity of real estate, variations in market activity and performance, differences in terms and conditions of sale, and questions of comparability add up to a formidable group of problems requiring the application of hypotheses, assumptions, and judgments. This process is greatly magnified by the fact that there has been a conspicuous lack of organized factual information about real estate markets.

Market-Comparison Techniques

The market-comparison method can be applied to the valuation of vacant land or to the valuation of land and buildings in combination. Techniques will vary considerably according to the nature of the proposed or actual use of the land and according to the purpose of the valuation estimate.

Vacant Commercial Land   Great attention has been devoted in appraisal literature to the development of techniques for valuation of vacant commercial land. One reason for the extensive reliance upon the market-comparison method in the valuation of commercial land is found in the common agreement that the capitalization-of-income method can result in widely differing estimates of land value with relatively small changes in gross-income estimation.[11] The latter conclusion can be demonstrated by illustration of a case in which the valuation of a vacant site is to be determined by assuming the construction of a hypothetical building to cost one million dollars. As shown in table 5–3, a change in the income estimation by as little as 10 percent can result in a large percentage difference in capitalized value of the assumed residual returns to the land.

Table 5–3. Effect of a Change of 10 Percent in Annual Returns upon Land-Residual Values

	Estimate 1	Estimate 2 Increase 10%	Estimate 3 Decrease 10%
Total annual returns to property	$75,000	$ 82,500	$67,500
Assume 7% level return on investment in building	70,000	70,000	70,000
Residual returns to land	5,000	12,500	0
Value of land-residual returns capitalized as perpetuity at 6%	83,333	208,333	0

Characteristic of other branches of appraisal theory, there has been an increasing attempt to apply semimathematical techniques to the appraisal of land by the market-comparison method. The theory underlying these techniques, however, has undergone little or no change since the writings of Hurd in 1903 and McMichael and Bingham in the early twenties.[12] The latter authors recognized utility as the basis for value of urban sites and emphasized that "all land is individual and unique in character," and for that reason, warned that "valuing land cannot be classed as an exact science" since "sales can never be more than sign posts to mark the way towards a correct conclusion."

Babcock on Market-Comparison Method   Babcock restated the theory of the market-comparison method as follows:

> As in all other real estate valuation problems, utility is the basis of comparison. If a given site is appraised by the comparison method, the process consists of finding sites which have comparable services to offer and for which values have been established. . . .

How, then, are these comparisons to be made? First, the valuator considers the characteristics of the site under valuation — its potential uses, its size, its shape, its accessibility, its restrictions by deeds, zoning, and so forth. Then he tries to find other sites having the same or nearly the same characteristics. He selects sites which have been purchased in free and open sales. Then he ascribes a value to the site under appraisement, the value being indicated by and justified by the sale prices of the comparable properties.[13]

Babcock held, however, that because of the limitations of data and problems of comparability, downtown sites should almost invariably be appraised by the residual-income-capitalization method. For reasons illustrated above, few authorities today would agree with Babcock on the latter conclusion, and it is no doubt true that he was strongly influenced by an inherent preference for the capitalization-of-income method. He identified three methods for valuing commercial land by market comparison: (1) the chunk method, (2) the square-foot method, and (3) the building-plan method. These alternative methods, according to his book, were to be used in combination with the residual-income method for valuing downtown business sites.

The first, or chunk method, involves the overall comparison of sites for which sales data are available and the fixing of a value for the site under appraisal by application of percentage factors to the comparable sales. The percentage factors applied to the comparables are based upon judgment and observation rather than upon any mathematical weighting of such elements as size of lot, topography, and location. In this sense, the chunk method is the simplest of the three.

The application of the square-foot method requires the calculation of the number of square feet of space in each site used as a comparable and the assignment of some quality adjustment to these square-foot value factors to allow for differences in the subject property. The latter adjustment factors are presumably determined by the same judgment process used in establishing similar factors for use in the chunk method described above.

The building-plan method involves considerably more calculation and, in reality, provides the statistical basis for application of the land-residual-income method to a given site valuation problem. In this method, the appraiser is called upon to develop tentative building plans for each site under comparison and to determine the relative amounts and quality of rentable space for each property. In making these calculations, he must determine the amount of net rentable space which will result from a given gross floor area and estimate the relative rentability of the different kinds of space available. Babcock outlines a technique for applying percentage factors to the various grades of space to reduce them to common units of grade A space. Thus, grade B space is converted to units of grade A space by application of a 60 percent factor, grade C by application of a 50 percent factor, and so forth.[14] It can be seen that it is only a step from this set of calculations to the conversion of the space figures to an estimate of gross income and expenses and, thence, to the estimation of the value of the sites by the land-residual-income method outlined in chapter 6.

In the example Babcock gave, the application of the three methods described above to a problem of valuation of a hotel site results in closely similar estimates of value by the three variations of the market-comparison technique. It can be readily seen that the estimates by the chunk and square-foot methods depend almost wholly upon the percentage adjustment factors used and that minor adjustments of these factors could easily force resultant value estimates into close agreement. Although the building-plan method gives the appearance of the greatest accuracy, it is based upon several assumptions and requires a substantial degree of estimation.

Adjustment Technique in the Market-Comparison Method   The basic criterion in using the comparable-sales method is to assure comparability. The more numerous and important in dollar terms are the necessary adjustments to the sales prices of the comparable properties used, the greater is the possible error introduced. Table 5–4 illustrates the traditional adaptation of the market-comparison method to a single-family home in Oakland, California, in October 1969. The dollar adjustments used in this illustration were made after consultation with real estate brokers who were knowledgeable concerning the reactions of potential buyers to the elements such as number of rooms, baths, lot size, age, and square footage. It will be noted that all of the sales occurred within three years of the date of the appraisal. The so-called time adjustment used was based upon the market-trend index for single-family homes in the East Bay area by dividing the index as of October 1969 by the value of the index as of the dates of the individual sales.

The reader may appropriately ask, What conclusions can be drawn from table 5–4 concerning the value of the subject property? At first glance, it would appear that the arithmetic mean of the adjusted comparable sales price of $62,496 might represent an acceptable estimate of value for the subject property. However, the range of the comparable figures indicates that the price might fall somewhere between $60,000 and $66,000 if the adjustment parameters were accurately estimated.

The standard deviation, shown as $2,191 in table 5–4, is the "standard" measure of statistical dispersion. It is calculated by (1) squaring the deviations of individual values from the arithmetic mean, (2) summing the squares, (3) dividing the sum by $(n - 1)$, and (4) extracting the square root.[15]

Large numbers of individual observations of statistical data drawn from a universe generally tend to group themselves about the arithmetic mean in a "normal" bell-shaped curve. If such a distribution is normal and not "skewed," it can be expected that 68.27 percent of the cases will fall within

Table 5–4. Adaptation of Market-Comparison Method to Oakland Single-Family Home

Property	Number of Rooms	Square Footage	Baths	Lot Size	Age of House	Architecture
1	11	2,750	3½	113 x 85	25 yrs.	Spanish
2	9	2,500	3½	70 x 80	35	Spanish
3	11	2,800	1½	130 x 88	45	Tudor
4	7	2,200	2	130 x 125	33	Colonial
5	8	2,250	3½	70 x 84	42	Tudor
6	8	2,400	3½	120 x 70	35	Spanish
Subject	14	3,250	5	128 x 84	43	Spanish

Property	Date of Sale	Sale Price	Index[a] 10/69 / Index Date of Sale	Factor Quotient	Gross Sales Price	Baths	Lot Size	Age and Condition	Number of Rooms and Square Footage	Comparable Figure
1	1/67	$52,000	143.8 / 127.4	113	$58,700	1½ x $1,000	2,200 x $1	- $1,000	$5,000	$66,400
2	1/69	42,000	143.8 / 139.0	104	43,700	1½ x 1,000	6,100 x 1	+ 1,200	7,500	60,000
3	9/68	50,000	143.8 / 136.4	106	53,000	3½ x 1,000	300 x 1	- 700	4,500	60,600
4	9/67	47,000	143.8 / 129.6	111	52,200	3 x 1,000	- 5,500 x 1	+ 1,100	10,200	61,000
5	4/68	45,000	143.8 / 132.4	109	49,000	1½ x 1,000	5,900 x 1	0	7,000	63,400
6	4/68	45,000	143.8 / 132.4	109	49,000	1½ x 1,000	3,380 x 1	+ 1,100	8,500	63,480

Arithmetic mean: $62,496
Range: $60,000–$66,400
Standard deviation: $2,191

[a]"East Bay Market Trend Index," *Northern California Real Estate Report*, 4th quarter 1969, p. 54.

Source: Paul F. Wendt.

plus or minus 1 times the standard deviation, and that 95.45 percent will fall within plus or minus 2 times standard deviation.

If the sample of cases illustrated in table 5–4 was very large and the average represented the true mean of the population, an appraiser might expect that in 68.27 percent of the cases in which he collected a sample and adjusted the sales in the manner described, the resulting average estimate of value would fall within plus or minus $2,191 and in 95.45 percent of the cases within plus or minus $4,382 of the average $62,496.

The true range of variation may be higher than that shown, however, due to the small number of cases in the sample. Special statistical techniques are applicable in estimating probabilities for small samples. The ratio t, used in correcting for sampling errors, is defined as the deviation of the sample mean from the population mean expressed in standard error units. Most statistical texts include tables for values of t for different probability levels and so-called degrees of freedom which depend upon the size of the sample.[16] The t value at a 0.05 percent probability level (95 percent probability) with 5 degrees of freedom is 2.571. The upper and lower limits of estimated value for the sample of six cases in table 5–4 can be calculated from the formula:

$$\text{Upper limit of value} = \bar{X} + t\frac{s}{n}.$$

$$\text{Upper limit of value} = \$62,496 + 2.571 \times \frac{2,191}{\sqrt{6}} = \$64,794.$$

$$\text{Lower limit of value} = \$62,496 - 2.571 \times \frac{2,191}{\sqrt{6}} = \$60,198.$$

The foregoing examination of the results summarized in table 5–4 indicates that the appraiser can advise his client that successive samples of sales *adjusted in the same manner* will in ninety-five cases out of one hundred result in estimated values between $60,198 and $64,794.

Although this range of accuracy might be acceptable for some appraisal problems, others may dictate that the appraiser arrive at an estimate of value with a narrower range of probable variation. One obvious solution to this problem is for the appraiser to increase the number of comparable sales in his sample since the standard deviation and range of expected sampling variation will decline as the square root of the number of cases increases.[17]

The important point to emphasize is that the above procedure for estimating the expected *sampling* variation does not tell us anything about the quality of the data or the adjustment procedures, or about the *accuracy* of the resulting estimate of value. The inclusion of other property attributes, not considered in table 5–4, might result in a different valuation estimate. For example, the subject property may have one or more important characteristics (a panoramic view, a swimming pool, or proximity to a garbage dump) which may distinguish it from the other comparable properties studied. If appropriate adjustments were made for these property characteristics in table 5–4, the resulting value estimate would be different.

A "weighted feature" rating technique for processing comparables has been advocated recently by Ratcliff and Swan.[18] Reminiscent of the FHA Risk Rating System developed in the 1930s by Frederick M. Babcock, the method is a refinement of a value-ranking technique presented by Henry A. Babcock in his recent book.[19] This technique is based upon the theory that the appraiser can identify the property features affecting market value and is able to assign weights to each characteristic. The authors identify the feature-weighting plan as shown in table 5–5. Each of the comparables is ranked from one

Table 5–5. Illustration of Weighted Quality-Rating Technique

	Weight	Rating					Subject
		Comparables					
		A	B	C	D	E	
Locational convenience	15	8	7	3	10	1	6
Neighborhood	20	6	6	7	1	3	4
Lot	15	6	4	5	1	6	5
Exterior architecture	10	4	1	4	3	2	4
Physical condition	10	8	7	3	1	4	2
Interior plan	15	7	10	6	2	1	3
Interior attractiveness	10	2	2	1	2	3	3
Mechanical equipment	5	4	3	2	3	5	5
Total	100						

Source: *Appraisal Journal* 40 (January 1972): 72.

to six for each of the features listed in table 5–5 and a composite score derived by multiplying the weights for each feature times the score for each comparable. The authors observe a close relationship between the weighted quality rating score and sales prices for the comparables. This relationship is illustrated by a regression line showing the relationship between the weighted quality ratings for the comparables and market sales prices, which was fitted by visual inspection.

The authors drew attention to the major limitations of this and other grid weighting schemes in pointing out that the technique assumes that market price differentials are fully explained by the particular set of features identified. Further, both the weights and the rankings for each property are subjectively determined and experience has demonstrated that one appraiser's ranking may differ substantially from another's. It is not at all clear that the feature-rating technique is less subjective or more likely to produce accurate estimates of value than the more conventional methods of introducing dollar adjustments for adjusting comparables illustrated above.

It is obvious that there are important elements of judgment and subjectivity in the traditional methods of adjusting property sales for noncomparability. It will be pointed out that multiple regression analysis is a logical extension of the comparable sales approach. This technique permits the scientific measurement of the proportion of the variance in sales prices explained or accounted for by differences in the observed characteristics of the individual properties examined. If the number of comparable sales is large and the enumeration of the property characteristics is exhaustive, the multiple regression technique reduces substantially the problems of omission and subjectivity referred to above.

Recent Improvements in Market Data

The problems surrounding the use of the market-comparison technique have been considerably reduced in recent years as a result of two developments: (1) substantial improvements have occurred in the quality and availability of market data, and (2) new techniques of market data analysis involving the use of the computer have created new dimensions for the market-comparison method of valuation.

Market-Price Indexes Mortgage lenders, appraisal organizations, and government agencies have collaborated in the formation of local real estate research groups in several metropolitan areas during the past two decades. The *Northern California Real Estate Report*, formerly known as the *Bay Area Real Estate Report*, now provides a quarterly summary of real estate market statistics for the San Francisco, San Jose, and Sacramento metropolitan areas. Published data include loan and deed recordings, building-permit summaries, building costs, vacancies and unsold inventories, and estimated market-sales prices for a sample of over one hundred typical single-family residences and multifamily structures in the San Francisco Bay area. Similar data are available for the Los Angeles and San Diego areas through the Residential Research Committee of Los Angeles, which issues the quarterly *Residential Research Report*. Similar organizations have been established in Seattle, Miami, and Denver. Table 5–6, based on data from some of these reports, summarizes the market trend indexes for single-family homes in the San Francisco Bay area and in Los Angeles County.

In addition to these organizations, several of the major banking institutions have expanded their internal analysis of national and regional real estate markets in recent years. The recent reviews of the outlook for construction in the state of California by the Security First National Bank, the Bank of America, and the Wells Fargo Bank are typical of the improved data available for specific regions and states. The Chase National Bank has recently initiated annual reviews of real estate markets in collaboration with the American Institute of Real Estate Appraisers. Many individual Federal Reserve banks have recently expanded their collections and analyses of real estate market data.

The American Institute of Real Estate Appraisers and the Society of Real Estate Appraisers have recently inaugurated expanded cooperative market data programs which hold considerable promise for future availability of

Table 5-6. Market Trend Index for Single-Family Houses, San Francisco Bay Area[a] and Los Angeles County,[b] 1960-1971 1960 = 100

		San Francisco	Los Angeles
1960	April	100.0	100.0
	October	100.3	101.7
1961	April	102.0	103.5
	October	103.2	107.0
1962	April	104.7	110.1
	October	106.4	113.3
1963	April	109.7	117.1
	October	112.0	120.9
1964	April	115.6	121.0[c]
	October	118.5	124.0
1965	April	121.6	126.0
	October	124.0	128.0
1966	April	125.1	126.0
	October	125.1	126.0
1967	April	126.7	127.0
	October	128.0	128.0
1968	April	130.8	129.0
	October	134.6	131.0
1969	April	138.2	130.0
	October	141.6	135.6
1970	April	145.0	137.4
	October	148.6	139.4
1971	April	152.6	141.8
	October	156.0	144.3

[a] Includes the following counties: Alameda, Contra Costa, Marin, Napa, San Francisco, San Mateo, Santa Clara, Solano and Sonoma.

[b] Years 1957 through 1963 include Orange County in addition to Los Angeles.

[c] The Los Angeles sample includes Los Angeles, Orange, Riverside, San Bernardino, Ventura and Santa Barbara.

Source: *Northern California Real Estate Report,* 4th quarter 1970, p. 10. Residential Research Committee of Southern California, *Residential Research Report,* 3rd quarter 1963, p. 25; 3rd quarter 1964, p. 24; 3rd quarter 1966, p. 24; 3rd quarter 1967, p. 20; 3rd quarter 1969, p. 20; 3rd quarter 1971, p. 20.

continuing market sales data for single- and multi-family residences. The Society of Real Estate Appraisers inaugurated SREA Market Data centers in Los Angeles in 1968 and plans branch centers in seven metropolitan areas. These centers will provide monthly or quarterly computer summaries including sales price, room description, condition and location of single-family, commercial, and industrial properties.[20]

Market Data Improvements in England The British system of valuation has traditionally favored the concept of years purchase, which is a variation of the concept of payout period, or what is often referred to as the net-income-multiplier technique in the United States. In recent years the Co-operative Permanent Building Society in London has published semiannual indexes of house prices and house building costs for new houses, modern houses, and older houses by regions and for the United Kingdom as a whole.[21] It is of some interest to observe in figure 5–2 that prices of old-er houses have risen more rapidly in the past four years than the so-called modern or new houses. This probably reflects market preference for more traditional design, as well as quality adjustments in the market. The average compound annual rate of increase in house prices from 1965 to 1971 was approximately 8.25 percent per annum, almost twice the observed rate of increase for single-family houses sold in Oakland, California, during the same period.[22]

Multiple Listing The resurgence of market prices as the primary evidence of real estate value can be attributed in important degree to the expansion of multiple-listing activity in the 1950s and 1960s. Although the importance of multiple listing as a percentage of total transactions varies widely among different sections of the country, it has provided a central source of compara-ble sales data for residential properties in many cities. Case, in a study of multiple-listing data in Los Angeles County, found that multiple-listing sales recorded in seven multiple-listing systems rose from a total of 13,652 sales in 1953 (representing 6.1 percent of total deeds recorded) to 17,557 sales in 1960 (representing 8 percent of the total number of deeds recorded).[23] Single-family home sales accounted for 70 to 80 percent of all sales in the seven multiple-listing systems studied. The average single-family residential property sales price for the combined multiple-listing systems rose from $12,572 in 1953 to $18,237 in 1960 – a 45.1 percent increase. Case reported that market condi-tions in each of the individual multiple-listing systems at various times "showed distinctly individual patterns."[24] He concluded that the multiple-listing average sales price index would probably be a much more sensitive measure of changes in average sales prices than some of the indexes currently in use, although the level of the multiple-listing prices tended to be somewhat below that reported by other indexes.

Using a somewhat different methodology, Schaaf employed multiple-listing data from Oakland, California, to measure the mean percentage price increase from 1961 to 1963 and from 1964 to 1966. He identified 147 identical houses which had sold in 1961 and again in 1963 and 64 houses which had sold in 1964 and 1966 as a basis for concluding that average house prices had risen by 8.58 percent from 1961 to 1963 and by 9.29 percent from 1964 to 1966.[25] Using tests of statistical significance, he concluded that the difference in price performance for all houses and for houses with resale price over twenty thousand dollars and under twenty thousand dollars were not statisti-

Figure 5-2. Indexes of House Prices and House Building Costs—Great Britain (quarter ended 12/31/65 = 100)

New houses _____ / Modern houses oooooo / Older houses ■■■■■■ / House building costs ••••••

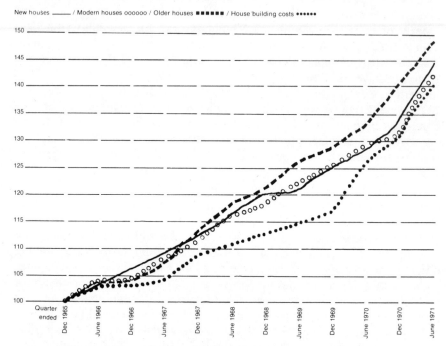

Indexes of House Prices and House Building Costs—Great Britain
(quarter ended 12/31/65 = 100)

Quarter ended	New houses	Modern existing houses	Older existing houses	House building (wages and materials) costs
12/31/65	100	100	100	100
6/30/66	103	104	104	103
12/31/66	106	104	104	103
6/30/67	109	108	107	104
12/31/67	112	111	113	109
6/30/68	116	116	118	111
12/31/68	120	118	121	113
6/30/69	121	122	126	115
12/31/69	125	125	129	117
6/30/70	128	129	133	126
12/31/70	133	131	140	131
6/30/71	144	142	148	140
12/31/71	161	160	166	142 a

[a] Provisional

Source: Nationwide Building Society, *Occasional Bulletin,* no. 105, August 1971 and no. 107, February 1972.

cally significant. He concluded, therefore, that used house prices in Oakland rose on the average 4.5 percent per year between 1961 and 1966.

Becker has found that multiple-listing data for Oakland can be used to represent house price trends with a high degree of statistical reliability.[26] Using average sales prices in multiple listings, Vidger reported that San Francisco's single-family house prices rose at an annual rate of 6.75 percent from 1958 to 1967.[27] More extensive use of multiple-listing sales data has been made by public agencies such as the Alameda County tax assessor. A sample of confirmed sales of residential property in Alameda County has been coded and analyzed by assessment map book areas and provides price trend data by districts surpassing any other previously available market data. These data, in the form of individual sales, are available in the public records of hearings before the Assessment Appeals Board of the county.

The adoption of the computer by many local tax assessors and the increasing attention in assessment practices to the analysis of actual sales data have opened up one of the most potentially valuable sources of market data for use in real estate appraisal. Local tax assessors have access to the public records of property sales, multiple-listing records, and direct questionnaire data received from individual property owners. Legislative and judicial pressure to improve assessment practices has provided a strong incentive to local assessment officials in many states to bring assessed values of real property more closely in line with market prices.

Multiple-Regression Analysis

The U.S. Department of Agriculture and the Bureau of the Census had used advanced statistical techniques for estimating farm real estate values as early as 1926.[28] More recently, William C. Pendleton described the potentials for the use of the computer in property assessment and valuation.[29] Multiple-regression analysis holds great promise for improving techniques in the market-data approach. The confluence of the greatly magnified flow of market data and improved computer hardware and software with a virtual revolution in the facilities within the real estate industry for storage and retrieval of listing information promises to make existing methods of analyzing comparable sales completely obsolete.[30]

Real estate appraisal can be viewed as an attempt, using some value concept, usually the most probable selling price or assessed value, to establish relationships between certain observed data, such as the area of the lot, costs, location, income, age, type of construction and size of house. For many years it has been possible to estimate the assessed value of property in certain jurisdictions by the use of the assessor's formula, which related the dependent variable, assessed value, to the age, original cost, location, and type of structure. More recently, the technique has been extended to the estimation of market sales prices.

109

Regression refers to the measurement of relationships among variables. If the selling prices of real estate depended on a single variable alone, let us say replacement costs, it would be possible to use simple regression showing the relationship between selling prices and replacement costs new to arrive at an estimate of value. However, it is known that many other factors influence market prices, such as age, condition, character of the neighborhood, financing, number of rooms, and lot size. This constitutes the argument in support of the use of multiple-regression analysis, which measures the simultaneous influence of a set of independent variables upon the dependent variable.[31]

To estimate the relationship between two variables of the population — say, selling price and size of house — statisticians use the method of least squares, a technique which assumes that deviations from the line of relationship follow the normal or Gaussian distribution.[32] The arithmetic mean of a series of observations is often referred to as a least-squares estimator since the positive and negative deviations of individual observations about the mean exactly offset one another, and their algebraic sum is zero. The sum of the squared deviations of individual observations about the mean is smaller than the sum of their squared deviations about any other point. The significance of the use of squared deviations is the elimination of the negative sign of deviations below the mean.

Under conditions of random sampling from a normal population, the arithmetic means of ninety-five samples out of one hundred (on the average) will lie within plus or minus two times the standard deviation (sometimes referred to as S_x), which is the square root of the sum of the squared deviations about the arithmetic mean divided by $(n - 1)$. For large samples drawn from the same population, 99 percent of the observations will normally fall within plus or minus 2.58 times the standard deviation. For samples of thirty observations or less, the ratio of a sample observation to its standard deviation does not follow the normal distribution. Special tables have been compiled based upon "Students distribution" or the *T-distribution*, as it is called, which show the expected variation in small sample observations.[33] Another measure, known as the *F-distribution*, is used in the analysis of variance to determine whether two samples are drawn from the same population. This ratio is calculated by the formula $F = S_1^2/S_2^2$, where S_1 and S_2, the standard errors of the samples, are adjusted for the size of the sample and for what is referred to as the *degrees of freedom*.[34]

Statisticians distinguish between simple regression, which describes the relationship between two variables, and multiple regression, which considers the relationship among several independent variables and a dependent variable (for example, the relationship between size of house, age, type of construction, property tax, and occupancy as independent variables, and selling price as the dependent variable). Multiple-regression analysis has increasing significance for the appraiser as the availability of market data with reference to real estate improves. Multiple-regression studies of house prices have shown that the selling prices of houses can be predicted within relatively close ranges of accuracy if the characteristics of the homes can be described in some detail.

Fortunately for the appraiser, so-called canned computer programs are readily available which produce as output the following information: the multiple-regression equation for any selected group of variables, the coefficients associated with each variable, the individual correlation coefficients for each of the independent variables with the dependent variable, and the percentage of variation in the dependent variable explained by the independent variables. Armed with this type of information, the appraiser is able to judge the influence of each characteristic included in the regression equation upon selling price and also the degree of variance in that relationship. If the sample he is using is small, he can refer to the T-distribution tables and F-distribution tables and ascertain whether the ratio of the sample observation to its standard error follows the normal distribution and whether the various samples appear to be drawn from the same population. In other words, statistical techniques make it possible for the appraiser to test his comparables scientifically.

These statistical techniques should be viewed as an aid to, rather than as a substitute for, the appraiser's judgment, but they represent a powerful and necessary assist when the volume of data requiring analysis becomes very large. Will these techniques produce appraisal estimates? Most certainly they will, and these estimates will have wide utility in many areas requiring analysis of large numbers of properties. These statistical techniques will also produce estimates of the range within which additional sample observations are likely to produce results which differ from those produced by one or more sets of observations. This represents an important aid to the appraiser because it makes possible his estimation of the probable range within which estimates of the most probable selling price will fall. The potential of a market-comparison technique which not only produces a mean estimate of value but also a measure of the probability that this estimate will differ by a given amount above or below that value should be of immeasurable value to mortgage lenders and investors. The use of multiple-regression techniques in the valuation of real estate is expanding rapidly under the impetus of changes in assessment practices and the increasing availability of high-speed computers to local tax assessors, mortgage lenders, and others. In many ways it can be said that the market-comparison method is on the threshhold of its greatest improvement in technique of application and broadened use.

Robert H. Gustafson described a multiple linear least-squares regression model used in Orange County, California, to estimate the selling prices for single-family properties.[35] Some 166 characteristics of 1,000 properties sold in five geographic areas of Orange County were tested and an equation was machine produced showing the contribution which each of 24 variables made, on the average, to the total selling price. Area 1 typically had relatively new homes selling for between $15,000 and $32,000 from 1,000 to 2,100 square feet on regular, flat lots. The estimated selling price for such a house and lot was $14,500 plus $14.32 per foot of lot width minus $637 if lot is irregular, minus $479 if lot is on a cul-de-sac, minus $412 if view is below standard, plus $876 if neighborhood value trend is above standard, plus $343 if available financing is above standard, minus $918 if condition is below standard, plus $193 if condition is above standard, minus $1,160 per bathroom, minus $809 if no central heating, minus $1,318 if no central cooling, minus $391 per quality class, plus $0.77 per square foot of living area, minus $1.46 per dollar of cost of uncovered patio, minus $3.29 per dollar of air conditioning cost, minus $0.48 per dollar of extra kitchen cost, plus $2.42 per dollar of extra plumbing cost, plus $222 if detached garage, plus $440 if attached garage, minus $0.93 per dollar of flat work cost, minus $1.18 per dollar of fence cost, minus $0.52 per dollar of miscellaneous cost, plus $1.082 per dollar of replacement cost new, and minus $50.57 per month for age of sale. The estimated replacement cost new for the property alone explained about 80 percent of the variation in selling prices among the 1,000 houses studied. Gustafson observed that "it is futile, and not always rewarding, to attempt to explain why certain variables were given certain weights. The machine has attempted to explain, with a series of additions and subtractions, the rationality of the market place in purchasing these properties."[36] The important observation for appraisers to note is that in 715 out of 993 cases, or in 72 percent of the cases, the estimated selling price differed from the actual selling price by less than 5 percent. In 932 cases, or 94 percent, the difference was less than 10 percent. It need not be emphasized that this range of accuracy would more than meet the criteria of most professional appraisal reports.

Although the reliability of the individual coefficients may be questioned and a high degree of multicollinearity among the variables must be assumed, these and other similar equations have demonstrated a high degree of reliability in predicting sales prices of single-family houses where they have been employed for some time. Lessinger has recently called attention to the problems of collinearity and interaction among the independent variables used in multiple-regression analysis.[37] He argued, "The price-per-unit of each component of real estate property is not fixed but depends on the other components which are present. For example: The price of an extra bedroom depends on the number of bathrooms—in other words, the components are interactive. The greater the degree of interaction among the components, the greater the degree of variation of price-per-unit of a component. This has an adverse effect on the assumption that the price determined by multiple regression has any meaning."[38] Lessinger argues well that the individual regression coefficients for the independent variables may be meaningless, and he rightly cautions the uninitiated appraiser not to make adjustments to the values of houses or other real estate based upon these coefficients. However, collinearity and interaction notwithstanding, high values for the square of the correlation coefficient – sometimes called the coefficient of determination – do measure the proportion of the dependent of Y variable explained by the supposed linear influence of the independent or X variables. The rationale for extending the use of multiple-regression techniques in appraisal work lies in the potential for testing the method employing varying dependent variables and monitoring the reliability of the correlation coefficients over time and under varying market circumstances.[39] The positive results of multiple-regression analysis in property assessment and valuation work are multiplying rapidly.

The application of multiple-regression analysis is not limited to the comparable sales approach since the technique permits the appraiser to measure the association between any characteristics of real estate and its selling price. As an illustration, it can be noted in the regression model for Orange County, California, illustrated above that the contribution of replacement costs new, age of the property, as well as financing terms available, are included as separate independent variables. In multiple-regression equations for use in valuation of income-producing properties, gross income would undoubtedly be used as one of the independent variables in the regression equation. Therefore, multiple regression represents a technique which can bring together the combined influence of any and, theoretically at least, all value determinants in a single approach to valuation. In this sense, it can be viewed as a composite substitute for the market comparison, cost and income approaches to value used separately. Needless to say, the technique can also be adapted to the estimation of loan value, condemnation value, investment value, or any other specialized concept. In each case the so-called independent variables might differ in their relative influence.

Illustration A single family home located in northern Atlanta, was appraised by means of a multiple-regression analysis in January 1971. The property is a five-year-old, single-family, owner-occupied residence, located in a well-planned subdivision of custom-built homes which feature a wide range of floor plans and elevations. It is a one-story brick veneer, colonial-style home containing nine rooms, including three bedrooms and three full baths, with a full, unfinished daylight basement containing the servants' facilities (full bath), laundry connections, and a fireplace. There is an attached, oversize double garage with an electric eye overhead door. The building is of high quality construction and is in excellent condition throughout.

Sales information was available for twenty-nine comparable properties in the same general neighborhood area of Atlanta, which is characterized by homes in the price range of fifty to ninety thousand dollars. The sales data are summarized in table 5–7.[40] A multiple-regression model for these twenty-nine sales was constructed using fifteen variables, seven of which were deleted from the computation as insignificant in establishing price. The partial correlation coefficients for these seven variables were low and the F values were extremely small. The multiple-regression equation shown below indi-

Table 5-7. Comparable Data for Twenty-nine Homes in Northern Atlanta Sold in Period 1966–1970

Number	Price	Age	Style	Const.	Carpets	Drapes	Stories	Sewer	Roof	Entry	LR	DR	Den	Fpl	Brk. Room	Porch	Pow. Room	Brs.	Baths	Bsmt.	Air Cond.	Serv. Facs.	Date	Finished Living Area
6005	51,500	0	Col.	Brick	No	No	1	X	cedar/shake	X	X	X	X	X	X	X	No	3	4	X	X	X	1966	2,600#
6005	57,500	1			Yes	Yes																	1967	
6005	58,500	2			Yes	Yes																	1967	
5975	52,500	0	Col.	Brick	No	No	2	X	c/s	X	X	X	X	X	X	No	X	4	3.5	X	No	X	1967	3,300#
5975	66,900	3																			X		1970	
6105	89,500	0	Col.	Brick	No	No	2	X	c/s	X	X	X	X	X	X	No	X	5	3.5	X	X	No	1970	3,600#
6260	86,500	0	French	Brk/Shingle	No	No	2	X	shake	X	X	X	X	X	X	X	X	4	3.5	No	X	No	1970	3,400#
6270	84,500	0	Spanish	Brick	No	No	2	X	c/s	X	X	X	X	X	X	X	X	4	3.5	No	X	No	1970	3,300#
6280	74,900	0	French	Brick	No	No	1	X	c/s	X	X	X	X	X	X	X	No	3	3	No	X	No	1970	2,400#
5945	65,000	0	Dutch	Brick	No	No	2	X	c/s	X	X	X	X	X	X	X		4	3	X	X	No	1968	
5945	76,500	2			Yes	Yes	1											3		No			1970	3,800#
5995	54,000	0	French	Brick	No	No	1	X	c/s	X	X	X	X	X	X	X	X	3	3	No	X	No	1966	2,400#
5995	58,000	3			Yes	Yes																	1969	
6020	60,500	0	French	Brick	No	No	1	X	c/s	X	X	X	X	X	X	X	X	4	4	X	X	X	1967	2,800#
6020	69,500	2			Yes	Yes																	1968	
6175	86,000	0	Col.	Brick	No	No	2	X	c/s	X	X	X	X	X	X	X	X	5	3.5	No	X	No	1969	3,600#
6175	87,250	1			Yes	Yes																	1970	
6145	72,000	0	Trad.	Brick	No	No	1	X	c/s	X	X	X	X	X	No	X	X	5	3	X	X	X	1969	2,800#
6145	82,500	1			Yes	Yes																	1970	
5720	58,000	0	Col.	Brick	No	No	1	X	c/s	X	X	X	X	X	X	X.	X	4	3	X	X	X	1968	3,400#
5925	64,500	0	French	Brick	No	No	1	X	c/s	X	X	X	X	X	X	X	X	4	3	X	X	No	1968	3,800#
5960	52,500	0	French	Brick	No	No	1	X	c/s	X	X	X	X	X	X	X	No	3	3	X	No	No	1967	2,900#
6000	56,000	0	Col.	Brick	No	No	1	X	c/s	X	X	X	X	X	X	No	No	4	3	X	X	No	1967	3,000#
5980	56,000	0	French	Brick	No	No	1	X	c/s	X	X	X	X	X	X	X	X	4	3	X	No	No	1966	3,100#
5980	70,000	3			Yes	Yes															X		1969	
6035	52,500	0	Col.	Brick	No	No	1	X	c/s	X	X	X	X	X	X	X	No	3	3	X	X	No	1966	2,600#
6055	52,500	0	Ranch	Brick	No	No	1	X	c/s	X	X	X	X	X	X	X	No	4	3	X	X	No	1966	2,300#
6115	95,350	0	French	Brick	No	No	2	X	c/s	X	X	X	X	X	X	X	X	4	3.5	X	X	No	1970	3,600#
5970	62,250	0	Col.	Brick	No	No	2	X	c/s	X	X	X	X	X	X	X	No	5	3	X	X	No	1967	3,100#

cates that the date of sale appeared to be of primary significance in estimating values based upon the sample selected, since it accounts for 86.85 percent of the variance accounted for. Following this variable in order of importance were age, number of baths, number of bedrooms, lot size, and servants' facilities.

Price (thousands of dollars) = − 489.22876 + 7.61837(date of sale) − 2.64424(age) − 0.00065(lot size) + 0.00684(square footage) + 3.31680 (number of bedrooms) + 9.31861(number of baths) − 4.58784(number of stories) − 4.27378(servants' facilities, yes or no).

Solving the multiple regression equation using data on the subject property resulted in an estimated price of $69,811.46 with a standard error of plus or minus $4,496.20. This would indicate that in approximately 68 percent of the cases drawn from the same sample group the price would fall within the range of $65,315.26 to $74,307.66. These variables accounted for 96 percent of the variation in observed selling prices. The F ratios, calculated from the coefficients of the independent variables and their standard errors, adjusted for the size of the sample, indicated that the regression coefficients met the tests of statistical significance at the 95 percent level. A review of the results suggested that the addition of a variable reflecting the financing terms would have added to the explanatory power of the regression equation. When the variable interest rate was added, it displaced the date of sale as the variable with the highest single multiple-regression coefficient, with a coefficient of 0.875 and a standard error of $6,754. The expected high degree of collinearity between date of sale and interest rate was confirmed.

It can be recognized that multiple regression provides a valuable assist to the appraiser in eliminating the need to adjust comparable sales for large numbers of variables. It aids first in identifying the variables which are statistically significant and ranks them in order of importance. In addition to providing an estimating equation, the technique identifies an estimated price, a range, and an estimate of the probabilities of variation in sale prices about that range.

Multiple-regression analysis is an aid to, rather than a substitute for, judgment in the appraisal process. If accurate square-foot costs for each of the twenty-nine sample properties had been available, it would seem highly probable that the addition of this variable in the regression analysis would have improved the estimating value of the resulting equation. It goes without saying that the quality of the data inputs is of even greater importance than is the number of variables employed. If the data for date of sale is inaccurate, any conclusions from this multiple-regression analysis about the relationship between date of sale and value are in error. The importance of comparability is not minimized by multiple-regression analysis. If, for example, one-half of the houses included were located in a neighborhood which differed substantially from the rest of the sample, the dispersion of sale prices around the average would be greater and the estimated range of probable price estimation would be wider. A shortcoming of the multiple-regression technique is that the appraiser is often caught in the dilemma of including incomparable properties in order to achieve a sample size which will permit estimation within acceptable ranges. For this reason, the technique is most adaptable where centralized market data systems are available.

The appraiser must use the results of multiple-regression analysis with a realization of their limitations. For many valuation estimates, the appraiser will use multiple-regression analysis to determine the approximate range of values applicable to a subject property. He will then pursue the appraisal through the more conventional market-comparison approach, where adjustments to value will reflect careful assessment of the influence of the individually important variables upon the subject property.

Vacant Residential Land　The high levels of subdivision activity in the post–World War II period and the consequent rise in subdivision land prices have brought about considerable interest in the appraisal of vacant land for subdivision purposes. Since most land with potential subdivision value is in agricultural use, appraisal techniques often require separate calculation of the value of the property for agricultural use during the transitional or ripening period and its appraisal as urban land when the land use is projected to change.

In a recent article, Weston and Ricks presented a theoretical curve portraying the gradual rise in prices of land as it reached the development stage.[41] The increases in value which they hypothesized appear adaptable to a growing area under conditions of gradual inflation such as have been experienced in California in the post–World War II years. It is axiomatic, however, that trends in the selling prices of land will vary in different regions and that local land taxation and zoning and land-use controls will have an important influence upon land-price trends. Some land ripe for residential development in Westchester County, New York (less than forty miles from New York City), has changed little in price over the past twenty years due to increasingly high tax rates and the very restrictive zoning, which has been in effect for the purpose of restricting residential development. However, Maisel, Mittelbach, and others have reported that the selling prices of residential lots in California have risen consistently and rapidly over the past two decades.[42]

Speculation and investment in unimproved land has become a major challenge for many appraisers in recent years when suburban land and farmland prices have risen rapidly. Opelka has developed a tabular technique for estimating the present value of sales income from lot development, which applies present value theory to the prospective flow of income from lot sales in the future after allowing for development and carrying costs.[43] Although he presents his chart technique as a method of developing "guesstimates," it has the realistic potential of providing more accurate present values for future subdivision land than many techniques based upon comparable sales approaches without reflecting the all-important rates of absorption. This technique, illustrated in table 5–8, represents the product of the sum of the "present value of a reversion" factors, taken from compound interest tables for varying years, multiplied by the estimated number of lots or "homesites" to be sold in each year of the prediction period. The present worth discount factor used (in this case 12 percent) represents the discount rate used by the appraiser in discounting the future income from lot sales. Thus, if an appraiser estimates that a purchaser would be able to sell five lots in the first year and five in the second, his profit in the sale of lots would have a present value of 8.45 times the average dollar profit per lot.[44]

Spurr and Bonini illustrate the estimation of lot values by use of multiple regression, based upon reported sales of twenty lots varying in price from twenty-nine hundred to seven thousand dollars. Using a stepwise regression program, they found that the following equation explained 92 percent of the observed variation in lot prices.[45]

Price (thousands of dollars) = 0.24021 + 0.09873 × area (in 000's of square feet) + 0.01068 × elevation (feet above sea level) + 0.02950 × slope (degrees) + 0.20487 × view (scale poor, − 1, to excellent, − 9).

The variable view alone explained 88 percent of the total variation in selling prices with a standard error of $588. The addition of the variable area increased the multiple-correlation coefficient to 91.35 percent with a small decline in the standard error. The addition of the variables elevation and slope had little effect on the multiple-correlation coefficients or the standard error. In discussing the tests of significance, the authors conclude that area and slope might just as well have been discarded and selling price expressed as a function of area and view alone. The equation for that relationship is shown as

Price (thousands of dollars) = 1.77976 + 0.10333 × area + 0.29475 × view.

Prof. William M. Shenkel identifies five general principles in using multiple-regression analysis in real estate valuation: (1) multiple-regression appraisal techniques are generally applicable to property commonly sold; (2) accurate valuation under multiple-regression analysis depends heavily on a refined sales sample; (3) multiple-regression procedures lend themselves to new techniques for refining sales samples; (4) descriptive statistics are required for each variable entered in the multiple-regression formula; (5) a field review of selected cases showing unusual variation between the computed

Table 5-8. Present Worth of Net Lot Development–Sales Income

Years	Present Worth $1 at 12%	Homesites Sold per Year									
		5	10	20	30	40	50	60	70	80	90
1	0.8929	4.465	8.929	17.86	26.79	35.72	44.65	53.57	62.50	71.43	80.36
2	0.7972	8.450	16.90	33.80	50.70	67.60	84.50	101.40	118.30	135.20	152.10
3	0.7118	12.01	24.02	48.04	72.06	96.08	120.10	144.12	168.14	192.16	216.18
4	0.6355	15.19	30.37	60.74	91.11	121.48	151.85	182.22	212.59	242.96	273.33
5	0.5674	18.03	36.05	72.10	108.15	144.20	180.25	216.30	252.35	288.40	324.45
6	0.5066	20.56	41.11	82.22	123.33	164.44	205.55	246.66	287.77	328.88	369.99
7	0.4532	22.82	45.64	91.28	136.92	182.56	228.20	273.84	319.48	365.12	410.76
8	0.4039	24.84	49.68	99.36	149.04	198.72	248.40	298.08	347.76	397.44	447.12
9	0.3606	26.64	53.28	106.56	159.84	213.12	266.40	319.68	372.96	426.24	479.52
10	0.3220	28.25	56.50	113.00	169.50	226.00	282.50	339.00	395.50	452.00	508.50

Source: F. Gregory Opelka, "Appraisal Report," *Savings and Loan News* (March 1969), p. 76.

value and sales price leads to final refinement of the valuation model.[46] Although the author cannot agree with those who predict that multiple-regression analysis will supplant more conventional valuation techniques in the near future, it would appear that the technique will most certainly gain greater acceptance as data retrieval systems improve and as appraisers gain greater sophistication in statistical analysis and interpretation.

Industrial Real Estate

The factors that must be taken into account in judging the comparability of industrial sites are probably more numerous than for any other class of property. According to Armstrong, they include the following: location of production material, labor, sites, industrial fuel, transportation facilities, market distribution facilities, power, water, living conditions, laws and regulations, tax structure, and climate.[47] This observation suggests that multiple-regression techniques may serve as valuable aids in industrial land-value analysis.[48] To make the matter of comparison more difficult, these factors are not of equal importance in every industry. Consequently, the appraiser cannot construct a table of weighted adjustment factors such as were illustrated for valuing downtown business sites and apply such factors indiscriminately to all industrial property. He must instead rely upon his general knowledge of industry requirements and upon his judgment to apply overall adjustment factors to comparable sales.

The difficulties of comparing industrial land sites can be observed from the estimates of the value of industrial land in twenty-two communities bordering on the San Francisco Bay as of 1955 and 1969. The prices shown in table 5–9 were quoted by members of the Society of Industrial Realtors as average prices per acre, quoted for parcels with spur, utilities, drainage, and sewage disposal facilities available. The lower range of values listed for 1969 is for larger, unimproved sites requiring some preparation for construction. Streets, water, sewer, and other services are adjacent but not within the property area. The higher range is for fully improved property, generally of smaller size – one-half acre to five acres. The tremendous rise in industrial land values in outlying areas reflects the substantial decentralization in employment growth in the San Francisco Bay area.

More recent studies of current sales prices of land in twenty-one industrial parks in the San Francisco Bay area indicate a range of prices between two and three dollars per square foot for selected industrial parks in San Mateo County, with a lower range of values in Santa Clara and Alameda counties.[49] The significant observation of this study, however, is that industrial land in well-planned industrial parks commands substantially higher prices than typical industrially zoned acreage. One explanation of this is found in the fact that a substantial percentage of the land in some of the larger industrial parks is used as office space or for combinations of engineering and

Table 5-9. Industrial Land Values

City	Price per Acre 1955		Price per Acre 1969	
	Low	High	Low	High
South San Francisco	$23,300	$45,850	$65,000	$110,000
San Bruno	25,000	45,000	40,000	80,000
Burlingame	22,500	35,000	65,000	130,000
San Mateo	15,000	27,500	40,000	100,000
San Carlos	15,000	23,250	35,000	80,000
Redwood City	14,000	35,000	35,000	80,000
Menlo Park	12,500	35,000	35,000	90,000
Mountain View	4,000	7,000	25,000	75,000
Sunnyvale	4,100	6,900	22,000	75,000
Santa Clara	5,300	8,300	15,000	75,000
San Jose	4,300	10,300	20,000	100,000
Milpitas	2,900	4,600	12,000	22,000
Hayward	6,000	11,200	25,000	45,000
San Leandro	8,100	20,200	45,000	75,000
Oakland (East)	17,300	38,100	50,000	110,000
Alameda	20,000	35,000	. . .	. . .
Livermore	800	2,500	6,000	15,000
Pleasanton	1,250	2,900	15,000	35,000
Richmond	4,500	8,800	15,000	60,000
Martinez	1,000	3,000	9,000	20,000
Pittsburg	3,600	6,500	8,000	17,000
Antioch	2,600	5,600	. 8,000	25,000

Source: *Bay Area Real Estate Report,* 1st quarter 1955; *Northern California Real Estate Report,* 3rd quarter 1969, p. 45.

research and development uses. In addition, many of the industrial parks have convenience commercial uses such as service stations, restaurants, banks, motels, and office buildings, which command high site values.

In the light of these studies, it is evident that substantial variation can be expected in land sales prices among different industrial land sold as acreage and similar land developed with the amenities of industrial parks. This emphasizes once again the key importance of comparability in the use of the market-comparison method and the potentials for use of multiple regression.

Evaluation of the Market-Comparison Method   The market-comparison method recommends itself in theory as the ideal method for establishing values of real estate and other goods in a competitive economy. The basic nonhomogeneity of real estate and the imperfections in its market structure are the principal factors which have thus far limited the application of the market-comparison method to problems of valuation. These difficulties have been somewhat compounded by the multiplication of fictional concepts such as "fair" market value, "justified" selling price, and "normal" value. The development of such concepts has opened the door to wholesale juggling of market price data.

Critics of the use of the market-comparison method hold that market prices are unstable and reflect too greatly the psychology of buyers and sellers. Upon examination, this criticism appears to be a weak rationalization for adopting other standards of value. Although this may be justified for certain purposes, such as for mortgage loan value, it does not alter the conclusion that market values should be sought in the marketplace.

Various mathematical techniques have been developed for adjusting comparable market sales prices. Examination of certain of these techniques revealed that many are based upon questionable hypotheses and assumptions. Although adjustments for differences in the timing of sales and for incomparability are certainly necessary, it might be contended that the overrefinement of mathematical adjustment techniques has frequently encouraged appraisers to lose sight of the basic principles of fixing values by reference to comparable sales. Some of the simpler and more straightforward techniques for adjusting comparable sales recommend themselves in terms of their logic and simplicity of application.

Organized price data are becoming increasingly available for various sectors of the real estate market. This improvement in the quantity and quality of market data should enhance the reliability of the market-comparison approach and encourage its more general application. As the knowledge of buyers and sellers increases and as the market structure becomes more efficient, less attention need be devoted to the adjustment of market-sales data. Viewing these developments as worthy objectives, the efforts of appraisal groups can be better given to the improvement of basic market data than to the continued refinement of mathematical procedures based, in the last analysis, upon judgment and opinion.

The use of gross-income multipliers, described in chapter 8, is a variation of the market-comparison as well as of the capitalization approach. This valuation technique, although highly useful for valuing income properties of similar type and age, is subject to the basic difficulty evident in the foregoing analysis of the market-comparison method, namely the determination of comparability. The solution of this problem, although troublesome, does not involve the many assumptions necessary in the replacement-cost and capitalization-of-income methods. The adaptability of the market-comparison method would appear to rest upon the frequency and character of the market transactions in properties of the subject type.

The combination of greatly improved market data through multiple listing and other sources and the adaptation of the high-speed computer to market-data analysis has accelerated the application of multiple-regression techniques to real estate valuation. In the author's view, this technique — used with a knowledge of its limitations — holds great promise for improvements in appraisal practice. Proponents of the use of multiple-regression techniques in real estate valuation have emphasized that the method is a logical extension of the comparable-sales approach. Properly used, it permits scientific measurement of the relationship between market sales prices and selected attributes of properties, referred to as the independent variables.

THE CAPITALIZATION-OF-INCOME METHOD

Real estate appraisal, by virtually unanimous agreement, is the process by which a present value is placed upon the future benefits from real property. The apparent logic of such an approach to real estate valuation has established the capitalization-of-income method in the eyes of many authors as central among the three approaches to valuation. The large segment of appraisal theory built around this method has already been noted in chapter 2. It is the purpose of this chapter to review briefly the origins of the capitalization-of-income method and to examine the assumptions underlying its use and the exposition of the method by its leading proponents. Attention will be given to the controversy over the selection of specific techniques. The position of the capitalization-of-income method in appraisal theory will be described, and its adaptability to practical problems of appraisal will be critically evaluated.

Origins

The origins of the capitalization-of-income method of valuation are found in writings on the theory of interest. As pointed out in chapter 1, economists of the nineteenth century laid the foundations for the income-capitalization method in developing the principle of "time preference." Böhm-Bawerk held that the explanation of interest lies in the valuation process — in the fact that men tend to value the same good more highly in the present than in the future. "Present goods invariably possess a greater value than future goods."[1]

The relationship between interest rates and capital value was also clearly recognized by John Stuart Mill, writing in the middle of the nineteenth century: "The rate of interest determines the value and price of all those saleable articles which are desired and bought, not for themselves, but for the income which they are capable of yielding. . . . The price of land, mines, and all other fixed sources of income, depends in like manner on the rate of interest."[2]

Alfred Marshall and Irving Fisher both considered interest the bridge between income and value. Marshall, writing at the turn of the century, said: "For the value of the capital already invested in improving land or erecting a building . . . is the aggregate discounted value of its estimated future net incomes (or quasi-rents); and if its prospective income-yielding power should diminish, its value would fall accordingly and would be the capitalized value of that smaller income after allowing for depreciation."[3] Irving Fisher pointed out that the interest rate could be used to calculate future from present values or present from future values. He emphasized that "the value of capital must be computed from the value of its estimated future net income, not vice-versa."[4] According to Fisher, the discount principle applied to the valuation of all property. Market values, in his words, would be "dependent solely on the same two factors, the benefits, or returns, expected by the investor and the market rate of interest by which those benefits are discounted."[5]

Fisher explored in some detail the various meanings attached to the terms *interest rate, discount rate*, and *capitalization rate*. He explained that in the valuation of capital goods the rate of interest refers to the ratio between the current annual income and the present capital value.[6] This ratio has been described by Babcock and others as the *overall* rate. Fisher held that the rate of capitalization was the reciprocal of the rate of interest and should be expressed as the number of years during which the amount of income flow would equal the present capital value. "Thus if $25,000 will buy a perpetual annuity of $1,000 a year, the rate of capitalization is 'twenty-five years' purchase.' "[7] Fisher also distinguished the rate of discount and demonstrated that it equals the equivalent rate of interest less a small correction.[8]

Although the concept of years' purchase is still widely employed in British writings on valuation, the term *capitalization rate* has gradually supplanted it in appraisal literature in the United States, where it refers to a theoretical risk rate of interest applied by valuators in calculating the present value of future returns. It is used synonymously with the term *discount rate* in the valuation field. The latter, however, continues to have the more specialized meaning employed by Fisher in the commercial banking field.

Leon Walras, a French economist writing in the latter part of the nineteenth century, emphasized the unity of capitalized values and market prices under conditions of equilibrium:

> From our point of view there can be no prices other than market prices. . . .
> The price of a capital good depends essentially on the price of its services, that is to say, on its income. . . . We must remember that the price of capital goods varies . . . by reason of expected changes in gross income and . . . expectations differ from individual to individual.[9]

The apparent close relationship between the capitalization-of-income and the market-comparison methods caused some writers to reject the view that there is such a thing as capitalized value distinct from market value. Medici said:

> Capitalization value does not constitute an independent aspect to be sought, because it is not distinguishable from market price. In fact, in every case capitalization value emanates from a market price represented by the

return (price of use) from a source of wealth and from a number (capitalization rate) which serves to translate that price into capital.

It is well to remark at once that from a theoretical standpoint, there is not just one capitalization value for a certain object, there are as many as there are possible rates. Among these is one which permits a coincidence of the capitalization value of the object with that of its market value.[10]

It is important to note, however, that Medici advocated the use of the capitalization-of-income method as a means of determining market value, even though he maintains the unity of capitalization and market values.

Development of Mathematical Techniques   The parallel development of mathematical techniques for establishing the present values of future expected incomes is described in the work of Grimes and Craigue, published in 1928.[11] Mathematical tables for establishing the present value of a future payment (the fundamental cornerstone of the capitalization-of-income method) appear to have been developed as a part of early actuarial science as early as 1716. The so-called sinking-fund method of valuation, employing two rates of interest for valuing speculative income, was advocated by Hoskold in a book published in 1877. Variations in this method were advanced by such writers in engineering valuation as George King, T. A. O'Donohue, and D. B. Morkill, who wrote in the decades from 1890 to 1920.[12]

Grimes and Craigue presented mathematical methods for valuing any type of income – increasing, constant, or decreasing – under a variety of assumptions about interest and amortization rates. Their work is important because it furnished the mathematical basis with which Frederick M. Babcock, the foremost proponent of the capitalization-of-income method in appraisal theory, forged the link between the theories of interest and value developed by Fisher and other economists and the actuarial science of valuation. The elaborate mathematical techniques developed by Grimes and Craigue and others contrast with the relatively unadorned theories of valuation advanced by economists. As a result, capitalization-of-income theory today is replete with highly technical mathematical rationalization. For this reason, in the discussion that follows, primary attention will be given to the assumptions underlying the use of the method and the determination of the key unknowns required rather than to the exposition of the mathematical techniques and formulas employed.

Assumptions and Unknowns in the Capitalization Approach

It is commonly agreed that mathematical formulas are merely mechanical aids in the valuation process and that the quality of an estimate of value by the capitalization-of-income method will depend upon the judgment of the appraiser with respect to four factors: (1) the annual future income which will accrue to the property; (2) the selection of an appropriate capitalization rate or rates; (3) the probable duration of the income (which usually requires an estimate of building life); (4) the terminal land value, assuming the end of the useful life of improvements. The difficulties which beset the appraiser in formulating judgments on these four factors vary with the nature of the appraisal problem. It will also be observed that the four factors vary considerably in their importance as influences upon the final estimate of value. It will be demonstrated below that the estimate of incomes for the years in the relatively near future and the capitalization rate chosen are key influences upon the resultant value figure. In contrast, wide variations in estimates of income in the far distant future, building life, or terminal land value are obscured by the capitalization process and affect resultant value estimates in lesser degree. To illustrate the varying degrees of difficulty in the estimation of future incomes and in the selection of capitalization rates, a series of three examples is presented below.

Example 1 – Simplest Case   The appraisal of a level, certain, terminable annuity represents the simplest type of capitalization problem. Reference to the formula for calculating the present value of an amount due at some future time reveals that the present value of a known return at a known date in the future is dependent on only one factor – the rate of discount. Given the income for a given year, S, and the number of years' wait, n, the discount rate is all that is required to determine the present value, P:

$$P = \frac{S}{(1 + i)^n}.$$

The present value of each of a series of annual returns can be calculated in the same manner, and the sum of the individual values would equal the present value of the series of annuities for the entire period.[13]

Important assumptions underlie the use of a single rate of discount in the estimation of value by the above method. Although there is general agreement that a dollar of income in the future is of lower value than a dollar of income in the present, the scale of time preferences may have infinite variations. Fisher pointed out that the degree of impatience or time preference will vary with an individual's expected real income and the manner in which it is expected to be distributed over time. Since a prospective investor theoretically applies a different rate of discount to each year's prospective income, any single rate of discount applied to an income stream must represent an average of these rates. Similarly, since the galaxy of rates applied to future incomes will differ among individuals, any single rate selected must be an average of individuals' average rates. To determine the present value of the known, terminable, level annuity in the example, the appraiser must select a rate representing a weighted average of the individual rates a variety of different persons would apply to each year's income over the period. Because the subjective estimation of such a rate is obviously an almost impossible task, it is commonly observed that the rate is obtained in the market.

The market rate of discount used in valuing a level, certain, terminable income (such as that illustrated in the present example) would be obtained by calculating the yield on a riskless annuity or bond of similar maturity. Reference to the market for the rate of discount in this manner, however, is essentially obtaining the value of the property by the market-comparison method since, in a roundabout way, the property is assigned a value equal to the selling price of an annuity with the same income expectancy and risk. As will be noted presently, the determination of a capitalization rate and the estimation of value by the capitalization-of-income method is seldom so simple a task in practical appraisal work.

Example 2 – Removing Simplifying Assumptions In the first case it was assumed that no risk was involved in the receipt of a known, level annuity terminating at a definite time in the future. In relaxing these assumptions it might be supposed that a property has been leased for a fixed annual sum (say, one thousand dollars per year) for a ten-year period and that at the end of that time the land reverts to the landlord. Here it is not presumed that the returns are certain of receipt.

This problem can be represented as follows:

$$V = \sum_{t=1}^{10} \frac{\$1,000}{(1 + i)^t} + \frac{\text{Residual Land Values}}{(1 + i)^{10}}.$$

There appear to be two unknowns in this problem: (1) the rate of capitalization and (2) the value of the land when it reverts to the landlord ten years hence. The key to the selection of the proper rate of capitalization lies in the determination of risk. As in the first example, the appraiser seeks to learn from the market the going rate of return on comparable investments. Although rates are theoretically obtained from the market, actual selection of a rate becomes a highly subjective process since wide exercise of judgment is necessary in determining the comparability of risk.

The estimation of the reversionary value of an improved property is an equally hazardous undertaking. Assuming that the building has no value at the end of the lease, the determination of land value at that time would involve estimating the amount and duration of returns from an appropriate new improvement, selecting a capitalization rate, and discounting returns to land after allowing for building returns. Owing to the obvious difficulties involved in such estimation, it is more customary for appraisers to estimate the market value of the land at the end of the lease and discount this as the reversionary land value. Because this, too, involves hazards of estimation, appraisers frequently determine present market value of the land by comparison and make the assumption that it will be the same at the end of the lease period. The presumption of constant land value over the period of a lease will be recognized as dangerous guesswork.

It can be seen that the capitalization-of-income method in this example not only relies upon the market in the selection of a discount rate, but employs the market-comparison method to establish the reversionary value of the land. Both of these procedures are based upon highly questionable assumptions.

Example 3 – Fee Simple Valuation The two examples just discussed were based upon the expectation of known, level, terminable incomes. The valuation of a property with no leases in effect releases these assumptions. In this example the appraiser must estimate the income stream and its duration and also establish a rate, or rates, of discount. It can readily be seen that such problems could provide a wide range of difficulty. The estimation of income alone requires a forecast of business conditions and price levels. The estimate of the duration of the income stream involves not only judgments as to physical durability, but also forecasts as to maintenance, quality of management, and rate of obsolescence.

The following representation of this problem illustrates the difficult estimating problem of the appraiser, who must establish the economic life or holding period, the income stream, residual land value and an appropriate capitalization rate:

$$V = \sum_{t=1}^{n} \frac{\text{Income}}{(1 + i)^t} + \frac{\text{Residual Land Value}}{(1 + i)^n}.$$

It is apparent that the hazards in the application of the capitalization-of-income method are greatly increased by dropping the simplifying assumptions concerning the amount and duration of income. It is also evident that the market-price mechanism performs the functions of mass estimation of these many influences in the fixing of market prices.

It has been observed from these examples that the problems of estimation in real estate appraisal range from the selection of a discount rate in the simplest of cases to the estimation of the total income stream, the future value of land and/or buildings, and the capitalization or discount rate, in more complicated problems. The procedures for making these estimates are described in considerable detail in Babcock's treatise and in other appraisal textbooks, some of which will be reviewed here.

Selection of Capitalization Rates

What Is a Capitalization Rate? Appraisal theory and practice have long been handicapped by a complex dichotomy and confusion concerning the meaning and use of capitalization rates. In October 1952, Winnick said, "By net capitalization rate is meant the ratio between the expected net income from a real estate asset and its price. . . . One is not always sure of how to render an empirically useful definition of capitalization rate, much less of measuring its change."[14] The preceding example makes it clear that a capitalization or discount rate is a rate of interest, expressed in percentage terms, which equates a future amount or a future stream of income and its present value. This rate is widely employed in the field of finance, where it is known as the *internal rate of return*, and in the field of investments, where it is simply referred to as the *rate of return*.[15]

Corporations are often described as employing a measure of their *cost of capital* as a discount rate to any expected future income from a capital asset in determining its value. Similarly, investors are viewed as using their *opportunity cost*, that is, the rate of return they can secure in alternative investments, in valuing the dividends or other returns from a contemplated investment. In the same manner, real estate investors are viewed as determining capitalization rates to apply to the expected future returns from real estate. However, as in many other fields, a specialized vocabulary has been developed in real estate appraisal which has tended to obscure the fundamental identity of a capitalization rate and the internal rate of return.

This can be attributed primarily to the notion that the portion of returns assigned to buildings should bear a different capitalization of risk than the portion assignable to land. This has served to introduce the concepts of so-called split rates in real estate investment. The related concept of fractional rates is usually employed to distinguish between the interest return to the mortgage holder and the so-called equity rate or the return to the owner of the property. The weighted average of these fractional rates is often referred to as the *overall rate*. In appraisal literature, fractional rates are sometimes referred to in a somewhat different sense as representing different rates assigned by investors to returns for different periods of time or for portions of returns for any year. A lower capitalization rate, for example, might be applied to the basic minimum rentals from a shopping center investment than that applied to the "overages" in the form of percentage rentals. Frederick M. Babcock discussed the notion of a capitalization rate representing an overall rate made up of an average of "galaxies of rates" applied by investors to different portions of the returns from real estate investment.[16]

The mathematics and special computational techniques which have developed in real estate appraisal literature are a further source of confusion to the meaning and use of capitalization rates in real estate investment and valuation. Capitalization rates are sometimes referred to in the form of their reciprocals, termed *multipliers*, which are found in various present value tables.[17] Two of these sets of tables, which, as mentioned above, were originally developed in the field of actuarial science, are associated with the names of Inwood and Hoskold, who originally published tables of "present value factors" for future payments or incomes at different capitalization rates. This has given rise to the use of this expression to have a meaning similar to the term *capitalization rate*, since the multiplication of any estimated future income by a present value factor gives the same result as its division by a capitalization rate.

The basic assumptions or premises underlying the Inwood and Hoskold tables of present value factors are important. McMichael and others have shown that the present value of an income stream will be the same under the Inwood and Hoskold premises if it is assumed that the portion of the investor's returns representing a return of his original investment is invested at the original capitalization rate.[18] However, if it is assumed that this portion of the investor's returns is reinvested in a sinking fund at some safe rate of interest different from the capitalization rate, their value will be greater and the multiplier applicable to any future income stream will be a higher present value factor. In effect, Hoskold, in his sinking-fund method, implies that the investor maintains his original capital invested and assigns a lower rate of return on the portion of his estimated future returns, representing return to his capital.[19] Capitalization tables based upon the Inwood premise are widely available and can be prepared with the aid of the computer for any range of rates and periods.

These tables are all based upon the following basic compound interest formulas:

1. Compound amount of $1 ($P = \$1$) $\qquad S_1 = P(1 + i)^n.$

2. Present value of a reversion of $1 ($S_1 = \$1$) $\qquad P \text{ or } V_{\overline{m}} = \dfrac{S_1}{(1 + i)^n}.$

3. Present value of an annuity of $1 per annum $\qquad a_{\overline{m}} = \dfrac{1 - \dfrac{1}{(1 + i)^n}}{i}.$

4. Installment necessary to amortize a payment of $1 $\qquad 1/a_{\overline{m}} = \dfrac{i}{1 - \dfrac{1}{(1 + i)^n}}.$

5. Accumulated amount of $1 per period $\qquad S_{\overline{m}} = \dfrac{(1 + i)^n - 1}{i}.$

6. Sinking fund necessary to accumulate $1 $\qquad 1/S_{\overline{m}} = \dfrac{i}{(1 + i)^n - 1}.$

Compound interest tables show the values based upon one dollar for each of these expressions. It can be observed that all of the formulas are derived from the basic formula 1 for the "compound amount of $1." The present value of an annuity of one dollar per annum is derived from formula 2, since it represents the sum of a series of payments in the future. Formula 4, as can be seen, is the reciprocal of formula 3. The appearance of I in the formulas reflects the assumption that the one dollar payments are generally viewed as of the end of the period. Formula 5 represents the sum of a series of payments accumulating interest, and can be expressed algebraically as

$$S_{\overline{n}} = 1 + (1 + i)^1 + (1 + i)^2 + \underline{\qquad} (1 + i)^{n-1}.$$

Formula 6 is the reciprocal of formula 5 and solves for the annual payments. This formula, as will be noted below, is employed by Ellwood and Kiers to convert a known or estimated amount of dollar depreciation into a percentage rate per annum.

It can be observed that the installment to amortize one dollar (formula 4), less the interest rate, is equal to the sinking-fund factor (formula 6). Similarly, it can be demonstrated that the sinking-fund factor $1/S_{\overline{n}}$ (formula 6) times the compound amount of 1, S_1 (formula 1) equals the installment of $1/a_{\overline{n}}$ (formula 4).[20]

A new set of capitalization tables has recently been published under the title *Ellwood Tables*, adding to the growing dichotomy associated with the rate of return in real estate investment.[21] One distinguishing feature of these tables is that they represent capitalization rates rather than present value factors for income streams of varying levels under differing assumptions regarding mortgage financing terms and price appreciation or depreciation. Ellwood's rates are identical with the internal rates of return and with the Inwood factors which would result under the same assumptions.[22] However, they have added still another galaxy of terms to the vocabulary of the capitalization-of-income approach.

It has been observed that the *capitalization rate*, the *discount rate*, or the *internal rate of return* — however one wishes to term it — is subject to relatively straightforward definition as an interest rate which equates some future income stream or value and its present value.[23] However, it is not surprising to find that the term itself has a wide variety of meanings for different appraisers and, for this and other reasons, is more easily defined than determined.

Frederick M. Babcock states repeatedly that capitalization rates should be obtained from the market.[24] His exposition of the method of developing rates from the market, however, leaves the appraiser with a highly subjective code of procedure. At the outset, Babcock emphasized the difficulties of obtaining capitalization rates from the market. In describing the limitations of the market as a source of data on capitalization rates, he fails to point out that the market does not usually yield essential information needed in the determination of capitalization rates, namely, the estimated incomes from the property. He does remark that actual income histories of properties would be of limited usefulness because it is the *prospective* future income, not the actual realized income, which is subject to the discounting process. He observes that "brokers, bankers, and others familiar with the long-time real estate market have very similar opinions with respect to certain rates, and that these rates are more or less established in a given community. It is also true that rates seem to be relatively permanent or persistent and subject to little fluctuation through the years and . . . do not seem to vary greatly from one community to another."[25] Following this discussion, Babcock departs from this view of the capitalization rate as a kind of generalized opinion and sets forth detailed procedures for establishing rates. He maintains that the particular rate applicable to income from a property will be influenced by the following four factors: (1) degree of certainty with which prediction of future returns can be made, (2) stability of future returns, (3) composition of future returns, and (4) functional aspects of the property. The criticism might be offered that Babcock's four factors affecting the level of capitalization rates are actually only four ways of considering the same prospect, namely, the certainty of the income. The last three of the factors appear to be significant only insofar as they might influence the first. Following this line of reasoning, it might be held that the capitalization rate would be low for a given property if returns could be predicted with certainty even though the forecast was for unstable income and the building might be of low architectural and functional quality.

Babcock presents a series of rate charts to be used as mechanical aids in the determination of capitalization rates. Separate charts are presented for determination of land and building rates because of his support of the use of so-called split rates, a theory which will be discussed presently.

The kind of building, its condition, use, architectural style, quality of construction, and the reliability of the income prediction, all enter into the determination of the capitalization rate to be applied to the assumed building returns in Babcock's scheme. In his assignment of weights, type and condition of the building in the building rate charts and the location and type of improvements in the land charts receive the chief emphasis. In the concluding remarks of chapter 29 of his book, he cautions the reader regarding the use of this approach, pointing out that the relative effects of the different factors are unknown and that other considerations could affect rates.[26]

It is apparent that Babcock's rate charts are merely an aid to the appraiser in a highly subjective judgment process. He recognizes the capitalization rate as a market phenomenon. However, in spite of his earlier assurances concerning the excellence of the opinions of brokers regarding the proper capitalization rate to use in a given situation, he apparently sees the danger in such a procedure. The rate-chart techniques that he developed, although ingenious, cannot alter the basic conclusion that the selection of a capitalization rate or rates is based upon opinion and judgment.

The text of the American Institute of Real Estate Appraisers advises that "the rates should be selected with utmost care, on the basis of market experience."[27] The importance of the selection of the proper rate in the capitalization-of-income method is illustrated in the institute text as follows:

131

Net Income	Value at 7%	Value at 8%	Decreased Value	Increased Value
$500	$7,143	$6,250	12.5%	14.3%

The going market rate, according to the authors, is determined by current market conditions. The following approaches to determination of the capitalization rate to be used are discussed in the 1967 edition of the text: (1) band of investment theory, (2) comparison of quality attributes (quality of income), and (3) direct comparison. Two of these approaches are identical to the list in the 1952 edition. The comparison of quality attributes is a variation of the earlier technique identified as the summation method.

Summation Method   The summation method, as illustrated by Schmutz and in the 1952 edition of the institute text, views the capitalization rate as the sum of the following:

	Typical rates Assumed
Safe or nonrisk rate	3%
Allowance for risk	1½
Allowance for nonliquidity	1½
Allowance for burden of management	1½

It is apparent that the safe or nonrisk rate will vary with the general interest rate level, while the other components will vary over time and under varying economic conditions, as well as among different properties.

This method of estimating capitalization rates, admittedly highly subjective with respect to its components, was replaced in the 1967 edition of the institute text by a method of rate selection referred to as "Comparison of Quality Attributes." This technique involves the assignment of quality ratings to comparable properties sold in the market and the adjustment of something referred to as the "actual interest rate" on these comparables by application of the quality-rating scores.[28]

The quality criteria suggested in the institute text are

	weight
Reliability of income prediction	15%
Reliability of expense prediction	10
Likelihood of competitive construction	15
Salability of the property	15
Expense-income ratio	20
Stability of value	15
Burden of management	10
Total	100%

In using the technique, comparable properties for which sales data and estimates of "net income after depreciation" are available are assigned a quality rating based upon a weighted total score of the above attributes (or some other set). The so-called actual rates, representing net income after depreciation/sales price, are adjusted by multiplying them by the respective quality-rating scores as shown below.

Illustration of Use of Quality-Rating Scores to Determine Capitalization Rates

Comparables	Sales Price	Net Income after Deprec.	Percent 3/2	Compos. Quality Rating Score	Adj. Cap. Rate
1	$100,000	$8,000	0.080	100	0.0800
2	47,000	4,300	0.091	87	0.7917
3	57,000	6,000	0.105	83	0.0871
4	38,000	2,750	0.072	95	0.0757

The resulting numbers in column 6 are referred to in appraisal literature as *interest rates*, to which some allowance is added for "recapture" to obtain an overall capitalization rate. What is "recapture"? The concept has its origins in the notion of loan amortization payments, which can be viewed as a sinking fund, representing the gradual return of the lender's capital. It will be recalled that the compound interest factor for the installment of one, $1/a_{\overline{m}}$, is equal to the sinking fund factor $1/S_{\overline{m}}$ + the interest rate i. It is assumed that an investor will separate a fraction of each payment he receives from a real estate investment and identify it as a return of his capital, as in the Hoskold premise described above, with the balance viewed as earned interest on his investment. The measurement of recapture in appraisal literature is usually based upon some assumed rate of depreciation on the portion of the investment represented by improvements. It is, so to speak, the portion of the investment "used up" in each year and represented by a straight line depreciation rate.

The notion that the typical real estate investor assigns some annual rate of loss in value to his property is at best unrealistic. In fact, we know that many investors do not anticipate any decline in the value of their property at all over their anticipated holding period. The age-life method of calculating possible future depreciation in value is highly unreliable, particularly during periods of prolonged inflation. Further, the assumption that investors actually separate the dollars returned from real estate in different piles is equally unrealistic. Capital withdrawals are in fact made by real estate investors from time to time, usually by refinancing, but in few cases are they viewed as annual recapture payments.

Further criticism of the above method for determining something called an *interest rate*, to which is added an allowance for recapture, is that the so-called interest rate is not an interest rate in the conventional sense as a rate paid on indebtedness, but it is a composite rate applicable to both the debt and equity interests in a property.

The notion that investors' capitalization rates will vary with the reliability of the income prediction, the operating ratio, burden of management, and other considerations was recognized in Babcock's writings in the 1930s and is also implicit in the summation method. The major problem in using these criteria for rate determination, of course, is that the weights assigned to the quality criteria and the quality rating scores themselves are highly subjective and will vary widely with the individual appraiser.

A more fundamental criticism of the method of determining capitalization rates identified as the "comparison of quality attributes" is that it omits from consideration the most important and relevant elements in rate determination, namely, the mortgage interest rate and the ratio of debt to total value. These are either known or are readily determinable in the market for properties under appraisal. Desired equity returns are less readily available, but can be approximated by surveys of investor opinions, or, as will be shown below, by cash-flow analysis.

For these reasons, most appraisal theorists advocate the derivation of overall capitalization rates by some technique of averaging debt and equity rates of return. The use of net income (itself a highly flexible calculation), adjusted for depreciation and further adjusted by the subjective judgmental process of comparing quality attributes, must be viewed as incorporating all of the weaknesses of the so-called summation method which it replaced. Another apparent problem in the method, as illustrated, is that the so-called actual interest rates are not actual at all. They are obtained by calculation of something called "net income after recapture," which is probably net income before income taxes and mortgage interest, less some arbitrary depreciation percentage assigned by the appraiser, the result expressed as a percentage of the sales price. What, if any, relation this might bear to the after-tax rate of return an investor would expect from any of the subject properties is not clear. In this author's view, an appraiser would be much better advised to consult with purchasers of comparable properties and ascertain at first hand the before- or after-tax rates of return they expected on their purchases and then use some average of these rates as his capitalization rate obtained from the market.

Rate selection from gross-rent multipliers is also advocated as a method of obtaining a reliable estimate of the market interest rate in the 1967 edition of the institute text.[29] This technique appears to assume that market capitalization rates equal the reciprocals of net income multipliers, which usually represent net income before mortgage interest and income taxes expressed as a percentage of market sales prices. This technique uses the all-too-familiar "broker's yield," which has been the subject of criticism in appraisal literature for years. If an investor is primarily and only interested in his after-tax yield on required equity investment, this is the only significant figure to use in capitalizing the value of an equity investment. If an overall capitalization rate is required, it can be approximated by the band-of-investment technique and estimated more precisely by the Ellwood method if the income is level, or by the use of the computer in the case of varying annual returns.

The consistent preoccupation with depreciation recapture in appraisal literature generally appears to rest upon an illogical conception of the nature of the capitalization process and of capitalization rates. Capitalization rate is a percentage number which equates an expected income and its capital value. This number, as the author and others have pointed out elsewhere, automatically makes provision for the return *of* and the return *on* capital. The addition to a capitalization rate of something called recapture is double-counting, to the extent that return of capital should already have been included in the capitalization rate and process. Similarly, the deduction from the expected income of an amount which is referred to as recapture installment represents an unjustified deduction from an expected income stream in the capitalization process.[30]

The effect of this is often hidden in professional appraisal reports by the purposeful selection of capitalization rates designed to offset this error. The author prefers to term this *the law of compensating error*. If, by virtue of adding something to the capitalization rate, or deducting something from the income for so-called recapture, valuation is lowered unjustifiably, the error can be corrected by specifying a capitalization rate which is reduced by an offsetting amount. This is one explanation for the great disparity between known investor yields on real estate and the low capitalization rates commonly used in appraisal practice. This observation may also explain why many appraisers alter their expression and refer to the rates used in the capitalization-of-income method as "interest rates."

Band-of-Investment Method This method of establishing capitalization rates involves the calculation of the rates as a weighted average of the fractional rates applicable to portions of the total investment. Assuming that rates at which mortgage funds will be available can be determined and that the going return on equity investments can be approximated, the capitalization rate is calculated as noted below.

Illustration of Band-of-Investment Method

First mortgage	0.05 × $7,000	=	$350
Second mortgage	0.08 × 3,000	=	240
Equity	0.10 × 2,000	=	200
Total investment in property	$12,000		
Total return			$790

$$\text{Capitalization rate} = \frac{\$790}{\$12,000} = 0.0658$$

Ellwood

The publication of the *Ellwood Tables for Real Estate Appraising and Financing* in 1958 and their revised publication in 1967 resulted in major modifications and improvements in the technique of developing a capitalization rate by the band-of-investment method. Ellwood presents the following formula which incorporates the equity rate, mortgage interest rate, and an adjustment for any expected appreciation or depreciation in the residual value of the investment:

$$R = Y - MC \pm \% \, App \, / Dep \times 1/S_{\overline{m}} \qquad (1)$$

where:
R = Overall rate applicable to any estimated level income.
Y = Equity yield rate to be estimated by the appraiser.
M = Ratio of mortgage to total investment as a percentage.
C = Mortgage coefficient which varies with mortgage terms.
App/Dep = Expected percentage appreciation or depreciation in the residual sales price of the investment.
$1/S_{\overline{m}}$ = Sinking-fund factor at the equity yield rate for the period of assumed holding of the investment.

The basic similarity of Ellwood's technique to the band-of-investment method of obtaining capitalization rates can be demonstrated by comparing the formula for what Ellwood terms his *basic capitalization rate* (which includes all the ingredients except provision for appreciation or depreciation during the income projection term) with the band-of-investment formula.

Ellwood's formula $r = Y - MC$ results in an identical value for r, where the values for MC are equal, in the band-of-investment formula:

$$r = MY + MC.$$

Assuming that the equity yield rate Y is 12 percent and the ratio of mortgage is 70 percent and equity 30 percent, it can be seen that the capitalization rates would be identical on a 6 percent mortgage yield basis:

$r = 0.12 - 0.70 \times 0.06$ or 7.80% Ellwood.
$r = 0.30(0.12) + 0.70(0.06)$ or 7.80% band-of-investment.

It should be emphasized that this assumes that there is no loan amortization, which is the principal element accounting for the difference between Ellwood's basic capitalization rates and rates obtained by the more conventional band-of-investment method.

Akerson has shown that Ellwood's adjusted band-of-investment rates can be derived very simply by substituting the installment factor $1/a_{\overline{m}}$ for the mortgage interest rate and by subtracting an allowance for return at the equity rate on the fraction of the mortgage amortized over the projection period, which he calls equity buildup.[31]

Under the assumption of a 70 percent loan for 30 years at 6 percent interest, he shows that the appropriate Ellwood rate for a 15-year holding period would be calculated as follows:

Mortgage loan at 6% for 30 years for 70% value
Monthly payment of
    Principal and interest   = 0.70 × 0.0720 = 0.0504
    Equity (down payment) = 0.30 × 0.12   = 0.0360
    Weighted average   = 1.00   = 0.0864
    Less credit for equity buildup (loan amortization)
(% of loan amortized) × (ratio loan to value) × (sinking-fund factor at equity rate)
0.2896 × 70 × 0.0268 = 0.0054.
       basic rate = 0.0810.

This basic rate agrees exactly with the Ellwood rate calculated from the equation:

$r = Y - MC.$
$r = 0.12 × 0.70 (0.0558).$
$r = 0.0810.$

Ellwood's capitalization rate (R) is derived by adjusting r for appreciation or depreciation, using the sinking-fund factor $1/S_{\overline{m}}$ at the equity rate.

The algebraic explanation of the derivation of Ellwood rates is much more difficult to follow than the simpler exposition by Akerson.

Ellwood's mortgage coefficients are calculated from the formula:[32]

where: $$C = Y + P \, 1/S_{\overline{m}} - f \tag{2}$$

P = Fraction of the mortgage amortized during the projection period.
$1/S_{\overline{m}}$ = Installment factor necessary to amortize $1 over n periods @ equity rate.
f = Interest rate on the mortgage times 1 plus the ratio of the fraction of the mortgage paid off to the percentage increase in the accumulated interest on the loan.

Formula 2 for the so-called mortgage coefficient represents the core of Ellwood's technique, since it is here that he allows for the return on what he calls capital recapture resulting from loan amortization. The mortgage coefficient again is represented in this formula as the difference between the equity rate Y, adjusted upward to allow for a return on the fraction of the mortgage paid off during the holding period, and f, which represents the annual requirement including principal and interest on a loan for any specific terms. The values of f are derived from the formula $1/a_{\overline{m}}$ described above, which equals the sinking-fund factor plus the applicable mortgage interest rate.

Ellwood represents this in the following equation:

where:
$$f = \left(1 + \frac{P}{Sp - 1}\right)I \tag{3}$$

P = Fraction of the mortgage amortized during the income projection period.

Sp = Compound amount of 1 for the number of periods in the projection.

I = Interest rate on the mortgage.

It can be noted that the value of f depends upon the ratio of the amount of the loan amortized to the accumulated interest due on the loan and upon the interest rate. The first ratio

$$\left(1 + \frac{P}{Sp - 1}\right)$$

varies of course with the interest rate and term of the loan.

The final term in Ellwood's basic equation (1), $\% \ App/Dep \times 1/S_{\overline{m}}$, represents a final adjustment to achieve what is referred to as the overall capitalization rate R. Essentially, this step converts an estimated or actual percentage change in value as of the end of an assumed holding period into a compound rate of interest which is added to or subtracted from the so-called basic capitalization rate r to obtain R. This step eliminates the need to treat the residual sales price independently of the annual returns in the conventional capitalization formulas referred to above.

The basic problems with the use of Ellwood rates are that, first, they are useful only when level returns are applicable and, second, since they are not adaptable to cash flow after taxes, they bear no direct relationship to rates actually received by either the lender or the equity holder.

The Ellwood method can be illustrated by assuming an investment property is expected to produce an annual stabilized income of five thousand dollars over a twelve-year holding period. The property is financed by a twenty-year amortized mortgage payable monthly at 8 percent interest in the amount of 50 percent of value. The appraiser assumes that the property will experience a 30 percent decline in value over the twelve-year holding period and that the investor requires a 15 percent return on his equity investment. The Ellwood rates for a twelve-year holding period are not available in his printed tables so that it is necessary to use the Ellwood basic formula (1) shown above and solve for the capitalization rate by hand calculation or through the use of the computer. The relevant inputs are:

$Y = 0.15$
$I = 0.08$
$M = 0.50$
$n = 240$ months (term of mortgage)
$N = 144$ months (holding period of 12 years)
$D = 0.30$ depreciation assumed over 12-year period
$1/S_{\overline{m}} = 0.0344808$ sinking-fund factor at 0.15 for 144 months
$Sp - 1 = 1.60339$ compound amount of 1 less 1 at 0.08 for 144 months.

Ellwood's equations are as follows:

$C = Y + P\ 1/S_{\overline{m}} - f$	0.0637.
$P = (f/I - 1)\ (Sp - 1)$	0.40832.
$f = (1 + P/Sp - 1)\ I$	0.1004.
$r = Y - MC$	0.1181468.
$R = Y - MC + Dep\ 1/S_{\overline{m}}$	0.1284910.
$V = d/r \qquad \$5,000/0.12849$	\$38,913.21.

Hand calculation of these numbers is burdensome and frustrating without the aid of mechanical equipment and patience. Computer programs have been developed which make the necessary calculations in only a few seconds, eliminating all need for hand calculation.

The above solution to the problem can be compared with that resulting from the use of the conventional capitalization formula.

$V = I_t(1 + r)^t + \text{Residual}/(1 + r)^n.$
$V = \$5,000/(1 + 0.115)^t + \text{Residual}/(1 + 0.115)^{12}.$
$r = MY + MC.$
$r = 0.50 \times 0.15 + 0.50 \times 0.08.$
$r = 0.115.$
$V = a_{\overline{m}} \times \$5,000 + 0.70V \times v_{\overline{m}}$
$V = 6.3405 \times \$5,000. + 0.70V \times 0.270833.$
$V = \$31,702.50 + 0.18958V.$
$0.81042V = \$31,702.50.$
$V = \$39,000.00.$

The results of the two methods are very closely similar in the example illustrated. A major shortcoming of the Ellwood method is that it can only be used when level incomes are assumed over some period in the future.

Conventional residual capitalization formulas can solve for value under assumptions of a varying income stream by trial and error methods or by use of the computer. These techniques, illustrated below, are described in detail in *Real Estate Investment Analysis and Taxation.*[33]

The author has demonstrated elsewhere that Ellwood's capitalization rates are identical with the Inwood capitalization rates and with the internal rate of return under similar assumptions.[34] His tables, therefore, become an aid to rapid calculation of capitalization rates under specific conditions, rather than any new application of the capitalization-of-income approach.

A simple example illustrates how valuation estimates may vary if capitalization techniques are used without careful consideration of the assumptions in the problem and their specific applicability to the problem at hand.

Example

Cost, income, and financing assumptions

Total cost of land and improvements (purchase price)	$10,000
Expected net income per annum (before interest, depreciation, and income taxes)	$1,000.00

Holding period – 5 years

No change in selling price during period of holding

Financing – 15 yrs. 0.75 mortgage @ 6%

Equity yield desired – 10%

Value of property by band-of-investment method

Debt 0.75 × 0.06 =	0.0450
0.25 equity × 10% =	0.0250
Weighted band-of-investment rate	0.0700

$1,000 × 4.100 = (P.V.* annuity @ 7%) (*present value)	$4,100
$10,000 × 0.7130 = (P.V. reversion $V_{\overline{m}}$@ 7%)	7,130
Estimated value	$11,230

Proof

Bank receives

$8.439* \times \$7,500 =$ \$63.29 per month
(*monthly constant payment factor @ 6%)

$63.29 \times 51.725561* =$ \$3,273.71
(*monthly P.V. of annuity @ 6% for 5 yrs.)

plus

$7,500 \times 0.76* = \$5,700 \times 0.7473** =$ <u>\$4,225.82</u>
(*remaining balance of loan; **P.V. reversion @ 6%)

Total received by bank   \$7,499.53

Investor Receives

$\dfrac{\$1,000}{12} = \$83.30 - \$63.29 = \$20.04$ per month

$20.04 \times 47.065 =$ 943.18
(P.V. annuity @ 10% for 60 months)

plus

$4,300 \times 0.6209 =$ <u>2,669.87</u>
(P.V. reversion $V_{\overline{m}}$ @ 10%)

Investor receives   3,613.05

Bank receives   <u>7,499.53</u>

Total received — estimated value   \$11,112.58

Value of property by Ellwood method

$Y - MC \pm App/Dep\ 1/S_{\overline{m}}$

$0.10 - 0.75 \times 0.0381* - 0.07147$ \$13,991
(*Ellwood mortgage coefficient — *Ellwood Tables*, p. 291 = 0.0715)

Does the Akerson method "Ellwood without Algebra"
provide a clue to differences in the valuation estimates?

Debt $0.75 \times 0.101268 =$ 0.07595
(0.008439 × 12 = constant payment factor @ 6%)

plus

Equity $0.25 \times 0.10 =$ <u>0.0250</u>

Weighted average   0.10095

less

Equity build-up:

% loan amortized $\times L/V*$ ratio $\times 1/S_{\overline{m}}.**$ @ equity rate $= \underline{0.029483}$
(*0.24 × *0.75 × **0.163797)

Ellwood rate by Akerson method   0.07147

Estimated value $= 1,000 - 0.07147 =$ \$13,991

An "Ellwoo" computer program developed at the University of Georgia was used to test the foregoing valuation by the Ellwood technique. The output of the "Ellwoo" program, which required only a few seconds of computer time, is self-explanatory. Reproduced below, the output indicates a valuation of $13,990.96.

Code 111 (Ellwoo)
I/12 .005000 f .101263 SP .34885 P .23990901 SF .1637975 C.03803367
r.0714747 R. 071474745 V$ 13990.96 M   .7500   I   .0600 n 180 d
$ 1000.00 N 60 D 0.   A 0.   Y   .10000 V   13990.96

With a .7500% mortgage available bearing interest at the rate of .0600000 per annum for a period of 180 months; an annual net income before mortgage amortization of $1,000.00 and the property is held for 60 months with an expected depreciation of 0% or app. of 0% in the value during ownership; an investor who desires a yield of .100% on his equity investment can realize his objective if total value paid for the property is $13,990.96.

There is only one correct valuation conclusion which meets the conditions of this simple problem: an investor who desires a 10 percent return on his equity investment and who purchases this property for $10,000, and sells it at the same price five years hence, and receives $1,000 per annum during the period of holding would be justified in assuming the property has a value to him of $11,230. (Note that this assumes no change in the purchase price as stated in the problem.)

The correct techniques for arriving at this conclusion are (1) capitalizing the annual return of $1,000 and the residual of $10,000 at the weighted average band-of-investment rate of 7 percent (this is generally termed an *overall rate*) or (2) capitalizing separately the returns to the lender at 6 percent and the returns to the investor at 10 percent and summing these (these rates are commonly called *fractional rates*).

The results of either of these techniques confirm the valuation of approximately $11,200, as shown above. The slightly higher valuation for the band-of-investment method arises because the band-of-investment rate was not adjusted for equity buildup. The application of the Ellwood technique results in an incorrect estimate of value because the mechanics of the techniques do not fit the problem. The Ellwood technique assumes that the cost to the investor is $13,991, not the $10,000 which is stated in the problem. This assumption also implies a residual sales price of $13,991 and a mortgage debt of 0.75 × $13,991 or approximately $10,493, rather than the $7,500 specified in the problem. The annual debt service on this mortgage alone would exceed the annual income flow. The assumptions necessary to justify a valuation of $13,991 are inconsistent with those stated in the problem. We can only conclude that the Ellwood technique is not adaptable to any valuation problem where the investor may wish to specify a purchase price or assumed cost different from the calculated value of the property under the debt terms and target yield originally specified.

Charles Akerson has suggested adjustments to the Ellwood technique which produce a solution to this problem consistent with the assumed purchase price of $10,000 and the valuation of $11,200. It can be observed below that two adjustments have been made: (1) the value for M in the Elwood equation has been changed to the ratio of assumed debt to the calculated value (V), and (2) an adjustment for *App/Dep* has been added based upon the difference between the calculated value (V) and the assumed selling price.

$V = 1,000/R$

$C = 0.0381$ from Ellwood tables.
$M = 7500/V \qquad 1/S_{\overline{m}} = 0.1638$.

$dep = 1 - 10,000/v$.

$V = 1,000/ [0.10 - (7,500/v) (0.0381) + (1 - 10,000/V) (0.1638)]$.

$V = \$11,084$.

Although Akerson's adjustments result in a value consistent with the Inwood technique employed by the author above, it is evident that they require basic modifications in the Ellwood formulation.

L. W. Ellwood, in a letter reviewing the apparent divergence in valuations, maintained that the value of the property in the above example is $10,000. He arrives at this conclusion by discounting the equity income and reversion at 22 percent. This obviously alters the basic assumption in the problem that the investor desires a target yield on his equity of 10 percent. Ellwood's letter, too long to quote in its entirety, stated, "To begin with, I cannot accept your premise that value of an investment for profit varies according to the technique used in processing the projected income and reversion. *Each technique includes implicit assumptions which are at variance with those of other techniques*" [italics mine]. The italicized sentence obviously accounts for the differences in valuations in the example shown and contradicts the previous statement. Ellwood's concluding paragraph, with which the author is in full agreement, is most significant: "I believe progress in appraisal education would only be retarded by text material which does not treat the capitalization process as an investment analysis tool. *Estimate value by market comparison and test it for yield prospects by use of the most applicable capitalization process*" [italics mine].

This example illustrates the substantial variation in valuation estimates which can result from the use of techniques which may be inappropriate to the problem at hand. A comparison later in this chapter of valuations resulting from use of land residual, building residual, and net cash-flow techniques illustrates the possible errors in using residual valuation techniques. Obviously, any mechanical capitalization procedure must be tailored to fit the problem, and any capitalization technique, if improperly used, may provide an unrealistic estimate of value. The potential danger and confusion in multiple-capitalization techniques is the basis for the author's argument that after-tax net cash flow is the most acceptable criterion of investor's return and that the discounted net cash-flow valuation technique should be used exclusively in the determination of investment value.

Beyond the contribution to computational ease, the major contribution of Ellwood's tables has been to refute the use of accounting concepts and methods of calculating depreciation in real estate investment and to emphasize the importance of mortgage-lending terms on market values of real estate. Ellwood's technique makes more explicit, even though it does not eliminate, the problem of subjective determination of capitalization rates, which is the source of much of the flexibility and confusion in the use of the capitalization-of-income approach. The most important element in the determination of the overall capitalization rate in the Ellwood procedure, as in other variations of the band-of-investment method and in grid techniques, is the equity rate reflecting risk assigned to any specific real estate investment. As pointed out earlier, authorities agree that this rate should reflect judgments of the market.

Estimating Future Income

Regardless of the specific capitalization-of-income technique employed, the appraiser must estimate the income expected to accrue to the property. This task may be easily accomplished in the exceptional case of a strong tenancy with a fixed, long-term, dollar rental. However, in most cases, such conditions are not present, and the appraiser must estimate income based upon month-to-month rentals, short-term leases, various types of tenancies, or percentage leases. Obviously, the accuracy of an estimate of value by the capitalization-of-income method will depend upon the accurate estimation of income as well as the selection of an appropriate discount rate.

Babcock on Estimating Future Income   Babcock describes two alternative methods for estimating the future net income for a property: (1) the year-by-year forecast of future gross income and expenses and (2) the use of what he refers to as the four income premises. Babcock appears to understand the difficulties in the prediction of future incomes accruing to real estate and recommends the use of the above methods, either singly or in combination. The acceptance of lease-rental incomes at face value is an error, he cautions. In discussing the estimation of the percentage of occupancy in the future, he admits that "there is no such thing as normal occupancy except from the point of view of individual properties."[35]

Throughout his discussion of the techniques of estimating income and expenses, Babcock emphasizes the dangers of projecting historical figures into the future; yet he implies that the appraiser, through the skillful analysis of data and exercise of judgment, can establish an estimate of future net incomes which will fall within the limits of probable fluctuations. Babcock rationalizes the difficulties of predicting the long-term future by demonstrating that the earlier portions of the income stream account for a preponderant percentage of the total value of a property in the capitalization-of-income method. The effect upon valuations of a failure to predict correctly the remaining lives of long-life properties is not very considerable. With short-life properties, the effect is much more pronounced.

According to Babcock, it is much easier to estimate future expenses with accuracy than income. When it is not possible to forecast individual items of expense, he advocates the use of the expense ratio. Babcock considers the estimation of the duration of income expectancy, which is related to the determination of building life, as a part of the general problem of forecasting income.

The Four Income Premises The estimation of the duration of incomes is related to the determination of building life and to the so-called income premises developed by Babcock. He assumed that the value of buildings will decline over their lifetime and, hence, that incomes from improved property will decline with property depreciation. Recognizing that the estimation of future incomes and expenses as outlined above is difficult, he fashioned theoretical curves based upon certain assumptions regarding the constancy or rate of decline in incomes over time.[36] Although the reader is referred to Babcock's *Valuation of Real Estate* for a complete description of these premises, they can be identified briefly as follows: *premise 1* assumes that future incomes will occur in equal annual installments; *premise 2* assumes a very gradual decline in annual incomes for early years and more rapid decline in later life; *premise 3* assumes a more even decline over period than premise 2; and *premise 4* assumes that future annual incomes will decline by equal annual differences (a straight-line decline). In discussing the use of these premises, Babcock says, "It is contemplated that the appraiser in using the tables will select the one having the future income curvature which is most like the income expectancy of the building he is appraising."[37] It is evident that these premises are to serve as substitutes for, or as supplements to, the technique of estimating future incomes which he described in chapters 20 to 21. Babcock facilitates the use of these premises by calculating multipliers which represent the present values of one-dollar income assumed to decline in accordance with the premise notions at varying rates of discount.

The employment of such generalized assumptions regarding the prospective income from property is, of course, subject to all of the weaknesses of the method of estimating incomes discussed previously. The danger lies in the fact that the ease of calculation of present values under the premises from

Babcock's tables would tend to encourage their use. His basic assumption that the incomes from improved property will decline over the life of the property at any predetermined rate is subject to attack. Age does not appear to be the most important factor influencing the income from improved property. Although cases come to mind in which the processes of obsolescence and physical wearing out of properties result in declining incomes, almost as many occasions suggest themselves in which the influence of these depreciating factors has been more than offset by other influences, such as changes in purchasing power of money, improved locational advantage, skillful management, and many others. Therefore, although the general theoretical principle that the income from improvements will decline over their lifetime may have validity, we have no accurate criteria to employ for estimating probable useful life. Not only do we not know when the decline will commence and at what rate, but there also seem to be strong grounds for presuming that any such decline will not proceed in the even manner set forth in Babcock's income premise charts.

Other Developments in Income Estimation   The recommendations for estimating income presented in the textbook of the American Institute of Real Estate Appraisers appear to follow Babcock closely.[38] The authors emphasize the importance of the gross income estimate and the dangers of relying upon present or past incomes in estimating the future. Recent business history abounds with evidence that the estimation of property income is an extremely hazardous undertaking.

Index numbers representing changes in gross income, expenses and net income before financing, and income tax charges are published annually in the *Apartment Building Experience Exchange*.[39] Data for varying numbers of apartment buildings in the United States and Canada are reported on a per-square-foot and per-room basis. Unfortunately, the data do not represent a stratified sample for the United States as a whole and are reported on a consistent basis for identical buildings for only the three-year periods, 1957 to 1959 and 1959 to 1961. Differences in the age distribution of the reporting apartment buildings and in the number of buildings reporting from different cities make it very difficult to develop meaningful trends from the reported data.

Table 6–1 shows recent annual trends in the average dollar rents per room and in the average reported net operating income per room for all buildings reporting in the United States. Although the year-to-year changes probably reflect changes in the sample of reported buildings, as well as a unidimensional variation in financial reporting practices by the respondents, the data reveal a pronounced upward drift in rents per room and a less pronounced upward trend in net operating income per room over the period.

Table 6–2 shows trends in operating ratios by type of apartment buildings, as well as by age of structure. Higher maintenance and heating costs account-

Table 6-1. Average Dollar Rents and Net Operating Income per Room for Apartment House Properties, 1959–1970

Year	Elevator Buildings		Walk-up Apartments over 25 Units		Garden Apartments	
	Rents per Room	Net Operating Income per Room	Rents per Room	Net Operating Income per Room	Rents per Room	Net Operating Income per Room
1959	$435.97	$204.73	$306.31	$136.11	$204.65	$115.26
1960	433.32	212.35	305.61	140.77	237.44	129.27
1961	474.15	246.31	302.93	144.87	251.37	136.92
1962[a]	499.00	234.97	328.80	140.40	282.64	149.75
1963	488.24	240.75	323.28	136.25	281.75	142.35
1964	544.51	272.22	331.62	147.60	305.26	161.27
1965	553.84	279.66	346.16	154.69	322.70	166.80
1966	562.00	283.00	351.00	157.00	327.00	167.00
1967	597.00	290.79	369.66	161.33	339.85	169.74
1968	601.19	296.36	389.00	161.78	361.71	184.09
1969	610.49	321.46	413.25	180.77	366.02	188.74
1970	640.80	324.21	464.30	224.92	399.17	204.96

[a]Weighted averages for North, South, West, calculated by the author.

Source: Institute of Real Estate Management, *Apartment Building Income/Expense Analysis*, annual issues, 1960–1971.

ed for the major portion of the higher operating expense ratios for older buildings. Buildings constructed before World War II reported operating ratios between 55 and 64 percent from 1967 to 1970, as compared with operating ratios of 47 to 49 percent for buildings built after 1960. The higher operating ratios for low-rise apartments in the North probably reflects the older average age of reporting apartment units in that region.

Figure 6–1 shows the relative trend in gross rental income and total operating expenses for seven FHA apartment properties in San Francisco from 1952 to 1967. It is apparent that the rise in operating expenses had a significant impact upon net operating income over the period. It should be observed, however, that since gross rental income is roughly twice the magnitude of total operating expenses, the rise in rental income over the period more than offset the larger percentage increase in operating expenses. For this reason, the actual net operating income for the seven FHA apartment properties rose gradually over the period and was reflected in higher cash flows and higher market sales prices.

A more recent study of changes in gross income and operating expenses for seven other newly constructed apartment buildings in Berkeley, California, during the period from 1963 to 1968 revealed that although gross income and operating expenses rose continuously over the period, showing the same percentage increase of 10 percent, net operating income rose during the period. It is apparent from this and other information that net operating income has not declined for apartment properties over recent years in accordance with declining income premises or in accordance with notions of a

Table 6-2. Comparison of Operating Ratio

1. By Age Group, 1967–1970

Trends: All building types unfurnished		All Expenses Divided by Actual Collections U.S.A. and Canada				
Building Type	Year	1961 to Date	1946–1960	1931–1945	1921–1930	1920 or Before
Elevator	1970	49.2%	52.8%	57.5%	60.1%	64.2%
	1969	47.2	53.8	57.8	62.4	60.5
	1968	46.7	52.3	54.9	64.2	59.5
	1967	47.0	51.5	55.8	61.9	59.0
Low-rise 12–24 units	1970	46.5	54.8	55.8	63.2	60.2
	1969	46.6	52.7	55.1	64.1	63.9
	1968	45.6	52.8	57.3	63.9	63.8
	1967	44.7	52.4	56.8	61.9	59.0
Low-rise 25+ units	1970	43.3	50.8	60.2	62.7	61.8
	1969	49.1	55.0	61.9	63.2	62.0
	1968	46.8	55.1	56.5	62.4	65.2
	1967	49.5	52.2	58.3	62.6	62.2
Garden	1970	45.8	52.7	56.7	71.4	64.7
	1969	45.3	52.6	55.5	57.2	. . .
	1968	45.3	53.3	53.8	58.5	. . .
	1967	44.2	53.1	53.8	58.1	. . .

2. All Ages, 1969–1970

Trends: All building types unfurnished					By Region					
	North		South		West		Canada		Average	
Building Type	1970	1969	1970	1969	1970	1969	1970	1969	1970	1969
Elevator	51.0%	50.7%	51.3%	47.7%	53.5%	51.1%	44.2%	46.9%	51.0%	49.7%
Low-rise 12–24 units	60.0	60.8	49.7	46.7	48.3	45.6	48.0	47.4	57.4	56.0
Low-rise 25+ units	54.7	57.0	47.3	56.0	43.5	44.7	41.5	50.0	50.3	55.3
Garden	48.5	49.1	47.8	47.0	45.4	46.3	43.1	42.2	47.8	47.6

Source: Institute of Real Estate Management, National Association of Real Estate Boards, *Apartment Building Income-Expense Analysis, 1971* (Chicago, 1971).

Figure 6-1. Gross Rent and Total Operating Expenses for Seven FHA Properties, 1953–1967

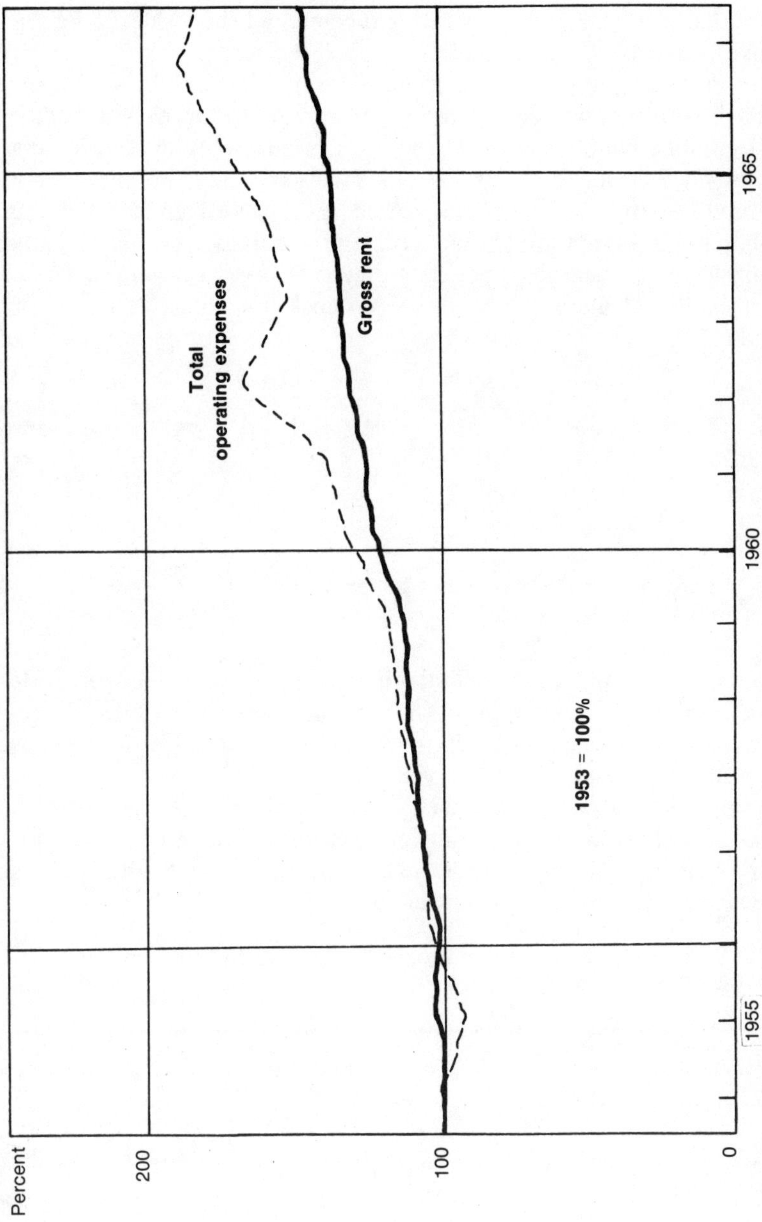

Source: Gilbert Tully, *Real Estate Investment Performance Study* (unpublished report to the faculty of the Graduate School of Business Administration, University of California, Berkeley, 29 August 1968), p. 48.

stabilized income-forecasting technique but, on the contrary, has risen for most properties, particularly for relatively new buildings. By the same token, it would not be necessary to go far back in history to find periods when both gross rental income and net operating income had shown declining tendencies over relatively long periods.

Unfortunately, the task of the appraiser using the capitalization-of-income approach is to estimate net operating income in the future, not in the past. Two techniques which have relatively wide applicability in security analysis recommend themselves for use in this situation. First, the uncertainties in long-run estimation can be circumvented, in large measure, by reducing the time horizon of estimation to manageable proportions. Few security analysts attempt to forecast earnings per share beyond a five-year period. Therefore, they usually calculate the value of a stock by some variation of the formula:[40]

$$V = \sum_{t=1}^{5} \frac{D(1 + g)^t}{(1 + g)^t} + \frac{M(E)}{(1 + i)^n}$$

where:

g = Growth rate.
M = P/E multiplier.
E = Earnings per share at end of holding period.
i = Rates of return.

The appraiser has the same flexibility in valuing an income property. He can estimate its value by discounting the income expectation over a five-year period and adding to it his expectation of the discounted value of its expected sales price at the end of the five years.

Second, the appraiser can and should use probability analysis in developing his forecasts of net operating income and future sales price. For an existing building, this might represent a simple balancing of alternative probabilities such as those stated in table 6–3.

Table 6–3. Illustration of the Use of Probability Analysis in Estimating Net Operating Income

Probability that NOI will show the following annual rate of change over five-year period	Percentage of weight assigned to each possible outcome	Product of probability x weight
+ 5%	10%	0.005
+ 2	20	0.004
no change	10	0.000
- 2	20	-0.004
- 5	20	-0.010
-10	20	-0.020
		-0.025

On the basis of the subjective analysis in table 6–3, the appraiser might conclude that he should forecast that net operating income would decline at a compound annual rate of 2.5 percent per year for the next five years. For a new building, he might wish to refer to reported net operating income per room or per square foot, as summarized in the *Apartment Building Income – Expense Analysis* for specific cities, and forecast the trend, using a similar method of analysis.

The appraiser's assignment of probabilities to various estimates of change in sales prices over the period should, of course, be consistent with his assignment of probabilities to changes in future net operating income. In other words, if the probabilities are low in his estimation that net operating income will rise, it would follow that the probability of a large expected price rise would not be great.

Estimating the Future Value of Land

Implicit in the assumption that the value of improvements will decline over time is the conclusion that the value of an improved property at some future time will be represented by the value of the land. As noted earlier, this necessitates assumptions in the income-capitalization process as to this future value, which, in theory, would be represented by the capitalization of the future returns expected from the use of the land in combination with some new improvement at the conclusion of the life of the present improvement.

Discussing this problem, Babcock stated, "In a new property the useful life predicted is usually so long that the appraiser cannot make any close prediction of the reversion value of the land and the most plausible assumption is the one which predicts the land income upon reaching normal occupancy to continue at the same level to perpetuity."[41] In essence, therefore, Babcock assumed that land will have a constant, perpetual income at a level equal to the current returns (assuming the property is developed with a suitable improvement). This assumption that land will have a constant return is used as the basis for the further assumption that land will have a constant value. Babcock and others fail to defend the implicit assumption in this chain of reasoning that capitalization rates, as well as land return, will remain constant in future.

Some have held that the above assumptions are "as usable as any where definite trends are not in view."[42] However, since it is generally acknowledged that land values do not remain constant over time, the notion of constant land values appears to be highly questionable and speculative. Defense for the assumptions seems to rest on the view that any other prediction would be subject to the same weaknesses. Further rationalization is found in the contention that since most improvements are long-lived, the reversionary value of land in the far-distant future is a small element in the present value of improved real property.

The unacceptability of the assumption that land values will remain constant in the future is supported in that the values have not been static in the past. Rising land values have been a worldwide phenomenon in recent decades. Following their collapse during the depression of the 1930s, downtown land values in major cities in the United States returned to their predepression peaks by 1950 and have risen sharply in most cities since then.[43] Values of commercial land on the peripheries of large cities have increased at even higher rates, while suburban land for residential development has skyrocketed in the past decade.[44]

The National Commission of Urban Problems published *Three Land Research Studies* in 1968. The first of these, based upon examination of changes in assessed values adjusted by use of assessment ratios, concluded that the market value of real estate in the United States approximately doubled from 1956 to 1966, rising from $269 billion at the beginning of the period to $523 billion in 1966.[45] The third study in this series reported on an experiment by the California State Board of Equalization in estimating changes in California land values from 1957 to 1966, based upon multiple-regression analysis. The authors found that changes in school enrollment, retail sales, wage payments, and population provided the best predictors of land value changes. During the decade ending in March 1966, the value of urban land in California rose from $29.5 billion to $63.4 billion; urban and rural land together rose in value from $35.7 billion to $77.9 billion; and the value of all land in the state, including timber, mineral, and water rights, rose from $39.7 billion to $81.4 billion. Based upon these data, it can be seen that land prices rose at a compound annual rate of approximately 7.5 to 8.0 percent during the decade preceding March 1966.[46]

Another monograph which treats land value increases is based upon a study of 248 parcels of land of ten acres or more in the Philadelphia metropolitan area. Milgram reported that the average price for these parcels rose from $1,030 per acre in 1945 when they were vacant to $13,300 per acre in 1962.[47]

Whatever may have been the causes of the rising land values documented in the above studies — and the general adoption of an inflationary psychology appears to be an important factor — it would seem obvious that any estimates based upon the presumption that land values would remain constant over long periods in the United States would be seriously in error. The indeterminacy of residual land or property values at some long-term future date provides one of the strongest arguments for shortening the time horizon used in the capitalization approach. Hazardous as it may appear, an estimate of market sales price five years in the future is almost certain to prove more reliable than an estimate for twenty years hence. The dynamics of property tax rates alone would appear sufficient reason to adopt the alternative of short-term forecasts for property income and sales prices.

The assumption of constant land values in the capitalization-of-income method appears to be one more in the long chain of hypotheses upon which this method rests. The possibilities of introducing error in assuming constant land values seem to be of greater importance when they are considered in conjunction with the limitations already observed in the estimation of discount rates and future income.

The Residual Approaches

In the discussion of capitalization rates it was noted that Frederick Babcock recommended the use of different rates of capitalization for land and building returns. The argument over the use of split rates versus a single rate of capitalization has been carried on with varying degrees of intensity since Hoskold first advocated the use of two rates of interest for valuing speculative income in 1877.[48] The argument was carried on vigorously during the early years of formation of the American Institute of Real Estate Appraisers and found such appraisers as Mark Levy and Phillip W. Kniskern in favor of using a single rate, while Babcock, Register, and others held to the theory of the split rate.[49] The dispute appeared fairly well resolved in favor of the split rate at the time it was reopened in 1950 by Prof. Richard U. Ratcliff.[50] The question is of added significance in the present discussion because the use of split rates is associated with the so-called residual methods of capitalizing income. The presentation of these methods is accorded substantial attention in modern appraisal literature.

Frederick Babcock, the foremost advocate of the use of split rates, said:

> The various portions of a property's return flow sometimes have different characteristics which are predictable. For example, land can be assumed to have a return which extends indefinitely into the future, while buildings can be assumed to have terminable lives. Thus, if the investment qualities of the land and the building are separately considered and the land returns and building returns are capitalized at different rates, the resulting valuation can be expected to be more nearly correct.
>
> The term "split rate" or "fractional rate" is used to apply to the rates used in determining the present worths of the returns anticipated from or attributed to fractional parts of the property.[51]

It is evident from these quotations that Babcock's advocacy of the use of split rates was founded on two hypotheses: (1) that the returns from land and buildings are separable and (2) that generally a lower risk attaches to the portion of returns from land because land is more durable than buildings. From these two assumptions, he developed elaborate techniques for separating land and building incomes and capitalizing them at different rates. The techniques are quite simple in their basic conceptions.

In the so-called land-residual method, the appraiser assumes that the building has a value based upon its replacement cost and assigns returns to the building by applying a selected capitalization rate to the replacement cost (after depreciation) of the building. These returns subtracted from total net income to the property yield residual returns to the land, which are capitalized as a perpetuity to yield land value. The sum of the land value so calculated and the replacement cost of the building is assumed to equal the total value of the property.

In the so-called building-residual method, the land value is determined by comparison with sales of other land and an assumed capitalization rate is applied to the assumed land values. The so-called land returns are then deducted from total returns to yield residual returns to the building. These, in turn, are capitalized by applying a building rate to determine building value. As above, the sum of the land value determined by comparison and the building value calculated by capitalization is assumed to equal total property value. The land and building residual techniques can be illustrated simply in table 6–4.

Table 6-4. Comparison of Land- and Building-Residual Methods

Land-Residual Method	Building-Residual Method
Total net income to property	Total net income to property
less	less
returns to building	returns to land
(calculated as a percentage of the replacement cost of building less depreciation). Apply assumed building rate	(calculated as a percentage of the value of land obtained by comparison). Apply assumed land rate
equals	equals
residual returns to land. Capitalize as perpetuity at land rate (results in land value).	residual returns to building during building life. Capitalize at building rate (results in building value).
Sum of	Sum of
building value by replacement cost and land value by capitalization of residual returns	land value by comparison and building value by capitalization of residual returns
equals	equals
property value.	property value.

It will be seen that these two methods will provide approximately the same estimate of value if the same capitalization rates are used in capitalizing assumed land and building returns since the total net income is the controlling figure in both cases.

Although both of these methods are widely employed in appraisal practice in combination with split rates, there is only limited discussion of the rationale for the practice in appraisal literature. John C. Tredwell, writing in the syllabus for *Course I* of the American Institute of Real Estate Appraisers in 1938, criticized the arbitrary use of split rates by appraisers and called attention to the influence of widely differing rates for land and building returns upon the resultant property valuation estimate. The fifth edition of the institute text states that split rates on land and building "can be justified only where a higher capitalization rate on the building reflects the additional rate necessary to provide for the projected recapture of the investment in depreciating improvements."[52]

If this argument were accepted, split rates would be used on all improved properties. Again, the persistent preoccupation with "recapture" is allowed to obscure the basic argument of whether an investor would assign a different risk or capitalization rate to some arbitrary division of the total returns. Ratcliff maintains that the basic hypotheses supporting the use of split rates are in error and that the use of the land- and building-residual methods "may result in substantial valuation error." Criticizing the theory, he wrote:

> At the base of the issue is the strong implication of common appraisal terminology and method that the income stream produced by improved urban real estate is assignable in part to land and in part to building. At its worst, the presumption is that determinable fractions of the income are *produced* by each of the two physical components, land and building. Equally misleading is the notion that certain portions of the income stream are mathematical functions of the present values of land and of building.[53]

Ratcliff not only held that it was impractical to determine the fractions of real estate income produced by land and building, but also that investors do not in fact assign portions of the income stream to these two factors. He continued:

> The investor in a bond and the investor in income-producing real property are basically interested in only two items — what will the investment produce in net income and what will it be worth at the end of the income-producing period. The Appraisal formula in both cases is simple — the present value of the net income at the appropriate capitalization rate plus the present value of the Liquidation Value. The sum is the measure of dollars which the investor is justified in committing. . . .
> The risk to be reflected in capitalizing net income is the uncertainty in the

forecasts of the gross income and expenses of the enterprise. This risk affects with equal force each dollar in the net income prediction.[54]

Ratcliff's argument that the total income from land and building in combination is exposed to the same risk is not only logical, but is probably so regarded by most investors. Babcock appears to have recognized this fact in his presentation of cases illustrating the use of split rates, for he advocates the use of closely similar rates when the forecast is for a long building life. The mere fact that land returns may be considered of longer duration than building returns does not furnish grounds for determining the relative risk over the period of their life in combination. The acceptance of Babcock's views regarding the use of split rates would make it necessary to employ the residual approaches in most problems.

The method of valuation by the capitalization-of-income method recommended by Ratcliff has long been recognized in appraisal theory as the "property reversion" or "property residual" method. Charles B. Shattuck described this method as early as 1938 in the syllabus for *Course I* of the AIREA.[55] The evaluation and treatment of the residual techniques are substantially unchanged in the 1967 edition of the institute text. In discussing their application, the authors say noncommittally:

> The methods of capitalization produce different answers because the inherent assumptions as to recapture, income, and interest differ in each of three methods.
>
> It is therefore apparent that the only reason for preferring one of these residual techniques to another is to enable the appraiser to complete his appraisal process with those assumptions (as to behavior of income) which he can best support.[56]

The smorgasbord of capitalization methods presented in the institute text contributes to confusion in the appraisal process. The methods of discounting a future estimation of an income stream and a residual value are straightforward and clearly set forth in present value theory. The use of *level* annuity tables to estimate the value of incomes which are expected to *decline* represents a makeshift adjustment process, which is wholly unnecessary with the use of modern computational techniques.

The source of much of the confusion, as pointed out earlier, is that practicing real estate appraisers have adopted certain cost accounting concepts into their jargon, and they can't let go. Depreciation and recapture haunt them like Caesar's ghost! The obvious flexibility inherent in the range of capitalization techniques presented in chapters 18 and 19 of the institute text may, in the words of the authors, be "perplexing to the uninformed." The reader is told, "There are basic assumptions made by the appraiser in the selection of one or the other. All of them cannot be correctly applied to one property. Usually only one method will be consistent with the appraiser's thinking concerning future income behavior, interest requirements, and recapture re-quirements."[57] The appraiser finds himself presented with a kaleidoscope of capitalization methods, each of which results in a different estimate of value.

Reduced to its simplest terms, the property-residual method, which ap-pears to enjoy wide support among appraisers and to be advocated strongly by Ratcliff and others opposed to the use of split rates, can be illustrated as in table 6–5.

Table 6–5. Property-Residual Method

Total net income to property

(discounted by use of a single rate for the duration of estimated life of building)

plus

the reversionary value of land

(or land and improvements, if the forecasting period is shorter than the estimated building life)

equals

property value

The problem of estimating the residual value of land or of land and improvements emphasizes once again the advantages of shortening the time horizon for income expectation and residual value. The shorter the period of estimation, the greater the reliability which can be attributed to both the income forecast and the residual value assumed.

The 1967 edition of the institute text illustrates the variations in valuations resulting from the selection of alternative residual methods and capitalization tables. The authors present guidelines to the selection of the various capitali-zation approaches illustrated, which appear to boil down to the conclusion that the land-residual method is to be used in connection with a hypothetical building in highest and best use; the building-residual method is to be most generally employed where land value has been satisfactorily estimated; and the property-residual method is used when property is under long-term lease, where sufficient data are available to employ direct capitalization, or where economic life is short.[58]

This author, and most academicians, would argue that the property-resi-dual method is the most logical technique to be employed for valuing im-proved property and that there is no justification for the assignment of varying capitalization rates to land and buildings in the building-residual method except where ground leases are in effect. The land-residual technique has applicability only as an aid in the determination of highest and best use of vacant land. Even then, the method must be used with extreme care because of the large differences in land value which may result in small changes in estimated total income to land and building combined. As illustrated below, the after-tax cash-flow yield is superior to capitalization of before-tax income and is the best criterion for determining the highest and best use.[59]

Recent Criticisms of Capitalization-of-Income Methods

The capitalization-of-income method has come under increasing attack in recent years. In a recent article, Ratcliff argued that "the capitalization formulas do not even closely replicate or simulate the real world system by which market price of income property is established," and "it follows that the conventional residual capitalization formulas are unlikely to produce a value figure which is market value."[60] This author contends that Ratcliff's indictments of the conventional capitalization-of-income techniques may, to a degree, be likened to "beating a dead horse," since traditional capitalization-of-income methods have been largely supplanted by more sophisticated methods of capitalizing projected after-tax cash flows. These techniques, it is argued, are of key significance in the determination of investment values and under certain circumstances may closely approximate market values.

Cash-Flow Analysis and Rate of Return

After-Tax Cash-Flow Analysis   This author has argued before, here and elsewhere, that capitalization rates are determined in the market by investors and represent a weighted band-of-investment percentage rate reflecting the going mortgage interest rates and the investor's desired return on the equity and residual returns. It is the determination of the latter components which provides the Achilles heel in capitalization-rate determination.

It can be shown that the only significant measures of the return to an investor in real estate are represented by the after-tax cash flow retained by the investor calculated as a percentage yield on his actual cash outlay or equity investment. This measure can be represented by the following equation:

$$V - D = E = \sum_{t=1}^{n} \frac{R_t - I_t - A_t - T_t}{(1 + r)^t} + \frac{P_n - GT - UM}{(1 + r)^n}$$

where V = Value of property.

R_t = Annual net income in period t.
I_t = Interest paid on mortgage in period t.
A_t = Mortgage amortization in period t.
T_t = Income tax allowance in period t.
P_n = Sales price or residual in period ($t = n$).
GT = Capital gains tax.

UM = Unpaid mortgage.
r = Rate of return.
E = Equity.
D = Mortgage debt.

This equation can be used to estimate the value of any equity interest in real estate, given the appropriate estimates of rental or other income, mortgage payments, income taxes, residual sales prices, capital gains taxes, unpaid mortgage at the end of the projection period, and the all-important capitalization rate.[61] It is obvious that the value of the subject property would be represented by the sum of the calculated equity value and the mortgage debt on the property.

The perceptive reader will note that the value of the numerator of the first term of the equation will change each year, since the owner's interest payments change annually on the usual amortized level payment mortgage and his income tax liabilities, represented by T_t, will also change accordingly. Hence, it can be argued that there is no such thing as a level income attributable to real estate investment, except in the case of so-called net-net after-tax leases. This observation outlaws the use of many capitalization techniques recommended in appraisal literature, including the Ellwood techniques which are specifically adapted to level, constant returns.

It is assumed in the above formulation that the entire property investment is subject to the same degree or risk and, hence, a single equity capitalization rate r is generally used. However, most valuation problems of any degree of complexity are solved through the use of the computer and there is no reason why a different rate might not be applied to the residual or even to returns for portions of the life of the property if the appraiser felt this to be justified.

The formulation is highly flexible, as can be observed, for it can be used to estimate the value of E on the left side of the equation if the other values are given, or, conversely, it can be employed to determine the equity rate of return r where the other values are known, or the value of the residual $P_n - GT - UM$, where the expected returns, equity investment, and capitalization rate are known.

The significance of this observation is that, assuming the market data and assumed residual values identified in the above equation are available to the appraiser, he can solve the equation for the troublesome return on equity, which is the key to rate determination. Illustration of this technique will be shown in the concluding section of this chapter.

It can be argued that the determination of the elements in the cash-flow equation involves a considerable degree of subjective estimation. This, of course, is implicit in the capitalization-of-income approach. However, given this formulation and the computer programs for its rapid solution, the appraiser can experiment at length, testing the sensitivity of the resultant rates to changes in his input assumptions, and by using subjective probabilities,

159

converge upon an acceptable rate for the problem at hand. As will be pointed out later, this formulation and technique also provides a means by which the appraiser can test any assumptions in the marketplace concerning future implied appreciation or depreciation, reflected in the value of the residual term.

Higgins and Cunningham used a formulation similar to that above to point out that risk in real estate investment can be measured by the degree of change in expected return with changes in estimated cash flows.[62]

The cash-flow technique, which is illustrated below, promises to sharpen the analytical tools available to the appraiser and real estate investment counselor in comparing the risks in various property investments. This, of course, is the key unknown in the subjective determination of capitalization rates of multipliers. This concept of risk has its close parallel in the concept of variance, which is widely used in securities portfolio decision models.[63]

Highest and Best Use   The use of residual methods and split rates is inextricably related to the classical determination of highest and best use. Babcock described this as "that available use and program of future utilization of a parcel of land which produces the highest present land value."[64] Dorau and Hinman described it as "that use which brings the largest net return in money and amenities over a period of time."[65] More recently, Fisher and Fisher define it as "a designated use of a spatial unit which will allegedly produce the largest net income over a given period of time."[66] Authors of *The Appraisal of Real Estate* define it as "that use which will develop fully the potential utility of the site . . . the highest and best utilization program . . . which will produce the greatest future benefits to the owner of the land."[67] Babcock's definition of the term appears to be not only the simplest, but also the most valid of those considered, since the other definitions fail to consider explicitly the importance of the timing of the receipt of future returns which is the essence of Babcock's present-value-of-land concept.

Agreement with Babcock's definition of the concept of highest and best use, however, in no way diminishes the difficulty of applying this concept in a specific case. To estimate the present value of vacant land, it is necessary to hypothesize an improvement scheme, estimate the future returns to the property over some time period, assign a portion of these returns to amortization of the building investment by applying an assumed building rate to the estimated value or cost of the improvements, and, finally, capitalize the residual returns to land as a perpetuity by applying some "land rate." (See table 6–6.) Problems in estimating land use and returns and in selecting capitalization rates have already been discussed.

As in many other aspects of appraisal theory and practice, it seems appropriate to consider how a real-life investor would determine the highest and best use for a parcel of vacant land. Theoretically, the market price of land should reflect the competition among users for each parcel. However, the

Table 6-6. Illustration of Land-Residual Valuation Method

Program of Utilization	Franchise Hamburger Stand (building lease)	25,000# Office Building	50-Unit Apt. Building
Estimated annual stabilized income-net operating income before depreciation & financing costs	$ 50,000	$125,000	$ 85,000
Cost of improvements	$ 75,000	$435,000	$300,000
Mortgage terms available, including land at $300,000	0.08 for 15 yrs. for 60%	0.09 for 30 yrs. for 60%	0.09 for 30 yrs. for 66%
Estimated economic life (yrs.)	15	30	30
Capitalization rate applied to building investment	0.10	0.15	0.12
Amortization of building investment	0.1315 × $75m	0.1523 × $435m	0.1241 × $300m
Returns to building (yearly)	$ 9,863	$ 66,251	$ 37,230
Net annual returns to land	$ 40,137	$ 58,749	$ 47,770
Capitalize as perpetuity-land value	$401,370 (0.10)	$391,660 (0.15)	$398,083 (0.12)
Add back cost of improvements	$ 75,000	$435,000	$300,000
Estimated total property value	$476,370	$826,660	$698,083
Total cost of land and improvements	$375,000	$735,000	$600,000

land market is notably imperfect and values are observed to change abruptly with changes in land utilization. For these reasons, the investor will almost invariably test going market prices by hypothesizing various improvement schemes.

It has already been argued that the investor is primarily interested in maximizing his after-tax cash flow as a percentage of any required equity commitment. Assuming that a parking lot or agricultural use does not represent the best economic use of the property, the investor is faced with the decision as to that combination of land and improvements which will maximize the difference between the discounted value of his after-tax cash flows and the necessary outlays. This can be represented as follows:

161

Maximize over all $\{J_k\} = \displaystyle\sum_{t=1}^{N} \frac{NCF_{(i,k,t)}}{(1 + r)^t} + \frac{\text{Residual}}{(1 + r)^N} - \sum_{t=1}^{N} \frac{\text{Equity}_{(i,k,t)}}{(1 + r)^t}$
i, k, N

where:

J_k = Value to be determined.
N = Holding period: to be varied from 1 to t.
t = Maximum investment horizon.
i = Investor type.
k = Property-use type.
$NCF_{(i, k, t)}$ = Net cash flow in year t from property-use type k to be received by investor type i.
r = Discount rate = "cost of capital."
Residual = Net cash flow upon final disposition of property in year $t = N$.
$\text{Equity}_{(i, k, t)}$ = Required capital commitments in year t to property-use type k which will be paid by investor type i.

Theoretically and practically, the highest value for J_k should represent the highest and best use since it should result in the highest present land value. This approach to the determination of highest and best use has these advantages: (1) returns are viewed as cash returns after all taxes (the most realistic concept for any investor); (2) the allowances for interest and amortization can be obtained from going financial terms available in the financial markets; and (3) the algorithm used for the solution of the problem can allow for any program of uses anticipated in the future. It is necessary to assume that the investor's financial capabilities will match the requirements of the property, so to speak, in determining the highest and best use by this technique. This assumption is consistent with the general principle of competition of uses for urban land.

The use of after-tax cash flows to determine highest and best use also assumes that highest and best use will differ among investor types. After some reflection, it will be seen that this is logical and consistent with price theory and with the principle of competition of uses. This means, in effect, that in competition among users for individual sites, that investor will prevail whose investment calculus satisfies the equation above. Investors for whom tax shelter is highly important will bid for sites matching their needs.

Case Example of Highest- and Best-Use Valuation   Alternative techniques for determining the highest and best use can be illustrated by hypothesizing the existence of a one-hundred-foot by two-hundred-foot lot on the main street of a growing city. The property is presently unimproved and zoned for office building, commercial, or multi-family residential use.

The application of the traditional land-residual technique for determining highest and best use is shown in table 6–6.

It can be observed that, under the assumptions of overall capitalization rates of 10 percent for the hamburger stand, 15 percent for the office building, and 12 percent for the apartment building, applied to land and buildings, the estimated land value in table 6–6 is highest for the hamburger stand alternative. The capitalization rates assumed by the investor are of course critical in the determination of land values by the land-residual method.

An additional problem in using the traditional land-residual technique is that it does not provide any representation of the actual decision motivations and processes of investors and it presupposes that some unknown use for the land at the end of the economic life of the improvements will produce a flow of continuous, level returns to the land.

The cash-flow model illustrated in tables 6–7, 6–8, and 6–9 provides a detailed and realistic representation of the considerations influencing an investor in choosing among the three alternatives. The REAL III computer program used in estimating the after-tax returns in tables 6–7, 6–8, and 6–9 requires explicit assumptions by the investor concerning: (1) gross income and operating expenses, (2) costs of the project, (3) future selling prices, (4) tax rates applicable to income earned, (5) financing terms available, (6) alternative holding periods, (7) depreciation rates applicable, and (8) target rates of equity return for different projects.

The results of this analysis show the relative after-tax cash flows and rates of return for alternative uses and holding periods. It can be noted that the output of the program includes a "reinvestment rate" which indicates the rate of return which would be required in a new alternative investment to justify sale of the property and switching to a new investment. The reinvestment rate for the last year is always shown as 0.00%, since it is assumed that the property is sold in that year. The relevant J_k values for the three uses for the differing holding periods under the assumed equity rates are as shown in table 6–10. Negative values for J_k indicate that the returns to equity are *below* the target returns shown.

What do these calculations tell us about the highest and best use of this site? First, for a five- or ten-year holding period, none of the proposed uses would provide the target rates of return under the cost, financing, income, residual sales price, and tax assumptions used, since all J_k values are negative. Second, the office building represents the best of the three alternatives for either fifteen-, twenty-, twenty-five–, or thirty-year holding periods. The apartment building shows the highest J_k values for five- and ten-year holding. Third, the output tells the investor how much he can afford to invest in each alternative use in order to achieve his target rate of return. Table 6–11 shows the total cost, including land, which could be justified for specified holding periods for each of the three uses. These are *lower* than the total estimated

Table 6-7. Cash Flow for Hamburger Stand

	(1)	(2)	(3)	(4)	(5)	(6)	(7)	(8)	(9)
Year	Equity	Before-Tax Cash Flow	Before-Tax Residual	Rate of Return	Reinvest. Rate	After-Tax Cash Flow	After-Tax Residual	Rate of Return	Reinvest. Rate
1	150,000	$24,197	$123,963	- 1.32%	20.82%	$10,901	$124,238	-10.26%	7.98%
2	0	24,197	121,481	7.52	21.56	10,113	121,763	- 2.62	8.22
3	0	24,197	120,098	10.96	22.18	9,299	120,388	0.17	8.45
4	0	24,197	119,863	12.92	22.67	8,490	120,153	1.68	8.66
5	0	24,197	120,828	14.23	23.01	7,678	121,118	2.65	8.84
6	0	24,197	123,052	15.18	23.19	6,856	123,342	3.35	8.99
7	0	24,197	126,603	15.91	23.22	6,276	126,893	3.90	9.08
8	0	24,197	131,551	16.47	23.10	5,647	131,841	4.37	9.11
9	0	24,197	137,977	16.91	22.86	4,966	138,267	4.76	9.08
10	0	24,197	145,968	17.25	22.51	4,229	146,258	5.09	9.00
11	0	24,197	155,620	17.52	22.09	3,430	155,910	5.37	8.88
12	0	24,197	167,038	17.73	21.62	2,540	167,338	5.61	8.72
13	0	24,197	180,336	17.90	21.12	1,571	180,636	5.81	8.54
14	0	24,197	195,640	18.02	20.62	522	195,940	5.98	8.35
15	0	24,197	213,087	18.11	0.00	- 615	213,387	6.13	0.00

164

Table 6-8. Cash Flow for Fifty-Unit Apartment Building

	(1)	(2)	(3)	(4)	(5)	(6)	(7)	(8)	(9)
Year	Equity	Before-Tax Cash Flow	Before-Tax Residual	Rate of Return	Reinvest. Rate	After-Tax Cash Flow	After-Tax Residual	Rate of Return	Reinvest. Rate
1	$204,000	$46,764	$159,989	1.51%	29.26%	27,892	160,279	- 8.29%	14.82%
2	0	46,764	152,436	12.28	30.72	27,310	152,726	1.10	15.27
3	0	46,764	145,361	16.44	32.23	26,735	145,651	4.56	15.73
4	0	46,764	138,784	18.77	33.78	26,167	139,074	6.43	16.20
5	0	46,764	132,732	20.32	35.34	25,593	133,031	7.63	16.66
6	0	46,764	127,232	21.44	36.90	25,008	127,532	8.48	17.11
7	0	46,764	122,315	22.29	38.43	24,422	122,615	9.14	17.55
8	0	46,764	118,013	22.95	39.89	23,830	118,313	9.66	17.96
9	0	46,764	114,365	23.48	41.24	23,231	114,665	10.08	18.33
10	0	46,764	111,411	23.90	42.43	22,620	111,711	10.44	18.66
11	0	46,764	109,198	24.23	43.42	21,995	109,498	10.74	18.91
12	0	46,764	107,775	24.50	44.15	21,622	108,075	11.00	19.07
13	0	46,764	107,197	24.71	44.59	21,214	107,497	11.23	19.10
14	0	46,764	107,525	24.88	44.70	20,767	107,825	11.43	19.00
15	0	46,764	108,826	25.02	44.48	20,278	109,126	11.61	18.77
16	0	46,764	111,173	25.13	43.91	19,744	111,473	11.77	18.42
17	0	46,764	114,647	25.22	43.02	19,160	114,947	11.90	17.95
18	0	46,764	119,336	25.29	41.85	18,516	119,640	12.01	17.39
19	0	46,764	125,337	25.34	40.45	17,794	125,647	12.11	16.76
20	0	46,764	132,758	25.38	38.89	17,003	133,068	12.19	16.08
21	0	46,764	141,714	25.42	37.22	16,139	142,024	12.26	15.38
22	0	46,764	152,334	25.44	35.51	15,193	152,644	12.32	14.67
23	0	46,764	164,758	25.46	33.82	14,159	164,779	12.36	14.02
24	0	46,764	179,140	25.48	32.18	13,028	178,635	12.40	13.42
25	0	46,764	195,649	25.49	30.64	11,791	194,589	12.42	12.87
26	0	46,764	214,469	25.50	29.22	10,437	212,823	12.44	12.36
27	0	46,764	235,803	25.50	27.94	8,957	233,538	12.45	11.91
28	0	46,764	259,873	25.51	26.79	7,337	256,959	12.46	11.50
29	0	46,764	286,920	25.51	25.79	5,544	283,327	12.46	11.14
30	0	46,764	317,212	25.51	0.00	3,545	312,909	12.45	0.00

165

Table 6-9. Cash Flow for Office Building

Year	(1) Equity	(2) Before-Tax Cash Flow	(3) Before-Tax Residual	(4) Rate of Return	(5) Reinvest. Rate	(6) After-Tax Cash Flow	(7) After-Tax Residual	(8) Rate of Return	(9) Reinvest. Rate
1	294,000	$82,419	$235,640	9.37%	34.98%	$45,816	$235,950	- 4.48%	17.05%
2	0	82,419	222,095	19.28	37.12	44,967	222,405	3.75	17.79
3	0	82,419	209,280	23.22	39.39	44,135	209,590	6.84	18.57
4	0	82,419	197,214	25.51	41.81	43,317	197,524	8.55	19.39
5	0	82,419	185,918	27.06	44.35	42,509	186,228	9.68	20.24
6	0	82,419	175,416	28.18	47.02	41,703	175,732	10.52	21.13
7	0	82,419	165,738	29.04	49.77	40,881	166,058	11.18	22.05
8	0	82,419	156,914	29.69	52.59	40,060	157,234	11.71	22.99
9	0	82,419	148,982	30.20	55.42	39,235	149,302	12.16	23.93
10	0	82,419	141,981	30.60	58.19	38,403	142,301	12.54	24.85
11	0	82,419	135,958	30.91	60.82	37,559	136,278	12.87	25.74
12	0	82,419	130,962	31.15	63.22	37,115	131,282	13.16	26.52
13	0	82,419	127,051	31.33	65.26	36,630	127,371	13.41	27.14
14	0	82,419	124,288	31.48	66.85	36,100	124,608	13.63	27.58
15	0	82,419	122,742	31.59	67.88	35,519	123,062	13.83	27.79
16	0	82,419	122,491	31.67	68.25	34,885	122,811	14.00	27.76
17	0	82,419	123,620	31.74	67.94	34,190	123,940	14.14	27.47
18	0	82,419	126,224	31.79	66.93	33,431	126,544	14.27	26.92
19	0	82,419	130,406	31.83	65.26	32,600	130,726	14.37	26.15
20	0	82,419	136,281	31.85	63.04	31,692	136,601	14.47	25.18
21	0	82,419	143,976	31.88	60.38	30,698	144,296	14.54	24.08
22	0	82,419	153,630	31.89	57.43	29,611	153,950	14.61	22.87
23	0	82,419	165,395	31.90	54.32	28,401	165,725	14.66	21.62
24	0	82,419	179,440	31.91	51.18	27,060	179,770	14.70	20.38
25	0	82,419	195,948	31.92	48.13	25,593	194,778	14.73	19.41
26	0	82,419	215,122	31.92	45.24	23,989	211,411	14.76	18.69
27	0	82,419	237,185	31.93	42.58	22,234	232,942	14.78	17.69
28	0	82,419	262,380	31.93	40.16	20,314	257,667	14.79	16.78
29	0	82,419	290,975	31.93	38.00	18,214	285,737	14.80	15.98
30	0	82,419	323,261	31.93	0.00	15,918	317,446	14.81	0.00

Table 6-10. Values of J_k for Three Alternative Uses and Holding Periods [a]

Hamburger stand—equity yield 0.08

Year	Sum of disc. NCF	(plus)	Disc. residual	(minus)	Equity	(equals)	J_k Value
5	$37,611.55	(plus)	$82,430.88	(minus)	$150,000	(equals)	-$29,957
Year 10	Sum of disc. NCF 53,087.96	(plus)	Disc. residual 67,745.75	(minus)	Equity 150,000	(equals)	J_k Value - 29,166
Year 15	Sum of disc. NCF 56,129.20	(plus)	Disc. residual 67,268.48	(minus)	Equity 150,000	(equals)	J_k Value - 26,602

Apartment building—equity yield 0.10

Year	Sum of disc. NCF	(plus)	Disc. residual	(minus)	Equity	(equals)	J_k Value
5	$101,776.67	(plus)	$82,601.78	(minus)	$204,000	(equals)	-$19,621
10	158,115.45	(plus)	43,069.43	(minus)	204,000	(equals)	- 2,815
15	189,181.93	(plus)	26,123.90	(minus)	204,000	(equals)	11,305
20	206,036.62	(plus)	19,779.71	(minus)	204,000	(equals)	21,816
25	214,076.08	(plus)	17,959.79	(minus)	204,000	(equals)	28,035
30	216,696.44	(plus)	17,932.36	(minus)	204,000	(equals)	30,628

Office building—equity yield 0.12

Year	Sum of disc. NCF	(plus)	Disc. residual	(minus)	Equity	(equals)	J_k Value
5	$159,818.47	(plus)	$105,670.77	(minus)	$294,000	(equals)	-$28,510
10	242,131.83	(plus)	45,817.11	(minus)	294,000	(equals)	- 6,051
15	284,726.25	(plus)	22,482.97	(minus)	294,000	(equals)	13,209
20	306,814.17	(plus)	14,160.98	(minus)	294,000	(equals)	26,975
25	317,486.58	(plus)	11,457.49	(minus)	294,000	(equals)	34,944
30	321,851.88	(plus)	10,595.69	(minus)	294,000	(equals)	38,447

[a]Based upon after-tax cash flows, residual values, and equities shown in tables 6-7, 6-8, and 6-9.

Table 6-11. Rates of Return for Alternative Uses and Holding Periods and Estimated Total Costs and Equities to Achieve Target Rates of Return

Hamburger stand:			
Holding Period in Years	Rate of Return	Reinvestment Rate	Equity
10	5.09%	9.00%	$150,000
15	6.13	0.00	150,000
Total cost to achieve target 8% rate of return for 15-year holding = $337,875			$135,150
Apartment building:			
10	10.44	18.66	204,000
15	11.61	18.77	204,000
20	12.19	16.08	204,000
30	12.45	0.00	204,000
Total cost to achieve target 10% rate of return for 30-year holding = $663,877			$225,718
Office building:			
10	12.54	24.85	294,000
15	13.83	27.79	294,000
20	14.47	25.18	294,000
30	14.81	0.00	294,000
Total cost to achieve target 12% rate of return for 30-year holding = $825,426			$330,170

costs of land and improvements indicated in table 6–6 for the hamburger stand, but *higher* for the office building and apartment building. This means that, assuming fifteen-year holding for the hamburger stand and thirty-year holding for the other uses, the investor could pay an amount above the original estimated costs for the apartment and office building and still receive his target returns on equity of 10 percent and 12 percent. Specifically, he could incur cost overruns on land and/or building costs of $63,877 on the apartment house and of $90,426 on the office building for thirty-year holding and still achieve his target rates of return. Conversely, he would have to reduce his outlays for the hamburger stand. *Assuming that his estimate of building costs was accurate, these numbers represent the excess over (or amount less than) the assumed land cost of $300,000 which an investor could pay.* The higher J_k value for the office building indicates that an investor buying the land for office building development would probably be the highest bidder and might pay as much as $390,000 for the land. Fourth, it can be seen in table 6–10 that the longer the assumed holding period, the more important the net cash flow term in the equation becomes relative to the residual term. From table 6–10 and the computer output, the investor can estimate the sensitivity of the J_k values to changed assumptions about residual sales prices and/or income. The computer program permits the appraiser or investment analyst to alter any of these assumptions to test the outcome, with a computer computation time of less than twenty seconds on the CDC 6400 for a complete rerun of any three alternatives. Fifth, the office building appears to represent the highest and best use among the alternatives considered. Further, the high reinvestment rates shown for the office building suggest that it would represent a desirable long-term holding, assuming, of course, the realization of the incomes and residual sale prices indicated. Obviously, conclusions with respect to highest and best use will vary with the assumed target rates of return on equity. A shift in assumed equity yields on the apartment and office building investments from 10 percent and 12 percent to 12 percent and 15 percent, respectively, would result in higher J_k values for the apartment building. This emphasizes the sensitivity of the J_k values to changes in the investor's desired equity yields.

The determination of highest and best use is the product of the exercise of judgment and analytical skill. Since this process involves a forecast of a wide range of alternatives over an uncertain future for most properties, the outcome must represent an opinion, not a fact to be found. Recently developed after-tax cash-flow programs represent a major refinement in techniques for determining highest and best use. Frederick Babcock's classical definition of highest and best use as that use resulting in the highest present land value is theoretically valid. However, traditional techniques for determination of highest and best use by the land residual method may prove misleading and inaccurate.

Capitalization — The Flexible Approach The variation in value estimates resulting from the use of conventional band-of-investment methods and the Ellwood technique was discussed earlier in this chapter.

The diversity and flexibility in the use of the capitalization-of-income approach can be further illustrated by comparing the results of the land-, building-, and property-residual techniques, using the data in tables 6–7, 6–8, and 6–9. It can be noted from table 6–12 that the value estimates by the building-residual method are very similar to those shown for the land-residual method in table 6–6. The essential difference is that in the building-residual method the land value is assumed to be represented by the market offering price and the residual returns to the improvements are capitalized over the expected economic life of the buildings. The same capitalization rates are used for comparative purposes. As in the land-residual method, the estimated building values are highly sensitive to changes in the income expectancy and to difference in the capitalization rates employed.

The values of the three hypothetical properties under the property-residual method are shown in table 6–13. The values by this technique are almost identical to those under the building-residual method. This will always be the case when the same capitalization rates are employed, since both methods capitalize the same net income stream over the identical building lives at the same assumed before-tax overall rates.[68] The reader may be interested to compare the valuations of the three hypothetical uses of the subject property

Table 6-12. Illustration of Building-Residual Method

Program of Utilization	Franchise Hamburger Stand (building lease)	25,000# Office Building	50-Unit Apt. Building
Established annual stabilized income (net operating income before depreciation & financing)	$ 50,000	$125,000	$ 85,000
Less land returns, based upon $300,000 market price	0.10 × $300m $ 30,000	0.15 × $300m $ 45,000	0.12 × $300m $ 36,000
Equals residual annual building returns	$ 20,000	$ 80,000	$ 49,000
Capitalized over estimated economic life of building	0.10 for 15 yrs.	0.15 for 30 yrs.	0.12 for 30 yrs.
Present value annuity	7.606 × $20,000	6.566 × $80,000	8.055 × $49,000
Equals building value	$152,120	$525,280	$394,695
Add land value	$300,000	$300,000	$300,000
Estimated property value	$452,120	$825,280	$694,695

Table 6-13. Illustration of Property-Residual Method[a]

Program of Utilization	Franchise Hamburger Stand (building lease)	25,000# Office Building	50-Unit Apt. Building
Established annual stabilized income	$ 50,000	$125,000	$ 85,000
Present value of annuity	0.10 for 15 yrs. 7.606 × $50,000 = $380,300	0.15 for 30 yrs. 6.566 × $125,000 = $820,750	0.12 for 30 yrs. 8.055 × $85,000 = $684,675
Add residual land value	0.10 for 15 yrs. 0.2394 × $300,000 = $71,820	0.15 for 30 yrs. 0.0151 × $300,000 = $4,530	0.12 for 30 yrs. 0.0334 × $300,000 = $10,020
Total estimated value by property residual method	$452,120	$825,280	$694,695

[a]See table 6-6 for further details and illustration of land-residual method.

THE CAPITALIZATION-OF-INCOME METHOD

Table 6-14. Comparison of Ellwood Before-Tax Valuations and VALUEL After-Tax Cash-Flow Valuations for Three Hypothetical Properties[a]

Hamburger stand:		
	Ellwood Valuation before Tax	Cash-Flow Valuation after Tax
R = 0.10781	Y = 0.10 = $463,778.87	r = 0.08 = $337,875
R = 0.12003	Y = 0.13 = 416,562.53	r = 0.10 = 306,474

Office building:		
	Ellwood Valuation before Tax	Cash-Flow Valuation after Tax
R = 0.11758	Y = 0.15 = $1,063,105.97	r = 0.12 = $825,426
R = 0.15390	Y = 0.24 = 812,215.72	r = 0.15 = $729,651

Apartment building:		
	Ellwood Valuation before Tax	Cash-Flow Valuation after Tax
R = 0.10399	Y = 0.12 = $817,386.29	r = 0.10 = $663,877
R = 0.12534	Y = 0.18 = 678,155.42	r = 0.12 = 610,800

[a]See table 6-1 for details of financing. Holding periods assumed—hamburger stand: 15 years; office building and apartment building: 30 years. The Ellwood rates are calculated from this formula:

$$R = Y - MC + App/Dep \times 1/S_{\overline{n|}}$$

by the Ellwood method using imputed before-tax equity yields, with the results of the after-tax cash-flow method, shown in table 6–14.

The purchase price is assumed to be the total cost of land and improvements as shown in table 6–6. The before-tax residuals in tables 6–7, 6–8, and 6–9 are used to estimate the percentage depreciation in selling price in the Ellwood calculations. The after-tax target equity yields are lower than the before-tax yields, as would be expected. Changes in these valuations would result from changes in the capitalization rates, estimated incomes, or building lives. The after-tax cash-flow technique resulted in significantly lower valuations than for any of the other capitalization methods using before-tax incomes. The basic reasons for the difference, of course, lie in the fact that after-tax cash flows are lower than before-tax net incomes. Both actual and target after-tax yields will generally be lower than those calculated on a before-tax basis except in circumstances where tax losses are offset against other taxable income. It may be seriously questioned whether investors are prepared to specify the difference between before-tax and after-tax equity yields in view of the complex tax implications of real estate investment. This represents a further argument in favor of using after-tax cash-flow yields in the determination of the investment value of income properties.

None of the capitalization techniques examined provides reliable clues to the estimation of the target equity yield rate, the principal factor influencing differences in valuations in table 6–14. The after-tax cash-flow method of valuation permits accurate calculation of past equity returns and is the most reliable method of estimating future yields. Computer techniques used in after-tax cash-flow analysis also permit tests of the sensitivity of future equity yields to changes in incomes, expenses and financing terms assumed. Since investors' target equity yields will vary with the expected sensitivity of cash flows and yields to such changes, the technique can serve to "bracket" desired equity yields.

Current appraisal theory recognizes the flexibility inherent in alternative capitalization techniques, but offers limited guidance in the specific selection of techniques or in the determination of the all-important equity yield. Alfred A. Ring, in his book *The Valuation of Real Estate*, concludes, "In appraisal practice, only one method of capitalization can logically be applied. The selection of the appropriate method of capitalization should not be made haphazardly, nor should the choice be influenced by attempts to obtain high, low, or conservative value estimates. Rather it is the appraiser's duty to study earning-to-price relationships at which comparable properties have exchanged in the open market and to use rates as well as methods of capitalization which reflect typical market practices and operations."[69] These observations, and the examples in chapter 18 of his book and those illustrated here, underscore the flexibility and diversity in capitalization-of-income techniques and their basic reliance upon the market as a test of their relevance.

The chapter which follows explores the use of the gross-multiplier method, which provides the "earnings-to-price" data referred to above as the basic link to the market place.

Summary and Conclusions

This examination of the capitalization-of-income method has drawn attention to the development of the theory of income capitalization by economists as a phase of the theory of interest and capital value and to their general assumption that the ideal measure of capitalized income value was to be found in the market price. Significant techniques for the application-of-capitalization theory to appraisal work were developed by Irving Fisher and by Craigue and Grimes and achieved an important place in appraisal theory as a result of the writings of Frederick M. Babcock in the early 1930s.

It was established by a series of examples that the application of the capitalization-of-income method in appraisal of real estate requires important assumptions, which, in many cases, are based upon the wide exercise of judgment. The most important of these assumptions are concerned with the selection of a rate or rates of discount, the estimation of the income stream and the duration of building life, and the estimation of the reversionary value of land at the end of building life.

Examination of appraisal writings revealed general agreement that capitalization rates should be obtained from the market. In the simplest case considered, it was noted that known, riskless, future incomes can be evaluated by reference to the selling prices of bonds or other income-bearing property with similar prospects and market conditions. In such cases, however, it was concluded that the capitalization-of-income method becomes a roundabout version of the market-comparison method. It was found that the discount rate is normally a conceptual rate applied to estimates of uncertain future incomes and that there is no ideal method for obtaining such risk rates from the market because of the diversity of real property and its income prospects and because of the intangible nature of capitalization rates. Consideration of grid charts and other mechanical aids used in the selection of rates resulted in the conclusion that the selection of capitalization rates is a highly subjective process and that difficulties in selection of rates can account for wide variations in estimates of value for an identical income stream.

The estimation of the future income stream also involved equally hazardous predictions. Such a forecast requires the determination of future business conditions and price levels as well as advance determination of the physical life of improvements. Examination of the results of selected empirical studies revealed that income streams do not follow the neat lines of prediction frequently employed in the use of income premises and other types of income forecasts.

Although the estimation of the reversionary value of land is of less overall significance in the capitalization-of-income method, particularly for long-lived properties, it was concluded that the commonly employed assumption that the market value of land will remain constant is fully as arbitrary as the assumptions necessary in estimating discount rates and future income.

The three basic problems of estimation in the capitalization-of-income method discussed above are all integrally related. The selection of a rate of discount will, of course, depend upon the degree of optimism in the estimation of the income or reversionary value. This interrelationship imparts a high degree of flexibility to the processes of discounting estimated future incomes.

A review of the controversy over split rates outlined the arguments for and against their use and drew attention to the nature of the assumptions underlying the so-called land-residual and building-residual methods. Although some of these assumptions will be discussed in further detail in connection with the estimation of depreciation in chapter 8, there appear to be good grounds for concluding that investors do not generally attribute different degrees of risk to fractions of the total income from property in their judgment of its value. This conclusion rules out the general acceptability of the land- and building-residual methods. Attention was drawn to the confusing and illogical presentation of variations of these methods in some of the more recent appraisal texts.

A description and review of several alternative capitalization techniques revealed that wide differences in value estimates result from their selective use. It appears to be true that many users of these alternative methods are not fully aware of the assumptions underlying the techniques and the effect upon valuation estimates of the selection of one or the other of them.

The relationship between the capitalization-of-income method and the market-comparison method is very close in theory. In practice, however, the capitalization-of-income method not only requires the exercise of highly subjective judgments for the determination of its key unknowns, but in its application requires extremely hypothetical assumptions regarding the valuation processes of individuals. The result is that a method which appeals to economists and appraisal writers as the only correct and logical method in theory provides a framework in practice for what many have referred to as "sophisticated guesswork."

Growing criticism of the subjective flexibility inherent in the capitalization-of-income method has led some academicians and others to advocate that the method be rejected in its entirety. Meanwhile, however, major modifications in the technique have been made possible through the substitution of the concept of after-tax cash flow for the previously used net income before depreciation, financing cost, and income taxes. This method, which has close parallels in the field of corporate security valuation, has provided a more realistic dimension to one of the key inputs in the capitalization-of-income method. The growing use of the computer in calculating rates of return and valuations has provided a flexible and efficient aid to the appraiser in determining probable investment values under varying income, financing, and tax assumptions. These techniques have opened up avenues for the appraiser to employ probability analysis in assigning values to real property, a subject which will be considered in more detail in chapter 10. They have also opened up new and fruitful approaches to the determination of equity capitalization rates.

The theory underlying the after-tax cash-flow technique and valuation method meets the tests of logic and of the market place. As long as the future remains uncertain, any technique which relies upon the estimation of incomes, expenses, and future sales prices will represent a judgmental estimate. As Van Horne says, "The really difficult problems are in specifying the appropriate degree of risk for an investment opportunity and in being consistent in these specifications from project to project and over time."[70]

After-tax cash-flow analysis provides a measure of return to investment which is both consistent and relevant. Modern computer techniques make it possible to test the sensitivity of this measure of the rate of return to alternative input assumptions and to weighted probabilities of their realization. The resulting valuations can then be compared with those in the marketplace, which provides the final testing ground for valuation estimates.

GROSS–RENT MULTIPLIERS

Gross-rent multipliers express a relationship between gross rentals (monthly or annual) and estimated capital value. They are used as a short cut to the capitalization method of estimating value. A gross-rent multiplier is derived from the principle that an average percentage relationship exists between the sum of dollar allowances for property taxes, management expense, depreciation, and maintenance costs and the capital value for particular classes of property.

Origins

The method of developing gross-rent multipliers was set forth in the 1924 edition of *Real Estate Principles and Practices* by Benson and North as follows:

> It is generally recognized that if property is suitably improved its rental is a safe guide to value. . . . The net rental is of course the amount of net income received by the owner and this sum capitalized at an appropriate percentage gives the value. . . .
>
> A shorter method than the foregoing is that of estimating the value from the amount of the *gross* rents. The following table gives percentages of gross rents to values of some standard building types.

Dwellings	12%
Cold-water flats	12% to 15%
Steam-heated flats	15% to 20%
Elevator apartments	18% to 25%
Loft buildings	15% to 20%
Office buildings	20% to 25%

> The amount of service given to the tenants must be considered in determining which rate to use for any particular property. . . . The necessity of care in capitalizing gross rents to get a value is apparent.
>
> Sometimes a rough estimate is made by traders by multiplying the gross rent by a certain number. Thus the value of an ordinary apartment is approximated at five, five and one half, or six times the (annual) rent.[1]

The technique Zangerle described in the 1924 edition of his *Principles of Real Estate Appraising* is as follows:[2]

> Appraisers frequently adopt a rough and ready method of deducing a value of improved and fully rented property through capitalizing monthly

rentals. The most common method as to residences is to consider a month's rental as 1 percent of the value. For example, a rental of $75.00 a month would probably indicate a capital value of $7500. This method pre-supposes that 12 percent per annum is sufficient return to continue the investment of capital in the industry, which as to 1919 and 1920 conditions was entirely insufficient. A prominent real estate expert after a study of the problem finds that a gross rental of 15 percent is a proper charge made up as follows:

2.30%	Taxes	
1.70%	Management	
2 %	Depreciation	
2 %	Maintenance	
7 %	Interest	
15 %	Gross Annual Allowance	
1¼ %	Gross Monthly Allowance	

Zangerle demonstrated that the capitalization of any given monthly rental at 1¼ percent as a perpetuity will result in an estimated capital value which will equal eighty times the monthly rental. Zangerle illustrated the derivation of *multiplying factors*, as he termed them, in table 7–1.[3]

Table 7-1. Rough Table of Computing Capital Value from Given Rentals

Monthly Rental	Yearly Allowances	Monthly Allowance	Multiplying Factor Monthly	Capital Value
$75	12%	1 %	100	$7,500
75	15	1-1/4	80	6,000
75	20	1-2/3	60	4,500
75	24	2	50	3,750

Source: John A. Zangerle, *Principles of Real Estate Appraising* (Cleveland: Stanley McMichael, 1924), p. 56.

The gross-rent multipliers are in actuality capitalization rates to be applied to gross income as distinct from net income. They are readily calculated as the reciprocals of gross capitalization rates. Thus, a gross capitalization rate of 12 percent is equivalent to an annual gross-rent multiplier of 8.3 times, while a gross capitalization rate of 20 percent is equivalent to an annual multiplier of 5 times. Annual gross-rent multipliers can be readily converted to monthly multipliers by multiplying them by 12, the number of months in a year.

The use of gross-rent multipliers has been criticized by many appraisal theorists and condoned by others. Their use, however, has persisted, and gross-rent multipliers are widely employed in the market as a means of estimating capital value from gross rentals. One of the principal reasons for their continued use is that gross rentals are more generally ascertainable than net income. In addition, the capitalization process is much simpler than generally advocated for the capitalization of net income.

Use in Security Analysis

It is of some interest to note that multipliers are widely used in the investment field. Benjamin Graham's explanation of the use of multipliers sheds interesting light on the use of the capitalization process in common-stock evaluation:

> The ideal form of common-stock analysis leads to a valuation of the issue which can be compared with the current price to determine whether or not the security is an attractive purchase. This valuation, in turn, would ordinarily be found by estimating the average earnings over a period of years in the *future* and then multiplying that estimate by an appropriate "capitalization factor." As a concrete example, an analyst might have estimated the future average earnings of General Motors in 1958 at about $3.50 per share versus average past earnings of $2.73. If he applied a "standard multiplier" of 13 to these expected earnings he would obtain a current valuation of about 45, as against an average price of 43 and a low price of 34 in that year. He would then have called the stock undervalued at its lower levels during 1958. But he could hardly have anticipated that its net earnings would advance to a record of $1.6 billion in 1963, or $5.50 per share, and its price to a lofty 102 in 1964.[4]

Variations in the multiplier approach to common-stock valuation are found in an article in the *Analysts Journal*:

> Generally speaking, however, we believe that the approach described here can be successfully employed in estimating the present investment value of most electrical utility common stocks. That is to say, the current or prospective near-term dividend might be capitalized at, say, 6%, and the expected increase in earnings over perhaps the next five years capitalized at some considerably higher figure. *Or, alternatively the earnings level expectable in two to three years might be used with a multiplier of from 12 to 14 times* [italics mine].[5]

Gross Multipliers in Recent Theory

Babcock made short shrift of the multiplier technique: "Another form of short-cut sometimes used in practical valuation is the multiplying of estimated gross revenues by selected factors. . . . The method should not be used even for quick estimating except for very typical properties. It ignores the importance of the expense ratio. . . . The principal objection to the method is, then, that it treats gross revenues rather than net incomes."[6]

Charles Shattuck in 1938 held that "the gross income multiple or conversion factor" was one of four basic methods in the capitalization-of-income process.

> The gross income multiple, which is sometimes called a conversion factor, is merely a ratio of rent to sales price. . . .
> This method of converting income to a capital value estimate is the simplest of many capitalization processes and has its most general use in the appraisal of the single-family residential property. However, it is also commonly used in the appraisal of multi-family residential properties such as apartments, both furnished and unfurnished. . . .
> A study of sales prices and rents obtaining at any time will indicate a similarity of the ratio of rent to sales price, or the gross income multiple, for properties of the same kind in the same general area. . . . It is important that the compared properties be similar in every essential respect.[7]

The 1951 edition of the AIREA text omitted any reference to the use of gross-rent multipliers as one of the basic capitalization methods and expressed a strong note of caution on the use of such multipliers: "Multipliers are useful only as general guides, and chiefly in tests of comparability in the market data approach. They must be used with great care and only under highly comparable conditions as to age, size, gross income ratio, etc. Variations in local conditions and the rate of return expected may give grounds for sale prices and values varying widely from the commonly accepted multipliers of income."[8]

It is significant that the fifth edition of the institute text devotes considerably more space to the discussion of gross-rent multipliers, a recognition of the fact that the gross-multiplier technique has become increasingly used in the appraisal of income properties. The authors reiterate, however, that gross multipliers are useful only as "general guides."[9]

Trends in Gross Multipliers

Winnick has pointed out that gross-rent multipliers are so generally relied upon in real estate market dealings for certain classes of property that market prices tend to cluster around a relatively narrow range in the gross-rent multipliers.[10] Winnick's summary of the long-run trends in gross-rent multipliers for major classes of properties appears in table 7–2. He called particular attention to the gradual decline in the gross-rent multiplier over the past half-century, explaining this as mainly resulting from the long-run decline in the ratio of net to gross income, reflecting increasing taxes and expenses as well as a tendency for increased services to be included in gross rentals. Winnick also noted a tendency for gross-rent multipliers to fall during depressions and rise during periods of business prosperity. This tendency is apparently attributable to the more optimistic capitalization of a given level of rentals during periods of prosperity.

Table 7-2. Gross-Rent Multiplier at Bench Mark Dates 1890–1949

Year	Single-Family	Tenement	Apartment House	Other
1890–1892	14.1	9.5	10.1	
1900	12.5	9.1		
1905	11.1			
1912		10.5	10.6	
1912	11.0		9.9	
1912	11.1		9.3	
1913	12.1		9.0	
1913	11.8			
1919	9.8			
1923			6.2	
1925		8.0	6.9	
1936	8.3			
1937			7.5	
1937–1938	8.3			
1937–1940		4.5		6.3
1939	7.4			
1940			7.2	
1940–1941	8.6			
1941	7.9		4.1	
1941		5.1		6.5
1941–1942			5.5	
1942		5.1		6.6
1943		3.2	4.8	
1948	10.1		8.3	
1949		4.6	5.6	

Source: Louis Winnick, "Long-Run Changes in the Valuation of Real Estate by Gross Rents," *Appraisal Journal* 20 (October 1952): 487, table 1. Footnotes are omitted above.

Winnick pointed out that various concepts of gross income are employed in the development of gross-income multipliers. In some cases, actual gross rentals for the current year are employed, while in others a forecast of so-called stabilized gross rentals is used. Obviously, these variations in the precise definition of gross rentals make it necessary to exercise great caution in the comparison of gross-rent multipliers. It is important to recall in interpreting the data in table 7–2 that federal and state rent controls were operative during and immediately following World War II.

The basic assumption in the use of gross-rent multipliers as a means of establishing most probable selling prices is that properties with the same gross income will have the same net-income expectancy or future cash flow to the investor and hence will have the same dollar value per dollar of expected future cash flow. This underlines the most important criterion in the use of this technique; namely, that the properties must be similar in their future cash-flow expectancy. This in turn implies that the ratio of net income to gross income should be the same and that properties should have the same outlook for gross income and expenses, including property taxes. Viewed in this light, it can be seen that the gross-multiplier method is a variation of the market-comparison technique of valuation. The use of the gross-multiplier method makes it possible to compare properties which are otherwise similar, but may be of varying size or quality and have different gross dollar incomes.

There is considerable evidence that the ratio of operating expenses to gross income is closely similar for the same type of property in the same general area. Table 7–3 summarizes the gross-rent multipliers which have prevailed for unfurnished apartment buildings in the San Francisco Bay area over the past twenty years. It has been observed that the gross-rent multipliers have varied with the age, condition, and location of apartment properties. The most significant observation, however, is that the gross-rent multiplier is

Table 7-3. Apartment House Gross-Rent Multipliers, San Francisco Bay Area, 1950–1970

Year	Mean	Range
1950–1951[a]	8.7	7.2–10.2
1951–1952[b]	7.7	6.0–12.0
1952–1953[b]	8.5	5.0–12.0
1953–1954[c]	6.5	4.9–11.7
1954–1955[c]	6.4	4.5– 7.8
1955–1956[c]	7.0	5.3– 8.6
1956–1957[c]	7.1	6.8– 8.5
1957–1958[c]	8.0	6.4– 9.7
1958–1959[c]	7.3	6.1– 9.6
1959–1960[c]	7.7	5.4– 9.7
1960–1961[d]	7.9	5.1– 9.9
1961–1962[e]	7.9	5.7– 9.0
1962–1963[f]	8.0	5.5–11.8
1963–1964[e]	8.2	7.5– 9.1
1964–1965[g]	8.5	7.7–10.0
1965–1966[h]	7.0	5.5– 8.2
1966–1967[i]	6.7	5.2– 8.0
1967–1968[e]	6.5	5.7– 7.2
1968–1969[e]	7.1	6.1– 7.7
1969–1970[h]	7.4	7.2– 7.9

[a]Eugene S. Cox, "Operating Expenses for San Francisco Area Properties," *Bay Area Real Estate Report,* 3rd quarter 1952.

[b]Records of Bay area realtors.

[c]Donal Hedlund, "Survey of Gross Rent Multipliers for Apartment Buildings in Alameda County, 1959–60" (thesis, University of California, Berkeley, 1963).

[d]*Bay Area Real Estate Report,* 1st quarter 1961.

[e]Northern California Chapter of AIREA, "Apartment Sales Analysis."

[f]*Bay Area Real Estate Report,* 4th quarter 1963.

[g]Richard U. Ratcliff, "Current Practices in Income Property Appraisal—A Critique" (Berkeley: Center for Real Estate and Urban Land Economics, Institute of Urban and Regional Development, University of California, 1967).

[h]Arthur Grandy, "Real Estate Rate of Returns Sensitivity Study" (thesis, University of California, Berkeley, 1969).

[i] Estimated by the author.

regarded as a key relationship by purchasers in the market, as indicated by the prominence accorded to this ratio by real estate brokers and investors.

This reflects a basic lack of confidence in reported net income figures, which are subject to wide interpretation and vary widely with the depreciation and financing charges used by individual brokers and owners. Knowing the financing terms he can secure, the ratio of operating expenses typical for properties of a certain class, and his tax position, an investor can construct a hypothetical after-tax cash-flow statement, provided he is given reliable current gross income figures and a good notion as to the level of stabilized future gross income. The gross multiplier has become, therefore, a key analytical tool for real estate investors and brokers, and its broad usage has an important influence on the market. If unfurnished apartment properties are known to sell at about 8 times stabilized gross income, it is difficult for a seller or buyer to secure prices much above or below this level.

The parallel with the securities markets is obvious. If price-earnings ratios for food manufacturing or petroleum companies with similar business and outlook are in the range of 15 to 16 times earnings, investors generally will expect the stocks of similar companies to sell within the same range.

Although gross-rent multipliers generally are given short shrift in appraisal literature, Ratcliff reported recently that gross- or net-multiplier techniques, which he refers to as direct conversion ratios, were used as a part of valuation analysis in 77 percent of a sample of income property appraisals he studied in 1968. He concluded, "One might infer that many appraisers place primary reliance on the direct conversion ratio and that in the 'correlation' step, they adjust the other approaches to produce value figures of respectable consistency." Ratcliff reported a range of multipliers in twelve samples of apartment properties selected in Alameda County, California, and Chicago between approximately 7.5 and 10 times gross income. His results, which are summarized in figure 7–1, showed that selling price of the properties studied could have been predicted with considerable accuracy by using gross income as the sole independent variable in a simple regression analysis.[11]

It can be noted that the observed standard deviations about the arithmetic means and the Student t and the F coefficients all indicate that even the smaller samples studied provided regression equations with high reliability of prediction. Ratcliff cautioned that "the regression equation derived from any one sample is useful in application only to properties which have the same characteristics as the cases which make up the sample."[12]

Shenkel reported on the relationship between gross income and sale price for forty-eight apartment buildings with twelve or more units each which were sold in 1968 in Fort Lauderdale, Florida.[13] He found that gross income, with a coefficient of 0.970, had the highest correlation with sale price among fourteen characteristics analyzed. High correlation coefficients were also found for the total floor area (0.967) and total number of units (0.941).[14] Based upon analysis of the forty-eight apartment sales, he found that the following

Figure 7-1. Regression Analysis of Twelve Samples of Apartment Properties in Alameda County and Chicago, 1963–1966

Sample 1: Four-plex apartment sales in Alameda County, California

Number of cases in sample: 25
Primary basis of selection: Annual gross income
Age range: 1 to 10 years
Date of sale range: 1963 to 1966

Regression statistics:

Independent variable: Gross income
Regression equation: Price = $1,323 + 8.395 (earnings)
Coefficient of multiple determination: R^2 = 0.666
Significance of multiple correlation: $F(1,23)$ = 48.768
Student t of regression coefficient: 6.983

Actual and predicted results:

Actual price, mean = $45,158
Deviation, mean = $610
Percent of predicted = 1.35

Sample 2: Four-plex apartment sales in Alameda County, California

Number of cases in sample: 25
Primary basis of selection: Date of sale
Age range: 1 to 10 years
Date of sale range: 1963 to 1965

Regression statistics:

Independent variable: Gross income
Regression equation: Price = $3,552 + 8.076 (earnings).
Coefficient of multiple determination: R^2 = 0.812
Significance of multiple correlation: $F(1,23)$ = 104.827
Student t of regression coefficient: 10.238

Actual and predicted results:

Actual price, mean = $45,738
Deviation, mean = $546
Percent of predicted = 1.19

Sample 3: Four-plex apartment sales in Alameda County, California

Number of cases in sample: 25
Primary basis of selection: Age
Age range: 1 to 6 years
Date of sale range: 1963 to 1966

Regression Statistics:

Independent variable: Gross income
Regression equation: Price = $3,755 + 8.0262 (earnings)
Coefficient of multiple determination: R^2 = 0.802
Significance of multiple correlation: $F(1,23)$ = 98.366
Student t of regression coefficient: 9.918

Actual and predicted results:

Actual price, mean = $45,738
Deviation, mean = $560
Percent of predicted = 1.22

Sample 4: Apartment sales in Alameda County, California

Number of cases in sample: 25
Primary basis of selection: Date of sale
Size of apartments: 5 to 10 units
Age range: 1 to 6 years
Date of sale range: 1963 to 1964

Regression statistics:

Independent variable: Gross income
Regression equation: Price = $7,851 + 7.551 (earnings)
Coefficient of multiple determination: R^2 = 0.950
Significance of multiple correlation: $F(1,23)$ = 458.481
Student t of regression coefficient: 21.412

Actual and predicted results:

Actual price, mean = $81,162
Deviation, mean = $1,156
Percent of predicted = 1.42

Sample 5: Four-plex apartment sales in Alameda County, California

Number of cases in sample: 15
Primary basis of selection: Annual income
Age range: 1 to 10 years
Date of sale range: 1963 to 1966

Regression statistics:

Independent variable: Net income
Regression equation: Price = $2,166 + 10.4285 (earnings)
Coefficient of multiple determination: R^2 = 0.702
Significance of multiple correlation: $F(1,13)$ = 33.963
Student t of regression coefficient: 5.828

Actual and predicted results:

Actual price, mean = $46,700
Deviation, mean = $664
Percent of predicted = 1.42

Sample 6: Four-plex apartment sales in Alameda County, California

Number of cases in sample: 18
Primary basis of selection: Date of sale
Age range: 1 to 10 years
Date of sale range: 1963 to 1965

Regression statistics:

Independent variable: Net income
Regression equation: Price = $2,367 + 10.4764 (earnings)
Coefficient of multiple determination: R^2 = 0.830
Significance of multiple correlation: $F(1,16)$ = 84.261
Student t of regression coefficient: 9.179

Actual and predicted results:

Actual price, mean = $46,014
Deviation, mean = $611
Percent of predicted = 1.33

Sample 7: Four-plex apartment sales in Alameda County, California

Number of cases in sample: 16
Primary basis of selection: Age
Age range: 1 to 10 years
Date of sale range: 1963 to 1966

Regression statistics:

Independent variable: Net income
Regression equation: Price = $4,227 + 10.0811 (earnings)
Coefficient of multiple determination: R^2 = 0.819
Significance of multiple correlation: $F(1,14)$ = 68.797
Student t of regression coefficient: 8.294

Actual and predicted results:

Actual price, mean = $46,953
Deviation, mean = $639
Percent of predicted = 1.36

Sample 8: Apartment sales in Alameda County, California

Number of cases in sample: 14
Primary basis of selection: Date of sale
Size of apartments: 5 to 10 units
Age range: 1 to 6 years

Regression statistics:

Independent variable: Net income
Regression equation: Price = $4,383 + 10.049 (earnings)
Coefficient of multiple determination: R^2 = 0.884
Significance of multiple correlation: $F(1,12)$ = 99.865
Student t of regression coefficient: 9.993

Actual and predicted results:

Actual price, mean = $68,860
Deviation, mean = $967
Percent of predicted = 1.41

Sample 9: Apartment sales in Alameda County, California

Number of cases in sample: 24
Size of apartments: 6 to 10 units
Age range: 1 to 10 years
Date of sale range: 1958 to 1959

Regression statistics:

Independent variable: Gross income
Regression equation: Price = $4,180 + 7.2654 (earnings)
Coefficient of multiple determination: R^2 = 0.954
Significance of multiple correlation: $F_{(1,23)}$ = 479.131
Student t of regression coefficient: 21.889

Actual and predicted results:

Actual price, mean = $64,802
Deviation, mean = $673
Percent of predicted = 1.04

Sample 10: Low-Rise elevator apartment sales in Chicago area

Number of cases in sample: 12
Size of apartments range: 26 to 80 units
Age range: New to 4 years
Date of sale range: 1964 to 1966

Regression statistics:

Independent variable: Gross income
Regression equation: Price = $34,088 + 5.8987 (earnings)
Coefficient of multiple determination: R^2 = 0.959
Significance of multiple correlation: $F_{(1,10)}$ = 262.113
Student t of regression coefficient: 16.120

Actual and predicted results:

Actual price, mean = $554,500
Deviation, mean = $9,096
Percent of predicted = 1.64

Sample 11: Walk-up apartment sales in Chicago area

Number of cases in sample: 15
Size of apartments range: 12 to 38 units
Age range: 1 to 10 years
Date of sale range: 1964 to 1966

Regression statistics:

Independent variable: Gross income
Regression equation: Price = $18,442 + 7.1211 (earnings)
Coefficient of multiple determination: R^2 = 0.898
Significance of multiple correlation: $F_{(1,13)}$ = 124.730
Student t of regression coefficient: 11.168

Actual and predicted results:

Actual price, mean = $221,833
Deviation, mean = $6,035
Percent of predicted = 2.72

Sample 12: Walk-up apartment sales in Chicago suburbs

Number of cases in sample: 15
Size of apartments range: 12 to 98 units
Age range: 2 to 8 years
Date of sale range: 1964 to 1966

Regression statistics:

Independent variable: Gross income
Regression equation: Price = $18,576 + 6.1349 (earnings)
Coefficient of multiple determination: R^2 = 0.964
Significance of multiple correlation: $F_{(1,13)}$ = 374.007
Student t of regression coefficient: 19.339

Actual and predicted results:

Actual price, mean = $277,033
Deviation, mean = $8,971
Percent of predicted = 3.24

Source: See chap. 7n11.

equation resulted in computed values which, on the average, differed from actual 1968 sales prices by only 5.4 percent.

$$\text{Value} = \$6,047 + 6.22 \text{ (gross income)}.$$

Gross income provided a highly reliable indicator of actual sales prices (within limits of 0–15 percent difference) in thirty-eight of the forty-eight cases. In only two cases were the differences between the computed and actual sales prices above 25 percent.[15] Shenkel's conclusions regarding the potentials of multiple-regression analysis and the strong influence of gross income upon property values confirm the findings of Ratcliff and the judgments of the market place, where gross multipliers have long been used in valuation of income properties.

Federal Housing Administration

The Federal Housing Administration has long employed gross-rent multipliers in the valuation of residential property. The rationale for their use is set forth in the valuation section of the *Underwriting Manual*, which was revised in February 1966:

Income returns realized from ownership of real property are comprised of dollar amounts available from its operation or letting out to others to occupy or operate, or from the rights and privileges (often termed amenities) of ownership and occupancy, or from combinations of the two. Relationships between these returns and values are discernible, maintain reasonable degrees of uniformity within types of property, neighborhoods and housing — or investment — market areas, and may prove the best criteria available in estimating value.[16]

Elsewhere, in discussing the capitalization-of-income method, the revised sections of the manual state, "In amenity income neighborhoods amenity motivation on the part of purchasers will clearly dominate the market. Sales and values will relate to the gross income available, capitalized through the use of a rent multiplier, and to direct comparison with similar or equivalent properties."[17]

The Federal Housing Administration places more reliance upon the use of gross-rent multipliers in the valuation of single-family dwellings than for multiples, as indicated in the *Underwriting Manual*: "In the case of single-family properties, the FHA relies upon the Gross Rent Multiplier as a realistic income approach for both rental and amenity income properties. The advantages of this approach are the ease of deriving the appropriate rent multiplier from rental comparables and the ease with which the indicated rent multiplier can be applied to the subject property. Another advantage is its relative accuracy when adequate data is [*sic*] available."

The gross rent multiplier is described in the FHA manual as an overall capitalization factor, developed from gross rent-to-sales price relationships:

> Its major limitation is that it relies upon the availability of comparable properties which are similar to the subject property as to expense and income characteristics. Although this is also true of any valuation analysis, it is of even greater importance with the GRM. The interplay of the many forces which influence the GRM complicate the development of reliable rent multipliers from dissimilar comparison data. For this reason, the FHA recommends that the rent multiplier not be used in the appraisal of multi-unit properties where the chance of finding very similar properties is not as great.[18]

It is difficult for the author to accept the premises upon which the above conclusions seem to rest. The volume of multi-unit construction has greatly increased nationwide over the past decade. Much of the new construction has, for different market areas, been of closely similar characteristics. The four-story walk-up, termed the *Dingbat* in the San Francisco Bay area, has probably accounted for over 75 percent of new apartment construction in the area since 1960. In other areas, the two-story cluster development has predominated. These properties represent a distinctive market for which gross-rent multipliers are often readily available. Since these units have their primary appeal to investors, the gross-multiplier technique appears better adapted to this category of multi-unit housing than to single-family housing which is usually predominately owner-occupied.[19] The determination of rentals in many single-family neighborhoods represents a difficult task for the latter reason. There appears to be inadequate recognition in the *Underwriting Manual* that the gross-rent multiplier method is, in reality, a variation of the market-comparison method and not, as would appear from the manual, solely an adjunct to the capitalization-of-income approach.

Estimated gross-rent multipliers, calculated from data submitted under Federal Housing Administration section 207 loan application forms from 1950 to 1967, are summarized in table 7–4. These data reveal trends generally similar to the San Francisco Bay area data shown in table 7–3. The sharp decline in gross multipliers for newly insured section 207 FHA loans in 1968, 1969, and 1970 from the peak in 1967 reflects the abrupt rise in mortgage interest rates during those years accompanied by a decline in the median ratio of mortgage to value. This trend was further accentuated by the rise in the median monthly rents. The multipliers in table 7–4 represent FHA appraised values divided by scheduled annual income.

Table 7-4. Estimated National Gross-Rent Multipliers
(based on loan/value ratios reported on FHA 207 loans)

Year	Median Monthly Rent	Median Mortgage Amount	Median Ratio Mortgage/Value	Multiplier[a]
1950	$ 71.13	$ 6,366	85.6%	8.7
1952	81.15	6,554	83.0	8.1
1954	115.60	8,031	74.4	7.8
1955	120.27	8,506	80.0	7.4
1956	92.02	7,431	88.7	7.6
1957	144.16	11,618	90.0	7.5
1958	150.81	12,009	89.1	7.4
1959	154.98	12,384	88.7	7.5
1960	171.31	14,088	89.6	7.6
1961	186.79	16,002	89.5	8.1
1962	198.70	16,323	88.8	7.7
1963	196.47	15,964	89.0	7.2
1964	224.72	17,095	90.0	7.0
1965	187.57	16,116	89.4	8.0
1966	172.29	12,990	89.0	7.1
1967	171.82	16,894	90.0	9.1
1968	246.60	17,340	86.9	6.7
1969	227.50	14,299	86.3	6.1
1970	227.24	15,172	90.0	6.2

[a]Calculated by the author FHA Appraised Value/Scheduled Annual Rent.

Sources: Federal Housing Administration, *29th Annual Report,* 1962, p. 44; U.S. Department of Housing and Urban Development, *Annual Report,* 1965, p. 122; and U.S. Department of Housing and Urban Development, *Statistical Yearbook,* 1970, p. 239.

Techniques for Adjusting Gross Multipliers

Sonnenschein points out that rent multipliers are variations of the capitalization-of-income method. He calls attention to the fact, however, that error frequently occurs from the application of rent multipliers to properties with varying life expectancies. Sonnenschein recommends that adjustment factors be applied to rent multipliers based upon the percentage of value calculated as remaining for various periods in a property's life.[20]

Although his technique is ingenious, the reader wonders at the rationality of calculating an adjustment factor in the manner outlined to be applied to a gross-rent multiplier. The latter is admittedly a technique for obtaining a rough preliminary estimate of value by a variation of the capitalization approach. The attempt to refine this approach as outlined by Sonnenschein is, in reality, a substitution of one of the more detailed capitalization techniques for the rough rule of thumb method of the gross-rent multiplier.

Gross-rent multipliers are, in the last analysis, a market phenomenon, and their use is as much an adaptation of the market-comparison as of the capitalization-of-income method. Market sales prices are estimated from gross rents by reference to relationships between sales prices and rents of comparable properties.

Advantages of Gross Multipliers

The use of gross-rent multipliers as a means of estimating market values seems to have certain advantages over the capitalization-of-income method. First, the value data required are usually available in the market place — namely, gross-rental income and selling prices. Second, assuming comparability of properties, the use of the gross-rent-multiplier method eliminates some of the more subjective processes of estimation which are implicit in the use of the capitalization-of-income method. Third, the process of estimating market value by the use of gross-income multipliers is simpler and more easily comprehended than are many variations of the capitalization-of-income method. Fourth, gross-rent multipliers are widely employed in practical valuation. There is a tendency, therefore, for actual sales prices to adapt themselves to the relationships presumed by gross-income multipliers.

Conclusions

Taken together, the advantages noted above furnish a strong basis for advocating the use of gross-rent multipliers for many classes of valuation. It was observed, however, that historical market data descriptive of trends in gross multipliers are, at best, imperfect and that wide variations may exist in multipliers for similar classes of property. It is obvious that the technique can only be used when the following conditions are present: (1) rent-value relationships are known to be similar for major classes of property, and (2) the subject property is similar in all essential respects to the properties used in developing the gross-rent multipliers. It necessarily follows that classes of property which enjoy a poor market generally will not be adaptable to the use of gross-rent multipliers.

The gross-multiplier method of valuation is a variation of both the capitalization-of-income and market-comparison methods and represents the true meeting place of these methods in the market. Evidence is mounting to indicate that the gross-multiplier method is widely used by real estate brokers, investors, mortgage lenders, government mortgage-insuring agencies, and professional appraisers. There is still strong opposition to the use of the method in some appraisal circles, but it appears to be diminishing.[21] The fact that gross multipliers are so extensively used by participants in the real estate market becomes self-justifying in a sense. If four-story, unfurnished multiples in a certain age bracket and location sell for about seven or eight times gross income, sales prices and appraised values tend to gravitate in that direction.[22]

The gross-multiplier method of valuation will undoubtedly become of increasing importance as the availability of market sales and gross-income data increases and becomes accessible to analysis with the aid of the computer. Further, the problems of comparability which have plagued the technique in the past should be greatly reduced as computer-selection techniques become generally available to the appraisal profession.

THE REPLACEMENT–COST METHOD

The replacement-cost method occupies an important place in appraisal theory and practice. It is the primary method used in establishing value for fire insurance and property taxation purposes and, as noted in chapter 2, it has been increasingly relied upon by the government in fixing values for insurance and guaranty of mortgage loans. Reference has already been made to the illusory nature of the concept of normal cost and to the flexibility in estimates of value by the replacement-cost method. In the present chapter, following a brief review of its origins, the replacement-cost method will be examined in further detail to determine its rationale, the circumstances in which it is applicable, and the problems in its interpretation and use. Commonly employed techniques in the application of the method will be described and critically evaluated.

Origins

It will be recalled that cost-of-production theories of value occupied the central position in economic theory until the middle of the nineteenth century. Although economists of the Austrian school placed a great deal more emphasis on demand as an influence upon value, the neoclassical economic doctrine developed by Alfred Marshall, Gustav Cassel, and others held that values in the long run would tend to equal average costs of representative firms under conditions of pure competition. The relationships between costs and observed values (or prices) in economic theory has become increasingly obscure as the complex nature of the process of cost and price determination has become evident. After extensive empirical investigation, economists have concluded that "the long-run cost curves of representative firms" of economic theory are not observable in the study of costs of existing firms.[1] Pure competition, the counterpart of the neoclassical theory of long-run average costs and the representative firm, has also been relegated to limbo in modern economic theory. Irving Fisher and others, in advocating the theory that value is represented by the present worth of future returns, drew attention to the fallacy in confusing historical costs with present value.

However, as pointed out earlier, the replacement-cost method received early and wide acceptance in appraisal theory because of the persistent and somewhat belated influence of neoclassical economic theory. The broad acceptance of the method in practice can be attributed to five factors: (1) the need for standardized valuation techniques, (2) the acceptance of replacement cost as a ceiling upon value estimates, (3) the relative ease of calculation of replacement costs, (4) the difficulties in the application of the capitalization-of-income method, and (5) the rejection of market sales as a measure of value.

The Need for Standardized Valuation Techniques The acceptance of the replacement-cost method has progressed as the need developed for standardized methods which could be applied to mass appraisals. Bonbright, tracing the evolution of the use of replacement cost as a basis for the general property tax and the wide acceptance of the replacement-cost standard by the courts, concluded:

> Perhaps the most strikingly distinctive feature of *judicial* valuation, in this country at least, is to be found in the proneness of the courts to single out the estimated replacement cost of replaceable property, minus certain allowances for depreciation, as the most reliable index or measure of value. . . .
>
> . . . In all but a small fraction of the cases [on fire insurance valuation], cost of replacement, with allowances for depreciation, has been accepted either as the measure of loss or else as the dominant evidence of this loss. This statement holds good despite the fact that in most cases the courts do not directly state that replacement cost is the test, but instead indicate that "market value" or "actual cash value" is the criterion.[2]

Attempts to establish uniform systems of appraisal for tax assessment purposes were led by W. A. Somers and John A. Zangerle during the period from 1910 to 1924. Zangerle commented on the desirability of standardized assessments and the problems of establishing values by the replacement-cost method in the 1924 edition of his appraisal book:

> From any viewpoint, it is therefore highly desirable that some uniform method of establishing values be adopted, and that particularity of appraisement be, so far as possible, eliminated. No greater asset accrues to the appraiser than uniformity in appraisal. . . .
>
> It is not claimed that every building of any description will cost exactly the figure shown in the schedules for that particular type . . . for it is a well-known fact that contractors estimating the cost of a building may vary as much as 100 percent in the amount of their bids.[3]

Replacement cost is generally accepted as the standard of value for tax assessment purposes and for establishing the measure of loss in fire insurance valuations. This results from the apparent ease of calculation of replacement costs as much as from any other single factor.

Although statutes governing assessment practices continue to refer to fair market value, most jurisdictions continue to use replacement cost less depreciation as the primary criterion for determining assessment values for property tax purposes. Amendments to the laws of the state of California in 1966 provide that local property must be assessed at not less than 25 percent of its market value, and that the State Division of Assessment Standards is required to report on the assessment ratios for separate assessing jurisdictions annually.[4]

The State Board of Assessment Standards makes regular sample studies of market values in each county which, in effect, require that local taxing authorities in the state give increasing attention to analysis of market sales of real property in establishing assessed values. Since counties which fail to meet the standards of a 25 percent ratio of assessed to market value are penalized financially by a reduction in state grants, the adjustment to use of market sales as a criterion of value is moving forward rapidly.[5]

It was noted in chapter 2 that the requirements of the federal government for standardized methods of establishing home loan values on a large scale resulted in substantial reliance upon the replacement-cost method by the Federal Housing Administration and the Veterans Administration. This emphasis upon replacement costs in federal government appraisal policies brought about a similar trend throughout the mortgage loan field. A circular effect of this reliance upon replacement costs in the mortgage loan field has been to cause market prices to adjust themselves to replacement costs, since lenders' appraisals are important influences upon market price.

Mortgage Lenders The post-World War II experience of mortgage lenders has undoubtedly caused some disillusionment with replacement cost as a criterion of value. The scandals surrounding FHA section 608 loans drew attention to the unreliability and the ease of juggling reported builders' costs. The credit crunches of 1966 and 1969 following the building boom of the early 1960s found many mortgage lenders with loans on their books in amounts exceeding current market values, many of which had been made on the basis of certified builders' costs. Mortgage lenders and others have finally become aware of the economic truism that *cost* is not value, and frequently is also not actual cost. As pointed out in chapter 2, with this realization, they have shifted their emphasis to alternative methods of estimating values for loan purposes. Mortgage lenders are relying increasingly upon current market values in their loan appraisals.[6]

The Acceptance of Replacement Cost as a Ceiling on Value Estimates
It was pointed out in chapter 2 that replacement cost has generally been accepted as a ceiling upon market price. This doctrine emanates from the principle that an intelligent buyer will pay no more in the market for a property than he can replace it for by constructing a substitute property. The Federal Housing Administration gives expression to this principle:

> Costs are related to value only in the sense that they establish an upper limit of value, since a typical buyer acting intelligently would not be warranted in

paying more for a property than the cost of producing an equivalent property. The value of a property may be equal to its cost only in the case of a building which is new, represents the highest and best use of the site, and when there is a balanced relationship between supply and demand. Since value and replacement cost can be equal, estimates of replacement cost in new condition are used as upper limits for estimates of value, thereby acting as controls on the judgment of the valuator.[7]

As will be noted below, there are many theoretical and practical problems in the definition of a substitute and in the measurement of replacement costs. However, these methodological problems have not reduced the basic reliance in practice upon cost of replacement as a ceiling upon value estimates.

The Relative Ease of Calculation of Replacement Costs The calculation of an estimate of replacement costs is misleadingly simple. Estimated square-foot costs for various types and grades of buildings are available from many statistical sources. It is generally agreed, however, that such cost indexes indicate in only a very general way trends in costs which may be expected to vary widely for individual builders, types of structures, and grades of construction at any one time and over a period of time. In spite of these basic shortcomings, the fact remains that replacement costs are sought as a measure of value and that a variety of sources furnish square-foot or cubic-foot cost figures which can readily be translated into an estimate of replacement cost for a structure. Although the problem of estimating depreciation is theoretically more difficult, the assumption is generally made that buildings will depreciate in some uniform manner with age. Based upon this assumption, schedules of accrued building depreciation are widely used in establishing values for tax assessment, fire insurance, and other purposes.

The Difficulties in the Application of the Capitalization-of-Income Method Serious shortcomings in the use of this method were discussed in chapter 6. These difficulties have been particularly apparent in the estimation of value for owner-occupied residences, since rental-income data are usually unavailable for such properties. The growing importance of owner-occupied single-family homes in recent years has highlighted these difficulties in establishing values. As a result of this, there has been increasing reliance upon the replacement-cost method in establishing such values. The ease of calculation and facility of establishing standardized values for such properties by the replacement-cost method have been important factors in furthering the method's use.

It should also be observed that many other classes of property do not produce measurable income streams which can be translated into value by the capitalization process. Among these are many factory buildings and institutionally owner-occupied structures. Many of these do not enjoy a ready market, and hence the replacement-cost method has been resorted to by default.

The Rejection of Market Sales as a Measure of Value The wide fluctuations in market prices for real estate during the depression years caused many institutions to reject market sales prices as a measure of value. It has already been seen that governmental agencies also were influenced by the apparent disorganization in the markets at that time and so they relied upon other methods of estimating values. The rejection of market prices was particularly evident in the early valuation policies of the Federal Housing Administration. The wide movements in residential real estate prices following World War II served to continue this tendency in governmental and institutional appraisal policies. Some large life insurance companies established as a policy that loan values of residences would not be recognized at more than 150 percent of the estimated 1940 replacement costs. The Federal Housing Administration and the Veterans Administration established reasonable costs for each region as standards of appraised value. Market prices were disregarded as evidences of value if they rose above these standard costs. The net result of these influences was to focus increased attention upon replacement costs in the valuation process.

This brief outline of the origins and growing prevalence in use of the replacement-cost method emphasizes the importance of the following review of the rationale for the use of the method and the problems in its application.

Rationale of the Replacement-Cost Method

This method may be defined as a means of determining the value of a property by reference to the cost of replacing it, or of an acceptable substitute. The method rests on a dual theoretical foundation. First, it is held that market values in the long run will tend to equal so-called normal costs of production. Second, it is maintained that replacement costs represent a ceiling upon market values since investors will pay no more for an improvement than the cost of obtaining the same or a substitute in the market.

A review of appraisal literature on the replacement-cost method reveals both stern critics and loyal supporters. Frederick M. Babcock devoted an entire chapter to an exposition of the distinction between *value* and *cost*. Following closely the writings of Irving Fisher, he maintained:

> Cost in the investment sense is not value. A standard illustration which makes this assertion clear is the one which assumes a 30-story hotel to have been built in a remote and inaccessible spot in a desert. It is self-evident that the building is not worth an amount represented by the investment which would be required to replace it. There is rarely, in fact, any connection between the cost of replacement of a building and its value. The notable excep-

tion and the only exception is the case of the building just completed which represents the highest and best use of its site. In the latter case a building is worth precisely its cost of replacement. However its value at any future time may not bear any relation to either its replacement or original cost of construction. . . .

The fact that in most kinds of real estate the values at a given time cannot greatly exceed replacement cost in no way modified the general statement that cost and value are distinct and that the cost method of valuation is unsound. . . .

A building is worth its cost of replacement provided it is new, represents the highest and best use of the site, and provided its construction is justified by the expected returns which it will produce. In all other cases its value must be discovered by some other process.[8]

Bonbright appears to be considerably more tolerant toward the use of the replacement-cost method, but upon close examination, his views are very similar to those of Babcock. He finds the theoretical basis for the method in the so-called law of competitive price and in the principle of substitution, which have been discussed in chapter 3. He views the principle of substitution (which is the basis for the premise that replacement cost ordinarily fixes the upper limit of value) as "one of the most useful single generalizations in appraisal theory."[9] However, the application of the principle, in his judgment, does little more than establish the value of a property between zero as a minimum and replacement cost, after allowance for depreciation, as a maximum. Bonbright apparently concurs that the operation of competitive forces in the economy seldom results in an equivalence between cost of production and market price.

Agreeing with Babcock, Bonbright concludes that the appraiser should accept an estimate of the replacement cost of property, with proper allowance for incidental loss and for depreciation, as the best available measure of its value when the appraiser is justified in thinking that if the property were lost or destroyed, the owner would rationally replace it. Upon reflection, this statement is seen as something of a truism, since, with market value as the desired object, the appraiser is advised to accept replacement cost as the measure of value when it is equal to market value. The full significance of this difficulty will be explored below.

As might be expected, stronger support of the replacement-cost approach is found in books on engineering valuation and property tax appraisal. Marston and Agg, although according primary weight to the income method of valuation, indicate that in the case of uncertain future earnings prospects, replacement cost should be given equal weight with the capitalization-of-income method. Echoing the doctrine of competitive price, they say: "In the long run, owing to the effects of competition and the principle of fair prices, the cost (reproduction or replacement cost) of a nonregulated enterprise may be a better indicator of future earnings than are averages of the past earnings and expense."[10]

Assessor's Handbook, published by the California State Board of Equalization, includes the following discussion of the replacement-cost method:

> Replacement cost is the cost, as of a particular date, of replacing the existing structure with a similar one that has equivalent utility. A structure of equivalent utility is one that will offer comparable shelter and amenities, provide similar services, and produce equal net income. The replacement cost concept is the most meaningful one as far as the principle of substitution is concerned and consequently has the closest relationship to market value.
>
> The replacement cost is the cost concept generally used by California assessors. However, because of the nature of the appraisal process and the sequence in which the three approaches to value are usually employed, a rigorous replacement cost approach cannot always be used. Obvious aspects of a building that would clearly and unequivocally not be replaced are excluded from the costs. When dealing with items that may or may not be replaced, the questionable items should in general be included in the cost estimate. The exact procedures to be followed in replacement cost estimating vary somewhat depending upon whether the property is industrial, commercial, rural, or residential.
>
> . . . In the case of new buildings, replacement, historical, and reproduction costs will usually coincide, and therefore there is no question as to what should or should not be included in the cost approach. Depreciation, in most new or almost new buildings will be small or non-existent, and this decreases the significance of another subjective portion of the cost estimate. In such cases, the appraiser should attach greater weight to the cost approach in the value conclusion.[11]

Modern appraisal literature, although generally following the views of Babcock and Bonbright on the adaptability of the replacement-cost method, accords only limited attention to the justification for the use of the method. Seemingly avoiding the basic question, May said, "While cost is not value, it is an element in value." He went on to point out that the appraiser must be able to judge the relative reliability of the replacement cost and other approaches and place the emphasis in his valuation accordingly.[12] Schmutz was more precise in saying: "Cost and value may or may not be the same. They may be, in the case of a new building, although there are exceptions. However, the estimated depreciated cost of an old building may be misleading. The older the building, then the greater the danger of error because of the nature of the depreciation computation, especially if estimated by the use of conventional age-life guides."[13]

The 1967 edition of the AIREA text recommends the use of the cost approach as one of the three approaches to value, pointing out that "the reproduction cost, new, normally sets the upper limit of value, provided that the improvement represents the highest and best use."[14] Most authorities would argue that reproduction cost should *always* set the upper limit of value and that the cost method has little or no relevance in circumstances where the improvements are not adapted to the site. The authors of the institute text continued: "The value indicated by the cost approach will be valid if the land value estimate is sound, if the reproduction cost has been estimated accurately, and if the estimate of depreciation from all causes is correct. But physical deterioration and functional and economic obsolescence cannot be measured precisely as a physical object can be measured. Its measurement — or better, its estimate — depends largely on the experience and judgment of the appraiser."[15] This statement acknowledges the subjective nature of the processes of estimating depreciation in the cost approach, which is the basis for its rejection by this author and many others. Sackman recommends that cost should only be used as evidence of value where: (1) the property is unique, (2) it is a specialty, or (3) there is competent proof of an absence of market data.[16]

The distinction between *cost* and *value* has been further emphasized in recent studies of apartment house investment in the San Francisco Bay area. Prof. Wallace F. Smith found that market sales prices of newly built, low-rise apartment buildings exceeded their costs of construction by substantial margins in the early 1960s, which he identified as attributable to entrepreneurial profit.[17]

The significance of Smith's findings for the appraiser is that he found no evidence of the assumed equivalences between market-sales prices and builders' costs of assembling land and building in a substantial number of cases. These and other findings not only fail to support the notion that replacement costs should be used as a ceiling upon market value, but suggest that market sales prices will generally exceed costs, for reasons similar to those governing pricing policies in the economy for most manufactured goods.

It is of interest to note that the Federal Housing Administration, an agency which has done much to encourage the use of replacement costs as the basis for establishing mortgage loan values, clearly distinguishes between cost and value, holding that "costs are related to value only in the sense that they establish an upper limit of value" and that "estimates of replacement cost are of greatest significance in the case of new, or nearly new, structures."[18]

In general, there seems to be agreement that the replacement-cost method must be used with extreme care and selectivity. Its principal usefulness appears to rest on the doctrine that cost of replacement represents a ceiling upon value. This doctrine is valid only under perfect competitive conditions because, as has been well established in economic theory, value can be above cost under conditions of imperfect competition. Writers are agreed that the possibilities of error in the use of the replacement-cost method are substantially greater for older properties or for properties which have experienced depreciation for reasons other than age. Few appraisal theorists today hold to the view that the operation of competitive forces in the economy results in an equivalence between cost of production and market price. To these fundamental theoretical limitations must be added the problems which arise in application of the method.

The Meaning of Replacement The identification of the term *replacement cost* with the cost of acquiring an acceptable substitute property opens up a wide vista of difficulties for the appraiser. Bonbright held that in few cases would an owner elect to replace a property with one identically the same. He identified three choices which might fit the definition of an "acceptable substitute":[19] (1) a new, but otherwise substantially identical, replica; (2) an equally depreciated substitute; (3) the most advantageous new and modern substitute. Rapidly changing building techniques and architectural styles magnify this problem for the appraiser. Broadly speaking, the appraiser usually must consider the replacement cost of a new and modern substitute property. The greater the differences between the subject property and its new and modern substitute, the greater is the problem of comparison between the two.

Dean Robert O. Harvey of the University of Connecticut recognized the difficulties in selecting a suitable substitute property in the replacement-cost method. Although he made his position clear in the following quotation from his article, he does not so easily resolve this difficult problem:

> The shift from reproduction to replacement was meant to give recognition to the point that it is sometimes impossible to reproduce buildings which were built with materials and methods no longer either available or desirable. The word "replacement," however, does not give an appraiser license to create a replacement structure fundamentally different from the one being appraised. The replacement structure used as the basis for estimating the value of an existing building must duplicate the existing building as nearly as possible. If this is not the case, the attempt to determine the cost of improvements which duplicate the productivity of existing real estate is defeated at the outset.[20]

Harvey fails to recognize that the fundamental reason for the shift from reproduction to replacement costs was because the investor is concerned with a suitable substitute and *not* with a replica. Contrary to the opinion expressed in his last sentence, a suitable substitute, differing in important degree, may duplicate the productivity of existing real estate. It would appear that because the consideration of a suitable substitute property involves the appraiser in comparative judgments, Harvey would have him reject all substitutes in favor of a substantial replica of the subject property.

Dr. Harvey's comments notwithstanding, the use of the replacement-cost method requires at the outset a judgment determination of what constitutes an acceptable substitute for the property under appraisal, and it is upon this judgment in part that the acceptability of replacement cost as a ceiling upon value must rest.

Problems in Cost Determination Having decided upon an acceptable sub-stitute, one must consider some of the important problems in the measure-ment of replacement costs. It is commonly agreed that builders' costs vary widely for identical structures. Should the appraiser seek the costs of the most efficient builder, the marginal builder, or some imaginary "typical" builder — or should he disregard current costs and seek long-term or "normal" costs of builders as an appropriate measure of replacement costs? The question might be raised whether builders' costs are significant to value determination since it might be argued that the replacement costs to the purchaser are the facts to be found. These questions must be resolved against a background of meager statistical information available about costs in the building industry.

Reference to the theory of replacement costs suggests that the costs to be determined represent those which would actually be incurred in replacing a property or its substitute. The determination of costs, therefore, involves something in the way of prediction rather than historical record. If an ap-praiser seeks to determine the replacement cost of a new single-family tract home, he comes face to face with the question of whose costs he is going to use. Although the homes in the tract may have been built in volume at costs typical for large builders, it cannot be assumed that such cost advantage would accrue in the future to the owner seeking to replace one of these homes. By the same token, the appraiser may not be justified in employing cost factors for individual custom-built homes to the appraisal problem. The use of such high-cost figures would certainly provide a ceiling upon value, but it would probably result in an estimate of value far above the cost of a reason-able facsimile of the subject home in another tract. In practice, as will be presently seen, the appraiser usually accepts offering prices in the market as indicative of builders' costs, recognizing that some builders are operating at a loss at these prices while others are making a substantial profit. Such costs represent replacement costs to the purchaser, rather than builders' costs. How carefully the replacement-cost method, thus applied, can be distinguished from the market-comparison method will be explored later in this chapter.

The measurement of replacement costs implies that a decision be made as to what should be included in costs. The simple dictum that all costs necessary to replace a property should be included is of only partial assis-tance. Illustration of this difficulty is found in the treatment of marketing and financing costs. As the *Underwriting Manual* states:

> The FHA estimate of replacement cost of on-site improvements includes the cost of materials, labor, subcontracts, workmen's compensation insurance, public liability insurance, unemployment insurance, social security tax, sales taxes, incidental job costs, finish grading, planting, general overhead and profit, and architectural services.
>
> Carrying charges during construction, the cost of financing, and fire and other hazard insurance during construction are not included in the estimate

of replacement cost of building improvements. However, appropriate allowance for these elements of cost is included by the valuator in the final Estimate of Replacement Cost of Property.[21]

Financing costs can vary widely over time, however, and among individual builders. This is illustrated by the fact that builders have frequently paid construction loan fees as high as 7 percent, and at times have been forced to absorb discounts on mortgage paper as high as 8 to 10 percent. Allowances for such items of cost are intimately tied in with the factors used for overhead and profits, since builders frequently absorb such charges as a deduction from profits. The appraiser must either know more about the structure of builders' costs than the builder himself, or he must rely upon some simple rule of thumb in handling these difficulties. Commonly, he does the latter and adds 10 percent for overhead and profit to his calculation of replacement costs, hoping that such a figure will prove a suitable allowance for what, in reality, are a series of significant unknowns.

Allowances for Difference in Quality Few problems in the replacement-cost method present greater difficulty than the allowances for differences in design, quality of materials, and workmanship in construction. Architectural style is largely a matter of personal choice; one appraiser may penalize a house with a flat roof, while another may consider contemporary design an added value feature. Even assuming the careful cataloguing of the grades of basic materials used in a building, the quality of workmanship in installing these materials is an important factor influencing the value of the improvements. The problem goes further than the mere identification of good as compared with poor workmanship because the appraiser must put a dollar value upon this difference. A good drywall interior job may be superior to a medium-quality plaster finish in the eyes of one appraiser and not another. No two appraisers may agree upon the penalties to be assessed against inferior quality, and the result is that at still another point the replacement-cost method hinges upon the individual judgment of the appraiser.

The influence of different production techniques upon the cost and value of structures is heightened by the rapid technological changes taking place in the early 1970s in housing construction. HUD's Operation Breakthrough program chose twenty-two producers of housing systems from among five hundred fifty submitted proposals to build prototypic models on specially selected sites in ten states.[22] The two thousand prototypic units include single-family, detached units; single-family attached; row houses; multi-family; low-rise units; and high-rise buildings. The building materials include concrete, wood, metal, and plastic.

Operation Breakthrough supports the development of new and innovative housing-system concepts and production methods, better management and maintenance methods, and seeks solutions to many problems impeding large-scale production of housing. The prospect of factory production of housing will most certainly add to the difficulties of applying the replacement-cost method. The costs of prototypes will often bear little relationship to the costs under conditions of large-scale production. The estimation of depreciation, building life, and quality of workmanship will prove difficult, and the determination of a suitable substitute structure will become more subjective.

Estimating Depreciation   The appraiser's troubles have just begun when he has established the replacement cost new for a subject property or for a suitable substitute. As noted above, such a figure is not acceptable as a measure of value unless the improvements are considered to be new and identical to those under appraisal, and, according to theory, they represent the highest and best use of the property. Obviously, the great bulk of appraisal problems fail to meet these conditions, and it is therefore necessary to make adjustments upward and downward. The estimation of depreciation presents a more difficult problem for the appraiser than any considered thus far. This accounts for the skeptical attitude of appraisers toward the replacement-cost method, particularly for old properties. This problem is complicated by a considerable amount of confusion with respect to the purpose to be served by an estimate of depreciation for use in the replacement-cost method. Simply stated, the appraiser seeks to establish the difference in value between a subject property presumed to be inferior and a new substitute or identical property. Two methods of obtaining such a differential value figure immediately suggest themselves: (1) the sale price of the old property can be compared with the replacement cost new of the substitute, or (2) the value of the two properties may be calculated by the capitalization-of-income method and the difference in value could be taken to represent depreciation.

Although both of these alternatives appear to be logical means of determining depreciation, they clearly involve the rejection of the replacement-cost method in favor of the market-comparison or capitalization-of-income methods. If the appraiser were satisfied that the value of the subject property could be determined by market comparison as in (1), he would determine value by this method directly rather than employ the market-comparison method to determine the key unknown in the replacement-cost calculation. Similarly, the determination of depreciation by comparing capitalized incomes for a new property involves primary reliance upon the capitalization-of-income method rather than upon the replacement-cost method.

Actually, as will be seen, neither of these methods is so summarily rejected. The so-called observed-condition method of estimating depreciation is based in large part upon the comparison of a subject property with a new substitute. Such a comparison relies heavily upon the appraiser's judgment as to the relative market values of the two properties. Similarly, relative earning power is frequently the basis upon which an appraiser determines the value of an old, as compared with a new, property. Bonbright said:

The ideal method of estimating depreciation would be a direct forecast of the differences, year by year, between the income of the enterprise with the old asset and the income of the same enterprise with the new asset. . . . In practice, however, it is usually hopeless to attempt such forecasts directly. The appraiser is therefore compelled to resort, partly to guesswork (usually misnamed "judgment"), and partly to mathematical formulas which make some plausible assumptions as to the discrepancies between the income streams derivable from the two comparable assets.[23]

The mathematical formulas to which Bonbright referred have been largely the product of accounting theorists and writers in the field of engineering valuation. Elaborate techniques have been developed in these fields for allocating the costs of physical assets over their assumed useful lives. These ready-made calculations have frequently been adopted by appraisers for use in estimating the accrued depreciation on improvements. Marston, Winfrey, and Hempstead, in a review of the various methods of estimating depreciation, distinguished two main classifications: (1) those not involving considerations of interest or time discounts, and (2) those involving the theory of compound interest.[24] Under the first heading, they identified several variations of the observed-condition method — the so-called sum-of-the-digits method, the declining-balance method, and the straight-line depreciation method. In real estate appraisal the observed-condition method, sometimes referred to as the direct appraisal method, is widely employed, although it has limited applicability in the accounting or engineering fields. The straight-line depreciation method is also widely used because of its simplicity. It assumes that depreciation accrues in equal annual amounts over the estimated life of a property. By this method, a property assumed to last fifty years would depreciate at the rate of 2 percent per year, while one assumed to last forty years would depreciate at the rate of 2.5 percent a year, and so on. The weaknesses of such arbitrary assumptions are readily apparent. Loss in value is dependent upon care and maintenance, neighborhood changes, other locational developments, economic trends, and many other factors not directly associated with age.

The second group of methods was designed to establish annual depreciation charges in the future rather than to estimate accrued depreciation. They are based upon the principle that past depreciation reserves will accumulate interest over the remaining life of the improvement or, stated differently, that future depreciation charges should be discounted because of their remoteness in time. In the sinking-fund method it is assumed that depreciation reserves will accumulate interest at a so-called safe rate. In the so-called annuity or present-worth depreciation principle, it is assumed that the amounts set aside for depreciation represent a direct reduction in the investment. Marston, Winfrey, and Hempstead demonstrated the wide variation in estimated accrued depreciation which results from the selection of alternative methods.[25] The significant point in the present discussion is that the appraiser is faced with a wide array of methods for estimating accrued depreciation which yield widely varying results.

Examination of the theoretical rationale for the use of the replacement-cost method, the consideration of the very meaning of the replacement concept, and the problems in its application destroy the aura of certainty and mathematical preciseness which surrounds the replacement-cost method in popular estimation. The problems of definition, interpretation, and judgment, to which attention has been drawn, emphasize the importance of a careful examination of replacement-cost techniques commonly used to evaluate their acceptability as means of establishing values.

Replacement-Cost Techniques

The estimation of replacement costs and of accrued depreciation, although integral parts of the replacement-cost method, are usually given separate treatment in appraisal literature. Substantial similarity and agreement with respect to the techniques of establishing estimates of replacement costs are lost in a heterogeneity of expression and nomenclature. For example, the Federal Housing Administration prescribes three methods of cost estimation:

1. The Inplace Unit Method comprises the measurement of component parts of the building, and the application of appropriate unit prices for the components erected in place. . . .
2. The Integrated Method comprises the use of a Basic Cost previously established for a typical dwelling and the application of adjustments to account for variations in the subject dwelling. . . .
3. The Repeat Case Method comprises the use of a lump-sum cost previously established for a basic structure, and the addition or deduction of lump-sum amounts to account for variations in the subject dwelling.[26]

Babcock identifies three very similar methods as (1) estimation by prices and quantities, (2) estimation by square- or cubic-foot unit prices, and (3) estimation by a combination of the foregoing methods. The authors of the textbook published by the American Institute of Real Estate Appraisers refer to three methods as (1) the quantity-survey method, (2) the unit cost-in-place method, and (3) the square-foot and cubic-foot methods. All express agreement that the in-place unit or quantity-survey method result in the highest degree of accuracy, and they urge caution in the use of the square-foot or cubic-foot methods. Particular caution is urged in the use of the latter methods because of the differences in ceiling heights, roof pitches, perimeters, and other elements of construction. The unit cost-in-place method enumerated in the institute text is sometimes referred to as a modified quantity-survey method since it employs dollar factors for various parts of a building.

The in-place unit method of cost estimation involves the painstaking calculation of the costs of putting the various components of a building in place. It is interesting to note that provision is made for quality adjustments by the application of percentage factors. The basis for such factors, of course, is a major problem in making such adjustments.

In the light of present knowledge concerning the wide variation in builders' individual costs, it is difficult to express agreement with those who claim that the in-place unit method (or the quantity-survey method) is the "most accurate and provable method" of the three mentioned. True, such a method is the basis for builders' cost estimates in competitive bidding. However, it is known that variations of as much as 30 to 40 percent are common in such bidding. The basis for materials' pricing alone presents an almost insuperable obstacle for the appraiser, since quoted prices of building materials are often at wide variance with actual sales prices to individual builders. Further, rapidly changing building techniques make it exceedingly difficult to develop labor output factors that are currently accurate – if there is any such thing as an accurate figure for such widely varying levels of productivity.

One apparent weakness of the in-place unit method as applied to home appraisals is that the dollar volume of subcontracts is approximately equal to the outlays for direct labor and materials on the typical house-building job. The appraiser using this method finds it necessary to determine not only the probable outlays for labor and materials by these subcontractors, but also to judge the competitive conditions in each subcontracting field that will influence bidding.

Because of the above limitations, a modified in-place unit system is widely employed in estimating replacement costs for single-family homes. By this technique, the exact specifications of a home considered typical in a locality are established, and the builder's direct costs of labor and materials are determined by regular interviews. These figures are then supplemented by the addition of subcontractors' bid prices for those portions of the home usually constructed in this manner. The regular canvassing of subcontractors' bid prices for the various house components is designed to reflect the competitive situation in the various lines as well as their outlays for direct labor and materials. The cost breakdown calculated in the above manner for one such house considered typical of the San Francisco Bay area for the period from January 1966 to January 1970 is shown in table 8–1. Complete description and the specifications for the house used as the basis for these calculations are found in the first quarter 1966 issue of the *Northern California Real Estate Report.*

This technique seems to solve some problems of cost estimation while it raises others. Since the figures apply to a specific house that, it can be assumed, usually differs from the one under appraisal, adjustments in the cost figures are required to reflect these differences. Frequently the differences are so substantial that the cost figures for the so-called typical home represent

Table 8-1. Cost Breakdown—Medium Quality Dwelling, Northern California

	1/1/66	1/1/68	1/1/70
Preliminary	$ 143	$ 143	$ 148
Excavation and site preparation	135	147	183
Concrete foundation	478	501	598
Lumber, rough	1,388	1,545	1,754
Lumber, finish	141	147	226
Carpenter labor, rough	1,368	1,556	1,852
Carpenter labor, finish	295	335	399
Doors (preassembled)	239	263	280
Wood windows and frames	168	185	244
Screens for wood windows	23	25	26
Aluminum windows and screens	125	133	137
Patio sliding glass door and screen	90	96	99
Cabinets	368	386	642
Hardware, rough	53	54	59
Hardware, finish	60	60	75
Roofing material & labor	810	810	1,064
Shower base	377	377	469
Ceramic tile			
Shower door			
Stucco, exterior	749	749	1,099
Interior finish (gyp. ed.)	777	848	908
Plumbing	1,772	2,154	2,447
Sewer line and connection	218	252	350
Heating	677	687	832
Sheetmetal and flashing			
Electric wiring	703	872	1,128
Electric fixtures	80	102	125
Hardwood floors	444	474	546
Linoleum floors	375	435	486
Painting	691	822	919
Bathroom accessories	45	45	45
Cleanup	72	80	85
Garage door	106	112	135
Concrete flat work	342	433	512
Driveway	334	386	458
Subtotal	$13,646	$15,214	$18,330
Insurance, comp., soc. sec., unemp., etc.	183	208	248
Overhead and profit—15%	2,115	2,358	2,841
Plans and specification	150	150	150
Total construction cost	$16,094	$17,930	$21,569
Cost per sq. ft. (house area)	11.54	12.85	15.46

Summary	Area	Sq. Ft. Cost	Total	Sq. Ft. Cost	Total	Sq. Ft. Cost	Total
House	1395 sq. ft.	$9.77	$13,629	$10.85	$15,135	$13.06	$18,216
Porch	74 sq. ft.	2.78	205	3.06	226	3.66	271
Garage	435 sq. ft.	4.08	1,775	4.68	2,039	5.58	2,427
Walks	190 sq. ft.	.51	97	.56	106	.69	131
Driveway	760 sq. ft.	.51	388	.56	424	.69	524
			$16,094		$17,930		$21,569

Additives		1/1/66	1/1/68	1/1/70
Fireplace		$475	$550	$570
Range, oven, and cabinets		300	300	330
Hood and fan		60	60	60
Ext. wall shth.		275	290	350
Lath and plstr. int. fin.		650	650	788

Source: *Northern California Real Estate Report,* 1st quarter 1966, p. 51; 1st quarter 1968, p. /1; 1st quarter 1970, p. 59.

little more than a convenient reference point. It must also be recognized that the cost figures make no allowances for differences in labor or management efficiency or for the builders' competitive pricing policies.

Appraisers generally rely upon the square- or cubic-foot method in establishing replacement costs. This method is also described in the *Underwriting Manual*. The square-foot cost factor used is based upon costs of nearly identical type structures, thus obviating the need for ex̲nsive adjustments. The problem of selection of builders for cost sampling ̲d the problem of quality adjustment percentages remain, of course. The technique, however, is so much simpler than the in-place unit system or its modification already described that it is widely employed in home appraisal work.

The application of the square- and cubic-foot methods to all types of improvements is facilitated by the regular publication of cost factors to be applied to various type and quality structures by such firms as the Dow Service, Marshall and Stevens, and others. These services usually furnish photographs and brief specifications for various classes and grades of structures, square- and cubic-foot factors, and various adjustment factors to be used in modifying cost factors for changes in specifications.[27] Such cost data are widely employed in appraisals for establishing values for general property tax and insurance purposes, but they serve only as rough rules of thumb for other types of appraisals. Since costs vary geographically, data may not be pertinent to the area. In addition, these cost factors are subject to all the limitations of cost indexes discussed previously. It is also probably true that appraisers would find it difficult to justify going appraisal fees if it became obvious that their estimates were based upon widely published cost factors available to any subscriber.

The third method, referred to in the *Underwriting Manual* as the repeat-case method, is based upon the principle that the same, or nearly same, structure will tend to have stable costs. Hence, if the costs of building a specific structure are known, it can be assumed that its replacement cost will be the same or similar. Although this method appears disarmingly simple and direct, closer examination reveals that it is subject to most of the limitations that have been discussed. Changes in scale of operation and in specific items of cost may occur with surprising swiftness. The appraiser is therefore forced to rely upon his judgment concerning the future in making appropriate adjustments to known historical costs for a given structure.

Although there are many modifications to the methods of estimating replacement costs which have been described, they are all subject to similar limitations. Structures differ individually. Builders' costs are indeterminate and vary widely over time among individual builders and for different types of structures. Because of the nature of the building process, the methods of cost estimation which seem to recommend themselves in terms of their precise attention to the details of costs can frequently err widely. Modifications of the in-place unit method represent an improvement but have limited applicability owing to nonstandardization of structures. The integrated square-foot and cubic-foot methods, when based upon careful analysis, probably represent the simplest and best adapted methods to most appraisal problems. This is particularly evident when the wide range of accuracy which must be imputed to any replacement-cost figure is considered.

Techniques for Estimating Depreciation

It will be recalled that the problem of making proper allowance for depreciation represents a key difficulty in the use of the replacement-cost method and the reason why the method is considered by many authorities as applicable only to new properties. There is undoubtedly more confusion about depreciation than about any other single segment of valuation theory. Part of this difficulty is accounted for in that the concept of depreciation is cast in a dual role in appraisal theory. In the capitalization-of-income method, as noted in chapter 6, it is used to establish rates of building amortization, while in the replacement-cost method, the concept of depreciation refers to the difference in value between an old or obsolescent building and its new replacement. Bonbright drew attention to the sources of some of the confusion on the matter of depreciation:

> Following the tradition of accountancy, most appraisers *talk* about depreciation in terms of a fall in value. Indeed, they really think in these terms on those somewhat rare occasions when they determine the present value of an asset by adding to or subtracting from original cost. Far more frequently, however, depreciation is treated as a deduction from replacement cost new, estimated as of the date of the valuation. Here the definition "fall in value" is quite erroneous, and the fact that it is still current has given rise to serious confusion. Depreciation should now refer to the difference between the present worth of the old and obsolescent asset and the present worth of the hypothetical new and modern asset. This difference may be much greater or much less than the *decline* in the value of the former asset. To be sure, even in estimating the differential value, an appraiser must, in effect, compare the probable future decline in the value of the new one. But his ultimate objective is to contrast the values of two properties *as of the same date.*[28]

Most present-day appraisal authors distinguish between depreciation as a penalty to be assessed against an old or obsolete structure in comparison with its new replacement and depreciation as an annual charge for the amortization of building investment. An outline of the theory of depreciation in the AIREA textbook identifies these two concepts as (1) accrued depreciation and (2) future depreciation. Shades of the confusion referred to by Bonbright can be noted in this outline, reproduced as figure 8–1. Accrued depreciation is identified as "loss of capital to date of appraisal or capital already recaptured." Obviously, this interpretation is at variance with the definition directly below it identifying accrued depreciation as the difference

Figure 8–1. An Outline of the Theory of Depreciation

Future depreciation

DATE OF

Provision for capital recapture during the economic life of the improvements

It is an annually recurring amount over the economic life of the improvements

It is a deduction from the annual income, i.e., the annual amount necessary to provide for the return (amortization) of the value (proper capital investment) in the improvements (a wasting asset) during their remaining economic life

Caused by

APPRAISAL

Anticipated wasting away (depletion) of the improvements and hence the capital investment therein from all causes over a definite period, i.e., the estimated remaining economic life

Measured by

Straight-line method—a rate usually included in the capitalization rate as an addition to the risk rate

Annuity method—provided for in the annuity factor, Inwood tables

Sinking-fund method—provided for in the Hoskold factor in capitalization rate composed of risk and sinking-fund rate

Used in income approach only

Accrued depreciation

Loss of capital to date of appraisal
or
Capital already recaptured

It is a lump sum

It is a deduction from the cost of replacement new at the date of appraisal, i.e., the difference between the replacement cost of the improvements at the date of appraisal and the value of the improvements as of that date

Caused by

Physical deterioration	Functional obsolescence
Inherent	Inherent
Curable	Curable
Incurable	Incurable

Economic obsolescence
Extrinsic
Rarely if
ever curable

Measured by

Physical curable	—Cost to cure
Physical incurable	—Observed condition and estimated remaining useful life
Functional curable	—Cost to cure
Functional incurable	—Capitalization of rental loss due to this cause
Economic	—Capitalization of rental loss due to this cause

Used in cost approach only

Source: American Institute of Real Estate Appraisers, *The Appraisal of Real Estate,* 5th ed. (Chicago, 1967), p. 198.

between the replacement cost of the improvements at the date of appraisal and the value of the improvements as of that date. It represents the inapplicable transmutation of an accounting theory of depreciation or amortized cost to valuation theory, where it has no relevance. It probably has its roots in the notion of loan amortization payments, which, in fact, represent the return or recapture of loan principal.

The outline in figure 8–1 follows custom in grouping the causes of depreciation under headings of physical deterioration, functional obsolescence, and economic obsolescence. The segregation of curable from incurable depreciation is designed to facilitate measurement of depreciation. Depreciation referred to as curable is usually measured by calculating the "cost to cure" it. Incurable depreciation may be measured by alternative methods, three of which are recommended: (1) the observed-condition method, (2) the age-life method, or (3) the capitalization-of-rental-loss or difference method. The institute text recommends that, in actual practice, methods (1) and (2) may be used in combination. The first requires the careful observation of the property by the appraiser and his expression of judgment about the dollar amount or percentage of incurable depreciation which exists in comparison with a new substitute replacement.

The second method relies upon tables purporting to represent the percentage depreciation assumed to accrue for particular types and classes of buildings over specific periods of building life. Marshall and Stevens provides subscribers with tables of "normal depreciation" for seven categories of property, classified according to quality of construction and price class. These tables present normal depreciation as a percentage for varying effective ages and life expectancies.[29] They are also subject to all of the weaknesses of the straight-line depreciation method.

The third, or capitalization method, is advocated by Babcock and Bonbright as the preferred method for estimating depreciation, and it is recommended for use in combination with the cost-to-cure method by May and Schmutz and the authors of the institute text.[30]

Figure 8–1 portrays the technique for estimating depreciation recommended in recent appraisal texts. It involves separate consideration of the various sources of loss in value and their addition to equal total estimated depreciation. The combination of methods recommended possesses some advantages as well as serious disadvantages. Its advantages lie in the convenient itemization of various factors contributing to depreciation; its disadvantages accrue from the fact that the basic objective sought is lost in the multiplicity of mathematical calculations and sophisticated guesses involved in the estimates. One might list as an advantage or disadvantage the fact that the numerous assumptions and judgments required throughout the estimating process make the resultant estimate of total depreciation easy to adjust so as to agree with an estimate reached by other means.

The distinctions between physical depreciation and functional obsolescence are more imaginary than real and do little more than make the estimation of depreciation needlessly complicated. It is easy to agree with Bonbright and Babcock, who held that the distinction between physical depreciation and functional obsolescence is seldom clear and of little or no significance in the valuation process.

Practically all modern appraisal texts suggest that something called economic obsolescence be added to physical deterioration and functional obsolescence to equal total accrued depreciation. This charge is essentially a penalty against a structure because it is not ideally suited to the land on which it is situated. The market value of the land, which assumes ideal improvements, is added to replacement cost of improvements after deduction of accrued depreciation to equal total estimated value of the property. It will be recalled that the fundamental criticism of the replacement-cost method by many is based on the principle that the summation of land and building values cannot be accepted as a measure of value unless the building is ideally suited to the land, that is, unless it represents what is termed the highest and best use of the site. The problems in definition and determination of the highest and best use of land were discussed in chapter 6. It was shown there that highest and best use represents an opinion rather than a fact and that it would vary over time and with the changing economic outlook and investors' forecasts. The criterion that the replacement-cost method is only to be used when property is in its highest and best use is seen to be highly nebulous, since its use would appear to rely upon land values determined by capitalization of expected returns and their comparison with market values.

The technique recommended for measurement of so-called economic obsolescence is similar in Schmutz, May, and the AIREA text. It is obtained by capitalizing the estimated difference in rental for the subject building, assuming all other deficiencies corrected, in its present location and in an ideal location, as illustrated in these steps: (1) estimate the monthly rental of subject property, assuming ideal location and assuming all physical and functional deficiencies corrected; (2) estimate monthly rental of subject property in present location, assuming all physical and functional deficiencies corrected; (3) estimate the difference in monthly rental $(A - B)$; (4) apportion this rental difference to land and buildings in ratio to their relative values; and (5) capitalize the difference in rental attributable to the building as economic obsolescence. Theoretically, this adjustment technique overcomes the objections to the use of replacement-cost method when the building is not the highest and best use. The reliability of the estimate of economic obsolescence, however, is subject to all the difficulties involved in the capitalization-of-income method and can hardly be referred to as a cost approach to valuation.

As pointed out earlier, the problem of estimating depreciation as a penalty against replacement cost new can be considered in its simplest form as either (1) the difference in market value between a subject property and a new substitute or (2) the capitalized difference in income accruing to the subject property as compared with a new replacement. Any final estimate of depreciation must approximate these values if it is to meet the "judgment" test. It is apparent that important segments of the depreciation-estimating techniques that have been described are subject to varying interpretations, particularly those dealing with the estimation of so-called incurable physical depreciation and functional and economic obsolescence. It has already been noted that the estimation of depreciation by capitalization of rental difference is actually the rejection of the replacement-cost method in favor of the capitalization-of-income method. For this reason it is common practice for appraisers to make elaborate calculations of depreciation by the methods outlined and then to test the result by comparison with an overall estimate of depreciation by the observed-condition method. When the estimates vary, appraisers usually adjust the "built-up" depreciation calculation to agree with their judgment estimate. This, of course, brings the replacement-cost method into very close relationship with the market-comparison method, a relationship to be considered in the following chapter.

In a series of articles on the subject of depreciation in appraisal theory, Charles F. Louie drew attention to the confusion in appraisal literature between depreciation viewed as the accountants' amortized cost and the more applicable concept of depreciation viewed as the difference between the value of two properties — one new and one old or obsolescent — on the same date.[31] He also drew attention to the difficulties in identifying depreciation by source or cause and to the inappropriateness of using the concepts of future depreciation in problems of valuation by capitalization of income.

The present author expressed similar criticisms in a review of Alfred A. Ring's presentation of the topic in the latter's recent book.[32] The term *depreciation* appears to have many identified causes and specialized meanings to professionals in various disciplines. The attempt of the appraisal profession to translate these into meaningful estimates for the purpose of assigning values has resulted in considerable confusion and an almost meaningless dichotomy. Most important, it has caused many appraisers to lose sight of the basic purpose and significance of making an estimate of depreciation in the replacement-cost method. Unfortunately, the overwhelming importance of accounting depreciation in determining tax shelter from real estate investment has added to the appraiser's confusion. Depreciation deductions for income tax purposes are significant only in their effect upon investors' cash flows and tax liabilities and have no relevance to deductions from replacement cost new in valuation.

Summary

The replacement-cost method has wide application in the field of valuation. Its acceptance has been influenced in large measure by the need for standardized techniques for estimating value and by the apparent ease of calculation of replacement costs. Most appraisal theorists accept cost as a ceiling upon value and consider the approach most adaptable to the valuation of new structures. Some adherents to replacement cost still cling to the idea of "normal" long-run costs as market-value determinants.

Upon examination, it was found that there are important unresolved problems in the application of the replacement-cost method, among the most important being the meaning of replacement and the measurement of costs and depreciation. Appraisal writings have not come to grips successfully with the important question of what constitutes a suitable replacement. The contention that the appraiser must consider only a substantial replica of the subject property narrows the adaptability of the method, while the admission of widely differing substitutes magnifies the difficulties of comparison.

It was concluded that replacement costs are, in fact, indeterminate. Furthermore, there is no agreement of whose costs are to be measured, or which items of cost to be included. In the face of the wide variation in builders' costs and the difficulty in their estimation, appraisers resort to fairly simple expedients of using square-foot factors which include percentages added for overhead and profit. At one point in the market these may represent something fairly close to the costs of efficient builders, while at other times they may represent the costs of high-cost producers. They appear to come closer to the replacement costs of purchasers rather than to those of builders.

The estimate of depreciation is a key unknown in the replacement-cost method. Depreciation is the subject of an extensive and sometimes confusing dichotomy in appraisal literature. Various techniques for estimating depreciation were described. It was concluded that the results of these techniques are usually tested by comparison with the observed-condition method, which, in practice, is based upon comparison of the market values of new and old properties. The wide range of depreciation estimates which can result from the application of the somewhat involved techniques recommended forces a strong reliance upon the observed-condition method, which is basically a variation of the market-comparison method of valuation.

Viewing these shortcomings and difficulties in the application of the replacement-cost method, it is difficult to make a strong case for the universal applicability of the method to appraisal problems. The method is clearly most adaptable in the valuation of new properties with no depreciation and with known and stable costs. Such cases would represent only a small fraction of the valuation problems facing the appraiser and, as Babcock maintains, even in these circumstances the market-comparison method is usually more reliable. The possibilities of large errors in the use of the replacement-cost method are greatly increased when it is used in the valuation of older properties. Here the appraiser becomes involved in questions of value differences between new replacement substitutes and older structures. The answers to these questions are founded to a large degree upon opinion and judgment. Continued reliance

THE REPLACEMENT-COST METHOD

upon replacement cost as a measure of value in the residential field results in an interaction between market prices and replacement costs, since market prices of purchasers are influenced by mortgage loan values based upon costs and costs, in turn, are influenced by market prices.

The dependence of the replacement-cost method upon market data and the relationships between the various methods of estimating value will be explored further in the concluding chapter. Although most authorities are in agreement that replacement cost has applicability in only special circumstances and for special classes of properties and, at best, provides a ceiling upon an estimate of value, the replacement-cost method continues to have wide application in appraisal practice. To a considerable degree, this appears to result from the facility with which calculations of replacement cost can be made and the general availability of cost data for use in valuation. The author regards the replacement-cost method as a useful supplement to the market-comparison method only in highly specialized circumstances where accurate cost data are available for new identical properties. The extent to which the method relies upon market data for estimation of depreciation in the case of older properties and the theoretical problems of defining a suitable replacement appear to be serious enough to outlaw the general use of the method over the broad range of real estate appraisal problems.

These criticisms do not imply that the appraiser should disregard cost data in the valuation process. It was pointed out in chapter 5 that costs represent one of many factors influencing market-sales prices. Viewed in this light, cost data represent significant inputs in multiple-regression analysis. The use of cost data in this broader context of valuation will be discussed further in chapter 9.

THE APPRAISAL PROCESS

The appraisal process forges the link between theories of value and valuation and the practical problem of establishing values. It has already been pointed out that the multiplication of value concepts and the confusion over the meaning of the term *value* have made it difficult to agree upon any central concept of value in valuation problems. The historical review of the development of appraisal theory in chapter 2 revealed considerable divergence in the views of appraisers about appropriate concepts, evidence, and procedure in establishing values. In spite of these difficulties, over the past two decades continued efforts have been directed toward the establishment of some broad and universally accepted framework for appraisal procedure. Because of the manifold nature of appraisal problems which such a framework must embrace and because of the differences in valuation procedure, this framework of necessity has had to permit maximum flexibility in procedure and results.

Figure 9–1 portrays an outline of the appraisal process as it has evolved and become generally accepted in appraisal literature over recent years. The reader will recognize that this outline is based upon the neoclassical theory of the equivalence of normal long-term costs, market value, and capitalized income. Before proceeding to a more detailed analysis of the individual steps in this procedure, it is significant to examine the origins and rationale for the present framework set forth in figure 9–1.

It has already been seen that appraisal writers generally agree that the technique of valuation and the value estimate itself will depend upon the nature of the valuation problem. A few have appealed unsuccessfully for a narrowing and sharpening of the value concept to serve as the basis for appraisal theory. Practical exigencies, however, have required that any outline of the appraisal process embrace a host of different types of valuation concepts and problems. An accurate portrayal of the appraisal process as it is actually carried out in certain problems of valuation, therefore, would provide that in certain cases (determination of insurable value, for instance) much of the process be eliminated and the appraiser determine value by calculating the cost to replace the building. In effect, consequently, the entire framework presented in the diagram would apply to only a fraction of the valuation problems presented to an appraiser.

The data program outlined in figure 9–1 attempts to encompass all the various forces which might conceivably affect values of a specific property. Variations of this diagram include analysis of international and national developments as part of the data program. The economic forces affecting

212

Figure 9-1.

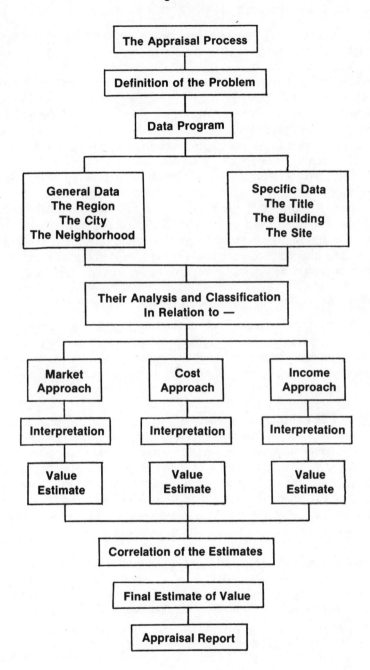

The Appraisal Process

Definition of the Problem

Data Program

General Data
The Region
The City
The Neighborhood

Specific Data
The Title
The Building
The Site

Their Analysis and Classification
In Relation to —

Market
Approach

Cost
Approach

Income
Approach

Interpretation

Interpretation

Interpretation

Value
Estimate

Value
Estimate

Value
Estimate

Correlation of the Estimates

Final Estimate of Value

Appraisal Report

Source: Arthur A. May, *The Valuation of Residential Real Estate*, 2d ed. (New York: Prentice-Hall, 1953), p. 27.

market value, costs, and incomes are of almost immeasurable complexity. They involve predictions of individual and corporate income, government fiscal policy, and international relations. As noted in chapters 2 and 3, the techniques for analyzing the economic and social forces affecting property values have been very imperfectly developed. The extent to which the validity of the whole valuation process hinges upon the accuracy of the exceedingly tenuous analytical procedures thus far developed for determining the economic and social background of real estate values will be considered later. It is obvious that the importance of the various portions of the so-called data program will vary widely with the nature of the appraisal problem and with the degree of emphasis given to each of the three approaches.

Figure 9–1 implies that the three approaches are universally employed with equal weight. It has already been indicated that the approaches to a valuation estimate frequently will vary with the definition of the valuation problem. It is important to trace below the evolution of the idea that the three approaches should be generally employed in real estate appraisal.

The Three Approaches in Economic Theory

As noted in chapter 1, the origin of the three approaches was in the neoclassical economic theory of the relationship between costs, market values, and capitalized income under conditions of stable equilibrium. It was from this same theory that the doctrines of normal value and normal cost, which have assumed important places in appraisal practice, were developed.

Principle of Substitution   Alfred Marshall, as mentioned earlier, was the first economist to express the view that the replacement-cost, market-comparison, and income methods would result in equal estimates of value for newly developed sites. This equivalence in value was to be effected through the operation of the important principle of "substitution," which was central to the neoclassical system of economics. The theory of the operation of this principle in the real estate market is based upon hypotheses with respect to the actions of consumers on the demand side and producers on the supply side. In other words, when property is replaceable, consumers will offer no more on the market than the cost of replacing the property itself, or a comparable substitute. By the same principle, if replacement costs are below market prices, producers will be induced by prospective profits to construct buildings for sale. These tendencies will bring market prices into line with new construction costs.

Since the basis for value of all real property lies in the prospects for future returns, consumers, in establishing demand prices in the market, will theoretically offer prices which represent the discounted value of the expected future returns. Similarly, owners of existing properties and builders will establish supply prices for properties based upon their evaluation of future returns.

According to neoclassical economic theory, the functioning of the principle of substitution would result in an equivalence among cost, market, and income values only under certain hypothetical assumptions. First, it was assumed that the theory would hold only for the pricing of new production and hence would not be applicable to the pricing of used assets. Second, it was assumed that conditions of perfect competition would prevail in the markets. Third, actual equivalence between the three value approaches would be achieved only under conditions of economic equilibrium. Examination of the significance of each of these assumptions will make it apparent that the economic theory of the equivalence among cost, market, and income values can have only limited applicability to the problem of establishing values in the real world.

Pricing of New versus Used Assets A theory which applies to the pricing of new production only is of limited applicability in real estate appraisal work. Since real estate is highly durable and long-lived, most valuation problems apply to used properties. As Bonbright points out, the bulk of properties, being old, are inferior to a new substitute and the calculation of the degree of inferiority is itself a baffling problem.[1] Even though one may minimize the problem of estimation of the depreciation, the necessity of such an adjustment in the preponderant number of appraisal problems disrupts the equivalence theory. Real estate is something of a misfit to this doctrine in another sense because land seldom has a cost of production in the usually accepted sense. Although some would argue that the fair market value of a comparable piece of land represents a fitting substitute for its cost of production, others would maintain that such a substitution represents the abandonment of the cost principle as applied to real estate.[2]

Assumption of Perfect Competition The assumption of perfect competition carries with it the assumption of uniformity of product, perfect knowledge on the part of large numbers of buyers and sellers, and a highly organized market structure. The very nature of real estate precludes the existence of perfect competition in this sense, since it is a highly differentiated product. Its bulk and immovability contribute to the imperfections in the real estate market. Because of the nature of the product and its market, the knowledge of both buyers and sellers is very incomplete. These general limitations are reflected in substantial errors in the estimation of market prices and building costs for similar products in the same markets. The incomparability of individual parcels of real estate magnifies such errors. Owing to these limitations alone, it would appear that the theory of the equivalence of cost, market, and income values would have less applicability to real estate than to almost any other commodity.

215

Meaning of Economic Equilibrium   Consideration of the importance of the assumption of economic equilibrium underlying the equivalence doctrine administers the *coup de grace* to the employment of this theory in real life. The concept of equilibrium is primarily a theoretical tool employed by economists. In neoclassical economics, the concept was associated with the so-called static state or uniformly progressing society. In such a state, the principle of substitution under perfect competitive conditions would operate with free rein. There would be no maladjustments among the various agents of production and their shares in distribution. Price levels would be constant. There would be no excessive amount of installment buying, no inflation or deflation, no wars, floods, disaster, and government would exercise no unbalancing influence upon incomes and expenditures. The economic system would function with the changelessness of a large electric generator. Samuelson has said:

> Prices keep moving as a result of the readjustments of behavior. If outside factors such as inventions, wars, or tastes were to remain constant long enough, then we might finally approach the "general equilibrium set of prices," at which all the forces of supply and demand, value and costs, might just be in balance, without any tendency to further change. Of course, in the real world, outside factors never stand still so that as fast as equilibrium tends to be attained it is disturbed. Still, there is always a tendency — at least in a "perfect" competitive system — for the equilibrium to re-establish itself, or at least to chase after its true position.[3]

Economists generally agree that neither conditions of perfect competition or economic equilibrium can be expected to prevail over any period of time. Hence, few economists would expect to find close equivalence at any time among the replacement cost of a real estate asset, its market value, and its capitalized income value. Indeed, as has been pointed out by another author, economists never troubled to define these concepts with sufficient precision to permit empirical testing of the theoretical hypothesis.[4] Because of these limitations, there is no logical reason for expecting that the three approaches to value will yield identical or nearly identical value estimates. This of course does not invalidate the principle of substitution, which affects the decisions of investors under real as well as theoretical market conditions. Recognition of this principle is the basis for the view, accepted by economists and appraisers alike, that an investor will pay no more in the market for a property than the replacement cost of a comparable substitute. The significance of this principle was examined in greater detail in chapter 8.

Normal Value   As will be noted presently, appraisal theorists have not maintained that the three approaches will yield identical estimates of value for a given property. There is wide acceptance of the view in appraisal literature, however, that long-run normal price will tend to be equivalent to normal cost of production. Owing to its importance in modern appraisal theory, the latter view and the assumptions underlying it must be examined in some detail.

It was noted in chapter 1 that the neoclassical concept of normal value was akin to "a perfect equilibrium value" and hence rested upon the assumptions of perfect competition and equilibrim already discussed. In his attempt to evaluate Marshall's theory of the equivalence between normal costs and normal value, Davenport found that the interpretation of the theory rests upon suitable definition of the terms *normal price*, *normal costs*, *representative firm*, *short run*, and *long run*, all of which are given kaleidoscopic meanings in Marshall's writings.[5]

Wesley C. Mitchell, keen observer of empirical economic data, concluded:

> There is no "normal state of trade." The phrase is common both in treatises upon economic theory and in the talk of business men. Yet the historical record shows no reality corresponding to this figment of the imagination.
>
> If "normal" is interpreted to mean usual, prevailing, that which exists in the absence of grave "disturbing causes," the annals show that the only normal condition is a state of change. . . .
>
> If "normal" means, not that which usually does prevail, but that which we think should prevail, it is equally a figment – though one of a useful kind.[6]

A critic of Marshall's and Cassel's theories of the equivalence between long-run cost and normal price in the housing field has said: "Marshall's round generalizations as to normality are unproved and unprovable, at least as applied to housing, and even the more careful assertion of Cassel, that 'the principle of cost in some degree represents a normal condition about which actual pricing oscillates' is only a statement of faith."[7]

The economic theory of the equivalence between long-run normal costs and normal prices not only lacks explicitness in the meaning attached to the words used, but appears to describe merely a tendency which might apply under assumed conditions which do not exist. Viewed in this light, the theory furnishes a highly insecure foundation for appraisal procedure.

The Three Approaches in Appraisal Theory

Early Emphasis on Market Sales   The evolution of the doctrine of the three approaches in appraisal theory has been fairly recent. Earlier writers recommended primary reliance upon the market-comparison method or the selective employment of alternative approaches.

Richard M. Hurd distinguished between what he called "intrinsic value" or that value obtained by capitalization of income and "exchange" or market value.[8] Although Hurd gave considerable attention to the capitalization-of-income method, he held that average sales prices were the best test of value. A similar emphasis upon market sales prices as the central method of valuation was found in McMichael and Bingham's book, published with

217

the endorsement of the National Association of Real Estate Boards in 1923.[9] Zangerle followed Hurd closely on the selection of method. He described the methods of determining what he called the "economic" value by reference to market sales. He expressed a strong preference for the use of the market-comparison method.[10] Zangerle emphasized the difficulties in the use of the building-cost method of estimating values owing to the wide variations which might be found in cost estimates for identical structures.

It is clear that these earlier writers recognized the differences which resulted from the application of each of the three methods of valuation. Reference to any neoclassical economic theories of equivalence between the cost, market, and income methods or to relationships between normal prices and long-run normal costs was notably absent.

Influence of Classical Economics Arthur J. Mertzke, whose book entitled *Real Estate Appraising* was published by the National Association of Real Estate Boards in 1927, centered his appraisal theory around the Marshallian equivalence between normal cost and normal value. As pointed out earlier, his work represents a key link between economic theory and appraisal theory. Mertzke translated the economic theory of the equivalence between long-run costs, normal value, and capitalized-income values (under specifically assumed conditions of perfect competition and economic equilibrium) into a working appraisal theory. Although he emphasized the three approaches to value and the central importance of long-run costs, he seemed to recognize the adaptability of specific methods to particular classes of property. For example, he advocated the use of the sales-comparison method for appraising vacant residential lots, the cost-of-reconstruction method for appraising the single-family home, and the capitalization-of-income method for appraising income properties. Apparently he did not consider that the three approaches had anything like universal applicability.

Pollock and Scholz, in their joint work published in 1926, reechoed the economic theory that "normal" price will tend to equal "normal" long-run costs:

> In the long run a decided increase in the price paid for a definite amount of a reproducible commodity (an increase in demand), without a corresponding increase in the prices paid for definite amounts of other reproducible goods, will invite increased production of this product, and by increasing the supply tend to lower the price so that the value-relationship between this and other reproducible goods may not be greatly modified. Competition among producers, wherever competition exists, will tend to keep the price of reproducible goods at or near costs of production. The long-run or normal price of such goods will not be far in excess of such costs, and at intervals may actually be below the costs of production. This is true in periods of forced liquidation during which business men sell their products at a sacrifice to realize immediate purchasing power. But in the long run the price of a reproducible good

will be determined primarily by the production costs, and this so-called normal price will not tend to vary to any great extent, unless new discoveries, new
inventions, should materially alter the production costs.[11]

The authors, however, deny the applicability of the normal value theory
to land because of the limitations upon the supply of urban sites. For this
reason, they concluded that the only scientific method of land valuation was
one based upon community expression of opinion, on a front-foot basis, with
the aid of depth tables and corner influence charts for adjusting values.[12] The
authors say little or nothing about the valuation of improved property. It is
clear from their work that they regarded the capitalization-of-income method
with distinct distrust. The quotation above would suggest that they placed
strong reliance upon replacement cost in the valuation of improvements and
market values (obtained in what they refer to as a scientific manner) in the
valuation of land.

Emphasis on Income Approach Frederick M. Babcock held that the income method is the only theoretically correct method of valuation. He ignored the doctrine of equivalence by the three approaches and specifically
rejected costs as suitable evidence of value under most circumstances. The
concepts of normal price and normal long-run costs are not mentioned in his
classic *Valuation of Real Estate*, published in 1932.

Babcock held that generally each property valuation problem required the
selection of a single method. He did, however, recommend a combination of
the income and market comparison methods for certain classes of appraisal
problems and the more or less general use of replacement costs to determine
the upper limits of valuation.[13]

Babcock identified seven methods of valuation. Upon examination, these
are found to be modifications of the cost, market, and income methods. He
identifies these by number, as shown in figure 9–2, which is reproduced from
his book. Methods numbered 1, 2, and 3 are variations of the capitalization-
of-income method. They can only be distinguished individually by the relative difficulty of measuring income to be assigned to the real property.
Babcock's methods numbered 4, 5, and 7 are adaptations of the replacement-
cost method, while he identifies the market-comparison method as number
6. Evidence of his strong preference for the capitalization-of-income method
can be seen in his assignment of greater accuracy to methods 1, 2, and 3. It
can be noted that he assigns the least degree of accuracy to the replacement-
cost methods (4, 5, and 7) and a wide range of accuracy to the market-
comparison method (6). The selection of the appropriate method, according
to Babcock's book, will depend upon the nature and measurability of the
returns from property. In all cases in which the returns are in dollars and
measurable, he recommends the selection of the capitalization-of-income
method. If the returns are not measurable, he recommends the use of method

Figure 9-2. Selection of Valuation Method

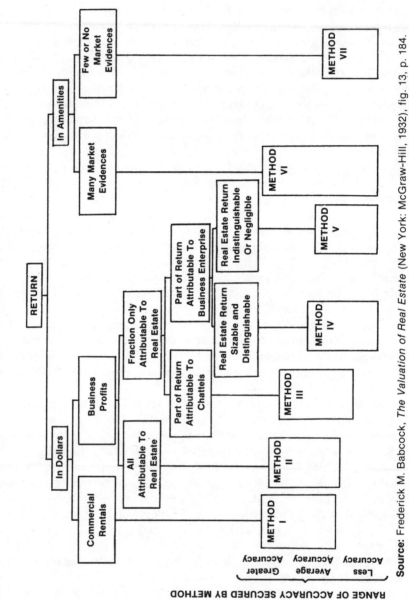

Source: Frederick M. Babcock, *The Valuation of Real Estate* (New York: McGraw-Hill, 1932), fig. 13, p. 184.

6, market comparison. Replacement-cost methods should only be resorted to as a last alternative, except for purposes of establishing a ceiling upon value.

Babcock broke the link established by Mertzke, Pollock, Scholz, and others between the normal price and normal long-run cost theories of neo-classical economics and appraisal theory. In its place he endeavored to forge a stronger link with Irving Fisher's theory that the present value of the future income stream is both the end and the means of establishing values.

Revival of the Three Approaches The doctrine of the three approaches did not die with the publication of Babcock's book. Harry Grant Atkinson, executive director of the institute, prepared the chapter entitled "The Three Approaches" for *Course I* of the American Institute of Real Estate Appraisers, published in 1938.[14] Stressing the controversy over the selection of method, the author pointed up the weaknesses in using each of the three methods alone and concluded that "all three of the primary factors of cost, income, and sales data are present to some extent at least in all appraisal problems." Although Atkinson did not revive the contention of Mertzke and others that the cost, market, and income methods would yield closely similar estimates of value and that normal costs would provide a good measure of normal value, he did single out those appraisal writers who recommended reliance upon a single method of valuation for particular criticism. In doing the latter he provided an excellent summary of the individual weaknesses of the three methods of valuation.

Stanley McMichael, whose *Appraising Manual* first appeared in the 1930s, dealt in cavalier fashion with the choice of method of valuation in his chapter entitled "Approach to the Valuation Estimate."[15] According to McMichael, homes and home sites should be valued by the market-comparison methods, while all investment properties should be valued by the income method, and service properties (schools, post offices, auditoriums, and so forth) should be valued by the replacement-cost methods. Although he did not describe the criteria of selection to be employed in choosing a method of valuation, it can be noted that McMichael's conclusions follow very closely those which would be reached by reference to Babcock's chart on the selection-of-valuation method (see figure 3–2) and the recommendations of this author and other modern appraisal writers.

Modern appraisal theory in the United States follows closely the views advanced by Atkinson in 1938 on the use of the three approaches to value. The textbook of the American Institute of Real Estate Appraisers advocates:

> The appraiser does not obtain his final estimate of value by averaging the three individual indications of value arrived at by means of the cost, market data, and income approaches. Rather, he first examines the spread between the minimum and maximum figures indicated in the three preliminary value estimates. Then, he places major emphasis on the approach which appears to

produce the most reliable solution to the specific appraisal problem. Then he tempers this estimate in accordance with his judgment concerning the degree of reliance to be placed on the other two indications of value.[16]

As this statement implies, the appraiser is given a wide rein in the selection of a method to suit a particular appraisal problem at hand. As indicated earlier, this has been the result of the multiplication of specialized value concepts for insurance, taxation, loan, and other purposes. However, there is strong implication here, as stated more vigorously by Mertzke and others, that the three approaches to value will yield closely equivalent results.

Similar recommendations on the use of the three approaches are found in *The Valuation of Residential Real Estate* by Arthur A. May. He described the appraisal process in diagrammatic form, as shown in figure 9–1, reproduced from his book. A similar diagram, although in somewhat greater detail, is presented in George Schmutz's *Appraisal Process*. Both May and Schmutz recommended the use of the three approaches as the foundation of the appraisal process. Schmutz comments that the income approach is adaptable only when the subject property produces measurable income returns, but he recommends the use of gross rent multipliers for residential properties as a variation of the income approaches.

The Three Approaches in European Theory   Reference to recent European writings in the field of appraisal reveals a totally different slant. Medici, head of the Department of Appraisal at the University of Naples, holds that there are only five economic concepts of value and only one basic method of valuation:

> All possible cases of appraisal can be worked out through the five possible economic aspects of the object to be appraised. . . .
>
> The analysis we have made permits us to . . . affirm that under conditions of equilibrium the five economic aspects considered: market value (capitalization value), cost, transformation value, substitution value, complimentary value, tend to coincide. Such conditions of equilibrium are only to be found in an economic regime of perfect *competition*. . . .
>
> In real life, and particularly where nonordinary firms are concerned, this perfect competition does not exist.
>
> . . . notwithstanding the *apparent* diversity of the various methods, essentially the method is only one, because it terminates inevitably in the two steps indicated: the forming of a scale of prices and the selecting of a level of the scale at which to place the object to be appraised.[17]

It is interesting to note that the doctrine of the three value approaches has little recognition in British appraisal literature. A widely read British book on valuation outlines a procedure for determining value:

A valuer required to find the market value of a particular property will proceed on the following lines:

1. He will determine the net rental value of the property.
2. He will determine the rate percent at which it should be valued.
3. He will multiply the net rental value by a figure of Year's Purchase based, by reference to tables, on his estimate of the appropriate rate percent. It may happen that there is little or no evidence of other transactions upon which the valuer may base his estimates. . . .

Accordingly the valuer may need to have recourse to other methods of valuation.

The principal alternatives are:
(a) Direct comparisons of capital value.
(b) Valuations based on cost.
(c) Valuations by reference to profits.
(d) The residual or development method.[18]

Where residential properties change hands frequently for owner occupancy, the authors recommend the direct comparison of capital value method. They caution that the cost of building is not necessarily a reliable guide to value. The strong reliance upon the capitalization-of-income method in British appraisal theory suggests a fairly close relationship to the framework of appraisal theory recommended by Babcock.

Even though it lacks acceptance in European appraisal writings, the theory of the three approaches to value apparently is securely anchored in American appraisal theory today. The initially close relationship of the theory to neoclassical economics, however, seems to have been lost since the writings of Mertzke and others in the 1920s. There appears to be at least tacit recognition in recent appraisal writings that the three approaches will seldom if ever yield identical or close to identical value estimates. Consequently, the three approaches more and more have their justification as scientific methods of orderly data collection. As a result of these trends, increasing attention is given to the need for "correlation" of the three approaches.

Principle of Correlation The principle of correlating the three approaches developed naturally from the observation that cost, market, and income methods seldom yielded similar values. The Home Owners Loan Corporation resolved this difficulty by requiring that valuation by the HOLC formula should equal the arithmetic average of the market price, capitalized value, and summation value.[19] According to McMichael's summary of HOLC appraisal policies, many other government agencies adopted similar standardized appraisal systems. Appraisers were quick to recognize the large possibilities of error in the method of employing arithmetic averages of values that might differ widely. For that reason, in the 1938 *Course I* text of the American Institute of Real Estate Appraisers, the appraiser was specifically advised not to average the three approaches, but to "co-ordinate" them. The 1967 edition of the institute text clearly rejects the traditional correlation approach and the notion of averaging: "The appraiser does not average the indications of value by the three approaches. He selects the one which is most applicable, and rounds to a final figure. He places the most emphasis on the approach which appears to be the most reliable and most applicable, as an indication of the answer to the specific appraisal problem. Then he tempers this estimate in accordance with his judgment as to the degree of reliance to be placed on the other two indications of value."[20]

Atkinson's instructions appear to cover all contingencies, since the appraiser is free to select a single method as primary in importance and presumably to rely almost exclusively upon it, using the other methods as mere checks. His comments about "narrowing the zone of reasonableness" and Hyder's similar discussion of the use of the three approaches to "narrow the zone of error" not only imply that the three approaches should be used, but also that they will result in closely similar value estimates.

Arthur A. May, in describing the correlation process, goes somewhat further in describing the relationship between the three valuation estimates: "We now have three value estimates resulting from the use of the three approaches. How shall these be rendered into one estimate? This is accomplished in step 6, in which the results of the three approaches are correlated each to the other. Each opinion is weighed in the light of the accuracy, importance, and relevancy of the data on which it is based, and these final opinions are compared and balanced."[21] The correlation process, as May describes it, appears to be essentially the weighing of the relative significance and adaptability of the three approaches to the problem at hand.

Schmutz makes even more clear the exact nature of the correlation process in his chapter entitled "The Correlation of the Estimates."

> The most important features of the correlation are: (a) the consideration of the reasonableness of the data; (b) the recomputation; and (c) the assignment of the relative degree of reliability to each indicated value. As regards the last point, if only two values had been developed, one at \$40,000 and the other \$30,000, and it was indicated that the higher figure was less susceptible of error of judgment, then and in such event the value to be reported would be closer to \$40,000 than to \$30,000.[22]

The reader might pause to wonder why Schmutz's decision in the problem illustrated was not that the value was exactly \$40,000. His insertion of the adjective "closer" before that figure appears to be a thin thread holding up the principle of the correlation of the three approaches.

Compression of Difference Schmutz's advocacy of the recomputation of the value estimates as part of the correlation process is designed to narrow the difference between the high and low estimates by the three approaches and involved "the making of a second appraisal (by each approach) after making reasonable changes in the basic data." In illustrating this technique, he demonstrates the simplicity with which an estimate of value by the replacement-cost method can be altered by changing the cost factors and estimate of accrued depreciation. Similarly, he demonstrates the flexibility in the income method by altering the estimate of gross income and expenses. Thus, he brings the estimates of value by the two former methods close to the market comparison result by what he calls the "compression of difference."[23] Clearly, Schmutz has adopted the view that the three approaches, properly applied, should give nearly identical value estimates and that the process of correlation is designed to force that equivalence. If this cannot be achieved gracefully, the appraiser is free to accept the figure which he regards as least susceptible to error.

The principle of correlation, as described by these authors, appears to involve little more than the process of deciding which of the three methods of valuation should be relied upon in each appraisal problem. The acknowledged need for correlating the three value estimates, therefore, would seem to validate the basic thesis of Babcock that in most cases only one method is ideal for use in a given appraisal and that in few cases are all three approaches applicable. The compression-of-difference doctrine advocated by Schmutz as part of the correlation process emphasizes the evident artificiality in presenting equivalent, or nearly equivalent, estimates of value by the three approaches.

Summary and Conclusions

Contrasted with the wide divergencies of opinion regarding theories of value and valuation, there appears to be considerable surface agreement in appraisal literature as to appraisal procedure. Examination of the successive steps outlined in the appraisal process revealed that the framework accepted is one with a substantial degree of built-in flexibility, providing the appraiser with a procedure which can be altered to suit the various types of valuation problems he encounters.

The outline of the general data program is so highly generalized that it provides little more than a list of some of the factors which can influence values. This phase of the appraisal process was subjected to a more searching examination in an earlier chapter.

The authors of recent appraisal literature appear to have rejected the early view that the market is the best test of value in favor of the neoclassical economic doctrine of the equivalence between cost, market, and capitalized income values. Examination of the assumptions underlying the theory revealed that it has negligible applicability to the problem of fixing values for real estate in actual economic life, since the theory is descriptive of only a tendency toward equivalence under hypothetical market assumptions. Nevertheless, this doctrine was lifted from the neoclassical economics and introduced as the foundation for the three approaches to value by Mertzke and others in the 1920s. At that time, this and the related theory of the equivalence between normal price and normal long-run cost were being subjected to critical reexamination by economists. As a result of this reexamination, economists have held that "normality" in economic life is a figment of the imagination and that the assumptions of perfect competition and economic equilibrium which underlie much of neoclassical economics deny most of its conclusions about relationships between costs and prices. Consequently, about all that was left of the neoclassical economic theory of aid to the appraiser was the principle of substitution, which has been interpreted to establish replacement costs as a ceiling upon value estimates.

As a result of the work of Mertzke, Atkinson, Hyder, May, Schmutz, and others, the doctrine of the equivalence of the three approaches to value has gained wide acceptance. Babcock, in his influential book on real estate appraisal, published in the early 1930s, advocated the rejection of the doctrine of the three approaches and recommended instead the selection of a single method which, according to his criteria of selection, was usually the capitalization-of-income method. The practical difficulties in fixing values by capitalization of income resulted in the gradual rejection of Babcock's principle that a single method be employed in favor of a return to the three approaches. The apparent rejection of Babcock on the selection of method appears to have been fundamentally a rejection of his emphasis upon the capitalization-of-income method rather than a basic difference with his view that a single method or a combination of two methods be chosen.

Members of the American Institute of Real Estate Appraisers were active in supporting the use of all three approaches to value, following the organization of that professional group in 1932. The doctrine of the three approaches has had little acceptance in European theory or practice. British appraisers rely heavily upon the capitalization-of-income method, while Italian theorists hold that there is no equivalence between cost, market, and income values in real life.

The doctrine of correlation evolved naturally from the use of the three approaches and the natural dissatisfaction with averaging techniques. A careful consideration of the real meaning of the term *correlation*, however, suggests that it describes the process of selecting one of the three approaches as most significant for a particular appraisal problem. So interpreted, there appears to be little fundamental difference between the views of Mertzke, Atkinson, Babcock, McMichael, and others on the selection of method, since they seem to be in general agreement that one method is usually best suited for a particular problem. Babcock and McMichael would recommend that this method be identified early in the appraisal process, while the others would favor the collection and interpretation of data by all three methods before any are rejected as unsuitable. Because the view is widely held that the three approaches to value should yield very similar value estimates, the process of correlation frequently resolves itself into the adjustment of data or factors used in one or more methods to obtain closer agreement with a preferred method or value estimate. This *compression of differences*, as it is called, is really the forcing of equivalence between the three approaches and frequently gives a misleading appearance of accuracy to an appraisal estimate.

Appraisers have required an appraisal theory flexible enough to meet the demands of a wide variety of special-purpose valuations. The retention of the three approaches and the doctrine of correlation have fostered that kind of flexibility. Armed with long lists of cost data, comparable sales, and complicated annuity calculations, the appraiser has freedom to exercise his judgment about the "accuracy, importance, and relevancy of the data" and can fashion an opinion of value to suit each specific occasion. Many would argue that all valuations are purposive and that appraisal is essentially a judgment process, hence this flexibility in a method is necessary. Others would maintain that requirements of flexibility cannot condone the maintenance of so tenuous, oblique, and unwieldy a body of appraisal theory. Evaluation of the merits of these opposing viewpoints must await more careful examination of appraisal theory and practice.

In *Real Estate Appraisal*, published in 1956, the author concluded:

1. Market value should be viewed as the central concept in real estate valuation. The doctrine of a willing buyer and a willing seller encourages the establishment of hypothetical market values and nurtures elements of flexibility in the appraisal process. Market prices are the most reliable indicators of market value and the market-comparison method should be the preferred approach to its estimation.

2. The doctrine that the three approaches to value should result in closely identical figures is false, and the technique of correlating the three approaches to value as a means of reconciling their differences introduces a large and undesirable area of flexibility and subjectivity in the appraisal process.

3. The gross-multiplier technique is a highly useful extension of the market-comparison method and provides excellent bench marks for certain classes of properties.

4. The theory of the economic base is crudely related, if at all, to the appraisal estimate in conventional appraisal theory and practice. Urban growth theories are also imperfectly integrated into appraisal theory. The principles of city growth which have provided a workable explanation of historical growth of American cities are unsatisfactory for predicting growth patterns of the future.

5. The capitalization-of-income method often results in wide variations in

valuation estimates, attributable in important degree to the arbitrary estimation of future incomes and subjective selection of capitalization rates. The employment of the so-called residual-approach, split-rates, straight-capitalization, and sinking-fund methods of valuation add little to the accuracy of valuations by the capitalization-of-income method.

6. The replacement-cost method has only limited and special applications in the valuation of real estate. The estimate of depreciation is often a highly significant element in the replacement-cost approach. Contrary to accepted appraisal theory, the division of depreciation between physical, functional, and economic is artificial and usually impossible to measure accurately.

7. The most promising future for appraisal research lies in improvements in market data that can serve to reestablish real estate appraisal on the firm foundations of the marketplace.

On the strength of these conclusions and recommendations, the author recommended a restructuring of the appraisal process as set forth in figure 9–3. The qualifications specified for the use of the replacement-cost and capitalization-of-income approaches are notable, as is the primary emphasis upon the market-comparison approach. Subsequent developments in appraisal theory lead the author to recommend that the appraisal process should be more specifically oriented to the particular value concept sought. It has been argued in chapters 1 and 2 that the two most generally used and important value concepts are most probable selling price and investment value. Replacement cost, it is maintained, represents a specialized method for use in considering new projects and for special-purpose valuation problems only. Figure 9–4 sets forth an outline of the appraisal process which is designed to emphasize the use of the market-comparison method and the related gross-multiplier method in the determination of the most probable selling price. The capitalization-of-income method is identified for use only in the determination of investment value. It is made clear that analysis of the economic base and long-term forecasts of the national and regional economies are relevant only in the determination of investment value.

The relationship between the concepts of most probable selling price and investment value are suggested by the notation toward the bottom of figure 9–4 that the two value measures may be the same or may differ, depending upon the degree of market activity and the characteristics of the property and of the investors considered.

It is assumed that an astute buyer would always consider the cost of replacing any real property which he is contemplating acquiring. In this sense, the replacement-cost method may be viewed as having relevance to the determination of the most probable selling price as well as to investment value. However, as noted in chapter 8, the problems of applying this method for other than new properties are so great as to justify, in the view of the author, the elimination of the replacement-cost method from general usage.

Figure 9-3. The Appraisal Process

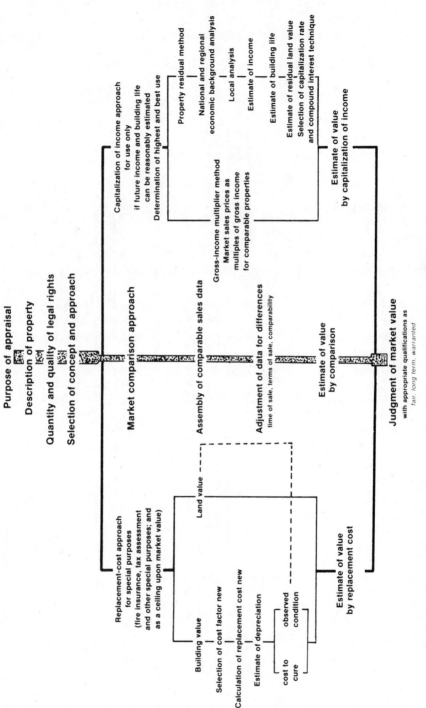

Source: Paul F. Wendt, *Real Estate Appraisal—A Critical Analysis of Theory and Practice* (New York: Holt, 1956).

Figure 9-4. The Appraisal Process

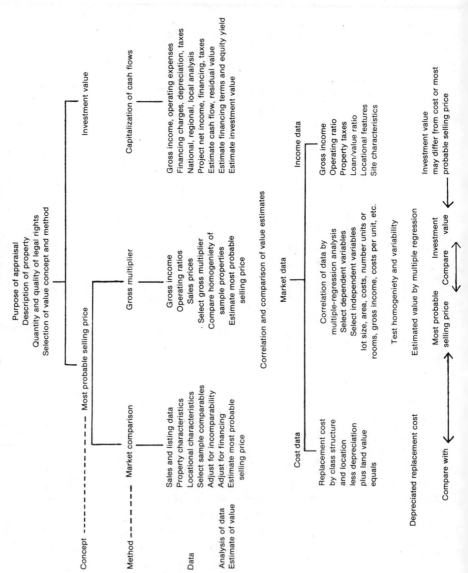

Purpose of appraisal
Description of property
Quantity and quality of legal rights
Selection of value concept and method

Concept - - - - - - - Most probable selling price   Investment value

Method - - - - - - Market comparison   Gross multiplier   Capitalization of cash flows

Data

Sales and listing data
Property characteristics
Locational characteristics
Select sample comparables
Adjust for incomparability
Adjust for financing
Estimate most probable
selling price

Gross income
Operating ratios
Sales prices
Select gross multiplier
Compare homogeniety of
sample properties
Estimate most probable
selling price

Gross income, operating expenses
Financing charges, depreciation, taxes
National, regional, local analysis
Project net income, financing, taxes
Estimate cash flow, residual value
Estimate financing terms and equity yield
Estimate investment value

Analysis of data
Estimate of value

Correlation and comparison of value estimates

Cost data   Market data   Income data

Replacement cost
by class structure
and location
less depreciation
plus land value
equals

Correlation of data by
multiple-regression analysis
Select dependent variables
Select independent variables
lot size, area, costs, number units or
rooms, gross income, costs per unit, etc.

Test homogeniety and variability

Gross income
Operating ratio
Property taxes
Loan/value ratio
Locational features
Site characteristics

Estimated value by multiple regression

Depreciated replacement cost   Most probable   Investment   Investment value
                                            selling price   value   may differ from cost or most
                                                  Compare   probable selling price

Compare with

The gross-multiplier method is assigned an important role in the outline of the appraisal process in figure 9–4. The justification for the emphasis upon the use of this method is found in its extensive use for certain classes of income property. The anticipated improved availability of market-sales and gross-income data for a wide range of property types and the present facilities for storage, analysis, and retrieval of these data through the use of the computer, promise even wider use and application of gross-income multipliers in the marketplace, as pointed out in chapter 7.

Figure 9–4 emphasizes the use of the market-comparison method to determine the most probable selling price. Recent improvements in market data availability and computer facilities make it possible to employ multiple-regression techniques more extensively and with greater reliability than in the past and, as pointed out in chapter 5, this variation of the comparable sales approach promises to supplant more traditional applications of this method of valuation.

The capitalization-of-income method occupies a more restricted position and role in the representation of the appraisal process in figure 9–4 than is customarily assigned to this technique. Explanation for this, dealt with more fully in chapter 6, lies in the high degree of subjectivity and flexibility with which values may be estimated by the use of this technique. The author finds it most applicable, therefore, where the basic inputs are related to a specific investor in the determination of investment value.

The representation of the appraisal process in figure 9–4 implies that econometric models of urban growth have great potential significance for use in real estate appraisal. Figure 9–4 incorporates the so-called specific data concerning the title, the building, and the site of the subject property as a part of the data bank. The figure introduces a new concept of correlation and comparison of value estimates, relying upon multiple correlation in a statistical sense, rather than in its traditional subjective adaptation in the appraisal process.

The integration of cost, market, and income data under the heading "Multiple-Regression Analysis" in figure 9–4 recognizes the joint contribution of these different types of data to the final valuation conclusion. The effect of this is to substitute a single valuation technique reflecting the joint contribution of cost, market, and income data for the traditional three separate data approaches. Some proponents of the use of multiple-regression analysis would contend that the technique should be regarded as a substitute for the more traditional applications of the market-comparison, gross-multiplier, cost, or capitalization approaches. The position accorded to "Multiple-Regression Analysis" in figure 9–4 reflects this author's views that the technique should be used as a supplement to the other techniques rather than as a substitute for them.

231

SUMMARY AND CONCLUSIONS

Earlier chapters have reviewed the development of appraisal theory, the rationale for the three approaches to value estimation, and problems in the application of these methods. It remains for the final chapter to summarize the findings and conclusions and to comment upon their significance for the student of real estate valuation.

Development of Appraisal Theory

The art of establishing property values is as old as the institution of private property. The systematic presentation of the principles of this art, referred to as appraisal theory, is of substantially more recent origin. It was noted in chapter 1 that theories of value and valuation were fully developed by economists by the end of the nineteenth century. The theory as they presented it was an integral part of what has been called neoclassical economics and was centered about the concept of the equivalence of cost, market, and income values under conditions of economic equilibrium. Mathematical techniques for discounting future returns had been developed over a century before and had wide application in the investment and accounting fields. The appraisers also inherited a formidable body of legal doctrine bearing upon the meaning of the term *value* and the techniques found acceptable by courts of law in establishing values for specific purposes. Any review of the historical antecedents of appraisal theory would not fail to mention its close links with real estate practice and with the phenomena of the marketplace.

It was the need for establishing values on a large scale for tax and loan purposes that gave rise to the integration of these various elements from 1910 to 1930 into what can be termed *appraisal theory*. During this incubation period, appraisal theory was nurtured by the real estate practitioner and thus relied closely upon the market process and market prices as evidence of value.

As appraisal theory commenced to assert its own individuality during the 1930s, it gradually severed its umbilical ties with economic theory and with real estate practice. In the process, however, appraisal writers clung to certain nineteenth-century economic theories that were no longer generally accepted among economists. These centered about the equivalence of cost, market, and income values under equilibrium conditions. In addition, appraisal theory was more or less permanently influenced by the work of Irving Fisher, an economist who early in the present century emphasized that value was represented by the present worth of future expected returns.

SUMMARY AND CONCLUSIONS

One explanation of the tenacity with which appraisal theory has clung to the idea of the equivalence of cost, market, and income approaches to value is found in the need for flexibility in the appraisal process. The meaning of value is one of the most widely discussed topics in appraisal literature. Many writers have contended that the term *value* is merely a generic expression and that the purpose and occasion for the value estimate must be known before the appraiser may estimate value. Others maintain that the several meanings of the word are aberrations and that market value should be the central concept in appraisal theory. Faced with the multiplicity of value concepts in use, the appraiser has needed a set of operating procedures that could be adapted to a variety of special-purpose valuations. The doctrine of the three approaches to value has provided such a framework.

Although each of the three approaches has had strong adherents over the few decades during which appraisal theory has developed, it seems fair to state that the greatest share of attention has been given to the theory and practice of the capitalization-of-income method. A publication of the American Institute of Real Estate Appraisers, which reproduced leading articles from the *Appraisal Journal* of the previous two decades, devoted less than one hundred pages to the techniques of the cost and market approaches as compared with over four hundred pages concerned with various phases of the capitalization-of-income method.[1] The emphasis in appraisal theory upon this latter method, and collaterally upon mathematical techniques for establishing values, can be traced to the influence of Frederick M. Babcock. He was primarily responsible for the synthesis of Irving Fisher's theory of value as the present worth of future returns with the mathematical contribution of accountants and engineers. Following its publication in 1932, his book *Valuation of Real Estate* dominated appraisal theory. Babcock's main tenet was that there is only one theoretically correct method of establishing the value of income-producing real estate – namely, by capitalization of expected income. This fundamental thesis has been rejected in both appraisal theory and practice over the past twenty years in favor of the doctrine of the equivalence of the so-called three approaches to value and their correlation.

A number of factors were noted in chapter 2 as contributing to this development. The obvious inapplicability of the capitalization-of-income method to certain problems in valuation and the difficulties in its use were undoubtedly of substantial influence. The need for standardized valuation techniques for taxation and other purposes gained support for the replacement-cost method. The collapse in property incomes and market values in the Great Depression of the thirties also resulted in added weight being given to replacement costs in estimating property values. This tendency was furthered by greatly expanded federal government activities in the residential mortgage field and increasing reliance upon replacement cost as evidence of value for mortgage loan purposes. As an outgrowth of these many influences, the

233

doctrine of the three approaches came into favor in appraisal circles during the 1930s. Its appeal has rested upon its apparent thoroughness as a scientific process of data assembly and, more realistically, upon its extreme flexibility.

The Three Approaches

The doctrine of the three approaches to value and their correlation was examined in some detail in chapter 9. The rationale for the use of the three approaches to value has changed substantially since it was first enunciated in the 1920s by Mertzke, Pollock, Scholtz, and others. Contrasted with these earlier rationalizations, which attempted to link appraisal theory with the neoclassical economic doctrine of normal costs and normal market values, recent proponents emphasize the weaknesses of each of the three approaches singly and maintain that the three approaches constitute a scientific data-collection technique. The logic of the contention that the use of the three approaches eliminates the weaknesses of the individual approaches used singly has been questioned.

The contentions that the three value approaches result in closely equivalent value estimates and that there is some observable relationship between normal costs and normal market values were examined in chapter 9. First, it was established that the assumptions underlying the doctrine of equivalence between the three approaches are quite out of keeping with real life circumstances. For this reason it was observed that economists seldom expect that the application of the three would result in closely equivalent value figures. Second, it was concluded that the concepts of normal costs and normal values have varying meanings over time and for different individuals, have little or no significance as observed phenomena in the real estate field, and hence furnish no support for the view that costs and market prices will be equal at any point in time.

Because of the wide variations typical in the estimation of values by the use of the three approaches, the key to the process of fixing values (according to modern appraisal theory) is found in the doctrine of correlation. A careful review of the meaning and significance of the term *correlation* revealed that it is, in fact, the process of determining which approach to value is best adapted to the problem at hand and of placing key reliance upon that approach. Viewed in this light, correlation involves merely a careful reconsideration of the method applicable to a valuation problem after all the data have been assembled. Here the doctrine that the three approaches to value should always be employed loses its position of sanctified universality. It was further observed in chapter 9 that the principle of correlation so interpreted returns modern appraisal theory to a position of agreement with Babcock, who had maintained that a single method of valuation, or a combination of two methods, was proper and that the three approaches seldom, if ever, should be employed. The apparent rejection of Babcock's theoretical framework was seen to have been a rejection of his view that the capitalization-of-income method is the only theoretically ideal method, rather than a true difference with his contention that a single method rather than the three approaches be employed in valuation.

Economic Background and Neighborhood Analysis

Important assumptions regarding the probable influence of economic factors underlie every appraisal of fair market value or estimate of future income or accumulated depreciation. The interrelationships among national, regional, and local economic factors and their influence upon real estate values were considered in chapter 3. It was observed that the importance of economic-base analysis is fully recognized in appraisal literature, but that little attention is devoted to the techniques for its analysis. Some explanation for the latter failure was found in the difficulty of the task and in the lack of well-integrated local and regional economic data.

Following a review of the characteristics of a local economy and the factors in its growth and stability, attention was drawn to the two key factors affecting the outlook for population and incomes in a local area: (1) the tendency for local and regional business conditions to reflect national business trends and (2) the importance to regional and local economies of so-called basic economic activities in attracting population and incomes to an area. These two elements provided the framework for the author's recommendations that in the analysis of the economic base, the appraiser give primary attention to forecasting national economic trends and changes in local basic employment. Case studies were examined that illustrated some of the techniques which can be used in such an approach. It was concluded that most of the techniques recommended furnish inadequate linkage between the national and regional economic analysis and the analysis of the local economic base. This area of knowledge, in the author's judgment, represents one of the weakest links in appraisal theory and practice.

The appraisal process also accords important attention to the analysis of neighborhood influence upon property values, since individual districts and neighborhoods of a city change and shift over time as the city grows and land-use patterns are altered. The process of urban growth and structural change and techniques for analysis of the internal structure of cities were described in chapter 4. It was concluded that, although the theories of city growth that have been developed furnish an acceptable account of the past growth trends in American cities, they provide a considerably less satisfactory basis for predicting urban growth patterns of the future. This conclusion was reached in spite of the observation that transportation and topography will probably continue to dominate the urban growth patterns of the future. Basic changes in the geographical concept of urban areas, fundamental alterations in transportation routes, technological changes, and greatly enlarged influence of public controls promise that future trends in urban development will be unlike those of the past.

Examination of the techniques recommended for the analysis of the internal structure of cities revealed a general failure to integrate the analysis of the urban districts with that of the urban economic base. Hence, principal attention is devoted in appraisal literature to characteristics of the neighborhood itself, rather than to the processes of urban change which are going on about it. An exception to this is found in the techniques recommended by Weimer and Hoyt, who emphasize that the future development of any district or neighborhood will depend upon the overall economic expansion in the urban area and the movements of major urban districts. It was concluded that the more detailed techniques of neighborhood analysis developed by Frederick Babcock, the Federal Housing Administration, and others can be used by the appraiser to better advantage if they are integrated with a careful historical view of past urban growth trends and with an economic analysis of the locational factors influencing current and future land-use trends.

The author drew attention to the potentialities in the use of the output of recently developed land-use simulation models as a means of integrating national, regional, and local economic forecasts. These models, which integrate economic forecasting, economic base, and location theory have extensive applicability to the appraisal process. Further, the economic assumptions underlying such models are explicitly stated and the models are so constructed that these and other inputs to the models can be altered to produce alternative forecasts with considerable ease. An important ancillary reason justifying the appraiser's use of such models is found in the fact that the results of land-use simulation models are being adopted increasingly as a basis for public policy actions.

Problems in Applying the Three Approaches

Chapters 5, 6, 7, and 8 were concerned with a more detailed consideration of the capitalization-of-income, replacement-cost, and market-comparison methods. The difficult problems of estimation in the capitalization-of-income method were portrayed through a series of examples illustrating the varying assumptions necessary in forecasting future incomes, selecting a rate or rates of capitalization, and estimating building lives and terminal land values.

Although writers on appraisal theory appear to be in agreement that capitalization rates should be obtained from the "market," examination of the various techniques for accomplishing this revealed that the process is essentially one of subjective estimation. Following Babcock, practically all modern appraisal texts advocate the use of some type of grid chart in the selection of rates. There proved to be relatively wide variation in the factors recommended for consideration in the various grid charts and their weightings. Rate grid charts are usually advocated for use in combination with an "ideal" rate for an investment of 100 percent quality. It is usually advocated that this ideal rate be represented by the percentage relationship between market prices and income for a given year. Although this represents a determinable statistic, the analysis in chapter 6 pointed out that there is little or no reason for using such a relationship to indicate a capitalization rate, which is generally understood to refer to the percentage relationship between future expected incomes and market price. It was concluded in chapter 6 that capitalization rates for properties with known fixed incomes may be approximated by comparison with bond yields, but that the determination of the capitalization rate for a property with an indeterminate future income is largely a matter of guesswork. The techniques examined make this guesswork appear more sophisticated but do not alter the important element of subjective estimation involved.

Other techniques for rate selection examined included the so-called summation and band-of-investment theories. The former method was viewed as a logical procedure for considering the factors influencing rates, although the key element – the percentage allowance for risk – remains a matter of judgment. The band-of-investment theory represents an attempt to obtain a weighted average of rates of return for the various interests in property ownership. The key to the determination of rates by this process, it was found, is in the estimation of the equity return, which is assumed to be the current rate of return on the equity interest. None of the techniques examined provide a scientific and objective method for establishing the capitalization rate for a given property.

The recent contributions of Ellwood to the technique of determining capitalization rates by the band-of-investment method were noted. Although he adds no clues to the determination of the most important element, the equity rate, Ellwood has developed an ingenious method for estimating an overall capitalization rate for level incomes where mortgage terms and estimated appreciation or depreciation are known.

It seems trite to say that capitalization rates must be obtained in the market. However, the broadened institutional and individual participation in real estate investment is forging stronger links between rates of return on real estate and on other classes of investments. As markets are broadened and analytical techniques are sharpened, it can be anticipated that the rates of return available for different classes of real estate will become a matter of general market knowledge. Here, in the author's view, lies the source and potential for analysis and development of rates to be used in the valuation of investment real estate. The techniques presented in chapter 6 for the empirical derivation of equity capitalization rates based upon projected after-tax cash flows should represent an important forward step in capitalization-rate determination.

The author has argued here and elsewhere that the rate of return on the after-tax cash flow to the equity investor is the most realistic and significant measure of true equity-capitalization rates.[2] Computer models designed to measure the internal rate of return, which was demonstrated to be identical to the so-called Inwood factors or Ellwood rates widely used in appraisal practice, were presented in chapter 6. The algorithms presented are capable of solving for rates of return on equity investment, a potent tool in determining the so-called equity rates, and more important, can be used to estimate values, under assumed financing terms and given target equity rates of return.

Capitalization-of-Income Method

The accurate estimation of future income is, of course, the key to sound valuation by the capitalization-of-income method. As pointed out in chapter 6, there are wide variations in the difficulty of forecasting incomes, depending upon the type and quality of the structure and tenure. Incomes from real estate have shown marked instability over the past several decades, while expenses have also been subject to wide fluctuations.

Because of the difficulties in estimating future incomes, tendencies were observed in appraisal literature to employ declining annuity tables as a substitute for year-to-year, forward-income estimates. These tables, which are based upon the premise that incomes will decline in some predeterminable manner with increasing age of structure, are not based upon known real estate income experience and represent highly theoretical and usually unreliable bases for predicting future incomes. The alternative to the use of such mathematical tables of prediction is for the appraiser to engage in careful economic analysis of trends in occupancy rates, rental incomes, expenses, and price levels. Although this procedure is obviously more sound, it requires an extensive knowledge of national, regional, and local economic conditions and is frequently beyond the capacities of the typical appraiser.

Faced with alternatives of merely projecting current incomes into the indefinite future, forecasting future incomes year by year, or employing declining annuity tables, the appraiser using the capitalization method cannot escape the fact that the best he can usually hope to produce is a sophisticated guess. Although the selection of the capitalization rate and the estimation of future income represent the key determinants in the capitalization-of-income method, it was pointed out in chapter 6 that the appraiser must also make an assumption regarding future land values and that the assumption of constant land value over the life of improvements is a highly questionable one. Added together, these three estimation problems account for the wide variations in estimated values based upon capitalization of income.

The problems referred to above are glossed over to some extent in appraisal literature, which accords greatest attention to the techniques and mathematical procedures to be used in capitalizing income. The rationale for the use of land and building residual methods and for employing various techniques for establishing the value of a future income stream was examined in chapter 6. It was concluded that investors infrequently assign different portions of an expected income stream to land and buildings separately and capitalize these conceptual income streams at differing rates. It was also questioned that investors do, in fact, employ the type of reasoning underlying the sinking-fund methods of valuation of future incomes. For these reasons, it was concluded that by and large the employment of the so-called residual approaches, split rates, and sinking-fund methods of valuation add little to the accuracy of valuations by the capitalization-of-income method. In some sense, they may have the opposite result, since the appraiser may be encouraged to look upon the valuation process as a mathematical calculation rather than the careful exercise of judgment. At best, it might be said that these processes add to the mystery of the appraisal process for the uninitiated.

Many practicing appraisers and academicians have expressed disillusionment with the capitalization approach to real estate valuation in recent years, and some have recommended the abandonment of the technique as outmoded and unrelated to real estate market determination. The author maintains that the capitalization-of-income method, properly employed, has an important place in the determination of investment value of real estate. It was pointed out in chapter 6, however, that the only realistic approach to the capitalization of income was through the concept of measuring the relationship between after-tax cash flow and investor's equity. This concept, which has wide practical use in real estate brokerage and investment circles, overcomes many of the former criticisms of the capitalization approach.

Use of Gross Multipliers

The estimation of values by employing gross-rental income multipliers was described in chapter 7. It was seen that this technique is, in reality, a variation of both the capitalization-of-income and market-comparison methods. The gross-multiplier technique is widely used in real estate and appraisal circles. Upon examination, it was concluded that it has certain advantages over the income-capitalization process since it avoids the difficult problems of estimating future incomes and building life and selecting capitalization rates. It also provides a useful adjunct to the market-comparison method. Great caution is required in its use, however, because of the differences in expense ratios among individual properties.

The gross-multiplier method of valuation is gaining adherents among real estate brokers, appraisers, investors, mortgage lenders, and government loan-insuring agencies. Its great strength, simplicity, appears to be its greatest weakness and accounts in considerable measure for its rejection by some professional appraisers. Improvements in the availability of market data promise further improvements and applications of this technique, which probably rests upon the firmest data foundation of any of the appraisal methods.

Replacement-Cost Method

The replacement-cost method is of great pragmatic significance since it is the basis for values established in the fire insurance and tax assessment fields and is relied upon extensively in both government and private mortgage loan appraisals. It was noted in chapter 8 that the replacement-cost method is considered to have only limited applicability by most appraisal theorists and that its general use has been heavily censured by Babcock and others. The explanation for the extensive use of this method appears to lie in the rejection of market prices as indicative of values and in its apparent ease of computation. There is, however, general agreement that replacement costs of a substitute represent a ceiling upon market value.

Important problems in the application of the method that were discussed in chapter 8 included the determination of the meaning of *replacement* and the measurement of costs and depreciation. Little difficulty is encountered in defining the term *replacement* and in the application of the replacement-cost method to the valuation of new and modern properties since it usually refers to the virtual reproduction of an existing building. Older properties, however, are seldom duplicated, and the appraiser is faced with the problem of determining the characteristics of an acceptable substitute. Obviously, individual views might differ widely on such a question, making the application of this method to such properties hazardous.

It was pointed out in chapter 8 that the structure of costs in the building industry is exceedingly complex and that the appraiser must determine whose costs are to furnish the basis for the estimate of value. This problem is particularly significant in the valuation of single-family homes because of the known variation of costs with scale of operation. Further problems were considered in connection with the question of including selling and financial costs, which might vary widely over time and among individual builders. It was concluded that appraisers generally employ costs as they find them reflected in market prices and that, so viewed, the replacement-cost method bears close relationship to the market-comparison method. Other important links were noted between market prices and replacement costs in residential appraisals. Market prices and replacement-cost estimates are usually similar for new residential construction since market prices are strongly influenced by appraisals for loan purposes which, in turn, are usually based upon replacement costs.

The greatest problem in the application of the replacement-cost method was found to be in the estimation of depreciation. It was concluded that the observed-condition method, in preference to various mathematical techniques and income-capitalization methods, is the most widely used and the most logical. The observed-condition method relies heavily upon the comparison of selling prices for a new property and for the older subject property. In this sense it furnishes another strong link between the replacement-cost method and the market-comparison method. Theoretically, replacement costs represent a ceiling upon value for all property. Actually, such costs can be determined only within broad limits of accuracy for new structures. The difficulties of establishing the characteristics of a structure to replace an older property and the hazards of estimating depreciation combine to eliminate the usefulness of this method for older properties. The techniques resorted to for estimating costs and depreciation bring this method into close relationship with the market-comparison method.

The replacement-cost method has fallen on evil times during the postwar decades, when building costs and methods changed rapidly and when the pressure of loan funds for employment encouraged many lenders to accept at face value the estimates of construction costs presented by speculative builders. Many of these lenders found out in the 1966 credit crunch that cost is not value, and some learned that there were wide differences between estimated costs – even certified costs – and actual outlays. Studies have been cited to show that market-sales prices have typically exceeded builders' costs by substantial margins during the recent years of high investor demand for real estate.

Changing styles and technology have heightened the problem of determining the characteristics of a replacement and have virtually outlawed the consideration of reproduction cost for many older-type dwellings. In these years, the subjective determination of depreciation is entirely speculative and the only real test lies in comparing the sales prices of old and new dwellings of similar type. More than ever, the replacement-cost method for older properties relies upon the market-comparison method for its most important inputs, the value of a new dwelling or property and the depreciation to be charged against the old.

This author can only conclude that cost is not only not value, but in most cases it is not even cost. It is a highly inferior method of limited general applicability.

Market-Comparison Method

The market-comparison method recommends itself as the most logical and simplest technique for establishing values of property, and it has long been recognized as such by economists. Although many would contend that the market has no monopoly over pecuniary valuations, the market prices of consumer goods and other income-producing investments are accepted as indicative of their value for most purposes. The nonhomogeneity of real estate, the imperfections in its market, and the wide variations which have occurred in market values of real property have all combined to cause some rejection of the market-comparison method in recent decades. This tendency has been encouraged by the lack of well-organized market data in the real estate field.

The appraiser using the market-comparison method is required to determine the comparability of the individual properties for which he has sales data and to ascertain the influence of the terms and conditions of the sales upon market prices. The individuality of real properties and the imperfections in the real estate market frequently make these processes difficult. It was noted in chapter 2 that market value is generally held to be the price for which a property would sell under certain idealized market conditions rather than the price for which it actually sells. This conception of market value has been nurtured by the courts and by federal government agencies engaged in mortgage-insuring and guaranteeing activities. It has, of course, imparted substantial flexibility to the term *market value*, since individuals' views as to what market value "ought to be" vary widely.

Assuming that the appraiser can judge comparability of individual properties and establish suitable criteria for evaluating the terms and conditions of sales, the market-comparison method requires that dollar adjustments be made in sales figures to reflect his judgments. A variety of techniques, many of them based upon the use of grids for rating of features of the individual properties, were examined in chapter 5. It was concluded that some of the more involved of these techniques apparently lose sight of the basic principle of the market-comparison method – namely, the selection of market sales of highly comparable properties as evidence of value for a subject property. It was also concluded that the usefulness of the market-comparison method could be greatly enhanced by the improvement in market information. This author concurs with his colleagues who advocate that the most probable selling price is a superior concept of value to the traditional hypothetical fair market value adhered to in appraisal literature and in the courts. Improved data sources and techniques of analysis have been cited in support of the more extensive reliance upon the market-comparison method. The method not only stands on its own feet as the most reliable and logical one for establishing values, but it provides the foundation upon which both the capitalization approach and the replacement-cost approach rest.

The use of the multiple-regression analysis is viewed by some as representing a variation of the market comparison technique and by others as a *fourth* valuation approach integrating all of the variables influencing value into a single equation representing the weighted influence of each variable. Although the multiple-regression technique has been applied successfully in many areas for a number of years, it represents something new that is little understood and thus is mysterious and suspicious to the average practitioner without statistical training. Nevertheless, the application of multiple-regression analysis to problems of valuation of real estate is inexorable and inevitable. Its usefulness in mass appraisals for assessment purposes has already been demonstrated. Its progress will, of necessity, go hand in hand with improvements in market data collection and retrieval and with professional education. The author views multiple-regression analysis in appraising as the research opportunity of the present and the hope of the future. It is to be hoped that within a decade appraisers will no longer refer to the three approaches but rather to three (or more) types of data (variables) influencing values. A new meaning will attach to the traditional *correlation* of the three approaches to value.

SUMMARY AND CONCLUSIONS

Problems in Appraisal Theory and Practice

The appraisal of real estate is an art, not a science! Many problems in the field of appraisal theory and practice stem from attempts to apply mathematical and engineering techniques to the appraisal of property. The needs for standardized methods and consistent valuation results for a variety of purposes have resulted in a multiplication of value concepts and encouraged resorting to mathematical and engineering methods.

The view that an estimate of value will vary with the purpose of each appraisal has had great influence upon the development of appraisal theory since it has encouraged the retention of the doctrine of the three approaches and resultant flexibility in establishing estimates of value. Babcock's efforts to establish a theory of appraisal were handicapped by his refusal to accept market prices as evidence of value and by his zealousness in translating Fisher's theory of value into a technique for valuation.

By far, the largest number of real estate appraisals is directed toward the determination of market value. Although admittedly imperfect, the real estate market represents the most reliable source of information bearing upon market value. Compared with the market-comparison method, the capitalization-of-income and replacement-cost methods have extremely limited applicability and rely upon the market for key elements in the valuation process. Generally, the possibilities of substantial error in valuations appear to become larger as the methods employed diminish their reliance upon market prices. Recent years have witnessed an improvement in the flow of real estate market information. This development lends support to the view expressed here that market value should represent the central appraisal concept and market prices the basic evidence upon which value estimates should be based.

The author has argued in chapter 1 and elsewhere that the most probable selling price represents the most unambiguous definition of market value, is free from most of the subjective reasoning that surrounds the hypothetical willing buyer–willing seller concept, and should be regarded as the central-value concept. It was pointed out that investment value may or may not equal the most probable selling price, since the tax positions, access to financing, and risk parameters of individual investors will vary. For this reason, it was argued that investment value should be regarded as a separate concept of value. At the conjuncture of market price, investment values and market values will be the same for particular investors, but many appraisal problems require the estimation of values for a specific investor, and these may differ substantially. This conception of the valuation process brings the appraiser into the sphere of valuation sometimes professionally associated with the real estate counselor. The author argues that the replacement-cost method should be reserved for special problems and eliminated as a generally used approach. Acceptance of this dichotomy of value concepts would have the following beneficial results of (1) releasing appraisal theory from the straitjacket of the three approaches and their equivalence, (2) clarifying the market value con-

243

cept by relating it more directly to market data and the market-comparison approach, (3) bringing appraisal theory into a more logical relationship with value concepts which have meaning in the marketplace, (4) retaining the capitalization approach but specifying the areas of its applicability, (5) giving clear recognition to the widely acknowledged shortcomings of the cost approach to value, and (6) simplifying the overly cumbersome structure of appraisal theory.

The link between appraisal concepts and methods is close, and the author recommends revision of the appraisal process in chapter 9. The outline of the appraisal process in figure 9–4 in that chapter emphasizes the distinction between the concepts and methods appropriate to the estimation of the most probable selling price and investment value. The gross-multiplier approach is viewed in figure 9–4 as an important adjunct to the market-comparison method, a role which is consistent with the use of that method in real estate markets. The discounted cash-flow method recommended overcomes many of the criticisms of more traditional capitalization-of-income approaches.

The dominant characteristic of the appraisal process, as traditionally conceived, was its inherent flexibility. This made it ideally suited, in some ways, to a wide range of value concepts, appraisal problems, preconceptions, and preferences of individual appraisers. The degree of this flexibility has led many to regard its elasticity as that ordinarily associated with the rubber band. In the judgment of the author, it is time to spell out in greater detail the guidelines to be used by the appraiser in approaching specific valuation problems. The framework proposed by the author in 1956, shown in chapter 9, had this as an objective, and he has pursued the same goal in the present work.

Some disapprove of the author's emphasis on market sales on the grounds that they eliminate the all-important element of the professional appraiser's judgment and make a statistician or "bean counter" out of him.

The outline of the appraisal process in figure 9–4 has a fourfold purpose: (1) to classify the major occasions for valuation and define the concepts unambiguously, (2) specify the methods best adapted to the estimation of value in each case, (3) integrate new techniques of economic and statistical analysis into the appraisal process, and (4) reestablish the basic link between investment analysis and appraisal theory.

Significance of Conclusions for the Student of Valuation

Even the most unlooked-for acceptance of the author's recommendations will only partially simplify the task for the student of valuation. As noted in chapter 1, specialized concepts of value and their related techniques are securely established in law and practice for an indefinite future. Therefore, the appraiser must recognize that the word *value* will continue to have a variety of meanings and related valuation procedures for special purposes — and these he must know.

The present framework of the appraisal process appears to be so firmly established in appraisal literature and education that acceptance of any major modifications will be slow. Viewing the present structure of appraisal theory and its rationalizations as a scientific data-collection process, the student of appraisal must be able to recognize the inapplicability of certain of the three approaches to specific problems in valuation. At the same time, he must realize both the apparent and hidden links between the income, replacement-cost, and market-comparison methods. With a knowledge of these relationships he will be able to understand the true manner in which the three approaches are "correlated."

The capitalization-of-income method has its major support in the theory that value should be measured by estimating the present worth of future returns. The appraiser must be prepared to defend such a theory of value. At the same time, he must understand the techniques of the capitalization-of-income method well enough to dismiss some of its results as involving too high a level of abstraction. He must also be able to perceive and demonstrate the key influence of market sales prices upon capitalization rates used in establishing values by the income method.

The wide-scale employment of the replacement-cost method would alone require that the student of appraisal comprehend the rationale for its use and the problems in its application. Its principal usefulness lies in the acceptance of replacement cost as a ceiling upon value. Carefully analyzed, the estimated cost of new residential structures is largely based upon market sales prices. Since estimates of depreciation for older structures are generally keyed to differences in market value between an old and a new property, it is apparent that the replacement-cost method is closely dependent upon market sales prices.

The market-comparison method provides the all-important link with economic realities for the appraiser. Although, because of market imperfections, it cannot be relied upon to reveal values with uniform precision, it is the central focus for the student of valuation. Significant improvements in real estate market data have been made in the post–World War II period, and this area of knowledge offers the most promising future for appraisal research. Concentration upon improvements in market data and refinements in the market-comparison method should bring real estate appraisal theory and practice much closer to the daily work of the real estate broker. Such a development may be objectionable to appraisers who have struggled to foster distinctive professional attitudes and levels of knowledge in the appraisal field. On the other hand, it may reestablish real estate appraisal on the firm foundations of the marketplace from which it was weaned and restore the exercise of wisdom and judgment to their true positions in appraising.

Many of the ideas expressed by the author can be found buried in the writings of Frederick M. Babcock, whose book *The Valuation of Real Estate*, published by McGraw-Hill in 1932, is still a giant in its field and in the writings of others. In many ways the history of appraisal theory is better than the theory itself. The problem is that theories become practice and, under the leadership of professional educators, soon become dogma. Textbooks sponsored by professional appraisal organizations become the dispensers of the received doctrine, which is soon echoed by courts of law and government administrative agencies. For the practicing appraiser or the neophyte, the spectre of passing the examination requirements of a professional appraisal society constitutes the principal barrier to assured economic success. The threat implicit in the existence of so-called appraisal review committees tends to encourage conformity in appraisal practice. However desirable this may seem as a means of improving the image of the professional organization, it most assuredly dampens innovation and the criticism of existing appraisal theory and practice.

The universities have had a relatively limited impact upon development and innovation in appraisal theory. Until recent years, university professors accepted the body of appraisal theory that had been developed largely by practicing appraisers. This was due in large measure to the dominance of professional appraisers and their organizations in the education of appraisers and to the general neglect of the entire field of real estate in academic curricula. A similar situation prevailed in the accounting field before the 1930s, when most university teaching of this subject was carried on by professional accountants on a part-time basis. Academicians have recently mounted a broad attack upon the traditional framework of appraisal theory, as noted earlier and elsewhere.[3] It is to be hoped that these efforts will result in the integration of university research results into the mainstream of appraisal theory and practice. The most promising aspect of this hoped-for development is that real estate brokers, mortgage lenders, and investors have moved ahead of the appraisal fraternity already in the adoption of many new techniques and approaches to real estate valuation.

A major evolution in institutional investment policies and practices is accompanying the technological revolution in valuation techniques. These developments are causing great changes in real estate valuation theory and practice and promise to merge real estate investment and valuation theory into the well-established structure of security analysis. The financial analyst, armed with the newest computer technology, promises to be a formidable competitor and participant in property valuation in the future.[4] The appraiser may very well find that his survival in a rapidly changing real estate market environment and organization will require that he adopt new techniques to meet the present-day needs of his clients.

NOTES

CHAPTER 1

1. *Southwestern Bell Telephone Company* v. *Public Service Commission*, 262 U.S. 276 at 310 (1923), as cited in James C. Bonbright, *The Valuation of Property* (New York: McGraw-Hill, 1937), 1: 5.

2. Ralph Barton Perry, *General Theory of Value* (New York: Longmans Green, 1926), p. 693. By permission from Harvard University Press.

3. Ibid., p. 21.

4. Herbert Joseph Davenport, *Value and Distribution* (Chicago: University of Chicago Press, 1908), p. 1.

5. Edwin R. A. Seligman, *Principles of Economics* (New York: Longmans Green, 1905), p. 174, as quoted in Davenport, *Value and Distribution*, p. 310.

6. Davenport, *Value and Distribution*, pp. 315–316.

7. Guiseppe Medici, *Principles of Appraisal* (Ames: Iowa State College Press, 1953), p. 17n.

8. Herbert B. Dorau and Albert G. Hinman, *Urban Land Economics* (New York: Macmillan, 1928), p. 524.

9. Richard Ruggles, "The Value of Value Theory," *American Economic Review* 44 (May 1954): 140–160.

10. Richard M. Hurd, *Principles of City Land Values* (New York: Real Estate Record Association, 1903), p. 2.

11. John A. Zangerle, *Principles of Real Estate Appraising* (Cleveland: Stanley McMichael, 1924), pp. 22–24.

12. Frederick M. Babcock, *The Valuation of Real Estate* (New York: McGraw-Hill, 1932), pp. 12–16, 160–161.

13. Stanley L. McMichael, *McMichael's Appraising Manual*, 3d ed. (Englewood Cliffs, N.J.: Prentice-Hall, 1944), pp. 6–7, 10.

14. Arthur A. May, *The Valuation of Residential Real Estate*, 2d ed. (Englewood Cliffs, N.J.: Prentice-Hall, 1953), p. 3. May does give his reasons for denying the use of the term *value* to the various concepts he lists, although he quite obviously subscribes to the generally accepted view that there may be an infinite number of value concepts. Later in his work, May appears to defend market value as the general concept.

15. Ibid., pp. 12, 13.

16. American Institute of Real Estate Appraisers, *Appraisal Terminology and Handbook*, 5th ed. (Chicago, 1967), p. 131.

17. George L. Schmutz, *The Appraisal Process* (North Hollywood, Calif., 1951), p. 29.

18. David M. Lawrance et al., *Modern Methods of Valuation of Land, Houses, and Buildings*, 5th ed. (London: Estates Gazette, 1962), p. 2.

19. Medici, *Principles of Appraisal*, pp. 33, 38.

20. Percival V. Bowen, "Shall Values Be Based on Past, Present, or Future," *Appraisal Journal* 2 (January 1934): 130.

21. Robert H. Armstrong, "Values and Fetishes," *Appraisal Journal* 18 (April 1950): 179–184.

22. "Willing Buyer, Willing Seller and Market Value," *Appraisal Journal* 14 (January 1946): 5–6, as reprinted in American Institute of Real Estate Appraisers, *Selected Readings in Real Estate* (Chicago, 1953), pp. 104–106.

23. Paul F. Wendt, *Real Estate Appraisal – A Critical Analysis of Theory and Practice* (New York: Holt, 1956), pp. 21, 306.

24. Richard U. Ratcliff, *Modern Real Estate Valuation, Theory and Application* (Madison, Wis.: Democrat Press, 1965), p. 48.

25. Henry A. Babcock, *Appraisal Principles and Procedures* (Homewood, Ill.: Irwin, 1968), p. 640.

26. Ibid., pp. 640–641.

27. Ibid., pp. 828–830.

28. William H. Husband and Frank Ray Anderson, *Real Estate Analysis* (Homewood, Ill.: Irwin, 1948), p. 410.

29. McMichael, *McMichael's Appraising Manual*, chap. 9.

30. Federal Housing Administration, *Underwriting Manual*, rev. ed. (Washington, D.C., 1952), sec. 1005.

31. Veterans Administration, *Lenders' Handbook*, pamphlet 4–3 (Washington, D.C., 1948), pp. 1, 34. The Federal Home Loan Bank Board recently proposed the following revised definition which it proposes to require in connection with appraisal reports prepared by or for all federally insured savings and loan associations: "The term market value shall mean the price in terms of cash, or in terms reasonably equivalent to cash, which a property will bring, if exposed for sale on an open market by an informed seller with a reasonable time to find a purchaser buying with

full knowledge of all the uses and purposes to which it is capable of being used, with neither buyer nor seller being under compulsion to buy or sell." Quoted from the *Appraiser* 26 (May 1970): 2.

32. Anson Marston, Robley Winfrey, and Jean C. Hempstead, *Engineering Valuation and Depreciation*, 2d ed. (New York: McGraw-Hill, 1953), p. 4.

33. Bonbright, *The Valuation of Property*, 1: 15.

34. Ibid., 1: 17, 64.

35. Ibid., 1: 56–63.

36. Ibid., 1: 65.

37. Herman D. Jerrett, *The Theory of Real Property Valuation* (Sacramento, Calif., 1938).

38. Ibid., pp. 81, 83, 89.

39. For a recent statement illustrating the calculation of investment values, see Robert C. Higgins and R. Hugh Cunningham, "Computerized Calculations – Rates of Return and Risks in Commercial Property," *Appraisal Journal* 38 (January 1970): 37–49.

CHAPTER 2

1. Arthur M. Weimer, "History of Value Theory for the Appraiser," *Appraisal Journal* 21 (January 1953): 8.

2. Lewis G. Haney, *History of Economic Thought* (New York: Macmillan, 1936). Davenport, *Value and Distribution*.

3. Adam Smith, *The Wealth of Nations* (New York: Collier, 1909), 1: 30 "The value of any commodity . . . is equal to the quantity of labor which it enables him to purchase or command." See also Adam C. Whitaker, *History and Criticism of the Labour Theory of Value in English Political Economy* (New York: Macmillan, 1904).

4. Davenport, *Value and Distribution*, chap. 14.

5. Alfred Marshall, *Principles of Economics*, 8th ed. (London: Macmillan, 1925), 5: chaps. 4, 11, 15; app. H.

6. Ibid., p. 441.

7. Ibid., app. G, pp. 447–450.

8. Ibid., p. 424n.

9. Ibid., p. 453. The residual process will be described in chap. 6.

10. Irving Fisher, *The Nature of Capital and Income* (New York: Macmillan, 1906).

11. Gustav Cassel, *The Theory of Social Economy*, trans. Joseph McCabe (New York: Harcourt, Brace, 1924), p. 127.

12. Laura M. Kingsbury, *The Economics of Housing* (New York: King's Crown Press, 1946),

pp. 31–33. A careful reading of Cassel makes it appear that Kingsbury's criticism was unjustified. In the case of valuing durable goods with limited lives, Cassel called attention to the need for including in the rent a proportion for the depreciation of the capital. However, in the next sentence he says, "Strictly speaking, the proportion for depreciation of capital is payment for part of the good itself, not rent, if we take it as net rent, or as the price that is paid for mere use, after striking off from the gross rent the cost of depreciation."

13. Dorau and Hinman, *Urban Land Economics*.

14. Ibid., pp. 525–530.

15. George Raymond Geiger, *The Theory of the Land Question* (New York: Macmillan, 1936); Harry Gunnison Brown, *Economic Science and the Common Welfare* (Columbia, Mo.: Lucus, 1936); Henry George, *Progress and Poverty* (New York: Schalkenbach, 1955).

16. John Bates Clark, *Distribution of Wealth* (New York: Macmillan, 1899); Richard T. Ely, *Outlines of Economics* (New York: Macmillan, 1908); Franklin A. Fetter, *Principles of Economics* (New York: Century, 1904); Seligman, *Principles of Economics*.

17. Raymond T. Bye, *Principles of Economics*, 3d ed. (New York: Crofts, 1934), pp. 331–332, 340.

18. Edward Chamberlin, *The Theory of Monopolistic Competition* (Cambridge: Harvard University Press, 1933); Joan Robinson, *Economics of Imperfect Competition* (London: Macmillan, 1933); Joe S. Bain, "Price and Production Policies," in *A Survey of Contemporary Economics*, ed. Howard S. Ellis (Philadelphia: Blakiston, 1938); Committee on Price Determination for the Conference on Price Research, *Cost Behavior and Price Policy* (New York: National Bureau of Economic Research, 1943).

19. Lawrence Chamberlain and George W. Edwards, *The Principles of Bond Investment*, rev. ed. (New York: Holt, 1927). The author has in his possession a set of bond value and interest tables prepared for S. A. Kean and Company, a Chicago banking house, in 1888.

20. John Burr Williams, *The Theory of Investment Value* (Cambridge: Harvard University Press, 1938).

21. Arthur Stone Dewing, *The Financial Policy of Corporations*, 5th ed. (New York: Ronald Press, 1953), pp. 277, 300–301.

22. James C. Van Horne, *Financial Management and Policy* (Englewood Cliffs, N.J.: Prentice-Hall, 1968).

23. Paul F. Wendt, "Current Growth Stock Valuation Methods," *Financial Analysts Journal*,

April 1965, pp. 91–103. Writing on the subject of security evaluation in the *Financial Analysts Journal* for November-December 1969, W. Scott Bauman presents three concepts of value: cash value, comparative value, and normative value. These can be viewed as parallels to concepts of value widely used in real estate appraisal. W. Scott Bauman, "Investment Returns and Present Values and an Appendix of 45 Tables," *Financial Analysts Journal*, November-December 1969, pp. 107–123.

24. Eugene Fama, "Random Walks in Stock Market Prices," *Financial Analysts Journal*, September-October 1965, pp. 55–59.

25. John B. Canning, *The Economics of Accountancy* (New York: Ronald Press, 1929).

26. Commenting upon the capitalization of income theory of value, Canning said, "The economist, in general, calmly assumes the existence of data that never have been available and never will be." Ibid., p. 197.

27. C. Rufus Rorem, *Accounting Method* (Chicago: University of Chicago Press, 1930), as quoted by Kingsbury, *The Economics of Housing*, pp. 146–147.

28. Dewing, *The Financial Policy of Corporations*, p. 539n.

29. Bonbright, *The Valuation of Property*, 1: 187. See also S. S. Wyer, *Regulation, Valuation and Depreciation of Public Utilities* (Columbus, Ohio: Sears and Simpson, 1913); R. B. Kester, *Advanced Accounting*, 3d ed. (New York: Ronald Press, 1933).

30. Robert R. Sterling, *Theory and Measurement of Enterprise Income* (Lawrence: University of Kansas Press, 1970), pp. 155–156.

31. American Accounting Association, *A Statement of Basic Accounting Theory* (Evanston, Ill., 1966), pp. 76–77.

32. Marston, Winfrey, and Hemstead, *Engineering Valuation and Depreciation*.

33. Bonbright, in his two-volume work *The Valuation of Property*, has traced the evolution of these concepts and techniques as they have been employed in condemnation, insurance, and tax law. Educational work in the appraisal field was initiated in the 1920s under the leadership of the National Association of Real Estate Boards. The American Institute of Real Estate Appraisers was organized under the auspices of NAREB in 1932. Two years later the Society of Residential Appraisers was organized under the sponsorship of the United States Building and Loan League.

34. Clarence A. Webb and Arthur Hunnings, *Valuation of Real Property* (London: Macmillan, 1913).

35. Richard M. Hurd, *Principles of City Land Values*.

36. Ibid., p. 2.

37. Stanley L. McMichael and Robert F. Bingham, *City Growth and Land Values* (Cleveland: McMichael, 1923).

38. Ibid., p. 227.

39. Walter William Pollock and Karl W. H. Scholz, *The Science and Practice of Urban Land Valuation* (Philadelphia: Pollock, 1926).

40. Ibid., p. 27.

41. Zangerle, *Principles of Real Estate Appraising*.

42. Ibid., p. 24.

43. Raoul J. Freeman, "Real Estate Assessment and Electronic Computers," *Appraisal Journal* 27 (April 1959): 182–184. See also Robert H. Gustafson, "Data Banks and Computerized Annual Updating of Assessment Rolls," paper delivered before the International Association of Assessing Officers, Denver, 7–10 September 1969.

44. Arthur J. Mertzke, "Real Estate Appraising," mimeographed (Chicago: National Association of Real Estate Boards, 1927); Horace F. Clark, *Appraising the Home* (New York: Prentice-Hall, 1930); Frederick M. Babcock, *The Valuation of Real Estate*; Kingsbury, *The Economics of Housing*. The author is indebted to Miss Kingsbury for much of the analysis which follows of the writings of Mertzke and Clark, both volumes being out of print.

45. Mertzke, "Real Estate Appraising," as quoted by Kingsbury, *The Economics of Housing*, pp. 116–117. Kingsbury pointed out that Mertzke erred in his description of the capitalization-of-income process by deducting depreciation prior to establishing net income and by capitalizing the lump-sum income to land and buildings as a perpetuity. Ibid., pp. 113–114.

46. John Alden Grimes and William Horace Craigue, *Principles of Valuation* (Englewood Cliffs, N.J.: Prentice-Hall, 1928).

47. E. Holland Johnson, "Cost Approach to Value," *Encyclopedia of Real Estate* (Englewood Cliffs, N.J.: Prentice-Hall, 1959), p. 52.

48. Sanders A. Kahn, Frederick E. Case, and Alfred Schimmel, *Real Estate and Investment* (New York: Ronald Press, 1963), p. 82.

49. Sanders A. Kahn, "The Entrepreneur – The Missing Factor," *Appraisal Journal* 31 (October 1963): 476.

50. Wallace F. Smith, *The Low-Rise Speculative Apartment*, Research Report no. 25 (Berkeley: Center for Real Estate and Urban Economics, University of California, 1964), pp. 88–89.

51. Ratcliff, *Modern Real Estate Valuation, Theory, and Application*, p. 67.

52. Richard U. Ratcliff, "Capitalized Income Is Not Market Value," *Appraisal Journal* 36 (January 1968): 35.

53. Ibid., p. 39.

54. For a review of this and other recent court decisions the student is referred to the *Appraisal Journal* 38 (October 1970), "The Legal Angle" by Henry J. Kaltenbach, p. 616, and "The Appraisal Docket" by William R. Theiss, p. 624. These articles are regular features of the *Appraisal Journal*.

55. Wendt, *Real Estate Appraisal*. For a review of recent developments in appraisal theory by the author, see Paul F. Wendt, "Recent Developments in Appraisal Theory," *Appraisal Journal* 37 (October 1969): 485–500.

56. *Northern California Real Estate Report*, San Francisco Bay Area Council, San Francisco; *Residential Research Report*, Residential Research Committee of Southern California, Los Angeles.

57. Leon W. Ellwood, "Depreciation and Appreciation," *Appraisal Journal* 24 (July 1956): 351–360. See chap. 6 for discussion.

58. For a review of Ellwood's technique, see Paul F. Wendt, "Ellwood, Inwood, and the Internal Rate of Return," *Appraisal Journal* 35 (October 1967): 561–576. See also Paul F. Wendt and Alan R. Cerf, *Real Estate Investment Analysis and Taxation* (New York: McGraw-Hill, 1969), app. B, chap. 2.

59. William M. Shenkel, "Valuation by Multiple Regression Analysis: Selected Case Studies," *The Application of Econometric Methods to the Appraisal Process* (Chicago: International Association of Assessing Officers, 1971), pp. 95–112, and David W. Walters, ed., *Real Estate Computerization*, Research Report no. 35 (Berkeley: Center for Real Estate and Urban Economics, 1971).

60. For a discussion of the use of after-tax cash flow in determining investment value, see Wendt and Cerf, *Real Estate Investment Analysis and Taxation*, chap. 2. Valuation based upon cash flow analysis is illustrated in chap. 6.

61. Federal Housing Administration, *Underwriting Manual*, loose-leaf rev. ed. (Washington, D.C., February 1966).

CHAPTER 3

1. Richard B. Andrews, "Mechanics of the Urban Economic Base," *Land Economics* 29 (May, August, November 1953); 30 (February, May, August, November 1954); 31 (February, May, August 1955).

2. Arthur M. Weimer, Homer Hoyt, and George F. Bloom, *Real Estate*, 6th ed. (New York: Ronald Press, 1972), p. 202.

3. "Economic base or function . . . whether it is manufacturing, retail trade, wholesale trade, mining, government . . . [is] that [which] furnishes the major volume of employment in the city" (Grace K. Ohlson, "Economic Classification of Cities," *The Municipal Yearbook* [Chicago: International City Managers Association, 1950], p. 29, as quoted in Andrews, "Mechanics of the Urban Economic Base," August 1953, p. 265). Another definition is "the fundamental sources of income that may be available to the citizens in a particular community, from which they derive their livelihood and on which the community's activity as a whole depends" (Larry Smith, "The Economic Base of the Community," *Business Action for Better Cities* [Washington, D.C.: Chamber of Commerce for the United States, 1952], p. 44, as quoted in Andrews, "Mechanics of the Urban Economic Base," August 1953, p. 265). "The economic base of an era in its broadest aspect is the sum total of all those factors which influence people to locate their residences in a particular place. . . . The definition of the economic base of an area is a definition of those income opportunities located within a specified area" (Chester Rapkin, Louis Winnick, and David M. Blank, *Housing Market Analysis: A Study of Theory and Methods*, Report of Project O–E–48 for the Housing and Home Finance Agency [Washington, D.C.: Government Printing Office, 1953], p. 43).

4. Hans Blumenfeld, "The Economic Base of the Metropolis," *Journal of the American Institute of Planners* 1 (Fall 1955): 114–143. Ralph W. Pfouts, ed., *The Techniques of Urban Economic Analysis* (Trenton, N.J.: Chandler-David, 1960).

5. Charles M. Tiebout, "The Urban Economic Base Reconsidered," *Land Economics* 32 (February 1956): 98.

6. Richard B. Andrews, *Urban Growth and Development* (New York: Simmons and Boardman, 1962), p. 7.

7. Homer Hoyt, "Importance of Manufacturing in Basic Employment," *Land Economics* 45 (August 1969): 344–349. Although Hoyt cites partial data for fifty-seven metropolitan areas, his data are complete for only twenty-one metropolitan areas over one million population and for thirty-one under one million population. The regression coefficients are based on these fifty-two cases only.

8. Paul F. Wendt and Hal R. Varian, note on Hoyt's "Importance of Manufacturing in Basic Employment," *Land Economics* 46 (August 1970): 350–354.

9. Tiebout, "The Urban Economic Base Reconsidered," pp. 95–99. See also Wilbur R. Thompson, *A Preface to Urban Economics* (Baltimore, Md.: Johns Hopkins Press, 1965), pp. 141–147.

10. Ray M. Northam, "Population Size, Relative Location, and Declining Urban Centers: Coterminous United States, 1940–1969," *Land Economics* 45 (August 1969): 315.

11. Frederick M. Babcock, *The Valuation of Real Estate*, p. 79.

12. Ibid., p. 81.

13. Ibid., p. 56. Examination of population data for fifty-five cities in six counties of the San Francisco Bay area from 1900 to 1950 reveals that the simple projection of past rates of growth would have resulted in exceedingly large errors in future population predictions. It also appears that the assumption that population in individual cities would grow at equal rates would have been in error. Projections, therefore, on the assumption that a city would maintain a constant percentage of the population of the San Francisco metropolitan area would have resulted in errors of large magnitude. Highway Research Board, Special Report 11, *Parking as a Factor in Business*, pt. 5, "Trends in Economic Activity and Transportation in San Francisco Bay Area," table A–1.

14. May, *The Valuation of Residential Real Estate*, pp. 55, 59–60.

15. Kahn, Case, and Schimmel, *Real Estate and Investment*, p. 56.

16. American Institute of Real Estate Appraisers, *The Appraisal of Real Estate*, 5th ed. (Chicago, 1967), p. 80.

17. Henry A. Babcock, *Appraisal Principles and Procedures*.

18. Jerome Dasso, "Economic Base Analysis for the Appraiser," *Appraisal Journal* 37 (July 1969): 382.

19. Richard U. Ratcliff, *Urban Land Economics* (New York: McGraw-Hill, 1949), p. 42.

20. Weimer, Hoyt, and Bloom, *Real Estate*, 6th ed., pp. 219–220.

21. Roland Artle, "On Some Methods and Problems in the Study of Metropolitan Economics," *Regional Science Association Papers* 8 (1962): 71–87. Reprinted in *Land Using Activities*, Research Report no. 33 (Berkeley: Center for Real Estate and Urban Economics, University of California, 1970), pp. 69–85.

22. Ibid., p. 71.

23. Ibid., p. 71.

24. Department of Housing and Urban Development, Federal Housing Administration, *FHA Techniques of Housing Market Analysis — Revised Edition* (Washington, D.C., August 1970), pp. 18–19.

25. For an example of the FHA market analysis reports, see *Analysis of the San Francisco–Oakland, California, Housing Market as of October 1, 1968* (Washington, D.C.: Federal Housing Administration, March 1969).

26. For a review of the contributions to this work by Tinbergen, Klein, Dusenberry, Eckstein, Fromm, and others, see Karl A. Fox, *Econometric Analysis for Public Policy* (Ames: Iowa State University Press, 1958).

27. James S. Duesenberry et al., eds., *A Quarterly Econometric Model of the United States Economy* (Chicago: Rand McNally, 1965).

28. United States Council of Economic Advisers, *Annual Report*.

29. National Planning Association, Center for Economic Projections, *National Economic Projection Series* (1959–current); *Regional Economic Projection Series* (1962–current).

30. Department of Commerce, Office of Business Economics, *Growth Patterns in Employment by County, 1940–50, and 1950–60*, 8 vols. (Washington, D.C.: Government Printing Office, 1965).

31. Edgar S. Dunn, Jr., "A Statistical and Analytical Technique for Regional Analysis," *Regional Science Association Papers* 6 (1960): 97–112. See also Lowell D. Ashby, "The Geographical Redistribution of Employment: An Examination of the Elements of Change," *Survey of Current Business* 44 (October 1964): 13–20.

32. A mathematical representation of the method of calculating national growth, income component mix, and regional share, aids in understanding table 3–4. The following explanation is shown on p. 18n4 of Robert B. Bretzfelder's article in *Survey of Current Business* for August 1970.

33. Charles F. Floyd, *The Changing Structure of Employment and Income in the Coastal Plains Development Region* (Washington, D.C.: Office of Regional Development Planning, Economic Development Administration, 1 March 1969). Charles F. Floyd, *Economic Growth in the Upper Great Lakes Region, 1950–1967* (Washington, D.C.: Office of Economic Research, Economic Development Administration, April 1970). Charles F. Floyd, "Employment and Income: Its Structure and Change in Northeast Georgia," prepared for Northeast Georgia Area Planning and Development Commission (Athens, Ga., August 1970).

The national and regional estimates of employment and income published by the Regional Economics Division, Office of Business Economics, U.S. Department of Commerce are based upon county wage and employment data. The technique for division of regional employment growth between the national growth, industrial mix and regional share components is illustrated mathematically below.

Let: E_i^1 Regional employment in industry i in base period 1

        E_i^2 Regional employment in industry i in base period 2

        EG Percentage growth rate in U.S. all-industry

        EI_i U.S. industrial industry growth rate

        NG National growth component of regional growth

        IM Industrial mix component of regional growth

        RS Regional share component of regional growth

        TC Total change in employment in region period 1 to 2

Then:
$$NG = \sum_{i=1}^{32} E_i^1 \times EG$$

$$IM = \sum_{i=1}^{32} E_i^1 \times (EI_i - EG)$$

$$TC = \sum_{i=1}^{32} E_i^2 - \sum_{i=1}^{32} E_i^1$$

$$RS = TC - (NG + IM)$$

34. Floyd, *Employment and Income: Its Structure and Change in Northeast Georgia*, table A–18. For a critical evaluation of the shift share technique and a rebuttal, see H. J. Brown, "Shift and Share Projections of Regional Economic Growth: An Empirical Test," *Journal of Regional Science* 9 (April 1969): 1–18, and Christos C. Paraskevopoules and H. J. Brown, Comments and Reply, *Journal of Regional Science* 11 (April 1971): 107–114.

35. For a summary and evaluation of these studies, see *Jobs, People, and Land: Bay Area Simulation Study (BASS)*, Special Report no. 6 (Berkeley: Center for Real Estate and Urban Economics, Institute of Urban and Regional Studies, University of California, 1968).

36. John M. Mattila, *Estimating Metropolitan Income: Detroit, 1950–1969* (Detroit: Center for Urban Studies, Wayne State University, January 1970).

37. Ibid., p. 34.

38. Ibid., p. 35.

39. Victor Zarnowitz, *An Appraisal of Short-Term Economic Forecasts* (New York: National Bureau of Economic Research, 1967), pp. 4–8.

CHAPTER 4

1. Noel P. Gist and L. S. Halbert, *Urban Society*, 3d ed. (New York: Crowell, 1948), p. 95; Donald J. Bogue, ed., *Needed Urban and Metropolitan Research*, Scripps Foundation Studies in Population Distribution, no. 7 (Oxford, Ohio: Scripps, 1953), p. 80.

2. Bogue, *Needed Urban and Metropolitan Research*, p. 12.

3. Hurd, *Principles of City Land Values*, pp. 15–16.

4. R. E. Park and E. W. Burgess, *The City* (Chicago: University of Chicago Press, 1925), chap. 2.

5. Ernest W. Burgess, "The Ecology and Social Psychology of the City," in Bogue, *Needed Urban and Metropolitan Research*, p. 81. For a more recent reinterpretation of Burgess's theory, see Leo F. Schnore, "On the Spatial Structure of Cities in the Two Americas," in *The Study of Urbanization*, Philip M. Hauser and Leo F. Schnore, eds. (New York: Wiley, 1965), pp. 347–398. See also Leo F. Schnore, *The Urban Scene: Human Ecology and Demography* (New York: Free Press, 1965).

6. Homer Hoyt, *The Structure and Growth of Residential Neighborhoods in American Cities* (Washington, D.C.: Federal Housing Administration, 1939).

7. Weimer, Hoyt, and Bloom, *Real Estate*, p. 293.

8. Ibid., pp. 294–297.

9. Walter Firey, *Land Use in Central Boston* (Cambridge: Harvard University Press, 1947), chaps. 1, 2, 9; Lloyd Rodwin, "The Theory of Residential Growth and Structure," *Appraisal Journal* 18 (July 1950): 295–317. See also Homer Hoyt, "Residential Sectors Revisited," *Appraisal Journal* 18 (October 1950): 445–450.

10. Rodwin, "The Theory of Residential Growth and Structure," p. 301.

11. Dorau and Hinman, *Urban Land Economics*, p. 214.

12. Robert Murray Haig, *Major Economic Factors in Metropolitan Growth and Arrangement*, vol. 1, *Regional Survey of New York and Its Environs* (New York: Regional Plan Association, 1927), 39–42.

13. Paul F. Wendt, "Theory of Urban Land Value Trends," *Land Economics* 33 (August 1957): 228–240; "Urban Land Value Trends," *Appraisal Journal* 26 (April 1958): 254–269; "Economic Growth and Urban Land Values," *Appraisal Journal* 26 (July 1958): 427–443. See also R. U. Ratcliff's rejoinder, "Commentary: On Wendt's Theory of Land Values," *Land Economics* 33 (November 1957): 360–362.

14. William Alonso, *Location and Land Use: Toward a General Theory of Land Rent* (Cambridge: Harvard University Press, 1964), p. 105.

15. Michael A. Goldberg, "Transportation and Land Values," *Land Economics* 46 (May 1970): 159.

16. Ratcliff, *Urban Land Economics*, p. 410.

17. Ibid., chap. 5.

18. Ibid., p. 403.

19. Frederick M. Babcock, *The Valuation of Real Estate*, p. 59.

20. Lowdon Wingo, *Transportation and Urban Land* (Washington, D.C.: Resources for the Future, 1961), p. 115.

21. Ibid., p. 117.

22. William Alonso, *Location and Land Use: Toward a General Theory of Land Rent*.

23. Ibid., p. 128. See also Paul F. Wendt and William Goldner, "Land Values and the Dynamics of Residential Location," *Essays in Urban Land Economics* (Los Angeles: Real Estate Research Program, University of California, 1966).

24. For a review of recent literature on housing and intraurban location, the reader is referred to Alfred N. Page and Warren R. Seyfried, *Urban Analysis – Readings in Housing and Urban Development* (Glenview, Ill.: Scott Foresman, 1970), sec. 3. See also Robert D. Dean, William H. Leahy and David L. McKee, eds., *Spatial Economic Theory* (New York: Free Press, 1970).

25. Herbert Mohring and Mitchell Horwitz, *Highway Benefits: An Analytical Framework* (Evanston, Ill.: Transportation Center at Northwestern University, Northwestern University Press, 1962), p. 180.

26. Brian J. L. Berry, *Geography of Market Centers and Retail Distribution*, Foundations of Economic Geography Series (Englewood Cliffs, N.J.: Prentice-Hall, 1967), chaps. 3, 4, 5, 6.

27. Ibid., p. 123.

28. Donald J. Bogue, *The Structure of the Metropolitan Community: A Study of Dominance and Subdominance* (Ann Arbor: Horace R. Rackham School of Graduate Studies, University of Michigan, 1959), p. 48.

29. Robert B. Mitchell and Chester Rapkin, *Urban Traffic* (New York: Columbia University Press, 1954), chap. 1.

30. David L. Birch, *The Economic Future of City and Suburb*, CED Supplementary Paper no. 30 (New York: Committee for Economic Development, 1970).

31. Ibid., p. 8.

32. Ibid., p. 12.

33. Ibid., p. 26.

34. Hurd, *Principles of City Land Values*; McMichael and Bingham, *City Growth and Land Values*.

35. Frederick M. Babcock, *The Valuation of Real Estate*, pp. 64–65.

36. Frederick M. Babcock, Maurice R. Massey, Jr., and Walter L. Greene, "Techniques of Residential Location Rating," *Journal of the American Institute of Real Estate Appraisers* 5 (April 1938): 133–140.

37. Ibid., pp. 171–172. See also Federal Housing Administration, *Underwriting Manual* (1952), pt. 3, sec. 13, p. 140.

38. Federal Housing Administration, *Underwriting Manual*, loose-leaf rev. ed. (Washington, D.C., February 1968). Statistical analysis of substantial quantities of accurate sales data have made the earlier grid techniques used by the FHA in its mortgage risk rating system obsolete. They also promise to supplant the typical rating grids recommended for use in leading appraisal texts. The FHA recently advised the author that "we no longer complete the 'Rating of Property' or 'Rating of Location' grids in our appraisal process." Letter from Mr. Don L. Ralya, chief underwriter, Federal Housing Administration, San Francisco, 14 April 1970. For a test of the FHA rating technique, see Wendt and Goldner, "Land Values and the Dynamics of Residential Location," pp. 188–213.

39. May, *The Valuation of Residential Real Estate*, p. 91.

40. Ibid., p. 87.

41. Charles Abrams, "The 'New Greshams' Law of Neighborhoods – Fact or Fiction," *Appraisal Journal* 19 (July 1951): 324–337; Belden Morgan, "Value in Transition Areas: Some New Concepts," *Review of the Society of Residential Appraisers* 18 (March 1952): 5–10; Luigi M. Laurenti, "Effects of Nonwhite Purchases on Market Prices of Residences," *Appraisal Journal* 20 (July 1952): 314–329; E. F. Schietinger, "Race and Residential Market Values in Chicago," *Land Economics* 30 (November 1954): 301–308.

42. *Population and Employment—Analysis of Projections for the Atlanta Metropolitan Area* (Atlanta: Atlanta Region Metropolitan Planning Commission, March 1969).

43. *Jobs, People and Land: Bay Area Simulation Study (BASS)*.

44. For a critical review of this and other models, see Douglas B. Lee, Jr., "Requiem for Large-Scale Models," *AIP Journal* 39 (May 1973): 163–178.

45. Development Research Associates, *Economic Impact of a Regional Open Space Program for the San Francisco Bay Area* (Los Angeles, 1969).

CHAPTER 5

1. David Friday, "An Extension of Value Theory," *Quarterly Journal of Economics* 36 (1922): 197–219.

NOTES

2. Alfred D. Jahr, *The Law of Eminent Domain: Valuation and Procedure* (New York: Clark Boardman, 1953), pp. 98–99.

3. Bonbright, *The Valuation of Property*, 1: 63.

4. Arthur J. Mertzke, "Valuation Principles as Applied to Residential Property," *Appraisal Journal* 1 (October 1933): 2–3.

5. Ernest M. Fisher and Robert M. Fisher, *Urban Real Estate* (New York: Holt, 1954), p. 223.

6. Peter Hanson, "The Meaning of Value," *Appraisal Journal* 1 (July 1933): 296.

7. Federal Housing Administration, *Underwriting Manual*, loose-leaf rev. ed. (February 1966), pt. 4, sec. 13, 71305.

8. James L. Doherty, "Favorable Financing Effects on Values of Single Family Residences," *Appraisal Journal* 39 (July 1970): 398–405.

9. Ken Garcia, "Sales Prices and Cash Equivalents," *Appraisal Journal* 40 (January 1972): 1–16.

10. AIREA, *The Appraisal of Real Estate*, 5th ed., p. 346. See also Alfred A. Ring and Philip A. Benson, *Real Estate Principles and Practices* (Englewood Cliffs, N.J.: Prentice-Hall, 1967), p. 379.

11. Frederick M. Babcock, *The Valuation of Real Estate*, pp. 288–289.

12. Hurd, *Principles of City Land Values*; McMichael and Bingham, *City Growth and Land Values*, chap. 22.

13. Frederick M. Babcock, *The Valuation of Real Estate*, p. 456.

14. Ibid., pp. 460–464.

15. William A. Spurr and Charles P. Bonini, *Statistical Analysis for Business Decisions* (Homewood, Ill.: Irwin, 1967), p. 122.

16. Ibid., chap. 13, app. table J and p. 302.

17. Ibid., chap. 11, p. 25.

18. Richard U. Ratcliff and Dennis G. Swan, "Getting More from Comparables by Rating and Regression," *Appraisal Journal* 40 (January 1972): 68.

19. Henry A. Babcock, *Appraisal Principles and Procedures*, p. 217.

20. "All the Sales Data You Need – At Less Cost," *Savings and Loan News*, December 1968, pp. 38–39.

21. Nationwide Building Society, *Occasional Bulletin*, no. 107, February 1972.

22. A. H. Schaaf, "Price Behavior in Existing House Markets, 1961–66," *Appraisal Journal* 37 (April 1969): 289–295. The Alameda County Assessor has estimated that house prices rose at a compound annual rate of 4.5 percent from 1965 to 1969. These price trends were confirmed by analysis of multiple-listing sales by the author.

23. Fred E. Case, *Real Estate Market Behavior in Los Angeles: A Study of Multiple Listing System Data*, Real Estate Research Program, Research Report no. 5 (Los Angeles: Graduate School of Business Administration, University of California, 1963).

24. Ibid., p. 9.

25. Schaaf, "Price Behavior in Existing House Markets, 1961–66." See also Gabriel A. Zimmerman, "Analysis of Multiple Listing Data in the East Bay and San Francisco, 1956–1961," *Bay Area Real Estate Report*, 1st quarter 1963, pp. 65–71.

26. Boris W. Becker, "On The Reliability of Multiple Listing Data," *Appraisal Journal* 40 (April 1972): 264–267.

27. Leonard P. Vidger, *San Francisco Housing Markets: A Study of Price Movements in 1958–1967 with Projections to 1975*, Real Estate Research Program, Occasional Research Report no. 2 (San Francisco State College, 1969).

28. Raoul J. Freeman, "Real Estate Assessment and Electronic Computers."

29. William C. Pendleton, "Statistical Inference in Appraisal and Assessment Procedures," *Appraisal Journal* 33 (January 1965): 73–82.

30. An interesting application of this technique in estimating land prices in Tokyo is found in Shunsuke Ishihara, "Multiple Regression Analysis of Land Prices in Tokyo," *Real Estate Research Quarterly Journal* 8 (July 1966): 48–54. An English version of this article has been submitted to the *Appraisal Journal* for publication. See also William M. Shenkel, "Valuation by Multiple Regression Analysis: Selected Case Studies."

31. William A. Spurr and Charles P. Bonini, *Statistical Analysis for Business Decisions*, chap. 23. See also Theodore Reynolds Smith, "The Market as a Basis of Value: A Survey of Modern Appraisal Methodology," paper delivered before the Department of Revenue and Finance, Washington, D.C., 1970.

32. Karl A. Fox, *Intermediate Economic Statistics* (New York: Wiley, 1968), pp. 52–57.

33. Ibid., pp. 58, 554.

34. Ibid., pp. 59, 557–558.

35. Robert H. Gustafson, "E.S.P. and the Appraiser," paper prepared for delivery at the Thirty-fifth Annual Conference of the National Association of Tax Administrators, San Francisco, June 1967.

36. Ibid., p. 11. For an excellent discussion of the problems of collinearity and an illustration of the use of multiple regression analysis in estimating lot prices, see William A. Spurr and

NOTES

Charles P. Bonini, *Statistical Analysis for Business Decisions*, pp. 601–611.

37. Jack Lessinger, "Econometrics and Appraisal," *Appraisal Journal* 37 (October 1969): 501–512.

38. Ibid., p. 508.

39. See for example Robert A. Blettner, "Mass Appraisals via Multiple Regression Analysis," *Appraisal Journal* 37 (October 1969): 513–521.

40. The author is indebted to Miss Betty Isakson, a student in his appraisal course at the University of Georgia in the fall of 1970 for assembling the data and developing the regression model described.

41. J. Fred Weston and R. Bruce Ricks, "Land as a Growth Investment," *Financial Analysts Journal*, July-August 1966, pp. 69–78.

42. See articles by Sherman J. Maisel and Frank G. Mitelbach in *Housing in California—Appendix*, Governor's Advisory Commission on Housing Problems, Sacramento, April 1963, pp. 221–291.

43. F. Gregory Opelka, "Appraisal Report," *Savings and Loan News*, March 1969, pp. 76–77.

44. Ibid., p. 77. Bruce Ricks presented a similar model for determining the present values added by land development in this article, "New Town Development and the Theory of Location," *Land Economics* 46 (February 1970): 6.

45. Spurr and Bonini, *Statistical Analysis for Business Decisions*, pp. 593–611.

46. Shenkel, "Valuation by Multiple Regression Analysis: Selected Case Studies."

47. Robert H. Armstrong, "Valuation of Industrial Property, Part IV," *Appraisal Journal* 21 (October 1953): 526–527. The American Trucking Association cited substantially the same list of plant location factors in a 1963 study, cited in William N. Kinnard, Jr., *Industrial Real Estate* (Washington, D.C.: Society of Industrial Realtors, 1967), p. 66.

48. See William Shenkel, "Cash Flow Analysis and Multiple Regression Techniques," *Journal of Property Management*, November-December 1969, pp. 264–276. Professor Shenkel has been one of the leaders in advocating the use of multiple regression analysis in real estate appraisal. See "Computer Valuation by Multiple Regression Analysis," Proceedings of the Thirty-fourth Annual International Conference on Assessment Administration, 13–16 October 1968, St. Louis, pp. 26–39, and "Valuation Studies" in Proceedings of the Thirty-fifth Annual International Conference on Assessment Administration, 7–10 September 1969, Denver, pp. 98–115.

49. "Analysis of Bay Area Industrial Park Characteristics," mimeographed, project of the Real Estate Research Committee, Northern California chapter, American Institute of Real Estate Appraisers, 15 January 1970.

CHAPTER 6

1. Eugen V. Bohm-Bawerk, *Positive Theory of Capital*, trans. William A. Smart (New York: Macmillan, 1923), p. 259.

2. John Stuart Mill, *Principles of Political Economy*, 5th ed. (New York, 1897), p. 213.

3. Marshall, *Principles of Economics*, p. 593.

4. Irving Fisher, *The Theory of Interest* (New York: Macmillan, 1930), p. 14.

5. Ibid., pp. 17–18.

6. Irving Fisher, *The Nature of Capital and Income*, p. 192.

7. Ibid., p. 194.

8. Ibid., pp. 199, 364–365.

9. Leon Walras, *Elements of Pure Economics*, trans. William Jaffe (London: George Allen and Ungwin, 1954), pp. 267, 310–311.

10. Medici, *Principles of Appraisal*, p. 29.

11. Grimes and Craigue, *Principles of Valuation*, pp. vii–ix.

12. Ibid.

13. Paul R. Rider and Carl H. Fischer, *Mathematics of Investment* (New York: Rinehart, 1951), chaps. 1, 3; Frederick M. Babcock, *The Valuation of Real Estate*, pp. 142–146. Readers familiar with the use of annuity formulas will recognize that the present value of a known, terminable, level annuity can be calculated more rapidly by the use of tables showing the present value of an annuity. These are based upon the formula illustrated, and it is considered desirable to employ the simplest mathematical techniques for the present example.

14. Louis Winnick, "Long-Run Changes in the Valuation of Real Estate by Gross Rents," *Appraisal Journal* 20 (October 1952): 492.

15. J. Fred Weston and Eugene F. Brigham, *Managerial Finance*, 2d ed. (New York: Holt, Rinehart, and Winston, 1966), app. A to chap. 7.

16. Frederick M. Babcock, *The Valuation of Real Estate*, pp. 427–432.

17. Paul F. Wendt and Alan R. Cerf, *Tables for Use in Real Estate and Investment Analysis* (Berkeley: Center for Real Estate and Urban Economics, University of California, 1968). William M. Shenkel, *Capitalization Tables for Investment Purposes* (Athens: Department of Real Estate and Urban Development, University of Georgia, 1970).

255

18. Stanley L. McMichael, *McMichael's Appraising Manual*, 4th ed. (Englewood Cliffs, N.J.: Prentice-Hall, 1951), chap. 6.

19. Wendt, *"Ellwood, Inwood, and the Internal Rate of Return."*

20. Shenkel, *Capitalization Tables for Investment Purposes*, p. 26. Wendt and Cerf, *Tables for Use in Real Estate and Investment Analysis*.

21. *Ellwood Tables* (Chicago: American Institute of Real Estate Appraisers, 1970).

22. Wendt, "Ellwood, Inwood, and the Internal Rate of Return."

23. This same phenomenon is the subject of an extensive literature in the field of finance, where the sinking-fund is identified as the "reinvestment" rate. The reader is referred to Ezra Solomon, *The Management of Corporate Capital* (Chicago: Graduate School of Business, University of Chicago: 1959), chap. 2.

24. Frederick M. Babcock, *The Valuation of Real Estate*, pp. 138, 427, 438, 432.

25. Ibid., p. 429.

26. Ibid., p. 454.

27. AIREA, *The Appraisal of Real Estate*, 5th ed., p. 267.

28. Ibid., p. 273.

29. Ibid., pp. 275–276.

30. For an example of this, see ibid., p. 274. For a discussion of these issues, see also Charles F. Louie, "Depreciation and the Cost Approach," *Appraisal Journal* 29 (October 1961): 507–517, and "Depreciation and the Income Approach," *Appraisal Journal* 30 (January 1962): 40–48. For a lucid explanation of the relationship between "recapture" and investor's yield, see James E. Gibbons, "Impact of Yields on Value," *Appraisal Journal* 38 (October 1970): 495–509. William N. Kinnard, Jr., in chaps. 8 and 9 of his recent book *Income Property Valuation* (Lexington, Mass: Heath Lexington, 1971) draws attention to and reviews the "confusion and variety" in the use of rate terminology in appraising. The author argues that the *discount rate* is the investment rate of return excluding capital recovery, while the term *capitalization rate* includes an allowance for capital recovery. Contrary to his views, this author would argue that the terms *discount rate* and *capitalization rate* are and should mean the same thing in financial and appraisal literature.

31. Charles B. Akerson, "Ellwood without Algebra," *Appraisal Journal* 38 (July 1970): 332.

32. Leon W. Ellwood, *Ellwood Tables for Real Estate Appraising and Financing*, 2d ed. (Chicago: American Institute of Real Estate Appraisers, 1970), p. 79. This formula is explained on pp. 11–15 in the 1970 edition of *Ellwood Tables*.

33. Wendt and Cerf, *Tables for Use in Real Estate and Investment Analysis*, p. 28.

34. Wendt, "Ellwood, Inwood, and the Internal Rate of Return." See also Paul F. Wendt, David W. Walters, and Wallace F. Smith, *California Net Income Valuation Tables* (Berkeley: Center for Real Estate and Urban Economics, University of California, 1970).

35. Frederick M. Babcock, *The Valuation of Real Estate*, p. 236.

36. Ibid., pp. 413–414.

37. Ibid., p. 414.

38. AIREA, *The Appraisal of Real Estate*, 5th ed., chap. 15.

39. *Journal of Property Management, Apartment Building Experience Exchange*, annual issues, 1960–1969.

40. For an explanation of this and other stock valuation formulas, see Wendt, "Current Growth Stock Valuation Methods."

41. Frederick M. Babcock, *The Valuation of Real Estate*, p. 417.

42. Richard U. Ratcliff, "Net Income Can't Be Split," *Appraisal Journal* 18 (April 1950): 171.

43. Wendt, "Economic Growth and Urban Land Values." See also Michael A. Goldberg, "Transportation, Urban Land Values, and Rents: A Synthesis," *Land Economics* 46 (May 1970): 153–162.

44. Sherman J. Maisel, "Background Information on Costs of Land for Single-Family Housing," *Housing in California* (Sacramento, Calif.: State Printing Office, April 1963), pp. 221–281.

45. Allen D. Manvel, "Trends in the Value of Real Estate," in *Three Land Research Studies*, National Commission on Urban Problems, Research Report no. 12 (Washington, D.C., 1968), pp. 1–17.

46. Robert H. Gustafson and Ronald B. Welch, "Estimating California Land Values from Independent Statistical Indicators," in *Three Land Research Studies*, pp. 60–72.

47. Grace Milgram, *The City Expands* (Philadelphia: Institute of Environmental Studies, University of Pennsylvania, 1967). For purposes of comparison, it is interesting to note that the Japan Real Estate Institute has recently published price indexes for commercial, residential, and industrial land in Japan, showing that land prices, on the average, rose from an index level of 106.0 in September 1955 to 1073.0 in September 1968. Address by Mitsuo Kushita, president of the Japan Real Estate Institute, "The Guidepost System of Urban Land Prices and Its Background – Japan's Land Problem Today and Tomorrow," n.d.

48. Grimes and Craigue, *Principles of Valua-*

tion, p. vii.

49. *Journal of the American Institute of Real Estate Appraisers* 1 (1934). See articles by Mark Levy and Frederick M. Babcock.

50. Ratcliff, "Net Income Can't Be Split."

51. Ibid., pp. 155, 432.

52. AIREA, *The Appraisal of Real Estate*, 5th ed., p. 276.

53. Ratcliff, "Net Income Can't Be Split," p. 168.

54. Ibid., pp. 169–172.

55. Charles B. Shattuck, "Income Approach—Capitalization Processes," in AIREA, *Real Estate Appraisal Text Material, Course I* (Chicago, 1938), pp. 11–12.

56. AIREA, *The Appraisal of Real Estate*, 5th ed., p. 292.

57. Ibid., p. 314.

58. Ibid., pp. 313–314.

59. See p. 307 below.

60. Ratcliff, "Capitalized Income Is Not Market Value," p. 35.

61. For a complete exposition of this technique, the reader is referred to Wendt and Cerf, *Real Estate Investment Analysis and Taxation*, chap. 2. For an illustration of the use of a similar formulation in measuring the risk in real estate investments, see Robert C. Higgins and R. Hugh Cunningham, "Computerized Calculations—Rates of Return and Risks in Commercial Property."

62. Higgins and Cunningham, "Computerized Calculations," pp. 41–42.

63. Harry M. Markowitz, *Portfolio Selection—Efficient Diversification of Investments* (New York: Wiley, 1959), chap. 4.

64. Frederick M. Babcock, *The Valuation of Real Estate*, p. 57.

65. Ibid.

66. Ernest M. Fisher and Robert M. Fisher, *Urban Real Estate*, p. 481.

67. AIREA, *The Appraisal of Real Estate*, 5th ed., p. 122.

68. The overall rates in tables 6–6, 6–12 and 6–13 are applicable to before-tax estimated net incomes. The inputed before-tax equity band-of-investment rates based upon the financing terms assumed in table 6–6 would be substantially above 0.10, 0.12, and 0.15 as can be seen below.

Hamburger stand: Debt	- 0.60	× 0.08	=	0.0480
Equity	- 0.40	× 0.13	=	0.0520
Overall rate	-			0.1000

Office building: Debt	- 0.60	× 0.09	=	0.054
Equity	- 0.40	× 0.24	=	0.096
Overall rate	-			0.150

Apartment building: Debt	- 0.66	× 0.09	=	0.0594
Equity	- 0.34	× 0.1783	=	0.0606
Overall rate	-			0.1200

These "implied" before-tax equity yields can be compared with the pro-forma after-tax yields in col. 8 of tables 6–7, 6–8 and 6–9. It can be seen that the after-tax yields shown there bear no consistent relationship to the "implied" before-tax equity rates.

69. 2d ed. (Englewood Cliffs, N.J.: Prentice-Hall, 1970), p. 282.

70. James C. Van Horne, *Financial Management and Policy*, p. 68.

CHAPTER 7

1. Philip A. Benson and Nelson L. North, *Real Estate Principles and Practices* (Englewood Cliffs, N.J.: Prentice-Hall, 1924), pp. 170–171.

2. Zangerle, *Principles of Real Estate Appraising*, chap. 8.

3. Ibid.

4. Benjamin Graham, *The Intelligent Investor*, 3d ed. (New York: Harper and Row, 1965), p. 155.

5. Charles Tatham, Jr., "Investment Value of Electrical Utility Common Stocks," *Analysts Journal* 10 (November 1954): 14. See also Wendt, "Current Growth Stock Valuation Methods."

6. Frederick M. Babcock, *The Valuation of Real Estate*, p. 180.

7. Charles B. Shattuck, "Income Approach—Capitalization Processes," in AIREA, *Selected Readings in Real Estate Appraisal*, pp. 1060–1061.

8. AIREA, *The Appraisal of Real Estate*, 2d ed., p. 393.

9. AIREA, *The Appraisal of Real Estate*, 5th ed., pp. 336–337, 348, 351, 354–355, 360–362.

10. Louis Winnick, "Long-Run Changes in the Valuation of Real Estate by Gross Rents," *Appraisal Journal* 20 (October 1952): 484–498.

11. Richard U. Ratcliff, "Current Practices in Income Property Appraisal—A Critique," Report no. 30 (Berkeley: Center for Real Estate and Urban Land Economics, Institute of Urban and Regional Development, University of California, 1967), pp. 53–60. Ratcliff cites the following sources and characteristics of the twelve samples of sales data for which regression equations are shown in fig. 7–1:

Data Sources:

Samples 1 to 8: The primary market data were collected from the personal record files of

Mr. George Hoyt, an independent appraiser in Berkeley, who has been in active practice for the past fifty-eight years. The geographical coverage of the apartment sales was confined to the East Bay region in Alameda County, California. A total of 109 apartment sales was considered. The apartments selected were predominantly small properties, ranging in size from four-plexes to ten units. Their ages ranged from new to ten years old, and the dates of sale from 1963 to 1966.

Sample 9: A sample group of twenty-four apartment sales was selected from the Donol Hedlund MBA thesis, "Survey of Gross Rent Multipliers for Apartment Buildings in Alameda County, 1959–60." Hedlund's study was made in December 1960 and was carried on with the assistance of the Real Estate Research Program, University of California, Berkeley. The selected sample sales were comprised predominately of apartment properties of sizes ranging from six to ten units, of ages from one to ten years old, and sold in 1958 and 1959.

Samples 10 to 12: These apartment sales data were taken from the *Appraiser* 8 (April 1967): 10–11. This bulletin is published by the American Institute of Real Estate Appraisers. The statistical data were prepared by George L. Mercer, assistant vice-president and assistant manager of the Appraisal Division, Bell Savings and Loan Association of Chicago.

Sample 10: There were twelve low-rise elevator apartment sales located in the Chicago area. They ranged in size from twenty-six to eighty units, in age from new to four years old, and were sold from July 1964 to August 1966.

Sample 11: The sales covered fifteen walk-up apartments, located in the Chicago area, ranging in size from twelve to thirty-eight units, in age from one to ten years old, and were sold from 1964 to 1966.

Sample 12: The data consisted of fifteen walk-up apartment sales located in the Chicago suburbs, containing twelve to ninety-eight units, of ages from two to eight years old, and sold from 1964 to 1966.

Definitions for samples 1 to 8:

Annual gross income: potential rental income at 100 percent occupancy at current rental rates. Only unfurnished buildings were included in the sample.

Operating expenses: operating outlays as reported by the owners. Those cases included in samples 5 to 8, where net income was related to sales price, were selected from samples 1 to 4 and were limited to cases where the owner reported expenditures on each of five types of expense: real estate tax, hazard insurance, repairs and maintenance, trash collection, and utilities.

Net income: as used in samples 5 to 8, the difference between annual gross income and operating expenses as defined above.

12. Ibid., p. 47.
13. "Cash Flow Analysis and Multiple Regression Techniques."
14. Ibid., p. 31.
15. Ibid., p. 34.
16. Federal Housing Administrations, *Underwriting Manual*, loose-leaf rev. ed. (February 1966).
17. Ibid., sec. 71420.
18. Ibid. (April 1969), sec. 71510.1.
19. A prominent California developer has recently cautioned that gross multipliers based upon typical apartment buildings may not be applicable for newer developments incorporating many special amenity features, such as club houses, swimming pools, etc.
20. Frank E. Sonnenschein, "Effect of Life Estimates on Capital Values," *Appraisal Journal* 14 (January 1946): 62–68.
21. A well-known professional appraiser from the Washington, D.C. area recently wrote the author, saying: "The gross rent multiple for valuation of real estate . . . is completely out the window for all marketable investment properties above about $100,000 in price range in this part of the country, and is also no longer applicable to even the lowest priced single-family housing in the Washington, D.C. region for the simple reason that the investors or speculators in rental property cannot now compete with the demands from private owners (purchasers) during the present extreme shortage of lowest priced housing." Translated into valuation terms, this statement appears to say that gross-rent multipliers have risen substantially in that area due to a shortage of housing.
22. Ratcliff, "Capitalized Income Is Not Market Value," p. 39.

CHAPTER 8

1. Committee on Price Determination for the Conference on Price Research, *Cost Behavior and Price Policy*, p. 262.
2. Bonbright, *The Valuation of Property*, 1: 150, 402.
3. Zangerle, *Principles of Real Estate Appraising*, pp. 179, 235.
4. Statutes and Amendments to the Codes, State of California, 1966 Corporations Code. Chap. 147, pp. 649–683.
5. Andrew J. Hinshaw, "The Assessor and Computerization of Data," *Appraisal Journal* 37 (April 1969): 283–288.
6. R. E. Cady, "Appraising in a Saturated Market: The Lender's Viewpoint," *Appraisal Journal* 34 (January 1966): 27–31. See also Carey

Winston, "The Appraisal and Changes in Mortgage Banking," *Appraisal Journal* 32 (April 1964): 167–171.

7. Federal Housing Administration, *Underwriting Manual*, loose-leaf rev. ed. (February 1966), sec. 71307.

8. Frederick M. Babcock, *The Valuation of Real Estate*, pp. 36, 40, 477.

9. Bonbright, *The Valuation of Property*, 1: 175.

10. Anson Marston and Thomas R. Agg, *Engineering Valuation* (New York: McGraw-Hill, 1936), pp. 349–350.

11. California State Board of Equalization, Assessment Standards Division, *Assessor's Handbook, General Appraisal Manual*, 2d ed., rev. (Sacramento, October 1968), pp. 52–53.

12. May, *The Valuation of Residential Real Estate*, pp. 31–33.

13. Schmutz, *The Appraisal Process*, p. 81.

14. AIREA, *The Appraisal of Real Estate*, 5th ed., p. 61.

15. Ibid., p. 62.

16. Jules L. Sackman, "The Limitations of the Cost Approach," *Appraisal Journal* 36 (January 1968): 53–63.

17. Smith, *The Low-Rise Speculative Apartment*.

18. Federal Housing Administration, *Underwriting Manual*, loose-leaf rev. ed. (February 1967), pp. 1007, 1020.

19. Bonbright, *The Valuation of Property*, 1: 152.

20. Robert O. Harvey, "Observation on the Cost Approach," *Appraisal Journal* 21 (October 1953): 515.

21. Federal Housing Administration, *Underwriting Manual*, loose-leaf rev. ed. (Washington, D.C., January 1961), pt. 3, sec.8, 7080c.1–70806.2.

22. Department of Housing and Urban Development, *HUD News*, 70–104 (Washington, D. C., 26 February 1970).

23. Bonbright, *The Valuation of Property*, 1: 190–191.

24. Marston, Winfrey, and Hempstead, *Engineering Valuation and Depreciation*, chap. 9.

25. Ibid., pp. 201–204.

26. Federal Housing Administration, *Underwriting Manual*, loose-leaf rev. ed. (January 1961), pt. 3, sec. 8, 70811.1–70811.4.

27. Dow Service, Inc., New York; Marshall and Stevens, *Marshall Valuation Service*, New York; E. H. Boeck, *Manual of Appraisals*, 6th ed. (Washington, D.C., 1963).

28. Bonbright, *The Valuation of Property*, 1: 185.

29. Marshall and Stevens, *Marshall Valuation Service* (Los Angeles, 1968), sec. 97, p. 2.

30. Schmutz, *The Appraisal Process*, p. 120; Bonbright, *The Valuation of Property*, 1: 189–190; May, *The Valuation of Residential Real Estate*, pp.

157–158; AIREA, *The Appraisal of Real Estate*, 5th ed., p. 198.

31. Louie, "Depreciation and the Cost Approach" and "Depreciation and the Income Approach."

32. Paul F. Wendt, "Depreciation and the Capitalization of Income Method," *Appraisal Journal* 31 (April 1963): 185–193.

CHAPTER 9

1. Bonbright, *The Valuation of Property*, 1: 161.

2. "It is commonly said that land is irreplaceable and hence that the replacement-cost method is inapplicable. But the former statement is inaccurate, save with respect to those rare locations that can be called 'unique' — reservoir sites, mountain passes, preferred sites for resort hotels, etc. . . . With land, the values inferred from current sales of similar land are rough approximations to replacement cost no less than to realization price. The traditional land valuation is, therefore, not notably inconsistent with the replacement-cost theory." Ibid., 1: 169. Cf. Kingsbury, *The Economics of Housing*, pp. 53–56.

3. Paul A. Samuelson, *Economics* (New York: McGraw-Hill, 1948), p. 594.

4. Kingsbury, *The Economics of Housing*, chap. 13. See also Medici, *Principles of Appraisal*, pp. 44–45.

5. H. J. Davenport, *The Economics of Alfred Marshall* (Ithaca, N.Y.: Cornell University Press, 1935), p. 407.

6. Wesley C. Mitchell, *Business Cycles*, vol. 1, *The Problem and Its Setting* (New York: National Bureau of Economic Research, 1927), p. 376.

7. Kingsbury, *The Economics of Housing*, p. 80.

8. Hurd, *Principles of City Land Values*, p. 2.

9. McMichael and Bingham, *City Growth and Land Values*, chap. 22.

10. Zangerle, *Principles of Real Estate Appraising*, pp. 22–23.

11. Pollock and Scholz, *The Science and Practice of Urban Land Valuation*, pp. 16–17.

12. Ibid., pp. 44–45.

13. Frederick M. Babcock, *The Valuation of Property*, chap. 17.

14. AIREA, *Real Estate Appraisal Text Material, Course I.*

15. McMichael, *Appraising Manual*, chap. 10. For a similar recent statement, see Henry A. Babcock, *The Valuation of Property*, chap. 5.

16. AIREA, *The Appraisal of Real Estate*, 5th ed., pp. 66–67.

17. Medici, *Principles of Appraisal*, pp. 28, 29, 44.

18. Lawrance et al., *Modern Methods of Valuation of Land, Houses and Buildings*, pp. 119–120.

19. See chap. 1. See also McMichael, *Principles of Appraisal*, chap. 9.

20. AIREA, *The Appraisal of Real Estate*, 5th ed., p. 378.

21. May, *The Valuation of Residential Real Estate*, p. 28.

22. Schmutz, *The Appraisal Process*, p. 107.

23. Ibid., pp. 105–106.

CHAPTER 10

1. AIREA, *Selected Readings in Real Estate Appraisal*.

2. See chap. 6. See also Wendt and Cerf, *Real Estate Investment Analysis and Taxation*, chap. 2.

3. Paul F. Wendt, "Recent Developments in Appraisal Theory."

4. For an interesting forecast of the impact of the financial analyst on real estate investment, see Frank Lalli, "The Strategy Behind Wall Street's Move into Real Estate," *Institutional Investor* 4 (May 1970): 35–38, 78–88.

LIST OF WORKS CITED

Abrams, Charles. "The 'New Greshams' Law of Neighborhoods – Fact or Fiction." *Appraisal Journal* 19 (July 1951): 324–337.

Akerson, Charles B. "Ellwood without Algebra." *Appraisal Journal* 38 (July 1970): 325–335.

"All the Sales Data You Need – At Less Cost." *Savings and Loan News*, December 1968, pp. 38–39.

Alonso, William. *Location and Land Use: Toward a General Theory of Land Rent.* Cambridge: Harvard University Press, 1964.

American Accounting Association. *A Statement of Basic Accounting Theory.* Evanston, Ill., 1966.

American Institute of Real Estate Appraisers. *The Appraisal of Real Estate.* 2d and 5th eds. Chicago, 1951, 1967.

––––––. *Appraisal Terminology and Handbook.* 5th ed. Chicago, 1967.

"Analysis of Bay Area Industrial Park Characteristics." Mimeographed. Project of the Real Estate Research Committee, Northern California chapter. American Institute of Real Estate Appraisers, 15 January 1970.

Andrews, Richard B. "Mechanics of the Urban Economic Base." *Land Economics* 29 (May, August, November 1953); 30 (February, May, August, November 1954); 31 (February, May, August 1955).

––––––. *Urban Growth and Development.* New York: Simmons and Boardman, 1962.

Armstrong, Robert H. "Valuation of Industrial Property, Part IV." *Appraisal Journal* 21 (October 1953): 519–528.

––––––. "Values and Fetishes." *Appraisal Journal* 18 (April 1950): 179–184.

Artle, Roland. "On Some Methods and Problems in the Study of Metropolitan Economics." *Regional Science Association Papers* 8 (1962): 71–87. Reprinted in *Land Using Activities.* Research Report no. 33, pp. 69–85. Berkeley: Center for Real Estate and Urban Economics, University of California, 1970.

Babcock, Frederick M. *The Valuation of Real Estate.* New York: McGraw-Hill, 1932.

––––––; Massey, Maurice R., Jr.; and Greene, Walter L. "Techniques of Residential Location Rating." *Journal of the American Institute of Real Estate Appraisers* 5 (April 1938): 133–140.

Babcock, Henry A. *Appraisal Principles and Procedures.* Homewood, Ill.: Irwin, 1968.

Bain, Joe S. "Price and Production Policies." In *A Survey of Contemporary Economics*, edited by Howard S. Ellis. Philadelphia: Blakiston, 1938.

Bauman, W. Scott. "Investment Returns and Present Values and an Appendix of 45 Tables." *Financial Analysts Journal*, November-December 1969, pp. 107–125.

Becker, Boris W. "On the Reliability of Multiple Listing Data." *Appraisal Journal* 40 (April 1972): 264–267.

Benson, Philip A., and North, Nelson L. *Real Estate Principles and Practices.* Englewood Cliffs, N.J.: Prentice-Hall, 1924.

Berry, Brian J. L. *Geography of Market Centers and Retail Distribution.* Foundations of Economic Geography Series. Englewood Cliffs, N.J.: Prentice-Hall, 1967.

Birch, David L. *The Economic Future of City and Suburb.* Committee for Economic Development Supplementary Paper no. 30. New York: Committee for Economic Development, 1970.

Blumenfeld, Hans. "The Economic Base of the Metropolis." *Journal of American Institute of Planners* 1 (Fall 1955): 114–143.

Bogue, Donald J., ed. *Needed Urban and Metropolitan Research.* Scripps Foundation Studies in Population Distribution, no. 7. Ohio: Scripps, 1953.

––––––. *The Structure of the Metropolitan Community: A Study of Dominance and Subdominance.* Ann Arbor, Mich.: Horace R. Rackham School of Graduate Studies, 1959.

Bohm-Bawerk, Eugen V. *Positive Theory of Capital.* Translated by William A. Smart, New York: Macmillan, 1923.

Bonbright, James C. *The Valuation of Property.* 2 vols. New York: McGraw-Hill, 1937.

Bowen, Percival V. "Shall Values Be Based on Past, Present or Future." *Appraisal Journal* 2 (January 1934): 125–130.

Bretzfelder, Robert B. "Geographic Trends in Personal Income in the 1960's." *Survey of*

WORKS CITED

Current Business 50 (August 1970): 14–32.

Brown, Harry Gunnison. *Economic Science and the Common Welfare*. Columbia, Mo.: Lucas, 1936.

Bye, Raymond T. *Principles of Economics*. 3d ed. New York: Crofts, 1934.

Cady, R. E. "Appraising in a Saturated Market: The Lender's Viewpoint." *Appraisal Journal* 34 (January 1966): 27–31.

California State Board of Equalization. Assessment Standards Division. *Assessor's Handbook, General Appraisal Manual*. 2d ed., rev. Sacramento, October 1968.

Canning, John B. *The Economics of Accountancy*. New York: Ronald Press, 1929.

Case, Fred E. *Real Estate Market Behavior in Los Angeles: A Study of Multiple Listing System Data*. Real Estate Research Program, Report no. 5. Los Angeles: Graduate School of Business Administration. University of California, 1963.

Cassel, Gustav. *The Theory of Social Economy*. Translated by Joseph McCabe. New York: Harcourt, Brace, 1924.

Chamberlain, Lawrence, and Edwards, George W. *The Principles of Bond Investment*. Rev. ed. New York: Holt, 1927.

Chamberlin, Edward. *The Theory of Monopolistic Competition*. Cambridge: Harvard University Press, 1933.

Clark, Horace F. *Appraising the Home*. New York: Prentice-Hall, 1930.

Clark, John Bates. *Distribution of Wealth*. New York: Macmillan, 1899.

Committee on Price Determination for the Conference on Price Research. *Cost Behavior and Price Policy*. New York: National Bureau of Economic Research, 1943.

Dasso, Jerome. "Economic Base Analysis for the Appraiser." *Appraisal Journal* 37 (July 1969): 374–385.

Davenport, Herbert Joseph. *The Economics of Alfred Marshall*. Ithaca, N.Y.: Cornell University Press, 1935.

———. *Value and Distribution*. Chicago: University of Chicago Press, 1908.

Department of Housing and Urban Development. Federal Housing Administration. *Analysis of the San Francisco–Oakland, California, Housing Market as of October 1, 1968*. Washington, D.C., March 1969.

———. *FHA Techniques of Housing Market Analysis – Revised Edition*. Washington, D.C., August 1970.

———. *HUD News*, 70–104. Washington, D.C., 26 February 1970.

Development Research Associates. *Economic Impact of a Regional Open Space Program for the San Francisco Bay Area*. Los Angeles, 1969.

Dewing, Arthur Stone. *The Financial Policy of Corporations*. 5th ed. New York: Ronald Press, 1953.

Doherty, James L. "Favorable Financing Effects on Values of Single Family Residences." *Appraisal Journal* 39 (July 1970): 398–405.

Dorau, Herbert B., and Hinman, Albert G. *Urban Land Economics*. New York: Macmillan, 1928.

Duesenberry, James S.; Fromm, Gary; Klein, Lawrence R.; and Kuh, Edwin, eds. *A Quarterly Econometric Model of the United States Economy*. Chicago: Rand McNally, 1965.

Dunn, Edgar S., Jr. "A Statistical and Analytical Technique for Regional Analysis." *Regional Science Association Papers* 6 (1960): 97–112.

Ellwood, Leon W. "Depreciation and Appreciation." *Appraisal Journal* 24 (July 1956): 351–360.

———. *Ellwood Tables for Real Estate Appraising and Financing*. 2d ed. Chicago: American Institute of Real Estate Appraisers, 1970.

Ely, Richard T. *Outlines of Economics*. New York: Macmillan, 1908.

Fama, Eugene. "Random Walks in Stock Market Prices." *Financial Analysts Journal*, September-October 1965, pp. 55–59.

Federal Housing Administration. *Underwriting Manual*. Rev. ed. Washington, D.C., 1952.

———. *Underwriting Manual*. Loose-leaf rev. eds. Washington, D.C., January 1961, February 1966, February 1967, February 1968, and April 1969.

Fetter, Franklin A. *Principles of Economics*. New York: Century, 1904.

Firey, Walter. *Land Use in Central Boston*. Cambridge: Harvard University Press, 1947.

Fisher, Ernest M., and Fisher, Robert M. *Urban Real Estate*. New York: Holt, 1954.

Fisher, Irving. *The Nature of Capital and Income*. New York: Macmillan, 1906.

———. *The Theory of Interest*. New York: Macmillan, 1930.

Floyd, Charles F. *The Changing Structure of Employment and Income in the Coastal Plains Development Region*. Washington, D.C.: Office of Regional Development Planning, Economic Development Administration, 1 March 1969.

WORKS CITED

————. *Economic Growth in the Upper Great Lakes Region, 1950–1967.* Washington, D.C.: Office of Economic Research, Economic Development Administration, April 1970.

————. "Employment and Income: Its Structure and Change in Northeast Georgia." Prepared for Northeast Georgia Area Planning and Development Commission. Athens, Ga., August 1970.

Fox, Karl A. *Intermediate Economic Statistics.* New York: Wiley, 1968.

Freeman, Raoul J. "Real Estate Assessment and Electronic Computers." *Appraisal Journal* 27 (April 1959): 181–184.

Friday, David. "An Extension of Value Theory." *Quarterly Journal of Economics* 36 (1922): 197–219.

Garcia, Ken. "Sales Prices and Cash Equivalents." *Appraisal Journal* 40 (January 1972): 1–16.

Geiger, George Raymond. *The Theory of the Land Question.* New York: Macmillan, 1936.

George, Henry. *Progress and Poverty.* New York: Schalkenbach, 1955.

Gist, Noel P., and Halbert, L. A. *Urban Society.* 3d ed. New York: Crowell, 1948.

Goldberg, Michael A. "Transportation and Land Values." *Land Economics* 46 (May 1970): 153–162.

Graham, Benjamin. *The Intelligent Investor.* 3d ed. New York: Harper and Row, 1965.

Grimes, John Alden, and Craigue, William Horace. *Principles of Valuation.* Englewood Cliffs, N.J.: Prentice-Hall, 1928.

Gustafson, Robert H. "E.S.P. and the Appraiser." Paper prepared for delivery at the Thirty-Fifth Annual Conference of the National Association of Tax Administrators, San Francisco, June 1967.

Haig, Robert Murray. *Major Economic Factors in Metropolitan Growth and Arrangement.* Vol. 1. *Regional Survey of New York and Its Environs.* New York: Regional Plan Association, 1927.

Haney, Lewis G. *History of Economic Thought.* New York: Macmillan, 1936.

Hanson, Peter. "The Meaning of Value." *Appraisal Journal* 1 (July 1933): 289–297.

Harvey, Robert O. "Observations on the Cost Approach." *Appraisal Journal* 21 (October 1953): 514–518.

Higgins, Robert C., and Cunningham, R. Hugh. "Computerized Calculations — Rates of Return and Risks in Commercial Property." *Appraisal Journal* 38 (January 1970): 37–49.

Highway Research Board. Special Report 11.

Parking as a Factor in Business, part 5. "Trends in Economic Activity and Transportation in San Francisco Bay Area." Table A–1.

Hinshaw, Andrew J. "The Assessor and Computerization of Data." *Appraisal Journal* 37 (April 1969): 283–288.

Hoyt, Homer. "Importance of Manufacturing in Basic Employment." *Land Economics* 45 (August 1969): 344–349.

————. "Residential Sectors Revisited." *Appraisal Journal* 18 (October 1950): 445–450.

————. *The Structure and Growth of Residential Neighborhoods in American Cities.* Washington, D.C.: Federal Housing Administration, 1939.

Hurd, Richard M. *Principles of City Land Values.* New York: Real Estate Record Association, 1903.

Husband, William H., and Anderson, Frank Ray. *Real Estate Analysis.* Homewood, Ill.: Irwin, 1948.

Ishihara, Shunsuke. "Multiple Regression Analysis of Land Prices in Tokyo." *Real Estate Research Quarterly Journal* 8 (July 1966): 48–54.

Jahr, Alfred D. *The Law of Eminent Domain: Valuation and Procedure.* New York: Clark Boardman, 1953.

Jerrett, Herman D. *The Theory of Real Property Valuation.* Sacramento, Calif., 1938.

Jobs, People and Land: Bay Area Simulation Study (BASS). Special Report no. 6. Berkeley: Center for Real Estate and Urban Economics, Institute of Urban and Regional Studies, University of California, 1968.

Johnson, E. Holland. "Cost Approach to Value." In *Encyclopedia of Real Estate.* Englewood Cliffs, N.J.: Prentice-Hall, 1959.

Kahn, Sanders A. "The Entrepreneur — The Missing Factor." *Appraisal Journal* 31 (October 1963): 472–476.

————; Case, Frederick E.; and Schimmel, Alfred. *Real Estate and Investment.* New York: Ronald Press, 1963.

Kaltenbach, Henry. "The Legal Angle." *Appraisal Journal* 38 (October 1970): 616–623.

Kingsbury, Laura M. *The Economics of Housing.* New York: King's Crown Press, 1946.

Kinnard, William N., Jr. *Industrial Real Estate.* Washington, D.C.: Society of Industrial Realtors, 1967.

Laurenti, Luigi M. "Effects of Nonwhite Purchases on Market Prices of Residences." *Ap-*

praisal Journal 20 (July 1952): 314–329.

Lawrance, David M.; May, Harold G.; Rees, W. H.; and Britton, W. *Modern Methods of Valuation of Land, Houses, and Buildings*. 5th ed. London: Estates Gazette, 1962.

Lessinger, Jack. "Econometrics and Appraisal." *Appraisal Journal* 37 (October 1969): 501–512.

McMichael, Stanley L. *McMichael's Appraising Manual*. 3d and 4th eds. Englewood Cliffs, N.J.: Prentice-Hall, 1944, 1951.

————, and Bingham, Robert F. *City Growth and Land Values*. Cleveland: McMichael, 1923.

Maisel, Sherman J. "Background Information on Costs of Land for Single-Family Housing." *Housing in California*, Governor's Advisory Commission on Housing Problems. Sacramento: State Printing Office, April 1963.

Manvel, Allen D. "Trends in the Value of Real Estate." In *Three Land Research Studies*, National Commission on Urban Problems, Research Report no. 12. Washington, D.C., 1968.

Markowitz, Harry M. *Portfolio Selection — Efficient Diversification of Investments*. New York: Wiley, 1959.

Marshall, Alfred. *Principles of Economics*. 8th ed. London: Macmillan, 1925.

Marston, Anson, and Agg, Thomas R. *Engineering Valuation*. New York: McGraw-Hill, 1936.

————; Winfrey, Robley; and Hempstead, Jean C. *Engineering Valuation and Depreciation*. 2d ed. New York: McGraw-Hill, 1953.

Mattila, John M. *Estimating Metropolitan Income: Detroit, 1950–1969*. Detroit: Center for Urban Studies, Wayne State University, January 1970.

May, Arthur A. *The Valuation of Residential Real Estate*. 2d ed. Englewood Cliffs, N.J.: Prentice-Hall, 1953.

Medici, Guiseppe. *Principles of Appraisal*. Ames: Iowa State College Press, 1953.

Mertzke, Arthur J. "Real Estate Appraising." Mimeographed. Chicago: National Association of Real Estate Boards, 1927.

————. "Valuation Principles as Applied to Residential Property." *Appraisal Journal* 1 (October 1933): 298–309.

Milgram, Grace. *The City Expands*. Philadelphia: Institute of Environmental Studies, University of Pennsylvania, 1967.

Mill, John Stuart. *Principles of Political Economy*. 5th ed. New York, 1897.

Mitchell, Robert B., and Rapkin, Chester. *Urban Traffic*. New York: Columbia University Press, 1954.

Mitchell, Wesley C. *Business Cycles*. Vol. 1. *The Problem and Its Setting*. New York: National Bureau of Economic Research, 1927.

Mohring, Herbert, and Horwitz, Mitchell. *Highway Benefits: An Analytical Framework*. Evanston, Ill.: Transportation Center at Northwestern University, Northwestern University Press, 1962.

Morgan, Belden. "Value in Transition Areas: Some New Concepts." *Review of the Society of Residential Appraisers* 18 (March 1952): 5–10.

National Planning Association. Center for Economic Projections. *National Economic Projection Series*. "Report 68–N–1: National Economic Projections to 1978/79." Washington, D.C., January 1969.

Nationwide Building Society. *Occasional Bulletin*, no. 107. February 1972.

Northam, Ray M. "Population Size, Relative Location, and Declining Urban Centers: Coterminous United States, 1940–1969." *Land Economics* 45 (August 1969): 313–322.

Northern California Real Estate Report, San Francisco Bay Area Council, San Francisco.

Ohlson, Grace K. "Economic Classification of Cities." In *The Municipal Yearbook*. Chicago: International City Manager's Association, 1950.

Opelka, F. Gregory. "Appraisal Report." *Savings and Loan News*, March 1969, 76–77.

Page, Alfred N., and Seyfried, Warren R. *Urban Analysis — Readings in Housing and Urban Development*. Glenview, Ill.: Scott Foresman, 1970.

Park, R. E., and Burgess, E. W. *The City*. Chicago: University of Chicago Press, 1925.

Pendleton, William C. "Statistical Inference in Appraisal and Assessment Procedures." *Appraisal Journal* 33 (January 1965): 73–82.

Perry, Ralph Barton. *General Theory of Value*. New York: Longmans Green, 1926.

Pfouts, Ralph W., ed. *The Techniques of Urban Economic Analysis*. Trenton, N.J.: Chandler-David, 1960.

Pollock, Walter William, and Scholz, Karl W. H. *The Science and Practice of Urban Land Valuation*. Philadelphia: Pollock, 1926.

Population and Employment — Analysis of Projections for the Atlanta Metropolitan Area. Atlanta: Atlanta Region Metropolitan Planning Commission, March 1969.

WORKS CITED

Rapkin, Chester; Winnick, Louis; and Blank, David M. *Housing Market Analysis: A Study of Theory and Methods*. Report of Project O–E–48 for the Housing and Home Finance Agency. Washington, D.C.: Government Printing Office, 1953.

Ratcliff, Richard U. "Capitalized Income Is Not Market Value." *Appraisal Journal* 36 (January 1968): 33–40.

————. "Current Practices in Income Property Appraisal—A Critique." Report no. 30. Berkeley: Center for Real Estate and Urban Economics, Institute of Urban and Regional Development, University of California, 1967.

————. *Modern Real Estate Valuation, Theory and Application*. Madison, Wis.: Democrat Press, 1965.

————. "Net Income Can't Be Split." *Appraisal Journal* 18 (April 1950): 168–172.

————. *Urban Land Economics*. New York: McGraw-Hill, 1949.

————, and Swan, Dennis G. "Getting More from Comparables by Rating and Regression." *Appraisal Journal* 40 (January 1972): 68–75.

Residential Research Report, Residential Research Committee for Southern California, Los Angeles.

Rider, Paul R., and Fischer, Carl H. *Mathematics of Investment*. New York: Rinehart, 1951.

Ring, Alfred A. *The Valuation of Real Estate*. 2d ed. Englewood Cliffs, N.J.: Prentice-Hall, 1970.

————, and Benson, Philip A. *Real Estate Principles and Practices*. Englewood Cliffs, N.J.: Prentice-Hall, 1967.

Robinson, Joan. *Economics of Imperfect Competition*. London: Macmillan, 1933.

Rodwin, Lloyd. "The Theory of Residential Growth and Structure." *Appraisal Journal* 18 (July 1950): 295–317.

Rorem, C. Rufus. *Accounting Method*. Chicago: University of Chicago Press, 1930.

Ruggles, Richard. "The Theory of Value Theory." *American Economic Review* 44 (May 1954): 140–160.

Sackman, Jules L. "The Limitations of the Cost Approach." *Appraisal Journal* 36 (January 1968): 53–63.

Samuelson, Paul A. *Economics*. New York: McGraw-Hill, 1948.

Schaaf, A. H. "Price Behavior in Existing House Markets, 1961–66." *Appraisal Journal* 37 (April 1969): 289–295.

Schietinger, E. F. "Race and Residential Market Values in Chicago." *Land Economics* 30 (November 1954): 301–308.

Schmutz, George L. *The Appraisal Process*. North Hollywood, Calif., 1951.

Schnore, Leo F. *The Urban Scene: Human Ecology and Demography*. New York: Free Press, 1965.

Seligman, Edwin R. A. *Principles of Economics*. New York: Longmans Green, 1905.

Shattuck, Charles B. "Income Approach—Capitalization Processes." In *Selected Readings in Real Estate*, pp. 1060–1061. Chicago: American Institute of Real Estate Appraisers, 1953.

Shenkel, William M. *Capitalization Tables for Investment Purposes*. Athens: Department of Real Estate and Urban Development, University of Georgia, 1970.

————. "Cash Flow Analysis and Multiple Regression Techniques." *Journal of Property Management*, November-December 1969, pp. 264–276.

————. "Valuation by Multiple Regression Analysis: Selected Case Studies." Paper delivered before the Thirty-Sixth Annual International Conference on Assessment Administration, Las Vegas, October 1970. In *The Application of Econometric Methods to the Appraisal Process*. Chicago: International Association of Assessing Officers, 1971.

Smith, Adam. *The Wealth of Nations*. New York: Collier, 1905.

Smith, Larry. "The Economic Base of the Community." In *Business Action for Better Cities*. Washington, D.C.: Chamber of Commerce for the United States, 1952.

Smith, Wallace F. *The Low-Rise Speculative Apartment*. Research Report no. 25. Berkeley: Center for Real Estate and Urban Economics, University of California, 1964.

Solomon, Ezra. *The Management of Corporate Capital*. Chicago: Graduate School of Business, University of Chicago, 1959.

Sonnenschein, Frank E. "Effect of Life Estimates on Capital Values." *Appraisal Journal* 14 (January 1946): 62–68.

Spurr, William A., and Bonini, Charles P. *Statistical Analysis for Business Decisions*. Homewood, Ill.: Irwin, 1967.

Sterling, Robert R. *Theory and Measurement of Enterprise Income*. Lawrence: University of Kansas Press, 1970.

Tatham, Charles, Jr. "Investment Value of Electrical Utility Common Stocks." *Analysts Journal* 10 (November 1954): 11–14.

WORKS CITED

Theiss, William R. "The Appraisal Docket." *Appraisal Journal* 38 (October 1970): 624–626.

Thompson, Wilbur R. *A Preface to Urban Economics*. Baltimore, Md.: Johns Hopkins Press, 1965.

Tiebout, Charles M. "The Urban Economic Base Reconsidered." *Land Economics* 32 (February 1956): 95–99.

Van Horne, James C. *Financial Management and Policy*. Englewood Cliffs, N.J.: Prentice-Hall, 1968.

Veterans Administration. *Lenders' Handbook*. Pamphlet 4–3. Washington, D.C., 1948.

Vidger, Leonard P. *San Francisco Housing Markets: A Study of Price Movements in 1958–1967 with Projections to 1975*. Real Estate Research Program. Occasional Research Report no. 2. San Francisco State College, 1969.

Walras, Leon. *Elements of Pure Economics*. Translated by William Jaffe. London: George Allen and Ungwin, 1954.

Walters, David W., ed. *Real Estate Computerization*. Research Report no. 35. Berkeley: Center for Real Estate and Urban Economics, 1971.

Webb, Clarence A., and Hunnings, Arthur. *Valuation of Real Property*. London: Macmillan, 1913.

Weimer, Arthur M. "History of Value Theory for the Appraiser." *Appraisal Journal* 21 (January 1953): 8–22.

————; Hoyt, Homer; and Bloom, George F. *Real Estate*. 6th ed. New York: Ronald Press, 1972.

Wendt, Paul F. "Current Growth Stock Valuation Methods." *Financial Analysts Journal*, April 1965, pp. 91–103.

————. "Economic Growth and Urban Land Values." *Appraisal Journal* 26 (July 1958): 427–443.

————. "Ellwood, Inwood, and the Internal Rate of Return." *Appraisal Journal* 35 (October 1967): 561–576.

————. *Real Estate Appraisal — A Critical Analysis of Theory and Practice*. New York: Holt, 1956.

————. "Recent Developments in Appraisal Theory." *Appraisal Journal* 37 (October 1969): 485–500.

————."Theory of Urban Land Value Trends." *Land Economics* 33 (August 1957): 228–240.

————. "Urban Land Value Trends." *Appraisal Journal* 26 (April 1958): 254–269.

————, and Cerf, Alan R. *Real Estate Investment Analysis and Taxation*. New York: McGraw-Hill, 1969.

————, and ————. *Tables for Use In Real Estate and Investment Analysis*. Berkeley: Center for Real Estate and Urban Economics, University of California, 1968.

————, and Varian, Hal R. Note on Hoyt's "Importance of Manufacturing in Basic Employment." *Land Economics* 46 (August 1970): 350–354.

Weston, J. Fred, and Brigham, Eugene F. *Managerial Finance*. 2d ed. New York: Holt, Rinehart, and Winston, 1966.

————, and Ricks, R. Bruce. "Land as a Growth Investment." *Financial Analysts Journal*, July-August 1966, pp. 69–78.

Williams, John Burr. *The Theory of Investment Value*. Cambridge: Harvard University Press, 1938.

"Willing Buyer, Willing Seller and Market Value." *Appraisal Journal* 14 (January 1946): 5–6. In *Selected Readings in Real Estate*, pp. 104–106. Chicago: American Institute of Real Estate Appraisers, 1953.

Wingo, Lowdon. *Transportation and Urban Land*. Washington, D.C.: Resources for the Future, 1961.

Winnick, Louis. "Long-Run Changes in the Valuation of Real Estate by Gross Rents." *Appraisal Journal* 20 (October 1952): 484–498.

Zangerle, John A. *Principles of Real Estate Appraising*. Cleveland: Stanley McMichael, 1924.

Zarnowitz, Victor. *An Appraisal of Short-Term Economic Forecasts*. New York: National Bureau of Economic Research, 1967.

INDEX

INDEX

Marx, Karl, 17
McMichael, Stanley: on definition of value, 4; contribution to theory, 26; appraisal manual, 221
May, Arthur A.: definition of market value, 4; emphasis on economic base analysis, 44; analysis of neighborhood, 77; on correlation, 224
Medici, 5–6, 7, 124
Mertzke, Arthur J.: on general market conditions, 92–93; on normal value, 218
Milgram, Grace, 152
Mill, John Stuart, 17
Morkill, D. B., 124
Multiple-regression analysis, 230–231
Multiple-regression technique: use with comparable sales, 109–117; Shenkel on, 117; Spurr and Bonini, 117

National Commission of Urban Problems, 152
National Housing Act of 1934, 8
National Housing Act of 1954, 9
Neighborhood analysis, 235
Northern California Real Estate Report, 202, 203

O'Donohue, T. A., 124

Pendleton, William C., 109
Present value of reversion, 125, 129
Probability analysis, 150
Property-residual method, 157
Public Land Law Review Commission, 10

Quality-attributes method, 132

Ratcliff, Richard: on appraisal theory, 5, 6, 21; procedure for analyzing economic base, 47; on theory of urban land, 69; development of rating technique for comparable sales, 104; on conventional formulas, 29; on residual methods, 153–156
Recapture: and depreciation, 156
Replacement cost method: origins of, 188; ceiling on value, 190; evaluation of, 239
Residual approaches, 153–157
Residual land value, 127
Ricardo, David, 12
Ring, Alfred A.: on selection of method, 172; on depreciation, 209

Schmutz, George, 5, 222, 225
Servicemen's Readjustment Act of 1944, 9

Shenkel, William M.: principles of multiple regression, 117, 119
Sinking-fund factor, 130
Smith, Adam, 17
Smith, Wallace F., 29, 195
Society of Real Estate Appraisers, 33
Somers, W. A., 189
Split rates, 153
Stevens, Marshall, 204
Summation method, 132
Swan, Dennis G., 104

Three approaches: discussion of, 214, 234, 236; and economic equilibrium, 216; and appraisal theory, 217; European theory, 222; use of correlation, 223–225
Tiebout, Charles M., 37–38
Tredwell, John C., 155

Urban growth theory: development of theory, 66–67; recent developments, 72; impact of transportation routes, 73; neighborhood analysis, 75–78; author's observations on urban structure, 78–79; use of simulation models, 80
Urban Renewal Administration, 7
Utility theory, 13

Valuation of securities, 150
Value: meaning, 2; warranted, 3, 10; market value, 3, 4, 5, 8, 9, 10, 11; most probable selling price, 6; investment, 6, 16; market price, 6, 7, 9, 10, 11, 15; objective, 10; subjective exchange value, 10, 13; normal, 216–217
Value theory: economic concepts, 12; classical economists, 12; Austrian school, 13; neoclassical, 13; influence of economists, 19; influence of mortgage lenders, 21; influence of security valuation, 22; influence of economists, 27
Veterans Administration, 7

Walras, Leon, 123
Weimer, Arthur M.: analysis of economic base, 36; procedure for analyzing economic base, 47–48
Weimer, Hoyt, and Bloom, 236
Wendt, Paul F.: *Real Estate Investment Analysis and Taxation*, 140; *Real Estate Appraisal* (1956), 227
Wingo, Lawdon, 71

Zangerle, John A., 3, 19, 27, 189
Zarnowitz, Victor, 61